STRUCTURES OF FEELING IN SEVENTEENTH-CENTURY CULTURAL EXPRESSION

STRUCTURES OF FEELING IN SEVENTEENTH-CENTURY CULTURAL EXPRESSION

Edited by Susan McClary

Published by the University of Toronto Press in association with the UCLA Center for Seventeenth- and Eighteenth-Century Studies and the William Andrews Clark Memorial Library

www.utppublishing.com
Printed in Canada

ISBN 978-1-4426-4062-7

Printed on acid-free, 100% post-consumer recycled paper
with vegetable-based inks.

Library and Archives Canada Cataloguing in Publication

Structures of feeling in seventeenth-century cultural expression / edited by Susan McClary.

(UCLA Center Clark Library series)
Essays based on papers presented at four international conferences held at the UCLA Clark Library, 2005.
Includes bibliographical references and index.
ISBN 978-1-4426-4062-7

1. Arts, Modern—17th century—Congresses. 2. Emotions—History—17th century—Congresses. 3. Expression—History—17th century—Congresses. I. McClary, Susan II. William Andrews Clark Memorial Library III. University of California, Los Angeles. Center for 17th- & 18th-Century Studies IV. Series: UCLA Clark Memorial Library series

NX650.E46S77 2013 700'.4538 C2012-908145-0

This book has been published with the help of a grant from the UCLA Center for Seventeenth- and Eighteenth-Century Studies.

University of Toronto Press acknowledges the financial assistance to its publishing program of the Canada Council for the Arts and the Ontario Arts Council.

Canada Council for the Arts Conseil des Arts du Canada

ONTARIO ARTS COUNCIL
CONSEIL DES ARTS DE L'ONTARIO
50 YEARS OF ONTARIO GOVERNMENT SUPPORT OF THE ARTS
50 ANS DE SOUTIEN DU GOUVERNEMENT DE L'ONTARIO AUX ARTS

University of Toronto Press acknowledges the financial support of the Government of Canada through the Canada Book Fund for its publishing activities.

Contents

Acknowledgments

All books rely on a great many individuals from inception to finished product, and *Structures of Feeling in Seventeenth-Century Cultural Expression* is no exception. I wish to thank first the University of Toronto Press for making this publication possible. At Toronto, Richard Ratzlaff and Wayne Herrington shepherded the project along, Patricia Simoes arranged for the magnificent cover design, and James Leahy served as our painstaking copy editor. I am also grateful to the two anonymous readers who made invaluable suggestions for the improvement of all the essays.

The chapters in the book emerged from a series of four international conferences held at the UCLA Clark Library in 2005. It was my honour as Clark Professor that year to invite forty illustrious scholars of seventeenth-century history and culture to participate in those conferences, which surely count as the highlight of my own intellectual career. Although I would prefer to have had the work of all forty authors in this volume, I had to choose no more than twelve. I selected the papers finally included because of their natural clustering around particular topics. My heartfelt thanks to all those who made the conferences themselves so extraordinary.

I owe special thanks to the authors who agreed to revise their papers for publication in this book. As the reader can see, each of the writers makes important contributions with respect to her or his own field. It is my hope that together they will provide insights not easily available within separate disciplines, and I am delighted to see these interlocking chapters finally reaching the public.

But neither the conferences nor the book could have occurred without UCLA's Center for Seventeenth- and Eighteenth-Century Studies. The Center supported my research assistants, Ljubica Ilic and Eric

Wang, who helped me assemble and edit the book. The expert staff took care of organizing the conferences, ensuring that they unfolded with the elegance characteristic of the Clark. The Center provided the funding for the speakers' honoraria and, of course, for my own stint as Clark Professor.

My greatest debt, however, is to Peter Reill, the brilliant Director of the Center for Seventeenth- and Eighteenth-Century Studies for nearly twenty years. Peter helped recruit me to UCLA and became one of my dearest friends when I was on that faculty. At the committee meetings for the Center each year, Peter would ask us who wanted to be the next Clark Professor, and then he would glare daggers at me. I finally relented and embarked upon the adventure that has resulted in this book.

Peter and I both retired from UCLA in June 2011. He will always be my model of the engaged humanist who somehow manages to continue his own groundbreaking scholarship while coaxing the best efforts out of everyone around him. I dedicate *Structures of Feeling in Seventeenth-Century Cultural Expression* to Peter Reill.

Susan McClary
Cleveland Heights, OH
October 2011

Illustrations

Musical Examples

STRUCTURES OF FEELING IN SEVENTEENTH-CENTURY CULTURAL EXPRESSION

introduction

On Bodies, Affects, and Cultural Identities in the Seventeenth Century

SUSAN McCLARY

> They went to sea in a sieve, they did,
> In a sieve they went to sea:
> In spite of all their friends could say,
> On a winter's morn, on a stormy day,
> In a sieve they went to sea!
>
> —Edward Lear, 'The Jumblies'

Following the waning of the Renaissance and prior to the period of consolidation we call the Enlightenment, many fundamental aspects of human behaviour – for example, ideals of bodily deportment, theories for understanding and manipulating the passions, constructions of gender and the erotic, expressions of religious devotion, ways of experiencing time and space, conceptions of the self – changed radically and permanently. Historians who take the eighteenth century as normative often trace forerunners of various elements back into the previous period, and they have contributed a great deal to our collective knowledge, for the 1600s did indeed usher onto the cultural stage many of the practices we still count as our own: the rise of the empirical sciences, the increased emphasis on the individual, the invention of opera. But we can only identify these seventeenth-century manifestations as 'us' if we ignore such details as Isaac Newton's lifelong commitment to alchemy, the idiosyncratic utterances of religious mystics, or the internationally adored stars of operatic representation – the castrati.

How do we go about studying such ephemeral qualities as subjectivities when the people who embodied them lived 400 years ago? Some of the radical transformations of this period were explicitly acknowledged in verbal texts. Others, however, left their most vivid traces in cultural media – the visual arts, poetry, theatre, music, dance – that do not always explain their motivations in words. Instead, they manifest themselves through simulations of affective extremes, violations of traditional stylistic principles, or transgressions against officially sanctioned behaviours. So long as we demand verbal confirmation as evidence for historical arguments, we will continue to neglect some of the most profound changes that have occurred within the development of European thought.

The authors of the essays in this volume seek to explore various manifestations of seventeenth-century cultural expression, understood not as embryonic potentialities that later reached maturity but as ways for making sense of a world strikingly different from our own. The volume's title draws upon Raymond Williams's phrase 'structures of feeling,'[1] which yokes together dimensions of human experience often regarded as unique or subjective with scholarly methods of formal analysis and archival research. In Williams's words:

> For what we are defining is a particular quality of social experience and relationship, historically distinct from other particular qualities, which gives the sense of a generation or of a period. The relations between this quality and the other specifying historical marks of changing institutions, formations, and beliefs, and beyond these the changing social and economic relations between and within classes, are again an open question: that is to say, a set of specific historical questions . . . We are talking about characteristic elements of impulse, restraint, and tone; specifically affective elements of consciousness and relationships: not feeling against thought, but thought as felt and feeling as thought: practical consciousness of a present kind, in a living and interrelating continuity.[2]

Like Michel Foucault, Clifford Geertz, and others, Williams regarded 'feelings' as phenomena that shaped and that were also shaped by human societies. Hence they qualify as crucial elements of the historical record.

It is no news that the seventeenth century was a period of profound crisis: a time when the world had just become much larger (with the extension of European imperialism into the New World and elsewhere) and also much smaller (with Galileo's discovery that Earth may not be the centre of the universe after all). It was a time when intellectuals, theologians, and artists cast aside the received wisdom of centuries but agreed not at all about what to put in its place. Those radiant centres of Renaissance humanism, the courts of northern Italy, collapsed – some because of a failure to produce a male heir, some because of financial overextension. The whole of Europe and everything Europe touched became a battleground: given its religious wars and the indigenous resistance in its colonies, the 1600s saw almost no years of peace. Alternating between the heady arrogance inspired by new sources of power, riches, artistic innovation, and knowledge, on the one hand, and the acute anxieties produced by the absence of any shared certainties, on the other, seventeenth-century thinkers struggled to come to terms with a world that had become alien and frightening, in part because of their own endeavours. Too late to turn back after they had tasted the apple of modernity and too soon to know where they were headed, they performed their acrobatics without a safety net. Or, to pursue my epigraph, they navigated unknown waters without a compass and in a very leaky vessel.

And yet, the world we still inhabit today finds many of its roots in that chaotic period. We may wish to deny its relationship to us; indeed, as Richard Rambuss points out in his essay, Samuel Johnson and other eighteenth-century figures tried hard to distance themselves from the modes of expression they chose to disdain as 'baroque.' Art historians and musicologists have adopted this originally pejorative term to refer to the artistic practices of the 1600s, and although they often have defined the period through lists of neutral stylistic traits, the negative implications of the word continue to lie in wait, prepared at any time to cast aesthetic contempt on anything labelled as 'baroque.'

Several of the essays in this volume will present evidence aplenty for Johnson's horror of his predecessors' excesses. And, like him, we may prefer to view many aspects of this world as utterly unrecognizable, much as fundamentalists reject the possibility that they might have evolved from apes. Nonetheless, many elements of our contemporary culture first took shape in that quagmire, even if they appear distorted in retrospect as though through a fun-house mirror. Historians have sometimes tried to isolate those strands they want to value – the development of the centralized state, the invention of opera, the rise of empirical sciences, the spread of European civilization – separating them from the very mess that made them possible, shaking off the cooties that might bear witness to that sometimes unsavoury context.

But today's intellectuals and artists – especially those who tend to describe themselves as postmodern, poststructuralist, or postcolonial – often find themselves drawn more powerfully to the dark side of seventeenth-century culture. The affinities between Jacobean aesthetics of torture and the atrocities of Abu Ghraib, between justifications for imperialist incursions then and now, between gender-bending theatrics of Venetian opera and those of *Hedwig and the Angry Inch* or the late Michael Jackson, between attempts at understanding the relationship between mind and body in a newly secularized context and our own recent advances in neurobiology, between morbid fixations on dead bodies in early modern *Wunderkammern* and in today's *Bodyworks*: all these make the cultural expressions of the 1600s appear perhaps more like 'us' than those of the long-vaunted Enlightenment. It is like finding an uncanny resemblance between oneself and a distant relative, with traits that may have spared a few generations only to display themselves once again on our own faces.

All the essays in *Structures of Feeling in Seventeenth-Century Cultural Expression* concentrate in one way or other on the passions and on the brute materiality of the body. If a theologically governed society had dealt with affect and the corporeal dimensions of experience through the confessional and biblical guidelines to proper behaviour, the increasingly heterodox world of the 1600s found itself faced with the need to theorize *ab ovo* the mechanics of human emotions and physiology in order both to incite and to control them. In bringing together new work by prominent historians, philosophers, literary theorists, musicologists, and art critics in this collection, I hope to make this moment in our shared history both alien and uncomfortably close.

The Science of Affect

The volume begins with a cluster of essays that deal with the orderly side of seventeenth-century thought – with manifestations of projects that do, in fact, continue into the Enlightenment: the development of rigorous mathematical modelling, the early advances of medical science, the harnessing of music's vagaries to rational theories. Here we would seem to be on familiar ground. But when considered outside the usual teleological narratives that point securely forward to the Enlightenment, these projects, too, become strange.

The early triumphs of Galileo Galilei – many of them traceable back to the intellectual training he received from his father, the music theorist Vincenzo Galilei – set the terms for a wide range of new undertakings. Whereas previous generations had sought explanations compatible with the age-old wisdom of Aristotle and ecclesiastical authority, early seventeenth-century thinkers pioneered approaches based on measurement and empirical observation. But the applications of mechanical philosophy did not always pursue the paths we might have predicted. With so many variables now shaken loose from their usual paradigms came a plethora of mixes and matches between phenomena on the one hand and possible modes of theorizing on the other. Links between areas of knowledge that appear to us now as entirely unrelated often seemed then to offer potential solutions; analogies that may seem far-fetched to us were regarded as nearly self-evident. If such enterprises eventually got sorted out into categories familiar today, they did not necessarily start out that way.

Daniel Garber's essay focuses on Spinoza's theory of affect. Practitioners of standard mathematics had assumed that their objects of study remained immutable over time. But over the course of the seventeenth century, prominent thinkers increasingly focused on problems involving change, requiring the rapid development of the kinds of 'mixed mathematics' already associated with music theory. In his attempt to understand the mechanisms of emotional volatility within the human subject, Spinoza drew on the precise mathematical accounts of accelerating motion by Galileo and on Descartes's articulation of a philosophy *more geometrico* (in geometrical style). He proceeded step by step with graphs and theorems, thereby fashioning an approach to the passions, the relationships between mind and body, and temporality that appears to rely entirely on logical argumentation. In a world increasingly unsure of God's existence or willingness to intervene, Spinoza put the ability to negotiate between the poles of happiness and sadness in the hands of the individual, buttressing his position with the kinds of mathematical formulas we would expect to see in contemporaneous mechanical physics.

Historians who study the increasing application of mechanical argumentation to theories of the human subject in early modern science have tended to privilege the clock as the seventeenth-century machine par excellence. But although analogies to clockworks abounded, other important models existed as well. In her essay, Penelope Gouk examines closely the mechanical modelling that emerged among English thinkers (Robert Fludd, Timothy Bright, Richard Browne) as they dealt with the body and its relationships to mind. She finds that the English resurrected for their projects the ancient Pythagorean theory of *harmonia* – a metaphysics grounded in the phenomena demonstrable through physical acoustics. Just as two pitches can be heard to resonate in harmony, so body and soul, and even heaven and earth, might be brought into perfect balance. As Gouk demonstrates, physicians and early theorists of the condition known as melancholy made extensive use of this metaphor, comparing the mind-body complex to musical instruments as they sought ways of diagnosing and 'retuning' individuals whose passions had become discordant. Indeed, Richard Browne reported that patients benefit from contact with exposure to carefully chosen musical performances, making him an early advocate of the kind of music therapy practised today.

Music theory served, then, as a crucial structural model for early modern concepts of psychology, physiology, physics, and much more. Influences moved in both directions, however. Thomas Christensen's essay examines the ways Father Marin Mersenne laboured in his monumental *Harmonie universelle* to bring all of knowledge pertaining to music in line with the new mechanical philosophy and its empirical methods. Yet whereas some practitioners of mechanical philosophy eliminated the necessity of God from their epistemological terrains, Mersenne (much like the eighteenth-century philosopher George Bishop Berkeley) worked to fortify his faith through his scientific endeavours. In Christensen's words, 'By showing how the mechanical world of material bodies in motion and contact obey precisely quantifiable laws, Mersenne believes we must be persuaded of the beneficent and rational plan of God.'

Colonial Extensions

Thus far, I have discussed European culture as if it existed in a self-contained bubble, though earlier I alluded to underlying affective tensions between anxiety and arrogance. And one of the principal sources of both arrogance and anxiety was the colonial project that preoccupied, enriched, drained, and destabilized Europe throughout this period. It used to be possible to read histories of seventeenth-century culture that either positioned New World imperialism as a side show or else neglected to mention it altogether. But for much of the planet, the colonial condition had long since been an overwhelming fact of life. Moreover, the colonial enterprise had already produced lasting effects not only on the cultures of the indigenous peoples subjected to European control but also on those of the colonizers themselves.

Over the course of the 1600s, Europe extended tentacles of power across the seas, attempting to impose its languages, religions, and cultural priorities on those whose wealth and land it sought to appropriate. Yet the various colonial powers – Spain, France, England – deployed very different strategies and to quite different effects. In each instance, the relationship between colonizer and colonized became a two-way channel, as the practices Europeans attempted to suppress found their way back to the homeland.

The next three essays in the volume concentrate on strategies, policies, and ramifications of imperialist expansion from the points of view of France, Spain, and England. We begin with the most benign version – or at least the version most consonant with the rationalist essays presented in the previous section. Sara Melzer explores in her essay the self-justifications for colonization offered in French documents of the time. The French prided themselves on their 'soft' colonization: in contrast to the military incursions through which their rivals pursued their agendas, they attempted to seduce North American Indians by means of their superior culture and language. In describing contacts between French and Native American communities, narrators continually related how Indians pleaded – in statements presented as direct quotations – to be assimilated, to be allowed to share the obvious advantages displayed by the Europeans. These *relations de voyage* greatly influenced official policies at Versailles, as well as public opinion in France. With the natives begging for admission, how could the French deny them this 'voluntary subjection'? And how could the French not feel enormous pride in a culture that so easily won converts, even among 'savages'? The claim to the universality of French culture gained considerable support from these stories, and any potential criticism of the colonial project got nipped in the bud.

The Spanish strategy differed markedly from that of the French. Beginning immediately with Columbus's discovery of the New World, relatively small forces of Spanish soldiers undertook to conquer what came to be called Latin America. As they marched upon powerful urban centres in Mexico and Peru, they often experienced tremendous fear, not only because of the displays of military might and the pagan rituals they witnessed but also because of the sounds of singing and drumming that assailed them. Gary Tomlinson, in his 'Fear of Singing,' demonstrates how the documents by conquistadors and missionaries focus to a surprising extent on the musical activities of indigenous people, how they attempted to eradicate these cultural practices from the Indians, how confidence in the colonial project itself collapsed in the face of spontaneous eruptions of Native song. Tomlinson explains that in the decades following Luther's Reformation, Catholic missionaries came to interpret indigenous music-making not as residues of earlier cultural practices but rather as evidence of devil worship. In the age of the Inquisition and witch burnings, the dances and songs of Native Americans seemed but yet another manifestation of satanic infiltration, and Indians caught participating were duly punished.

In her essay, Olivia Bloechl reveals that English colonizers in North America made similar associations between Native ritual and devil worship. Particularly alarming to English missionaries were the trance states they observed in certain Indians during ceremonial activities. But the contagion spread back to England by way of drawings and descriptions that circulated widely. When groups of Protestant dissidents began exhibiting their own trance states, accompanied by 'quaking' and speaking in tongues, authorities condemned these practices with the same vocabulary and diagnoses they had developed for the description of North American Indian rituals. To their chagrin, the English found that attempts at imposing religion and culture on another people can have unexpected consequences with respect to the home population. Bloechl's essay recalls elements of Gouk's, especially in its concern with the effects of music on mind and body.

The Politics of Opera

Walter Pater once wrote that all art constantly aspires toward the condition of music, by which he meant the wordless sublimity of instrumental music. In the seventeenth century, however, all forms of expression aspired to the theatricality of Italian opera, the age's most splendid artistic invention. A descendent of multi-media Renaissance court entertainments, opera brought together the latest innovations of architecture, sumptuous costuming, dance, and theatre with music in all its available forms. Only the invention of cinema three centuries later would rival the seduction and sensory assault offered by this most extravagant of genres.

Its earliest manifestations took place at the court of the Medici, who guarded its new devices as jealously as state secrets. Commedia dell'arte troupes adopted bits and pieces of what they heard and saw into their travelling shows, thereby both instilling a taste for 'speaking in music' throughout the Italian peninsula and also incorporating their own shticks into the mix. By the 1630s, even the Princes of the Church had gotten in on the act: Giulio Rospigliosi (later Pope Clement IX) himself penned libretti for comic operas such as *Chi soffre speri* (1639) and *Dal male il bene* (1653), based on one of Boccaccio's ribald tales.

The genre as we know it today really coalesced, however, in Venice when a commedia troupe rented out a theatre and performed an opera for a paying audience during the 1637 carnival season. Guided by the marketing genius of Giulio Strozzi, who first honed the marketing and advertising strategies still used in Hollywood, public opera became a wildly successful enterprise. Eventually its apparatus would invade even the France of Louis XIV; although French artists had made a concerted effort to hold music drama at bay, they met the challenge by producing their own more dignified and ballet-oriented versions. But most of the rest of Europe was content to import the latest hits from Italy, somewhat like the way provincial cities now await the arrival of megamusicals exported from London and Broadway.

Wendy Heller's essay examines the explicit obsession with shape-shifting that dominated Italian opera during the seventeenth century. As she explains, Ovid's *Metamorphoses* served as one of the favourite sources for plots, for it allowed women to turn into laurel bushes (Daphne) or bears (Calisto), and it featured as its stars males who had been surgically altered so that they could sing in the soprano range. As soon as the singing body reached the stage, in other words, exploration of its infinite malleability became a primary goal. Heller examines two different treatments of the story of Daphne and Apollo, the first of which dates from the earliest experiments with *dramma per musica* in the context of the northern Italian courts, the second from the peak of commercial opera in Venice – then the Las Vegas of Europe where tourists came to sample the sexual licence for which the city was famous. Both versions of Ovid's tale put normative notions of gender and selfhood through the proverbial wringer.

Opera continued, however, to be an enormously expensive undertaking, and those who paid the bills often influenced its content. If the carnival audiences in Venice demanded explicit sex, comedians who specialized in playing stuttering hunchbacks, and a surfeit of tunes, Spanish-controlled Naples drew upon a different set of priorities and theatrical traditions. Because musicologists have tended to pay little attention to the Iberian peninsula itself in their narratives of musical development, this crucial moment of Spanish intervention in our favourite Italian genre has been largely underestimated.

Louise Stein's essay focuses on a remarkably enterprising Spanish viceroy, the Marquis de Heliche y del Carpio, who shaped opera in 1680s Naples in accordance with his own tastes. Long a significant producer of spectacle at the court in Madrid, Carpio brought with him to Naples the plays of Pedro Calderón, an erotic quality characteristic of Spanish music theatre, and a penchant for female performers. Under his patronage, artists such as the young Alessandro Scarlatti blended Italian opera with elements borrowed from Spanish royal theatre, helping to cultivate the conventions that soon emerged as *opera seria*, which would dominate the European stage throughout the entire eighteenth century. Stein offers extensive archival documentation to show how Carpio worked in Naples to provide opera suitable for sustaining the purposes of the Spanish sovereign while recruiting the best available talent – castrati, engineers of stage machinery, instrumentalists, composers – from all over Italy. Incidentally, the aforementioned Rospigliosi served as papal nuncio to Spain before he became pope, and he incorporated the plots and theatrical devices he had picked up in the course of his Iberian travels into Roman libretti. Stein's research here and elsewhere is making musicologists recognize the profound impact of Spanish modes of expression on Italy and the rest of the continent.

Baroque Bodies

Issues concerning 'the body' figure prominently throughout this collection: in philosophical treatments of the relationship between mind and body, in mechanical approaches to bodies by medical specialists, in the astonishment and apprehension of colonizers in view of the very different bodily behaviours of American Indians. In the first series of essays, we could imagine 'the body' as a transhistorical entity, even when the explanations offered at the time now seem quite bizarre; in the second cluster, problems of 'the body' involved only Others, whether abroad or (with respect to Quakers and Shakers) at home. But 'the body' as it was understood by European insiders does not appear to have come into question. Thus it may come as something of a shock to turn to representations of bodies in seventeenth-century European mainstream entertainment. In the third cluster of essays, Heller's essay on operatic metamorphoses demonstrates how both the bodies of performers and the characters they portrayed were pushed to extremes for the sake of titillation, arousal, and amusement.

Performances of the body were not limited to the stage, however. As Foucault never tired of reminding us, bodies, genders, and sexualities all have social and ideological histories. And any assumption that 'they' were just like 'us' vanishes quickly in the face of the very different assumptions that sustain these cultural projects – transparent to those of the moment, nearly completely opaque already to those in the eighteenth century who sought to hold them at arm's length by labelling them 'baroque.' The fourth cluster of essays scrutinizes seventeenth-century conceptions of the body manifested in literature, in legal policy, and in the intersection between the plastic and medical arts.

In his essay, Richard Rambuss concentrates on the Metaphysical poets, a group of English writers whose reputation has risen or fallen according to the ability of critics to stomach the vivid, corporeal imagery of their verse. Influenced by sources as diverse as the Jesuit Spiritual Exercises (which insisted that the believer strive to identify with the wounds of Christ), Spanish mystics such as St Teresa (who claimed to experience Union with the Divine Body), and exotic descriptions of recently conquered territories, the Metaphysical poets pushed their manneristic conceits to extremes bordering on blasphemy. Think of the violent homoeroticism of John Donne's 'Batter my heart, three person'd God' or his exclamation on uncovering his lover's private parts: 'O my America! my new-found-land, My kingdome, safeliest when with one man man'd.'

According to Rambuss, however, the place of honour for far-fetched imagery is held by Richard Crashaw, particularly his lengthy homage to Mary Magdalene in which he imagines her tears in a succession of metaphors that have disgusted critics for centuries. Crashaw hones his descriptions so as to engage and even assault the reader's body as directly as possible, given the limitations of the written word (the music of Divine Love by composers such as Alessandro Grandi, Claudio Monteverdi, Girolamo Frescobaldi, Chiara Margarita Cozzolani, and others attempted to produce its effects even more directly). These meditations, which work rhetorically to induce feelings of erotic arousal, ecstasy, voyeurism, and even disgust, deploy the mind's eye and corporeal imagination to break down the physical boundaries usually maintained for self-protection, ideally producing, in Rambuss's words, a 'metaphysical shudder.'

Crashaw's radical images operate on the virtual bodies of readers, but the theatricality exploited in opera and metaphysical verse also had literal corollaries. In her essay, Sarah Covington explores the ways English authorities in the seventeenth century engraved their laws on the faces, skins, and torsos of convicted malefactors. Presented as a kind of street theatre before mobs of curious onlookers, the carefully coded mutilation and execution of criminals qualified not only as a mode of deterring others from evil deeds but also as a form of mass entertainment. Moreover, as she explains, criminals themselves sometimes seized the opportunity to work the crowd, eliciting personal sympathy and even fomenting revolt through their wounds, potentially understood as badges of honour parallel to those of Christ himself. The forcible inscription of law on the surface of the body could thus turn against the intentions of the government, as the passive individual claimed agency and cried out for justice.

Kathryn Hoffmann's essay returns us to the issues of medicine raised by Penelope Gouk earlier in the volume. As the science of anatomy developed, so did an increased curiosity concerning the abnormally formed. Phenomena – for instance, conjoined twins – that in an earlier time might have been feared as signs of witchcraft began to attract the attention of collectors and entrepreneurs, as well as the casual gazes of curiosity-seekers. Although some of the resulting enterprises resemble what later came to be called freak shows, others fed into the growth of scientific knowledge. We owe our modern museums to the *Wunderkammern* assembled from displays that featured such bodies. Even today, the Museum of Jurassic Technology (about a mile from my house in Los Angeles) claims to possess one of the horns that kept appearing on the head of a seventeenth-century English woman named Mary Davis, one of the bodies Hoffmann discusses. This disquieting essay invites us to regard the histories of medicine and science museums quite differently.

Toward a History of Time and Subjectivity

Saint Augustine famously quipped that he knew what time was unless he was asked. The seventeenth century saw the emergence of new, sometimes mutually antagonistic ways of rendering and experiencing time, as well as space. Italian musicians of the period, for instance, experimented with ways of manipulating the temporal dimensions of their music – producing dizzying sequences of headlong propulsions into the future, balloons of hovering motionlessness, sudden dilations, and just as sudden compressions.

By contrast, the French court insisted on the kind of moderating regularity associated with geometrically arranged dance, and Italianate excesses were strictly prohibited. Musicians accustomed to the kinds of goal-oriented temporalities typical of eighteenth-century Italian and German composers (e.g. Vivaldi, J.S. Bach, Mozart) often hear the music composed for the court of Louis XIV as fussy and directionless, and they consequently dismiss it as inferior. In my own contribution to this collection, I examine Jean Henry D'Anglebert's *Tombeau de Mr de Chambonnières* and reflect on some of the reasons why the French worked to develop a very different way of experiencing time – in music as well as in the other arts and even in theology. For, as Thomas Christensen's essay reminds us, music and its theories still were understood in Neoplatonic France as direct evidence of divine perfection.

Richard Leppert's essay addresses a wide range of issues, making it ideal as a concluding piece. Concentrating on Dutch paintings of music-making and musical instruments, it brings together the visual and sonic arts. Leppert is especially concerned with the position of music and its trappings within the mercantile world of the Netherlands, for instruments counted as expensive commodities, advertising the affluence of those who could afford such luxury items. Yet recalling Gouk's essay, Leppert also analyses the still-resonant traces of Pythagorean symbolism registered in the very presence of the instruments, which remain eerily silent on the canvas. Early modern subjectivity, he argues, comes into particular focus in the contradictions between sight and sound, in the codes that determined who (according to gender or class) could play what instruments, in the different subject positions of performer and listener.

In the wake of the Second World War, Fernand Braudel wrote: 'With the Baroque a new light began to shine . . . new and more lurid colors now bathed the landscapes of western Europe.'[3] Over the course of the sixty years since Braudel penned that description, many aspects of early modern culture have been domesticated, bleached of their luridness, toned down to suit the priorities of progress-oriented historiographies.

As these essays demonstrate, however, the seventeenth century still stands as a profoundly alien universe. The authors presented here point to the need for greater critical scrutiny of this period, not only because of its historical significance as the turning point between the Renaissance and the Enlightenment but also because in many respects its expressions of exaltation, its excesses, its anxieties often resemble our own. Although the contributors to this volume do not claim to offer definitive answers or to resolve contradictions, we do hope to open paths for new research that takes into account *as evidence* the structures of feeling manifested in seventeenth-century expressive culture.

NOTES

1 Raymond Williams, *Marxism and Literature* (Oxford: Oxford University Press, 1977), 128–35.

2 Ibid., 131–2.

3 Fernand Braudel, *The Mediterranean and the Mediterranean World in the Age of Philip II*, 2 vols., trans. Siân Reynolds (New York: Harper Colophon, 1976; first published in 1949), 827.

PART I

THE SCIENCE OF AFFECT

chapter one

Disciplining Feeling: The Seventeenth-Century Idea of a Mathematical Theory of the Emotions

DANIEL GARBER

Introduction: Setting Up the Problem

The seventeenth century was fascinated both by mathematics and by the emotions. So, in a way, it is not surprising that in this period there emerged a mathematical theory of the emotions.

Modern mathematics, from algebra as we now know it, to analytic geometry, to the calculus, was born in the seventeenth century. It is also during this century that mathematical physics as we know it came into being. In the beginning of the century Galileo was the first to tame motion mathematically, with his mathematical account of free-fall and projectile motion; the century ended with Newton's monumental *Principia*, where he offers a derivation of the law of universal gravitation. Most curious is the application of strict mathematical reasoning where one would expect it least, to the phenomenon of chance. The new mathematical theory of chance, developed by Pascal, Fermat, and Huygens in mid-century, became a kind of cultural fad, and quickly passed beyond its initial application to the analysis of games of chance to applications in the calculation of annuities, the analysis of testimony, and even theology, with Pascal's famous wager argument.[1]

But it wasn't only mathematics, but also mathematical styles of argument, that became fashionable in the period. In 1635, the Paris astrologer Jean-Baptiste Morin published a little pamphlet, *Quod Deus sit*, in which he offered a proof for the existence of God in geometrical style, with definitions, axioms, and formal proofs.[2] This seems to have been the inspiration for something that Descartes published as an appendix to the second set of objections to his *Meditations*, a brief text in which he redid some of the main arguments of the *Meditations* 'more geometrico,' in geometrical style.[3] This way of doing philosophy impressed the young Spinoza greatly. His first publication was an exposition of Descartes's philosophy in geometrical form, rather fuller than Descartes's own brief exercise in the genre.[4] But his central philosophical work was his *Ethics*, published only after his death, in 1677.[5] And this, too, was in geometrical form.

Spinoza's full reasons for choosing to write in the form of definitions, axioms, and formal proofs are rather complex, and are deeply connected with the details of his philosophy.[6] But the form in which Spinoza chose to present his philosophy is one of its most striking features, both to us and to his contemporaries. What is particularly striking is that the heart of this work is an account of the human emotions. Spinoza begins the work with a metaphysical preface. In Part I he first outlines his conception of God, identical (in a sense) with nature, who acts from his nature with complete necessity to create a world without meaning or purpose. In Part II he then goes on to talk about human beings, whose minds are, in a sense, identical with their bodies, completely bound into this world governed by physical necessity. This is the starting point. The rest of the *Ethics* deals with human liberation, how we are to get ourselves out of this predicament in which we find ourselves, bound by necessity into a world without meaning. Parts III and IV deal with the passions that bind us. Spinoza, in full geometrical rigour, gives an account of all of the passions – desire, joy, and sadness – and all of the other passions that follow out of these basic three. The end of Part IV and the entire Part V are then devoted to showing us how we can liberate ourselves from those passions and find true freedom and happiness.

We won't be able to get to liberation in this short essay, but I would like to pause and reflect on Spinoza's geometrical account of the passions, and particularly his treatment of time and timelessness in those parts of the *Ethics*. Spinoza himself understands how odd it must seem to treat the passions in this geometrical way. Spinoza begins Part III of the *Ethics* as follows:

> Most of those who have written about the Affects, and men's way of living, seem to treat, not of natural things, which follow the common laws of nature, but of things which are outside nature. Indeed they seem to conceive man in nature as a dominion within a dominion. For they believe that man disturbs, rather than follows, the order of nature, that he has absolute power over his actions, and that he is determined only by himself. And

> they attribute the cause of human impotence, not to the common power of nature, but to I know not what vice of human nature, which they therefore bewail, or laugh at, or disdain, or (as usually happens) curse. And he who knows how to censure more eloquently and cunningly the weakness of the human Mind is held to be Godly . . . To them it will doubtless seem strange that I should undertake to treat men's vices and absurdities in the Geometric style, and that I should wish to demonstrate by certain reasoning things which are contrary to reason, and which they proclaim to be empty, absurd, and horrible. [E3pref.]

Spinoza justifies his project of a geometrical theory of the passions as follows:

> But my reason is this: nothing happens in nature which can be attributed to any defect in it, for nature is always the same, and its virtue and power of acting are everywhere one and the same, i.e., the laws and rules of nature, according to which all things happen, and change from one form to another, are always and everywhere the same. So the way of understanding the nature of anything, of whatever kind, must also be the same, viz. through the universal laws and rules of nature. The Affects, therefore, of hate, anger, envy, etc., considered in themselves, follow from the same necessity and force of nature as the other singular things. And therefore they acknowledge certain causes, through which they are understood, and have certain properties, as worthy of our knowledge as the properties of any other thing, by the mere contemplation of which we are pleased. Therefore . . . I shall consider human actions and appetites just as if it were a question of lines, planes, and bodies. [E3pref.]

The point here is that human beings (human bodies) are parts of nature, and as such, they are subject to the laws of nature, which govern the world with blind and geometrical necessity. Indeed, since minds are, in a sense, identified with bodies, there is a robust sense in which for Spinoza, all there is to the human being is the body. For that reason we can consider human actions and human appetites in a fully rigorous way, 'just as if it were a question of lines, planes, and bodies.'

Behind this statement is a development in earlier seventeenth-century thought that shaped Spinoza's position: the mechanization of the living body, including the human body. A central feature of the so-called mechanist revolution of the early seventeenth century was that living things, including human bodies, are just complicated machines, collections of smaller parts whose size, shape, and motion determine their behaviour, in just the way that the parts of a machine determine how it will behave. Philosophers like Descartes, Hobbes, and their followers rejected the idea of a soul as the principle of life and treated natural and artificial nature on the same terms. If the human being is a machine, the human body can be treated like a machine, through the science of motion and mechanics, itself mathematical.

We have moved from the passions of the soul, to the machine that is the human body, and from there to the science of motion and mechanics that governs the behaviour of the human body, something that can be treated mathematically. But behind all of this there is a bit of a paradox. Mathematics was thought to be the science of the unchanging and unchangeable world of pure mathematical objects, the Platonic forms. But how can there be a mathematics of change? If physics is the science that governs the world of change and changeable things, and mathematics is the science of the eternal, then how is a mathematical physics possible?

Galileo and the Mathematics of Motion

To understand how this could be possible, let me begin with a distinction between two conceptions of mathematics. There was a standard distinction between pure mathematics and mixed mathematics that dates far before the seventeenth century.[7] Pure mathematics, which included geometry and arithmetic, was the pure study of mathematical objects such as geometrical objects and numbers. Mixed mathematics, on the other hand, included such domains as astronomy, optics, music, mechanics, and, by the seventeenth century, motion. Mixed mathematics was mathematical insofar as it treated its subjects with the tools of mathematics, but it differed from pure mathematics insofar as it applied to the physical world. (It also differed from physics, properly speaking, but that is another matter.) Now, pure mathematics deals with an eternal and unchanging world of mathematical objects and their relationships. But mixed mathematics deals with change, particularly the theory of motion. How can that be?

To see how, let us look at Galileo and how he used mathematics to treat the theory of motion. Galileo may not have been the first to do so, but his work nicely illustrates how mathematics was adapted to the temporal world of physics. I want to look at a very simple theorem that Galileo proves at the beginning of the third day of his *Discorsi e dimostrazioni matematiche intorno à due nuove scienze* (Leiden: 1638) (*Two New Sciences*).[8]

Now, a body is in uniform acceleration if its speed increases at every moment by equal increments. (This, by the way, is not the obviously correct definition for uniform acceleration; why not equal increments of speed at equal distances from the starting place, rather than at equal moments? This is a crucial issue for Galileo.) Suppose that we have a body in uniform acceleration, defined in that way. Then, Galileo claims, in a given time it will move the same distance as it would have moved had it been moving at a constant speed of half the final velocity.[9] The diagram that he gives is shown in figure 1.1.

Such diagrams are familiar to all of us now, but we shouldn't lose sight of the real complexity of what it means to use a static geometrical diagram to represent change.[10] In this diagram, CD represents the distance traversed. Interestingly enough, it has no role at all to play in the actual argument; it is there presumably to give the imagination something to anchor onto, to visualize as the path of a body moving, falling perhaps a certain distance. All of the real action takes place in the diagram to the left. In that diagram, AB represents the time in which CD is traversed. That is, equal intervals of AB are supposed to represent equal time intervals, and the direction from A to B is supposed to represent earlier to

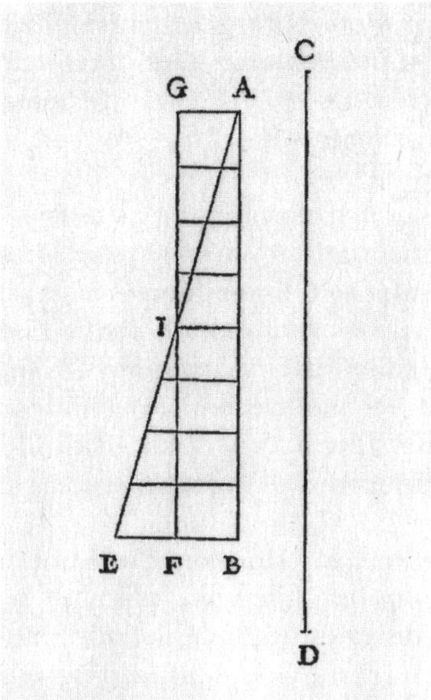

Figure 1.1 Galileo, *Discorsi* (1638), p. 170.

later. The line EB is supposed to represent the final speed of the body that is being uniformly accelerated. (It is drawn perpendicular to AB, but that is purely arbitrary; it can be at any angle that we like.) So, at time B, the speed of the body is represented by the length of the line EB. We then connect point E to point A. Galileo then tells us that the lines drawn to AE from every point of AB, parallel to EB, represent the speed of the body at a given moment of time. It is obvious from the geometry of the situation that in equal intervals of time, the line representing the speed will increase by equal increments.

What have we got here? First of all, a representation of uniform acceleration: as we progress along the line representing time, from earlier to later, we have another line that represents the speed of the body at that moment, a correlation between time elapsed (one line) and speed (another line). But we also have something more. When a body is moving at a uniform speed, the speed times the time equals the distance travelled. And so, for the accelerated body we can imagine summing tiny intervals of time with the speed at that time to get the distance travelled in that time interval. But geometrically, that will just be an area. And so it can easily be established that the area of the triangle ABE represents the distance travelled by the body as it moves during the time interval AB. Galileo goes on to show that this distance is the same as the distance that the body would travel if it moved uniformly at half the final speed BE, that is if it moved at speed BF for the entire period AB, by showing that the area of the triangle ABE equals the area of the parallelogram ABFG.[11]

In this way, Galileo has transformed a problem about motion, speed, and distance travelled in a time interval to a purely geometrical problem, one that deals with the relations between static areas in a static geometrical object. By representing motion through lines and geometrical objects, Galileo has converted a problem of temporal change into a geometrical problem. He has twisted geometry to represent a changing world: he has given us timeless truths about things in time. This is the power of mixed mathematics.

Spinoza on Time and the Emotions

Galileo illustrates how the eternal science of mathematics can be used to represent change. But at this point I would like to return to Spinoza and his mathematical treatment of the emotions. Before getting into the details of Spinoza's account of emotions, I would like to begin by reminding you of some features of Spinoza's thought. Earlier I talked about the central theme of liberation from the passions in Spinoza's thought. The details are complicated, but the idea is simple. The passions are, unsurprisingly, passive; they are states in which we are acted on by something external to ourselves. Actions are events that derive from ourselves as complete causes. Or, more formally, as he puts it in the beginning of Part III of the *Ethics*,

> I say that we act when something happens, in us or outside us, of which we are the adequate cause, i.e. . . . when something in us or outside us follows from our nature, which can be clearly and distinctly understood through it alone. On the other hand, I say that we are acted on when something happens in us, or something follows from our nature, of which we are only a partial cause. [E3d2]

Liberation for Spinoza involves the move from a state of being dominated by the passions and being acted on by things outside of us, and to a state in which we are genuine actors, in which our states have ourselves as causes, and not things outside of us. The difference between passion and action, Spinoza argues, corresponds to two different cognitive states. Imagination, the ability we have to form mental pictures, which involves both what we call sensation and what we more normally call imagination, is a state in which we are acted upon by things external to us: it is by virtue of bodies acting on us that we have these mental pictures that we call imaginations. On the other hand, reason is a purely active state for Spinoza. (There is a third kind of cognition – intuitive knowledge – that goes beyond reason, but we won't have to deal with that here.) And so, our liberation is connected with the move from knowledge based on imagination (from the senses, from testimony, from authority) to knowledge based on reason.

One other feature of Spinoza's thought is important to consider before we dive into the theory of the passions. As I have suggested earlier, mind and body are not exactly identical for Spinoza, as they are for Hobbes, for example. But then they aren't exactly separate either. Mind is not reducible to body insofar as mind is understood through thought and body through extension. But mind and body are in another sense, the exactly same item in Spinoza's ontology: they differ *only* in the way in which we understand them through different concepts. So, for all practical purposes, we can treat them identically. Indeed, everything Spinoza wants to say about the passions and about knowledge can be understood entirely in terms of the body alone, as if he were a Hobbesian materialist, in terms of the mind alone, as if he were a pure idealist, or in terms of a being that has both a mind and a body.

And at this point I would like to turn to Spinoza's account of the passions properly speaking, the passive emotions, the emotions that derive from things acting on us. What exactly does Spinoza's mathematical theory of the passions look like?

According to Spinoza, there are three basic emotions: desire, joy, and sadness; all other emotions 'arise' from these three [E3p11s]. Desire is connected to the basic urge we have to continue in our existence, something that pertains to all 'things': 'Unaquaeque res, quantum in se est, in suo esse perseverare conatur' ('Each and every thing, insofar as it can, strives to persevere in its existence)' [E3p6]. Despite the fact that Spinoza offers a formal proof of this proposition, it hasn't been entirely clear to commentators exactly what he has in mind here. The formal proof derives from the fact that the essence of a thing cannot contain anything contrary to the nature of the thing; that is, it cannot contain anything that could oppose its nature. Consequently, taken by itself, a thing will persist until it is destroyed by an external cause. But Spinoza wants something stronger, that 'it is opposed to everything which can take its existence away' [E3p6d].

I suspect that Spinoza is reasoning like this. An individual thing, for Spinoza, is something that has a nature; not every collection of randomly designated stuff satisfies this condition. And to have a nature for him means to have a stable structure, one that is sufficiently robust to maintain itself in the face of disruption. On such a homeostatic conception of the individual, a thing could legitimately be said to oppose 'everything which can take its existence away.'[12] This striving for continued existence is what Spinoza calls will, appetite, and desire:

> When this striving is related only to the Mind, it is called Will; but when it is related to the Mind and Body together, it is called Appetite . . . Between appetite and desire there is no difference, except that desire is generally related to men insofar as they are conscious of their appetite. So desire can be defined as appetite together with consciousness of the appetite. [E3p9s]

In practice, though, Spinoza uses 'desire' as his general term for the affect that is linked to the strive for continued existence.

Now, some outside impingements on a thing decrease its power to act, while others increase it. The former give rise to the passion of sadness, the latter to the passion of joy. And so Spinoza writes:

> By Joy, therefore, I shall understand in what follows that passion by which the Mind passes to a greater perfection. And by Sadness, that passion by which it passes to a lesser perfection. [E3p11s]

In this way, Spinoza identifies the affects of desire, joy, and sadness with particular states of the mind/body. Other emotions can be defined in these terms. And so, for example, Spinoza defines love as 'joy with the accompanying idea of an external cause' and hate as 'sadness with the accompanying idea of an external cause' [E3p13s].

And with these definitions in place, Spinoza can then begin the deductions that are supposed to display our emotional life with mathematical rigour. Insofar as the mind/body obeys certain definite laws, Spinoza can derive theorems concerning those states and their relations, and insofar as the passions are identified with particular states of body, these theorems will, ipso facto, be theorems about the passions:

> E3p13: The Mind, as far as it can, strives to imagine those things that increase or aid the Body's power of acting [i.e., which give it joy].
>
> E3p14: When the Mind imagines those things that diminish or restrain the Body's power of acting [i.e., things which make us sad], it strives, as far as it can, to recollect things that exclude their existence.
>
> E3p19: He who imagines that what he loves is destroyed will be saddened; but he who imagines it to be preserved, will rejoice.
>
> E3p20: He who imagines that what he hates is destroyed will rejoice.

In this way Spinoza can set our emotional life out in mathematical form.

But it is especially interesting to see the way in which time enters into the project. Two of the most important passions that Spinoza deals with in the *Ethics* are hope and fear. They are defined as follows:

> Hope is nothing but an inconstant Joy which has arisen from the image of a future or past thing whose outcome we doubt; Fear, on the other hand, is an inconstant Sadness, which has also arisen from the image of a doubtful thing. [E3p18s2]

These two passions are quite central to Spinoza's thought. Fear of punishment is what usually coerces the masses into obeying the laws set down by their governments:

> Nevertheless, since the true end of laws is usually evident only to a few, and since for the most part men are almost incapable of perceiving it and do anything but live according to reason, legislators, in order to bind all men equally, have wisely set up another end, very different from that which necessarily follows from the nature of laws, by promising to the defenders of the laws what the multitude most love, and on the other hand, by threatening those who would break the laws with what they most fear. In this way they have striven to restrain the multitude, like a horse with a harness, as far as they could.[13]

The hope for an eternal life of happiness and the fear of punishment in the afterlife are what induce the masses to live in accordance with morality:

> They are induced to live according to the rule of the divine law . . . not only by this hope, but also, and especially, by the fear that they may be punished horribly after death. If men did not have this Hope and Fear, but believed instead that the minds die with the body, and that the wretched, exhausted with the burden of Morality, cannot look forward to a life to come, they would return to their natural disposition, and would prefer to govern all their actions according to lust, and to obey fortune rather than themselves. [E5p41s][14]

Though hope and fear can certainly influence our behaviour, the fact that they deal with future states and events diminishes their power over our behaviour. Spinoza proves the following series of propositions that turn on the temporality of certain ideas:

> E4p9&c: An affect whose cause we imagine to be with us in the present is stronger than if we did not imagine it to be with us . . . Other things equal, the image of a future or past thing (i.e., of a thing we consider in relation to a future or past time, the present being excluded) is weaker than the image of a present thing; and consequently, an affect toward a future or past thing is milder, other things equal, than an affect toward a present thing.
>
> E4p10: We are affected more intensely toward a future thing which we imagine will quickly be present, than if we imagined the time when it will exist to be further from the present. We are also affected more intensely by

the memory of a thing we imagine to be not long past, than if we imagined it to be long past.

E4p16: A Desire which arises from a true knowledge of good and evil, insofar as this knowledge concerns the future, can be quite easily restrained or extinguished by a Desire for the pleasures of the moment.

In this way Spinoza proves, again with mathematical rigour, that people live for the moment, and while the hopes and fears of future pleasure and pain may play some role, it doesn't influence us as strongly as our present states do.

Once again we have the interesting situation we had with respect to Galileo: how can Spinoza represent this kind of temporality in a mathematical structure? How can we give timeless truths about a fundamentally temporal state of affairs? How can we represent the agent's relations with future (and past) at a given moment so that we can apply the timeless apparatus of the geometrical method of argument to derive these conclusions? Here is how Spinoza explains his conception of how we represent temporality:

Let us suppose, then, a child, who saw Peter for the first time yesterday, in the morning, but saw Paul at noon, and Simon in the evening, and today again saw Peter in the morning. It is clear . . . that as soon as he sees the morning light, he will immediately imagine the sun taking the same course through the sky as he saw on the preceding day, or he will imagine the whole day, and Peter together with the morning, Paul with noon, and Simon with the evening. That is, he will imagine the existence of Paul and of Simon with a relation to future time. On the other hand, if he sees Simon in the evening, he will relate Paul and Peter to the time past, by imagining them together with past time. And he will do this more uniformly, the more often he has seen them in this same order. [E2p44s]

Spinoza's strategy is this. The child represents time through an imaginary trajectory of the sun through the sky. Better, morning is represented by an imagination of the sun in the east; noon is represented by the sun overhead; evening is represented by the sun in the west. Peter-in-the-morning is represented as the conjunction of an imagination of Peter and an imagination of the sun in the east; Paul-at-noon is represented as the conjunction of an imagination of Paul and an imagination of the sun overhead; and Simon-in-the-evening is represented as the conjunction of Simon and an imagination of the sun in the west. This method of representing time has severe limitations, of course; it doesn't work at night, or on cloudy days, and it doesn't tell us how to represent a time period that goes beyond a single day. But it can easily be generalized. Time can be represented as a collection of ordered images. Galileo used the parts of an imagined line; Spinoza might imagine images of the hands of a clock in different positions, or the pages of a calendar (think of the way the passage of time was represented in old movies). And in just the way Galileo associated particular speeds with points on his time line, Spinoza associates particular events with the reference events that constitute the passage of time, Peter-is-present, or Paul-is-present, or Simon-is-present. In this way, just as Galileo took the time out of the temporal and gave a static representation of the passing of time, so does Spinoza allow us to treat the temporal at a given moment. Of course, Spinoza is not applying any sophisticated geometrical reasoning to these representations, unlike Galileo, but this static representation of the passage of time allows him to offer theorems about temporality and the passions in a mathematically rigorous way. In this way, one might say that Spinoza is offering us a kind of mixed mathematics of the passions, a kind of mathematical reasoning about the time-infused world of the passions.

Moving beyond Imagination, Moving beyond Time

The representation of temporality seems necessarily to involve the imagination: to conceive of things in time is to imagine them linked with other events that change in a regular way [E2p44s and E4p62s]. But the realm of the imagination is the realm of the passive, the realm of that which acts on us. What happens when we move toward Spinozistic liberation, give up the imagination, and move from the passive to the active, from imagination to reason? Well, one thing that happens is that we have to give up temporality, which is a feature of the imagination. Spinoza writes: 'It is of the nature of reason to perceive things *sub specie aeternitatis*' [E2p44c2]. What does this phrase mean, '*sub specie aeternitatis*'? Literally, it means 'under the gaze of eternity' or perhaps, 'from the point of view of eternity.' To have knowledge through reason, as opposed to the imagination, means to see things as outside the temporal. Spinoza defines eternity at the very beginning of the *Ethics*:

> By eternity I understand existence itself, insofar as it is conceived to follow necessarily from the definition alone of the eternal thing.

Exp: For such existence, like the essence of a thing, is conceived as an eternal truth, and on that account cannot be explained by duration or time, even if the duration is conceived to be without beginning or end. [E1d8]

In this way Spinoza would seem to distinguish rather sharply between the notion of eternity, and what has been called in the tradition 'sempiternity.' Sempiternity is temporal existence without beginning or end; it is existence for all time. Eternity, on the other hand, is existence outside of time altogether. Spinoza writes in the *Short Treatise on God, Man, and His Well-Being* (*ST*): 'in eternity there is neither before nor after.'[15] Later, in E1 he writes that 'in eternity there is neither *when*, nor *before*, nor *after*' [E1p33s2]. Eternal existence, he writes, 'cannot be defined by time or explained through duration' [E5p23s]. Insofar as reason deals with things *sub specie aeternitatis*, it deals with an eternal and timeless world, not the changing world of mixed mathematics, but the changeless world of pure geometry.

What this means, among other things, is that when we have conquered the passions, moved from imagination to reason, from being acted upon to acting, then there is no difference to us between past, present, and future: we are no longer in the tyrannical grip of the present moment.

E4p62: Insofar as the Mind conceives things from the dictate of reason, it is affected equally, whether the idea is of a future or past thing, or of a present one.

E4p66: From the guidance of reason we want a greater future good in preference to a lesser present one, and a lesser present evil in preference to a greater future one.

But even more importantly, when we abandon the imagination for reason, temporality for the eternal, then we abandon fear as well:

E4p63: He who is guided by fear, and does good to avoid evil, is not guided by reason.

In particular, the person guided by reason, what Spinoza calls the 'free man' in the *Ethics*, is not guided at all by a fear of death:

E4p67: A free man thinks of nothing less than of death, and his wisdom is a meditation on life, not on death.

Spinoza's goal is the liberation from hope and fear, the liberation from the passions themselves.

But the liberation from the passions is also the liberation from time itself, the step from the temporal to the eternal. Insofar as the mathematical treatment of the emotions in the earlier parts of the *Ethics* contributes to this goal, one might say that the mathematical treatment of change that it embodies plays a role in leading us out of time and toward that Platonic world of the unchanging that is, in a sense, the proper realm of the mathematical.

NOTES

1 On the history of mathematics in the period, see Michael Mahoney, 'The Mathematical Realm of Nature,' in *The Cambridge History of Seventeenth-Century Philosophy*, ed. Daniel Garber and Michael Ayers (Cambridge: Cambridge University Press, 1998), 1: 702–55. On the history of probability, see Ian Hacking, *The Emergence of Probability* (Cambridge: Cambridge University Press, 1975); and Gerd Gigerenzer et al., *The Empire of Chance: How Probability Changed Science and Everything Else* (Cambridge: Cambridge University Press, 1989).

2 Jean-Baptiste Morin, *Quod Deus sit* (Paris, 1635).

3 On this see Daniel Garber, 'J.-B. Morin and the *Second Objections*,' in Garber, *Descartes Embodied* (Cambridge: Cambridge University Press, 2001), 64–84.

4 See Benedictus Spinoza, *Renati Des Cartes Principiorum Philosophorum pars I & II more geometrico demonstratae* (Amsterdam, 1663). The Latin text can also be found in vol. 1 of Carl Gebhardt, ed., *Spinoza Opera*, 4 vols. (Heidelberg: Carl Winter, 1925). It is translated in vol. 1 of Edwin Curley, ed., *The Collected Works of Spinoza* (Princeton: Princeton University Press, 1985).

5 The *Ethica* is in vol. 2 of Gebhardt, and translated in Curley. In what follows I shall use transparent abbreviations to refer to the text. So, for example, 'E2p7s' refers to part 2, proposition 7, scholium, etc. Unless otherwise noted, the translations are taken from Curley. As much as possible I shall give the references to the *Ethics* in the body of the text.

6 For some speculations on this question, see Daniel Garber, '"A Free Man Thinks of Nothing Less Than of Death": Spinoza on the Eternity of the Mind,' in *Early Modern Philosophy: Mind, Matter and Metaphysics*, ed. Christia Mercer and Eileen O'Neill (Oxford: Oxford University Press, 2005), 103–18, esp. 114–16.

7 On this, see e.g. James G. Lennox, 'Aristotle, Galileo, and "Mixed Sciences,"' in *Reinterpreting Galileo*, ed. William A. Wallace (Washington, DC:

Catholic University of America Press, 1986), 29–51; and Gary I. Brown, 'The Evolution of the Term "Mixed Mathematics,"' *Journal of the History of Ideas* 52 (1991): 81–102.

8 The standard text is in A. Favaro, ed., *Opere di Galileo Galilei* (Florence: G. Berbèra, 1890–1909), 8: 208–9, translated in Galileo, *Two New Sciences*, ed. and trans. Stillman Drake (Madison: University of Wisconsin Press, 1974), 165–6. The really interesting result, the one that arguably founded the mathematical theory of motion, is not the one I will discuss here, but the one following, where Galileo proves that in free fall, the distance fallen is proportional to the time squared. But the basic issues concerning the geometrical representation of time come out just as well in the simpler example I have chosen to treat.

9 This theorem, often called the 'mean-speed theorem' seems to have been stated and proved for the first time in early fifteenth-century Oxford at Merton College. See Marshall Clagett, *The Science of Mechanics in the Middle Ages* (Madison: University of Wisconsin Press, 1959), ch. 5, for a history of the theorem, with many of the relevant texts. For an account of Galileo's relation to these earlier versions, see Edith Sylla, 'Galileo and the Oxford Calculatores: Analytical Languages and the Mean-Speed Theorem for Accelerated Motion,' in *Reinterpreting Galileo*, ed. William A. Wallace (Washington, DC: Catholic University Press, 1986), 53–108. Thanks much to Michael Mahoney for this last reference.

10 These kinds of diagrams were probably not altogether unfamiliar in the time of Galileo either. For the history of geometrical representations of change in connection with the mean-speed theorem, see Clagett, *The Science of Mechanics*, ch. 6, and Clagett, *Nicole Oresme and the Medieval Geometry of Qualities and Motions* (Madison: University of Wisconsin Press, 1968). Thanks again to Michael Mahoney for this last reference.

11 Actually, Galileo does something rather more interesting here. What he does is sum up the aggregate of all the parallels that make up the quadrilateral AGFB, and those that make up the triangle AEB, and show that they are equal. This suggests the kinds of procedures that Galileo's contemporary Buonaventura Cavalieri suggested for calculating areas, procedures that are sometimes seen as the ancestor to modern integration in the calculus. On Cavalieri, see, e.g., K. Andersen, 'Cavalieri's Method of Indivisibles,' *Archive for History of Exact Sciences* 31 (1985): 291–367.

12 On this, see Daniel Garber, 'Descartes and Spinoza on Persistence and Conatus,' *Studia Spinozana* 10 (1994): 43–67.

13 Spinoza, *Tractatus Theologico-Politicus* (1670), ch. 4, in Gebhardt, *Opera,* 3: 58–9. The translation is by Edwin Curley, who kindly shared with me his yet unpublished translation. See also the account of how Moses controlled the Jews in chapter 2, Gebhardt, 3: 40–1.
14 Cf. *Tractatus Theologico-Politicus,* ch. 16, Gebhardt, 3: 194–5.
15 Gebhardt, 1: 37; trans. in Curley, *Collected Works,* 1: 82.

chapter two

Clockwork or Musical Instrument? Some English Theories of Mind-Body Interaction before and after Descartes

PENELOPE GOUK

Introduction

The title of my essay refers back to an article I wrote about twenty years ago, 'Some English Theories of Hearing in the Seventeenth Century: Before and after Descartes.'[1] Then as now, it proved essential to discuss my findings about early modern English theories of perception in relation to Descartes's mechanical philosophy, especially his dualistic account of the interaction between material body and immortal soul. The two works that contained the essence of Descartes's model of man were *De homine figuris*, which he completed around 1633, and his final work, *Les passions de l'âme*, which was published in 1649. In fact, the latter work was known in England much sooner than the former, not least because it was translated into English and published as *Passions of the Soul* in 1650, the year Descartes died. Meanwhile, *De homine figuris* (Treatise on Man) was only published in 1662, and there was no contemporary English translation – although, of course, all university-educated men and a few rare women would have been able to read it in Latin. Descartes's mechanical philosophy certainly made an impact on the seventeenth-century philosophical community, not least because of its radical distinction between inert passive matter and active 'mind,' or soul. However, it is only with hindsight that we know that his mechanical system finally displaced Aristotle's natural philosophy in the late seventeenth century, not just at the University of Paris, for example, which was Catholic, but also at the University of Leiden, which was Calvinist.

From the historical perspective of this paper, which takes a before-and-after approach to Descartes's system in the English-speaking world, both the originality and dominance of his ideas were not so great as is popularly thought today. Here I propose to explore the thinking of three English authors in order to highlight similarities with, and differences from, Descartes's conception of the mechanical philosophy. These writers include two physicians, namely Timothy Bright (1550–1615) and Robert Fludd (1574–1637), and an apothecary, Richard Browne (fl. 1729). I will show that it is no coincidence that all three men were medical professionals whose understanding of the relationship between the body and soul was of paramount importance in the practice of their professional duties, a crucial skill being the ability to diagnose and moderate the passions of the mind (or emotions as they are called today).[2] Furthermore I will argue that my subjects shared an unusual interest in music, two (Bright, Fludd) and probably all three of them being competent performers themselves. Having a direct personal experience of music's power to restore inner harmony could well explain their attention to music's effects as well as their musical, rather than strictly mechanical, conceptions of mind-body interaction.

Of course, there are many scholars, including other contributors to this volume, who know that Descartes's ideas were vigorously challenged in his own time, notably by his own countrymen Pierre Gassendi and Marin Mersenne, and also by the notorious English philosopher Thomas Hobbes. Indeed, it is well known that the rejection of Cartesian dualism in favour of materialism, and especially the thesis that even the soul itself is mortal, gained Hobbes a reputation for atheism that clings to him even down to the present day.[3] Leaving aside this particular controversy, however, I still want to claim that scholars have too simplistic an understanding of what we all tend to describe as the 'mechanical philosophy' of the seventeenth century, namely the attempt to understand and explain the workings of nature in terms of artificial, man-made devices and the ways the various parts of these artefacts interact and move in relation to each other, the archetypal model being, of course, the mechanical clock.[4] There are three main reasons why I say this. First, to compare an animal, human being, or even the cosmos itself to a piece of machinery emphatically does not remove God or life from the system, even though early-twentieth-century historians of science and technology may have wished to interpret mechanical philosophy in this way. In fact, I want to argue that the model allows devout Christians to conceptualize life, the universe, and everything in it as the manifestation of divine artifice and, at the same time, to raise the skill and status of the artificer, or mechanic, to something approaching the divine.

The second reason for my claim is that too little attention has been paid either to the finer details of the various mechanisms invoked by early modern thinkers or to the specific explanatory functions these analogies are meant to serve. As I will show in this essay, all so-called mechanical models involve themselves with the immediate source of their motive power (e.g., whether the device is moved by the pressure of water, or of air, or by weights and pulleys, wheels, springs, or a combination of any of these), as well as with the precise effect or outcome that is intended by this exercise of power.[5] In short, we need to notice just where the differences in input and output lie before we can really claim to understand the mechanical philosophy.

The third, and most important, reason why I think our historical understanding of the mechanical philosophy is too simplistic is that some categories of 'artifical' devices that philosophers invoked to explain nature's workings were specifically designed to produce *musical* sounds.[6] So far, so good: many of these devices might be simply classified as musical instruments, in that all that they appear to do is play music. For example, the automatic virginal made around 1610 by the Dutch engineer Cornelius Drebbel was apparently a hydraulic device that relied on the sun to set its jacks in motion. According to John Wilkins's *Mathematical Magic* (1648), it 'would of itself render a soft and pleasant harmony, but being removed into the shade, would presently become silent.'[7]

More generally, however, the musical capabilities of these devices represented only one function among several, notably those that involved keeping track of time. For example, a surviving bracket clock made in the Lower Rhine some time around 1583 tells the time with a dial that indicates the phases of the moon, the hours, and quarter hours. It also has an hour-striking train and a carillon of six bells that is released hourly by the motion work, so that the jack bobs his head and strikes the bells.[8] By contrast, a device made by Hans Schlottheim in 1582 for the Duke of Barvaria is not a clock, but an automaton with trumpeters and drummers that has an organ with ten pipes in the base. The musicians are set in motion when the organ sounds, and the drum tones are produced through two clappers striking on a membrane in the base.[9] These two examples alone show that an indiscriminate emphasis on 'machinery' obscures the significant overlap between on the one hand all categories of machine and on the other all categories of musical instrument, most of which require direct pressure of a player's fingers, and/or mouth and breath, and the contact of other parts of his or her body, in order to produce organized sounds that musicologists call 'the music itself.'

Indeed, the production of 'the music itself' doesn't just involve instruments and a battery of techniques; it also requires an intentional creator and a responsive listener (who may of course be the same individual). This capacity to evoke absent presences and sympathetic resonances suggests there is always much more to these instruments than meets the eye – whichever way you look at them, they have enormous symbolic power to function at different levels of abstraction, all at the same time. Two of the best-known seventeenth-century images showing this process at work appear in the *Utriusque cosmi historia*, or *History of the Macrocosm and Microcosm*, published at Oppenheim between 1617 and 1619 by the English physician and Rosicrucian philosopher Dr Robert Fludd (figures 2.1 and 2.2).

As the work of Frances Yates has demonstrated, it was partly in response to Fludd's hermetic vision of a magical universe resonating with occult powers that Descartes constructed his so-called 'mechanical' system, a universe in which particles of matter remain inert until they are displaced by an external force, an essentially kinetic theory of motion.[10] And although my title refers to theories *before* and *after* Descartes, I propose to start with Fludd's ideas, which are really in the middle. Thanks to Fludd's innovative use of visual imagery to depict what is really a profoundly musical way of thinking, I have come to understand why there are some striking continuities in English medical thinking about mind-body interaction from the late sixteenth to the early eighteenth centuries.[11]

Once I have discussed Fludd's visualization of the harmonies of inner and outer space, I shall move back in time by approximately a generation to examine some interesting ideas of Timothy Bright, the author of the first English *Treatise on Melancholy*, printed in 1586 (Bright already had an MA from Cambridge the year Fludd was born).[12] After dealing with Bright, who died in 1615, I shall ruthlessly 'fast forward' right through the seventeenth century and end my essay with the first medical treatise in English to be wholly devoted to music and its therapeutic potential: *A Mechanical Essay on Singing, Music and Dancing . . . Demonstrating, by Clear and Evident Reasons, the Alterations They Produce in a Human Body* (London, 1727) by Richard Browne. Browne was an apothecary rather than a physician, although he seems to have been aware of the most up-to-date physiology of his time. Whatever his background, which I suspect included musical training, Browne shows remarkable insight into the inner transformations that singing, playing, and listening to music could work on the human machine.

Robert Fludd, *History of the Macrocosm* (1617)

The first of Fludd's images (figure 2.1) is a realization of the story told by Plato and his followers about Pythgaoras's discovery of the mathematical harmonies governing the heavens, as well as his apochryphal invention of the musical canon, or monochord.[13] One of the most vociferous critics of this particular interpretation of the Pythagorean myth was Mersenne, who smugly pointed out that Fludd's divine monochord was flawed, partly because the F should be sharp for the tones and semitones to be correct. For Johannes Kepler, another harsh critic, the real problem was that Fludd thought cosmic harmonies followed Pythagorean tuning, while his own calculations made him certain that the divine scale followed the syntonic diatonic of Ptolemy.[14] Nevertheless, despite his apparent indifference to both musical or astronomical experience, Fludd principally intends in this image to portray an emanationist theory of creation, whereby each level of existence (empyrean, ethereal, elemental) emanates from a transcendent One, the God who appears to be keeping a strong grip on his creation via the monochord's only peg. (The tones get higher farther away from the earth.)

Fludd's Neoplatonic image of 'man the microcosm' (figure 2.2), from the second book of the *History*, reveals the same musical proportions governing human as well as cosmic bodies This is where the connection between medicine and music becomes particularly important. In the Neoplatonic universe, the harmony of the heavens is maintained by *tonos* or tension, a dynamic property of *spiritus*, *pneuma*, or the world soul, which is represented here by Fludd as a musical string that stretches upwards from the earthbound body of man and connects it sympathetically to the empyrean or heavenly realms. And although it is represented as a string in this particular image, *spiritus* or *pneuma* was more often thought of as an extremely fine and active substance that mediates between God and his creation – as a manifestation of his divine breath, which is the very stuff out of which the universe is composed. This concept meshes well with the Galenic medical system with which Fludd, as a humanistically educated physician, was intimately acquainted. Within this system, health was construed as the balance or harmony of opposites within the body, a state of equilibrium which is again maintained through *tonos* or sympathy.[15] In fact, these kinds of musical analogies for body parts and

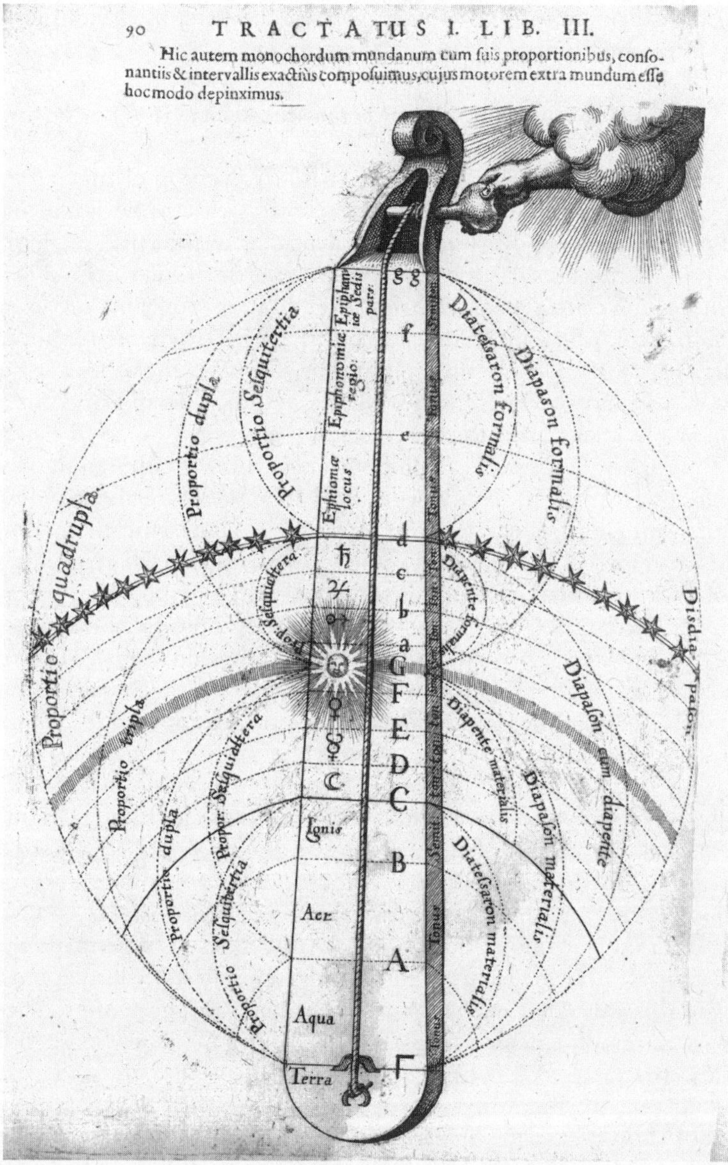

Figure 2.1 The universe as monochord, from Robert Fludd, *Utriusque cosmi . . . historia* (Oppenheim, 1617), I, tract. 1, p. 90. Wellcome Library, London.

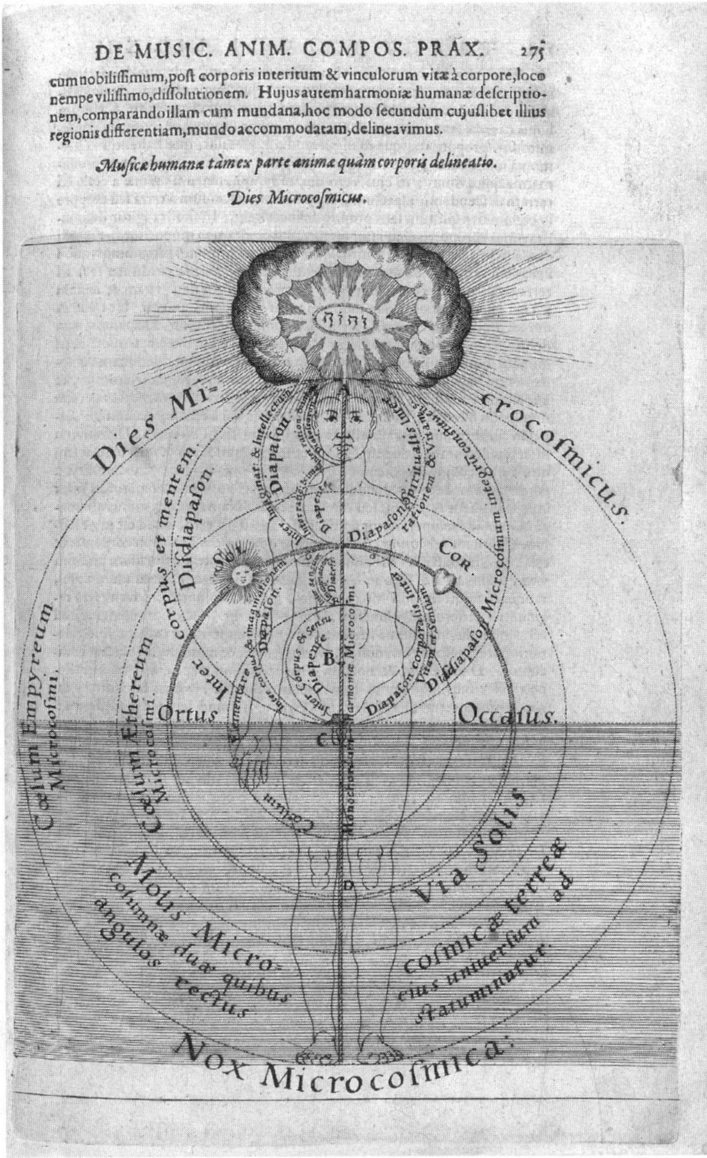
DE MUSIC. ANIM. COMPOS. PRAX. 275

cum nobiliſſimum, poſt corporis interitum & vinculorum vitæ à corpore, loco nempe viliſſimo, diſſolutionem. Hujus autem harmoniæ humanæ deſcriptionem, comparando illam cum mundana, hoc modo ſecundùm cujuſlibet illius regionis differentiam, mundo accommodatam, delineavimus.

Muſicæ humanæ tàm ex parte animæ quàm corporis delineatio.

Dies Microcoſmicus.

Figure 2.2 Man the microcosm, from Robert Fludd, *Utriusque cosmi . . . historia* (Oppenheim, 1618), II, tract. 1, p. 274. Wellcome Library, London.

functions were not confined to stringed instruments; the other kind most commonly invoked (e.g., for respiration or vocal exercising) was wind instruments.[16]

As far as I am aware, these engravings are the first detailed representations to appear in print of the cosmic and human harmonies alluded to in Boethius's *De musica* – that is to say, the higher levels of musical reality in the Neoplatonic universe, a system in which *musica instrumentalis* is only an imperfect imitation of the real harmonies that compose the heavens. Although Fludd's images were deliberately esoteric and available only to the privileged few who could afford to buy his *History*, I would argue that the concepts they communicate were potentially accessible to a much wider audience. This is because they are part of a distinctively Netherlandish tradition of visual art in which the transient nature of the sensible world and its pleasures is silently juxtaposed against a deeper reality – a hidden dimension that, no matter how skilful the artist, is always occluded from sight.[17]

In fact, Fludd's images were designed by Johann Theodore de Bry, a second-generation Flemish Huguenot whose father had fled from persecution and set up his publishing business in the more congenial Palatinate. As Richard Leppert demonstrates in his essay elsewhere in this volume, these images serve to remind contemplative viewers that just as a real musical instrument, or even a picture of an instrument (or part of an instrument), can bring to mind music that cannot be seen, so *music itself* may be thought of, or rather experienced, as an entity whose very existence signifies a meaningful interaction between ensouled or intelligent beings, who may not be physically proximate but are nevertheless communicating sympathetically with each other.[18]

Fludd is remembered for his visualizations of cosmic and human harmonies, but he was by no means the first English physician to grasp music's power to alter spiritual states. For my next example of an English theory of mind-body interaction I turn to the work of Timothy Bright, a Cambridge graduate who was among the first cohort of young gentlemen to travel and study in Queen Elizabeth's reign. Although Bright does not actually use pictures to help him describe the power of *spiritus* to animate the human frame, his verbal imagery is as effective as Fludd's visual imagery for communicating his ideas on this complex subject. The link between Fludd's picture of man the microcosm amd Bright's *Treatise of Melancholy* is Bright's claim that this disease or sickness comes from a loss of spirit, an affliction that signifies an imbalance within the body, and requires restoration of harmony between body, mind, and spirit.

Timothy Bright's *Treatise on Melancholy* (1586)

When Timothy Bright published his *Treatise on Melancholy* in 1586, he was physician to St Bartholomew's Hospital in London. Shortly afterwards, however, he gave up his professional medical practice, took holy orders, and spent the rest of his life as a (very negligent) pastor in Yorkshire.[19] Bright's *Treatise*, the first English work to deal with the causes and cures of melancholy, was completed only a few months after he and his wife Margaret suffered the death of one of their children. An important source for Robert Burton's *Anatomy* of 1621, it also predates the treatise on melancholy published by the French Huguenot physician André du Laurens in 1599.[20] For reasons I will reveal a little later, it is important to note that Bright himself was in France four years after graduating at Cambridge in 1568, at the age of eighteen. In fact he seems to have been studying medicine on the continent at the time he was caught up in the terrible events of the St Bartholomew's Day Massacre in Paris on 24 August 1572, when he took refuge in the house of the English Ambassador Sir Francis Walsingham, together with the latter's son-in-law Sir Philip Sidney. Surviving these horrendous events unscathed, Bright seems to have continued his medical studies in Europe, possibly in Italy and Germany, before returning to Cambridge, where he took his MB in 1574.

Bright tells his readers that he wrote the *Treatise of Melancholy* to reassure his friend 'M' that the latter's melancholy was not a form of soul sickness, the affliction of a troubled conscience that results from sin, a condition that can only be cured through religious means. Instead, Bright diagnoses M's condition as the 'natural' kind of melancholy that comes from disorder within the body and is therefore responsive to physic (the seventeenth-century term for 'medicine').[21]

In explaining how melancholy can affect people even if they have not sinned, Bright avers the existence of an extremely fine 'spirit' that flows through the body and functions as the soul's instrument. In contradiction to prevailing medical orthodoxy, Bright rejects the division between the natural, vital, and animal spirits that were thought to be localized respectively in the abdomen (liver), thorax (heart), and head (brain). In Bright's physiology there is only one, organical, spirit moved by an inward, forcible power that is sufficient to account for all life functions and bodily actions.[22] The transmission of motion from one part of a clock to another as if by an invisible spirit or indwelling principle serves as an apt model for traces of motions within the human body. To help his readers imagine how so many different operations can be performed through a single faculty, Bright uses the analogy of 'automatical instruments':

> We see it evident in automaticall instruments, as clockes, watches, and larums, how one right and straighte motion, through the aptness of the first wheele, not only causeth circular motion in the same, but in divers others also: and not only so, but distinct in pace, and time of motion: some wheeles passing swifter then other some, by divers rases: now to these devises some other instrument added, as hammer and bell, not only another right motion springeth thereof, as the stroke of the hammer, but sound also oft repeated, and delivered at certaine times by equall pauses, and that either larum or hourse according as the parts of the clocke are framed. To these if yet moreover a directory hand be added, this first, & simple & right motion by weight or straine, shall seme not only to be author of deliberate sound, and to counterfeit voice, but also to point with the finger as much as it have declared by sound. Besides these we see yet a third motion with reciprocation in the ballance of the clock. So many actions diverse in kinde rise from one simple first motion, by reason of variety of joints in one engine. If to these you adde what wit can devise, you may find all the motion of heaven with his planets counterfetted, in a small modil, with distinction of time and season, as in the course of the heavenly bodies.[23]

In other words, ten years before Descartes was even born, Bright was already able to assume his readers were sufficiently familiar with different kinds of mechanical timepieces to suggest that these automata can help them understand how many different controlled actions can result from a simple first motion, 'by reason of variety of joints in one engine.' I have already mentioned two examples of South German instruments that combine striking trains with automatic music and figurines. The same alluring combination of horology and automatic music was also fashionable in princely gardens of the period, sites where complex hydraulic devices were deployed in fountains and grottoes to create moving figures that appeared to play music. At the time Bright was travelling on the Continent, the most spectacular garden had just been designed and built at Pratolino for Francesco I of Tuscany by Bernardo Buontalenti (who incidentally went on to be the designer of the 1589 Florentine intermedii). Buontalenti purposely designed this to surpass the gardens of Quirinal Palace in Rome, which boasted a famous hydraulic organ with a variety of automated figures and other musical effects. This hydraulic organ was described and illustrated in Athanasius Kircher's *Musurgia*

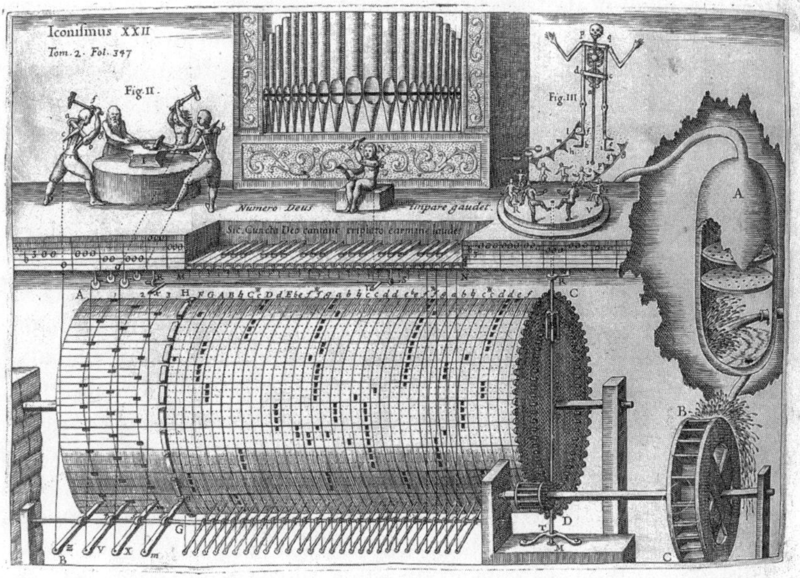

Figure 2.3 Hydraulic organ and forge from Athanasius Kircher, *Musurgia universalis* (Rome 1650), II, icon XII, f.p. 347. Wellcome Library, London.

universalis (Rome, 1650; see figure 2.3); it features an imaginative reconstruction of Pythagoras's visit to the smithy, where he reputedly made the discovery that different musical pitches were produced by hammers of different weights.[24]

In addition to clockwork devices, Bright further extends the metaphor of an all-purpose mover to include windmills that drain fens and grind grain simultaneously; he explains that to an 'American' (i.e., a native American) ignorant of the device it would seem to be wrought 'by a lively action of every part, and not by such a general mover as the wind is.'[25] Some examples of the kind of wind and water mills that Bright would have actually seen on his Continental travels are preserved in the engineer Agostino Ramelli's *Le diverse et artificiose machine*, published in Paris in 1588. In short, the most important point Bright wants to get across with his similitude is that a device like this (i.e., the human body) can malfunction even if the initial workmanship is perfect, an effect that may be due to problems with the soul's instrument rather than the outcome of a deliberate act of sin.

Apart from this striking image of a single spirit that animates the whole bodily machine, Bright's *Treatise* is also noteworthy for its remarks on music's value for calming the mind and as an effective cure for melancholy. He asserts that music acts like a 'magical charm' on the minds of men and, moreover, that the agreement between consent of music and affections of the mind is the reason why 'wise lawgivers in time past' (implicitly invoking Plato here) allowed certain kinds of music but rejected others 'as hurtful to their common wealths.'[26]

Unlike Browne (discussed below), Bright does not try to put into words the precise mechanisms by which music alters the spirit; the devices he describes are sufficient for the informed reader's imagination to grasp what is meant. And he is equally graphic in his explanation of the suitability of specific kinds of music for specific distempers, as would be possible only for one who had an intimate (I would say tacit or embodied) knowledge of the particular musical forms to which he alludes. The grounds for my claim are unusually strong, since Bright was not just qualified to practise medicine but was also by early modern definitions a true musician: that is, one skilled in both the theory and the practice of the art. We can infer this mix of medico-musical interests from Bright's will, in which he left most of his 'Bookes of Physic and philosophie' along with most of his (unspecified) 'Instruments of Musicke' to his younger son, Titus. To his brother William, however, Bright bequeathed his 'Theorbo, with its case,' and his Irish harp which he 'most usually played upon', along with his 'Hebrew Byble, the Syriac Testament, Josephus Zarlinus in Italian, in two volumes [probably the *Istitutioni harmoniche* of 1558 and *Dimostrationi harmoniche* of 1571], and Plato in Greek and Latin, translated by Marsilius Ficinus' [probably from the complete edition of Ficino's works published in Basel, 1576, rather than from an earlier edition of the late fifteenth century].[27] From this small body of evidence it is also possible to develop an understanding of Bright's broader intellectual and musical interests, which I propose to explore briefly here.

I think that this remarkable combination of books and instruments – the theorbo or bass lute invented by Antonio Naldi in the early 1570s to emulate the Greek kithara, the harp with its powerful links to King David – unmistakably connects Bright with the intellectual tradition of Florentine Neoplatonism as it was manifested in the court of France during the regency of Catherine de Medici, especially in the Neoplatonic salon of Claude-Catherine de Clermont, comtesse de Retz, and in the academy of the Pléiade under the leadership of Jean-Antoine de Baïf.[28] Indeed

I would even go far so as to suggest that Bright's particular interest in spiritual medicine for melancholics was fuelled while he was studying at Paris. In 1571, the lutenist and music publisher Adrien Le Roy printed his *Livre d'airs de cour*, which was dedicated to the comtesse de Retz. The *airs de cour*, simple strophic songs with lute accompaniment, were a new and extraordinarily fashionable genre just at that time.

As Jeanice Brooks has explained, with their capacity to communicate melancholic feelings inspired by love, pain, and loss, the *airs de cour* rapidly became an indicator of courtly nobility and virtue.[29] It was also in 1571 that le Roy's friend Jacques Gohory, another member of the comtesse's circle, set up a private academy devoted to philosophy, poetry, music, and the preparation of spiritual medicines and talismans according to the methods Ficino laid out in the *De vita*, or *Three Books on Life* (1489): a self-help manual for melancholic scholars looking for health and long life. It included conventional medical remedies but also incorporated the musical techniques reportedly used by Pythagoras and other ancient magi to draw down the 'natural' virtues of the stars.[30] Indeed, the *De vita* was actually the first Western work to suggest why music acts like a 'magical charm' (the phrase Bright uses) on the minds of men, and how musicians can alter people's mood through their ability to move the passions.

This brief digression should make clear why I think that Bright is speaking as a physician who has experimentally grounded evidence to back up his extremely precise observations about music's therapeutic potential. Thus he says that 'solemn music' is best for disordered rage and intemperate mirth, which are symptoms of madness. In particular Bright notes the virtue of 'dumps' and 'fancies,' which are quite specific forms of musical composition, for their treatment. Dumps (according to John Ward) were pieces written in memory of a deceased person, hence their solemnity, while fancies (a style originally imported from Italy) were composed improvisations for lute or keyboard.[31] Although Bright does not actually spell it out, his argument is that the movements of a disordered mind are repatterned by the particular organization of the music being attended to, a process that is mediated directly through the spirit. Also unspoken here is that the technique evidently produced a cure in the early modern medical sense: namely, that a striking effect immediately resulted from the treatment. Thus just as a potion was presumed to 'work' because it caused vomiting or diarrhea, for example, so the music caused a dramatic change in behaviour, as wild laughter or rage (i.e., symptoms of madness) gave way to calm composure.

By contrast, Bright is sure that 'cheerful music,' of the kind 'as most rejoyceth,' is best suited to melancholic ears, especially if it carries an 'odd measure.' I think by this he means that music in triple meter has a distinctive rhythmic pattern that should catch the attention of even the most introverted or withdrawn person, to bring them out of themselves, so to speak. However, he also observes that if the melancholic has skill in music (i.e., someone like Ficino or Bright himself, perhaps), the wise application of a 'deeper harmony' is required for 'alluring the spirits, stirring the blood and thinning the humours' in the effort to restore well-being.[32]

Even though some may now doubt such effects, we need to appreciate the theory underpinning Bright's idea that musically sophisticated melancholics might need something more complicated to alter their mood. Despite having some disagreements with it over some points of detail, the overall context for Bright's thinking was the Galenic humoral system that was fundamental to all medical education in early modern Europe.[33] In the detail, however, we see Ficino's *De vita* providing the explanatory context because it distinguishes between everyday melancholy, which anyone can occasionally suffer, and the affliction to which philosophers are constitutionally prone. (In the Galenic system there was no such category of special melancholy, which was simply an unpleasant disease.) According to Ficino, the philosopher's habit of introspection is an intense mental labour that requires the soul to draw in upon itself, and to stay immovable, as it were, at its own centre; as a consequence, the spirits become overheated and depleted. In turn, this loss of spirit results in an excess of black bile (melancholy) in the humoral mix, or constitution, of these deep-thinking individuals. This is because when the more subtle and clear parts of the blood (which contain spirit) dry up the rest of the blood is rendered dense, dry, and black and the brain becomes dry and cold, which is known as the earthy and melancholic quality.[34] Music has a special power to rebalance humours by virtue of its power over, and affinity with, the spirit.[35]

To conclude this necessarily brief summary of Bright's musical – but also mechanical – model of the body, let me just remind you that it is articulated not in a treatise about music but rather in the context of a 'medical' treatise explaining why feeling depressed is not a sinful state. In fact, the first medical treatise in English wholly devoted to music and its therapeutic potential – the anonymous *A Mechanical Essay on Singing, Music and Dancing. Containing Their Uses and Abuses; And Demonstrating, by Clear and Evident Reasons, the Alterations They Produce in a Human Body* –

did not appear until 1727. Two years later, a longer, revised version appeared with the title *Medicina Musica: Or, a Mechanical Essay on the Effects of Singing, Music, and Dancing on Human Bodies*, and this time its author was announced as Richard Browne, an apothecary of Oakham in Rutland – a small English county.

Richard Browne's *Medicina Musica* (1729)

We know nothing about Browne's life beyond the fact that he wrote the book during his apprenticeship, which means he was born in the early 1700s, and that his patron was Baptist Noel, the 4th Earl of Gainsborough (1708–51).[36] In fact, Browne dedicated *Medicina Musica* to the Earl, whom he described as having a 'Genius in Musick,' on the occasion of his twenty-first birthday.[37] I don't have space here to dwell on Browne's two very interesting treatises or to draw attention to the quite significant modifications made to the text between 1727 and 1729. Instead, I will treat them as a single entity, one which represents a coherent theory of disease and mind-body interaction dating from the early eighteenth century, with a view to drawing out both the similarities and differences between them and Bright's conception of the same things 140 years earlier.

With its emphasis on the medicinal effects of singing, of listening to music, and of dancing on the human body, Browne's *Essay* shares an affinity with Bright's much earlier *Treatise* in several interesting respects. First, although he does not explicitly call the body the soul's instrument, Browne understands that music's capacity to affect both mind and body is due to its effects on the spirits that flow through the nerves and, moreover, that this substance is the vehicle through which the soul processes sensory impressions and communicates its intentions to the body, which functions like a hydraulic instrument. Browne describes this interface between soul and spirits as a 'sympathy,' which can be seen in the way that the passions of the mind affect the body, just as distempered spirits can make impressions on the mind.[38] Unlike Bright, who imagined no difference between the natural, vital, and animal powers of the soul, Browne follows the more traditional view that animal spirits are particular to the nerves, but this in effect makes no difference to my argument. The important thing here is that Browne, just like Bright, thinks that it is music's effect on the spirit that allows it to be used to moderate the passions and to avoid disease, especially mental afflictions. Yet while Bright dedicated only one chapter of his *Treatise* to music, Browne makes music, or rather the effects of music (and singing and dancing), the thing that he proposes to explain in mechanical – i.e., what we would take to be scientific – terms.

In fact, this 'scientific context' is the single most important thing that distinguishes Browne's ideas from Bright's. For although they both present what might be described as a mechanical, or instrumental, model of mind-body interaction, what actually separates them is a fundamental transformation in thinking (and feeling) about the nature of bodies in general (i.e., physics) and human bodies in particular (physiology). In essence, Browne has the advantage of sounding 'modern' because he literally follows Newton, both in chronological and conceptual terms.

This debt is made immediately evident to the reader through six 'mathematical principles' or 'propositions' laid down at the start of the *Essay*.[39] It is from these principles that Browne's theories of mind-body interaction necessarily flow, just as the motions and interactions of planetary bodies inevitably flow from the three laws of motion Newton laid out in his *Principia mathematica* or *Mathematical Principles of Natural Philosophy* (first edition 1687, second edition 1713, third edition 1726).

Browne's conception of the body also draws more generally on the narrative of experimental and mathematical advances that elite physicians were associating with their research around this time. Indeed, although he may never have been to a university himself, Browne's physiology displays familiarity with the teachings of Herman Boerhaave (1668–1738), who was professor of medicine at Leiden from the late 1690s until his death in 1738.[40] Boerhaave's teaching was based on a mix of Cartesian and Newtonian principles. It was Cartesian because it effectively makes the 'soul' a black box that physicians have no duty to explain, and it assumes that all matter is inert unless it is receives motion transmitted by an external force. All sensations are caused by particles striking the external senses, which in turn transmit motion through the nerves; a chain of other reactions and movements result from these impressions. All bodily functions can thus be reduced to hydraulics, and all disease can be explained in terms of obstructions and impediments to flow.

What makes Boerhaave's model more than just Cartesian, however, is its emphasis on what appear to be peculiarly English ideas about the progressive nature of science, not just those embodied in Newton's laws. Thus Boerhaave's concept of physiology (and Browne's too) presumes a commitment to Baconian observation and empiricism, a knowledge of William Harvey's discovery of blood circulation (1628) and of Thomas Willis's anatomy of the nervous system (1672), as well as familiarity with Boyle's law (1662: pressure and volume are inversely proportional to temperature). Tempting as it is to place Browne in the vanguard of modern medicine, however, it is important to realize that he didn't need to understand physics or physiology at the level of a Newton to mobilize these ideas, which in any case were by no means dominant within the medical profession.

In fact, as far as trying to make medicine 'scientific' goes, I am inclined to see Browne's attempt to explain the effects of singing, music, and dancing on human bodies from another perspective altogether. In other words, it is not mechanics that is throwing light on music's effects on the body. Rather it is the effects of music that can persuade readers that the machine analogy really works to explain fundamental aspects of *human* behaviour, not just the action of machines.

Browne's central thesis is that singing, music, and dancing can be beneficial to people because they invigorate the spirits, a process he explains in hydraulic terms. Singing, for example, through the pressure exerted on the lungs causes stronger contractions of the heart, improves the circulation of the blood, and thereby increases the secretion and flow of the animal spirits. Regular singing is beneficial for most people, as long as they choose lively and vigorous tunes, rather than 'melancholy and languishing tunes,' which rather tend to their depression. Those with weak lungs are warned not to strain themselves, and those with inflammatory diseases (e.g., pleurisy, consumption) are to avoid it altogether.[41]

Unlike Bright, Browne does not foreground the concept of melancholy in his *Essay*, nor does he ascribe the condition to an excess of black bile accumulating in the spleen. Instead, he treats 'melancholy,' 'spleen,' and 'the vapours' as different symptoms of the same thing: namely, a lack of spirit and therefore a loss of pressure within the body's systems, a phenomenon he compares with the way that mercury falls in the barometer. (This instrument had not even been invented in Bright's time, but by the time Browne was writing they were being manufactured in and distributed from London.) Thus rage, frenzy, and madness are inevitable consequences of the pressure of too much spirit in the nerves – a fluid which, as Browne explains, is secreted from the blood when the heart contracts and the circulation increases accordingly.[42]

This emphasis on nervous energy rather than humoral imbalance marks what medical historians see as a shift from Renaissance humoral explanations of disease towards Enlightenment accounts that focus on the state of the nerves. In response to various stimuli, these nervous fibres move between extremes of tension and relaxation, of overexcitement and depression. Health is therefore construed as a state of

Figure 2.4 T. Cook, after William Hogarth, 'Credulity, Superstition and Fanaticism' (1798). Wellcome Library, London.

dynamic equilibrium within the body, while lack or excess of tension signals disease. The engraving in figure 2.4, a later copy of William Hogarth's original of 1762 entitled 'Credulity, Superstition and Fanaticism,' is a satire on the ever-dangerous world of fundamentalist religion, but in the bottom right-hand corner of the picture it also neatly shows a more general association Hogarth was making between temperature and emotional states, ranging from the heat of raving madness and lust through low spirits to despair and suicide, all of these conditions stemming from the diseased brain depicted beneath the thermometer.[43]

Browne tries to render the way that singing operates on the body 'clear and intelligible' by starting with the proposition that there is a sympathy between the soul and the animal spirits. This, he thinks, can be proven by observation, since we can clearly see how the passions of the mind affect the body. Fear produces a defect of spirits, anger produces their violent and irregular motion, while hope, mirth, and joy run between these extremes to produce a plentiful, but not excessive, secretion of spirits. (He does not explain how we can see these quantitative changes.) Conversely, we can observe how the body affects the mind, because when a person is distempered he is sometimes furious, sometimes dejected, angry, or pleased, according to the various impressions the spirits make on his mind.

Browne considers that no pleasure comes from music without the right kind of ear or without an idea in the mind.[44] However, he admits that the immediate pleasure experienced on hearing a well-played consort might come directly from the percussion of the vibrating air upon the auditory nerves. He infers that since musical instruments emit different sounds according to where they are touched, these sounds will produce differently pleasing sensations in the mind, thus variously influencing the motion of the spirits. In short, there is a direct correspondence, or sympathy, between the vibrations produced by musical instruments and the body, which is itself responding like a musical instrument.

This clear affinity between certain types of music and the condition of the spirits allows Browne to suggest how music could be deliberately used to moderate the passions and avoid disease. A defect of spirits caused by fear, melancholy, or despair might be prevented by a soft adagio, while if the soul is dejected there is nothing better to restore it than a brisk allegro. Alternatively an agreeable contrast of music might contribute to preserving health through its variety. As far as particular diseases go, Browne thinks that the spleen might be overcome by listening to an allegro, which would excite the mind and diffuse a 'corresponding vivacity' through the whole nervous system, while for madness only a 'soft, languishing adagio is to be admitted.'[45]

Conclusions

Browne's emphasis on the animal spirits as the vector of change between outer and inner states bears a distinct resemblance to Bright's claim that it is the flow of spirits through distinct pathways that causes movements of the body, both seen and unseen. And although there are crucial differences between the musical genres they recommend as likely remedies for mental afflictions (the dump and the fancy were effectively obsolete by Browne's time, when allegros and adagios in Italian operas were all the rage), both men appear to draw upon their personal soundworlds, the direct experience of actual music, to account for the experience of changing moods.

This continuity of ideas over nearly 150 years not only confirms that Descartes was far from original in his concept of the body as a hydraulic instrument, but also that there were always alternative physiological models available in his time. Moreover, it also seems apparent that 'mechanical' accounts of the body can actually be traced to the invention and use of real mechanical clocks and automatic devices that included musical sounds as part of their repertoire. For example, Bright's account of the similarity between the human frame and 'automaticall instruments' appears to be based on an eyewitness account of particular instruments which he probably saw on his travels in France. At the time he wrote, these devices were still new and remarkable, but they had become more commonplace by the early eighteenth century, when Browne was writing.

As I have already suggested in this essay, although the emphasis on the 'mechanical philosophy' as such distinctively captures important features of early modern physiological theory, it has also had the effect of obscuring the equally significant role of musical models for conceptualizing life functions and mind-body interactions. To be sure, thinking of the body as a musical device was compatible with Descartes's mechanistic belief that all matter is inert and requires an external motive force to put it into action. However, if we think of Fludd's diagrams in particular, it is clear that musical models have a special role to play in a cosmos where matter is animated even without any visible mechanism and spirit mediates between material and immaterial realms: a view of the universe that was by no means obsolete in Browne's time. Within such a paradigm, it is clear that one of the most important properties of music as a sonorous, viscerally experienced phenomenon is sympathy or resonance – the capacity of music to excite motion at a distance and to communicate between physical and mental states.

In the course of my research I have come to believe that the notion of sympathy is not so much a woolly substitute for more robust mechanisms as a valuable concept which can come into play at the very point where sight and discursive reasoning have their limits. The authors I have discussed show how sympathy can be invoked as a means of grasping through direct experience how external sense impressions may actually change inner states – a process that can be heard and experienced although hidden from view. Music serves as both a cause and explanation for changing mental states, a means of comprehending the world through sound rather than sight.

NOTES

1 Penelope Gouk, 'Some English Theories of Hearing in the Seventeenth Century: Before and after Descartes,' in *The Second Sense: Studies in Hearing and Musical Judgement from Antiquity to the Seventeenth Century*, ed. Charles Burnett, Michael Fend, and Penelope Gouk (London: The Warburg Institute, 1991), 95–113.

2 The passions of the mind comprised one of the six categories of 'non-naturals,' the conditions that early modern physicians and their patients knew needed to be regulated in order to achieve well-being and a healthy life. The other categories comprised light and air; meat and drink; exercise and rest; waking and sleeping; and expelling superfluities. For an introduction to the basic theoretical principles underpinning early modern medical practice see Vivian Nutton, 'Humoralism,' in *The Companion Encyclopedia of the History of Medicine*, 2 vols. (London: Routledge, 1993), 1: 281–91. For a historicized discussion of the passions and emotions *see* Thomas Dixon, From Passions to Emotions: The Creation of a Secular Psychological Category (Cambridge: Cambridge University Press, 2003), and Penelope Gouk and Helen Hills, 'Towards Histories of Emotions,' in *Representing Emotions: New Connections in the Histories of Art, Music and Medicine*, ed. Penelope Gouk and Helen Hills (Aldershot: Ashgate, 2005), 15–34.

3 Noel Malcolm, *Aspects of Hobbes* (Oxford: Clarendon Press, 2002).

4 See for example J.A. Bennett, 'The Mechanic's Philosophy and the Mechanical Philosophy,' *History of Science* 24 (1986): 1–28; John Henry, *The Scientific Revolution and the Origins of Modern Science* (Houndsmills and London: Macmillan, 1997).

5 Examples of different models can be found in Otto Mayr, *Authority, Liberty and Automatic Machinery in Early Modern Europe* (Baltimore/London: The Johns Hopkins University Press, 1986); and Jamie Croy Kassler, *Music, Science, Philosophy: Models in the Universe of Thought* (Aldershot: Ashgate, 2001).

6 Derek J. De Solla Price, 'Automata in History: Automata and the Origins of Mechanism and Mechanistic Philosophy,' *Technology and Culture* 5 (1964): 9–23; Jan Jaap Haspels, *Musical Automata: Catalogue of Automatic Musical Instruments in the National Museum 'from Musical Clock to Street Organ'* (Utrecht: National Museum, 1994).

7 John Wilkins, *Mathematical Magic* (London, 1648), 148–9.

8 The mechanical devices I describe here are discussed more fully in Klaus Maurice and Otto Mayr, eds., *The Clockwork Universe: German Clocks and Automata 1550–1650* (New York and Bristol: Neale Watson Academic Publishers, 1980). The illustration of the bracket clock appears on 168, while the automaton with trumpets is presented on 286–8.

9 Automaton with trumpets, Hans Schlottheim. Augsburg, 1582. Vienna, Kunsthistorisches Museum. Two black-and-white illustrations appear in Maurice and Mayr, *The Clockwork Universe*, 286.

10 Frances Amelia Yates, *The Rosicrucian Enlightenment* (London: Routledge and Kegan Paul, 1972). For a survey of Fludd's imagery, see Joscelyn Godwin, *Robert Fludd: Hermetic Philosopher and Surveyor of Two Worlds* (London: Thames and Hudson, 1979).

11 Penelope Gouk, 'Music, Melancholy and Medical Spirits in Early Modern Thought,' in *Music as Medicine: The History of Music Therapy since Antiquity*, ed. Peregrine Horden (Guilford: Ashgate, 2000), 173–94, and 'Raising Spirits and Restoring Souls: Early Modern Medical Explanations for Music's Effects,' in *Hearing Cultures: Essays on Sound, Listening and Modernity*, ed. Veit Erlmann (Oxford and New York: Berg, 2004), 87–105.

12 Geoffrey Keynes, *Doctor Timothie Bright, 1550–1615: A Survey of His Life* (London, 1962).

13 Robert Fludd, *Utriusque cosmi majoris scilicet et minoris metaphysica, physica atque technica historia*, 2 vols. (Oppenheim, 1617–19). This image appears in vol. 1 (1617), 90. In brief, Pythagoras is supposed to have discovered the harmonic proportions governing the consonances of the musical scale, namely the octave (1:2), fifth (2:3), and fourth (3:4), which can all be expressed as string length ratios on a monochord. In this system the interval of a major third is dissonant (64:81, consisting of two major tones, 8:9) and therefore excluded from the consonances.

14 The Pythagorean scale dominated theory until the late sixteenth century, when the music theorist Gioseffo Zarlino replaced it with the syntonic

diatonic of Ptolemy, a scale which allows the third to be harmonious (ratio 4:5, consisting of a major tone 8:9 and a minor tone 9:10). For further details of this profound shift in musical thinking see Daniel Pickering Walker, 'Kepler's Celestial Music,' in his *Studies in Musical Science in the Late Renaissance* (London: Brill, 1978), 34–62; H. Floris Cohen, *Quantifying Music: The Science of Music at the First Stage of the Scientific Revolution, 1580–1650* (Dordrecht: D. Reidel), esp. 13–29; and Penelope Gouk, 'The Role of Harmonics in the Scientific Revolution,' in *The Cambridge History of Western Music Theory*, ed. Thomas Christensen (Cambridge: Cambridge University Press, 2002), 223–45.

15 All early modern medical education was based on the system of humoral medicine codified by the ancient physician Galen of Pergamum in the 2nd century A.D. Briefly, this system was based on the doctrine of the four humours of blood, phlegm, yellow bile, and black bile (melancholy), the assumption being that disease was mostly caused by an imbalance of the humours. For fuller details, see Lawrence I. Conrad, Michael Neve, Vivian Nutton, Roy Porter, and Andrew Wear, eds., *The Western Medical Tradition 800 BC to AD 1800* (Cambridge: Cambridge University Press, 1995), as well as Nutton, 'Humoralism.'

16 Jamie Croy Kassler, 'Music as a Model in Early Science,' *History of Science* 20 (1982): 103–39, and 'Blowing the Organ: Willis, Hydro-Pneumatics and Hierarchy,' in *Music, Science, Philosophy: Models in the Universe of Thought*, ed. Jamie Croy Kassler (Aldershot: Ashgate, 2001), 125–64.

17 Linda P. Austern, '"All Things in This World Is but the Musick of Inconstancie": Music, Sensuality and the Sublime in Seventeenth-Century *Vanitas* Imagery,' in *Art and Music in the Early Modern Period: Essays in Honour of Franca Trinchieri Camiz*, ed. Katherine A. McIver (Aldershot: Ashgate, 2003), 287–332.

18 See Richard Leppert, 'Temporal Interventions: Music, Modernity, and the Presentation of the Self,' the last chapter of this volume; see also Leppert, *The Sight of Sound: Music, Representation, and the History of the Body* (Berkeley: University of California Press, 1993).

19 For fuller biographical details, see the entry on Bright in *Oxford Dictionary of National Biography*.

20 André du Laurens, *Discourse de la conservation de la veu: des maladies melancholiques des catarrhes, et de la vieillesses. Compossez par M. André De Laurens* (Rouen: Claude Le Villain, 1600).

21 Bright, *A Treatise of Melancholy* (London: John Windet, 1586), 'The Epistle Dedicatorie.'

22 Ibid., 43.

23 Ibid., 65.

24 Athanasius Kircher, *Musurgia universalis*, 2 vols. (Rome, 1650), II, f.p. 347. For an introduction to the devices of Pratolino and other gardens, see Joscelyn Godwin, *The Pagan Dream of the Renaissance* (London: Thames and Hudson, 2002), 173–80.

25 Bright, *Treatise of Melancholy*, 66.

26 Ibid., 241.

27 Quoted from W. Brown, 'The Will of Timothy Bright, M.D., Rector of Methley and Barwick-in-Elmet, 1615,' *Yorkshire Archaeological Journal* 17 (1903): 50–4.

28 Daniel Pickering Walker, 'The Aims of Baif's Académie de Poésie et de Musique,' *Journal of Renaissance and Baroque Music* 1 (1946): 91–100, and 'The Influence of *musique mesurée à l'antique*, particularly on the *airs de cour* of the Early 17th Century,' *Musica Disciplina* 2 (1948): 141–63.

29 Jeanice Brooks, *Courtly Song in Late Sixteenth-Century France* (Chicago: University of Chicago Press, 2000).

30 Daniel Pickering Walker, *Spiritual and Demonic Magic from Ficino to Campanella* (London, 1958), 96–106; Penelope Gouk, 'Harmony, Health and Healing: Music's Role in Early Modern Paracelsian Thought,' in *The Practice of Reform in Health, Medicine and Science, 1500–2000: Essays for Charles Webster*, ed. Margaret Pelling and Scott Mandelbrote (Aldershot: Ashgate, 2005), 1–19.

31 John Ward, 'The "Dolfull Domps,"' *Journal of the American Musicological Society* 4, no. 2 (1951): 111–21.

32 Bright, *Treatise on Melancholy*, 40–1.

33 See note 16.

34 Carol V. Kaske and John R. Clark, eds., *Marsilio Ficino Three Books on Life: A Critical Edition and Translation with Introduction and Notes* (Binghampton, NY: The Renaissance Society of America, 1989), 113–14. See also the classic work by Raymond Klibansky, Ernst Panofsky, and Fritz Saxl, *Saturn and Melancholy: Studies in the History of Natural Philosophy, Religion and Art* (Cambridge: W. Heffer and Sons, 1964).

35 Kaske and Clark, *Ficino*, 355–63; Walker, *Spiritual and Demonic Magic*, 3–24.

36 E.L. Wynder, 'Richard Browne,' *Preventive Medicine* 7, no. 1 (1978): 28–30.

37 Browne, *Medicina Musica* (London: John Cooke, 1729), iii–viii.

38 Ibid., 7–8.

39 Ibid., 7–14.

40 Andrew Cunningham, 'Medicine to Calm the Mind: Boerhaave's Medical System, and Why It Was Adopted in Edinburgh,' in *The Medical Enlightenment of the Eighteenth Century*, ed. Andrew Cunningham and Roger French (Cambridge: Cambridge University Press, 1990), 40–66; Rina Knoeff,

Herman Boerhaave (1668–1738: Calvinist Chemist and Physician (Amsterdam: Koninnklijke Nederlandse Akademie van Wetenschappen, 2002).

41 Browne, *Medicina Musica,* 14–15, 25–6.

42 Ibid., 11–12.

43 On Hogarth's treatment of mental illness, see Fiona Haslam, *From Hogarth to Rowlandson: Medicine in Art in Eighteenth-Century Britain* (Liverpool: Liverpool University Press, 1996), esp. 160. For more on fears and satires of religious fanaticism, see Olivia Bloechl, 'The Illicit Voice of Prophecy,' chapter 6 in this volume.

44 Browne, *Medicina Musica,* 31–51, 'Of Musick.'

45 Ibid., 48.

chapter three

The Sound World of Father Mersenne

THOMAS CHRISTENSEN

The Mayor grabbed a tom-tom. He started to smack it.
And, all over Who-ville, they whooped up a racket.
They rattled tin kettles! They beat on brass pans,
On garbage pail tops and old cranberry cans!
They blew on bazookas and blasted great toots
On clarinets, oom-pahs and boom-pahs and flutes!
Great gusts of loud racket rang high through the air.
They rattled and shook the whole sky!

—Dr Seuss, *Horton Hears a Who*

I

Marin Mersenne's friends must have wondered. For some ten years, the Minim father had been promising to his correspondents the publication of a major encyclopedia of musical knowledge, bits and pieces of which were tantalizingly dished out in a series of earlier publications. But when the *Harmonie universelle contenant la théorie et la pratique de la musique* finally appeared in two major volumes between 1636 and 1637, many of his impatient readers must have been perplexed by what they read. For the sprawling, multi-volume treatise was unlike any other work of music theory that had ever been published.

Running to some 1,500 pages, the *Harmonie universelle* was divided into a series of nineteen desultory 'books' containing a motley assortment of propositions, corollaries, and *avertissements* on diverse topics of musical acoustics, ancient harmonics, theory, practice, and instruments. Certainly, as the title promises, there is a strong Platonic ideal conveyed in Mersenne's writing that seeks to understand music as a paradigm of seemly proportion. But cheek and jowl with this traditional viewpoint that Mersenne would have inherited from his Renaissance precursors we also find a mechanistic model of music that does not always sit comfortably with the former.

Indeed, as a text of musical mechanics, the *Harmonie universelle* is arguably the most comprehensive work published during the whole of the seventeenth century. In it we find an extensive discussion of the physics of sound production and propagation, covering such diverse problems as the mechanics of string vibrations, the nature of sound waves, the measurement of the speed of sound, sound propagation in water or other dense media, and the geometry of reflecting sound waves.[1] (And it should be noted that not all discussions of mechanics deal with music; several whole books of the treatise were devoted to problems of pure mechanics recently tackled by Galileo: the acceleration of objects in free fall and on inclined planes, the trajectory of hurled objects, the motion of the pendulum, the geometry of the pulley and lever, and other classical problems of statics and kinematics).[2]

But for any reader who was familiar with Mersenne's many other publications, the mixture of music and mechanics found in the *Harmonie universelle* should have been no surprise at all. Virtually every one of Mersenne's earlier writings included discussions of music theory and mechanics. Indeed, in his inaugural magnum opus, a mammoth commentary on the opening chapters of Genesis published in 1623 (*Quaestiones celeberrimae in Genesim*), Mersenne folded together lengthy digressions on both topics amid the more orthodox discussions of Biblical hermeneutics, chronology, and church doctrine. And if musical readers were surprised by the presence of mechanics in the *Harmonie universelle,* his scientific friends might surely have been just as perplexed by the extensive musical discussions found in his publications dealing ostensibly with scientific matters, including *La verité des sciences* (1625), *Les nouvelles pensées de Galilée* (1638), the *Cogitata physico-mathematica* (1644), or the *Novarum observationum physico-mathematicarum* (1647).

Why this combining of music and mechanics? For Mersenne, the answer was self-evident. Using theories that can be traced back to Peripatetic teachings, he understood musical sound to be the result of pure physical motion. From the initial agitation of some musical instrument that sets the surrounding air molecules into periodic undulations, to the propagation of these undulations as air waves to the ear, musical sound can be analysed as a purely mechanical process that can be measured with precise geometric quantification. To begin understanding music, then, we must know the various kinds of motions that produce it. And this requires, naturally, the tools of mechanical analysis. The problem of the acceleration of a body rolling down an inclined plane was as much a part of the mechanical world as was that of the vibrating string, and it made perfect sense to Mersenne that each should be treated in the same treatise.[3]

Of course, Mersenne was not alone in these views. Music was only one of the many natural phenomenon that were then coming under the purview of the mechanical philosophy by which nature was being stripped of all Aristotelian qualities or occult properties and quantitatively analysed as but a geometric problem of moving and colliding material bodies (reduced to its manifest or 'primary qualities' as Robert Boyle would later put it). Already in 1585, the Italian physicist Giovanni Benedetti had offered a paradigmatic example of musical mechanization by suggesting a theory of consonance based upon the 'coincidence' of pitch frequencies: the more any two frequencies of a given interval coincided with each other, the more consonant the ear perceived them to be. Hence the octave, whose constituent frequencies stand in a duple relation [2:1], is heard as more consonant than the major third, whose constituent frequencies are in a sesquitertia [4:3] relationship.

The 'coincidence theory' of consonance, as H.F. Çohen has dubbed it, became a paradigm of musical mechanization, obviating any reliance upon discredited theories of Pythagorean numerology.[4] (Ironically, however, the coincidence theory had the effect of reinstating Pythagorean whole number ratios, although by situating them in the purely material process of intersecting frequency ratios – 'battements d'air' as Mersenne would describe it.) Little by little, music theory was pruned of the many numerological and naturalistic explanations by which it had previously been supported. Indeed, so easily did music become a model of mechanistic reduction that it seemed to have seduced a number of seventeenth-century natural philosophers into believing that most any natural phenomenon could be analogously treated. (One wonders if Descartes would have been so dogmatic in his conviction that phenomena ranging from magnetism, light, gravity, biological reproduction, and even the human passions could all be reduced to mechanical processes of moving and impacting rigid bodies had he not had the example of music about which he so avidly corresponded with Mersenne in the early 1630s.)

But Mersenne's project was not just to reduce music to mechanical principles. If anything, the opposite is truer: Mersenne hoped to subsume his mechanics within the paradigm of musical *harmonia*. Far from seeing the ancient Platonic ideal of heavenly harmony superseded by the new materialism, Mersenne was certain the two could be reconciled. For in the hard, material world of vibrating strings, resonating organ pipes, and trembling drum membranes, there were laws of motion and impact that were just as quantifiable, cogent, and universal as those governing the ratios of musical harmony. As Peter Dear has elegantly put it, Mersenne did not so much want to mechanize music as to musicalize mechanics, to make this new world of moving material bodies dance with the heavenly spheres in harmonic choreography.[5] The heavenly harmonia so extolled in Platonic tradition was seen – and now heard – in the hard corporeal world of impacting bodies. And it is in this polyphony of music and mechanics, I believe, that we may understand how our pious father was able to reconcile the threatening, corporeal science of Galileo and Descartes within his deeply orthodox Catholic beliefs. It is the paradox – and promise – of this dualism, the tension between music as a mechanical process and as sensual harmony, as acoustical stimulus and as spiritual edification, that I will try to tease out from the musical writings of Father Mersenne in this essay.

II

Mersenne's activities as a midwife of the new mechanical philosophy in music might not have been anticipated, as he certainly had no formal training as a musician. Still, as a young chorister he would certainly have learned the rudiments of *musica plana* necessary to sing chant. He also seemed to have picked up some music theory at the newly founded Jesuit college at La Flèche, which he attended as a student between 1604 and 1609. But it seems to have been acquaintance with the composer Jacques Mauduit that proved to be the greatest catalyst for Mersenne's enthusiasm for music.

Mauduit, the last member of the celebrated Académie de poésie et de musique founded in 1570 by Jean-Antoine de Baïf, lived near the convent of Minims (located by the Palais Royal) to which Mersenne had moved in 1619. Mersenne became fascinated by the Académie's project to recapture the powerful affects of ancient music and poetry, and the two soon struck up a close friendship. (Mersenne would repeatedly extol Mauduit's virtues as a musician in his writings, and he included a major necrology of his friend as an appendix to the 'Book of Percussion

Instruments' contained in the second volume of the *Harmonie universelle*).[6]

The project of the Académie was an obvious inspiration for much of Mersenne's own music theory. His quixotic obsession – repeated in almost all his publications – to discover if it was possible to compose the most beautiful song, to identify the most excellent consonances or ideal rhythms, and to determine how one might become the most perfect musician, are all really but inflections of the Académie's goal to recapture the affective power and beauty of ancient music. If Mersenne grew increasingly sceptical about attaining any of these goals (and we will return again to these questions below), they nonetheless constituted a vision that continued to haunt him until the end of his life. Still, for all of Mersenne's youthful enthusiasm for the project of the Académie, there was something else that attracted him to music: it seemed to be an ideal model of mechanical science.[7]

Mersenne became fascinated by the new mechanical philosophy that was beginning to stir in French intellectual circles in the 1620s. Shortly after moving into his monastic cell at the Palais Royal, he began to study seriously much of this new science. Most importantly, he began to correspond with many of the individuals throughout Europe who were sympathetic to the new philosophy, a correspondence that would eventually comprise over 1,800 letters and become, in effect, the single most important chronicle of scientific thought in the first half of the seventeenth century.[8]

Mersenne's contribution to science – like those he made to music theory – was not one of profound originality. While he did make some modest discoveries regarding the motion of the vibrating string and the theory of prime numbers, it was his role as facilitator and disseminator that stands out. He was one of the critical figures helping to promote the work of Galileo to a European-wide audience, even as Galileo was being persecuted by the Inquisition. Mersenne was also an able agitator for the new science; he was forever prodding his correspondents to solve certain problems and circulating the work of others for reaction and commentary. To the extent that Mersenne himself contributed to this conversation, it was more as an arbiter of empirical experimentation. Although he may not have had the genius of imagination and synthesis that someone such as Galileo possessed, he did have the patience and discipline to carry out careful experiments of quantitative exactitude or, in his own words, to offer models of 'expériences bien reglées et bien faites.'[9]

In the field of acoustics, a classical illustration of Mersenne's talent for experimental precision was his attempt to measure the speed of sound. Using differing sound sources as his subject (cannon and musket fire, trumpet calls, large bells, shrill whistles, and even thunder), Mersenne devised a number of imaginative experiments by which the speed of these noises might be precisely measured. So, for example, he would visually observe from a distance the blast of an *arquebuse* and mark that as a starting point by which to measure the time it took for the sound to reach him; in other cases he would measure the time it took for cannon fire to be reflected off a distant canyon wall as an echo. Through repeated experimentation, he was able to determine that sound travelled in uniform velocities independent of its pitch or loudness, although – to his great vexation – he was never able to arrive at a consistent value for this velocity.[10]

It was this painstaking attention to detail and precise measurement that was both Mersenne's virtue and vice as a scientist. On the one hand, it allowed him to verify or correct many of the findings reported by his scientific colleagues. (Galileo, who was otherwise Mersenne's scientific idol, came into sharp criticism for his notorious penchant to rely too much upon 'thought experiments' for his work in mechanics and not verify his conclusions through careful testing.)[11] On the other hand, as Charles Gillespie has noted, Mersenne's almost obsessive attention to 'the untidy facts of observation' seemed to hinder deeper theoretical synthesis and insight.[12]

As an example, we might cite Mersenne's observations of overtones. In a number of his publications, he reported hearing a series of faint tones above a vibrating string, a low organ pipe, and even his own voice.[13] Sometimes he heard a simple octave above the fundamental; sometimes a harmonic series up to the major seventeenth; and still other times he heard inharmonic overtones – particularly in bells. What could possibly explain these strange and inconsistent sounds? Although he prodded his many correspondents for help, Mersenne was never able to arrive at a satisfactory explanation. He later confessed this to be the most difficult problem in music he ever faced.[14] (This should not be surprising to us since the requisite mathematical tools by which composite harmonic vibrations might be analysed were not available until the development of partial differential equations a century later.) Oddly enough, Mersenne at one point came close to the right answer when he speculated 'it seems it is entirely necessary that [the string] beat the air five, four, three, and two times in the same time.' But he rejected the idea as 'impossible to imagine' and 'against experience.'[15] A too-strict reliance upon pure observation does not always serve the scientist well.

III

As already suggested above, Mersenne believed music to be an ideal science of mechanistic reduction, one to which the other physical sciences might even be subordinated:

> If one had a perfect knowledge of sounds, and mastered all of the things that could be known from their means, then one would have a science of all natural bodies that would be more general, more certain, and more particular than that of ordinary physics.[16]

But in stripping music of the many pernicious myths and dogmas it had accumulated over time, Mersenne by no means wished to deny the affective powers and moral authority attributed to music by the ancients (or by his friends in the Académie, for that matter). On the contrary, he hoped to verify and reinforce this authority by securing it more firmly in the new empirical science. Above all, he was convinced that the quantifiable order that was the foundation of the Pythagorean lore of sounding number was deeper and more far reaching than any champion of Rosicrucian knowledge such as Robert Fludd could have imagined.

Mersenne's study of the vibrating string was paradigmatic here. By showing how the frequency of a string's vibration is not only proportional to the square root of the tension of the string (which had been discovered by Vincenzo Galilei) but also inversely proportional to the square root of the string's weight or thickness (resulting in the formula today known as 'Mersenne's law'), he believed anyone should be convinced of the sublime rationality of God's universe – one far more profound and intricate than the mere iteration of simple whole-number ratios argued by the Pythagoreans.[17]

Indeed, so thoroughly rational and empirical were the mechanics of music that Mersenne was convinced that it could be used to convince sceptics, Pyrrhonists, and non-believers of the errors of their ways. For what could be more manifestly true and convincing than the truths of music theory? The precision by which intervals could be mechanically explained and precisely measured was surely a blow to the destructive scepticism of the Pyrrhonists, who argued that nothing certain could be known and that all judgments were ultimately groundless.[18] For those who argued that music was far too subjective an art and historically mutable, Mersenne responded in 1634 with a short treatise, the *Questions harmoniques,* in which he asks – and attempts to answer – a number of highly speculative questions related to music.[19]

Mersenne's actual stimulus for this treatise, it seems, was a lengthy essay sent to him by a humanist sceptic and follower of Montaigne named François de La Mothe Le Vayer. The essay, which Mersenne included in his publication under the title 'Discours sceptique sur la musique,' attempted to document the varying and often conflicting views held by ancient and non-Western authorities concerning the origins of music and its affects (84–171). The quantity of erroneous claims and sheer nonsense reported by the ancients and repeated by their acolytes today, La Mothe Le Vayer argued, coupled with the fallibility or our own judgments and knowledge should lead every sober Christian to recognize the limits of what we can know about music (164–5).[20]

Mersenne certainly had no argument with La Mothe Le Vayer concerning the hubris of human intellect. He regularly chided those writers who presumed to find final causes or occult properties in nature, let alone those who claimed to discern the plan and purpose God has for man.

> We cannot know the science or the true reasons for what occurs in nature, because there are always some circumstances or instances which make us doubt whether all the causes that we have believed are really true, or if any of them are true, or if there could be other causes altogether.[21]

But even if we can never penetrate to the ultimate causes of nature, Mersenne quickly added, we can still observe effects in nature, measure them with empirical precision, and perhaps derive from them some useful, moral application. (Richard Popkin has rightly characterized Mersenne's position here as one of 'mitigated' or 'constructive skepticism.')[22] While the kinds of delimited knowledge we gain from careful observation and measurement may not lead us to the ultimate truths known only to God, it is knowledge nonetheless, and a reasonable and honourable aim for all pious seekers.

There was real use to be had in music, too, Mersenne reminded La Mothe Le Vayer, by studying its physical origins and mathematical foundations. (Not by chance did Mersenne entitle the penultimate book of the *Harmonie universelle* 'De l'utilité de l'harmonie' – a text we will consider in more detail shortly.) And he attempted to use the rest of the treatise to make just this point. The *Questions harmoniques* might well be considered Mersenne's most explicit meditations on musical epistemology in that he tried to clear the deck, so to speak, and ask in unmistakable Cartesian rhetoric just what kind of certain knowledge ('principes certains et evidens' [80]) one could have about music. It turns out that theory can indeed lead to certain knowledge by applying tools of mechanics and geometry. While there is no doubt that the more intuitive understanding of music gained by practising musicians is also of value, Mersenne could not accept it as stable and profound as that gained by theory. For theory appeals to the dispassionate mind, whereas practice is guided only by fickle taste; the former is guided by the spirit, while the latter is seduced by the body, and it seeks the good and useful, not merely that which is delectable.[23]

> Practice is only an effect of theory, on which it depends entirely; and if there had been no theory there would have been no practice. And although an edifice is more useful to lodge in when it is made . . . the design of a building is the more excellent as it approaches nearer to that which the architect has conceived in his mind, following the rules of his art; and external moral actions which we call good and meritorious take their goodness from the internal acts that precede them or accompany them, without which they would have no moral goodness.[24]

Mersenne returned in his later writings to reconsider the relative merits of theory and practice in music, arriving always at the same conclusion. Again and again his Platonic sympathies were evident as he elevated the theory of art above the shadows of its practice:

> Because the mind of those who know only practice are limited by the scope of art, believing all else is useless and imaginary. It is nonetheless certain that theory is more excellent and more noble than practice, and that the essence of reason surpasses that of matter.[25]

Mersenne's confidence in the powers of reason applied to music inspired him to return in his later writings to some of the earlier speculative questions he had raised that were inspired by Mauduit's Académie: Can we determine what attributes the most perfect musician should have? Is it possible to learn through theory how to compose and sing the most perfect melody possible for any given subject? And is it therefore possible to know how to judge music perfectly?[26]

As for the question of composing a perfect melody, Mersenne thought that the science of combinatorics might be of help, since in order to know if a melody was perfect, one had to know first the number of possible melodies to begin with against which it might be compared. Hence Mersenne's fascination with Lullian *ars combinatoria* by which to calculate the number of permutations of a series of notes, rhythms, or voices.[27] Of course it was not possible to write out and perform – let alone to judge – all possible melodies on any given subject. In his own permutation tables, Mersenne reasonably limited himself to songs containing no more than the six notes of the diatonic hexachord (and thereby coming up with 720 permutations, each one of which was written out in *solfège* as well as staff notation). This limited exercise was proof enough that the number of practical melodies – especially when we take into account an extended gamut, repetition of notes, and rhythmic variety – exceeded by millions of times the number of grains of sand found on earth. 'All the people of the earth couldn't sing all of the possible songs contained in the harmonic hand [i.e., diatonic scale] . . . even if they sang a thousand different songs every day from the creation of the world until the present.'[28] With evident regret, Mersenne conceded that it would never be possible on this earth to compose a perfect melody, although he held out the happy prospect that the devout Christian might yet hear such perfect melodies sung by the angels in paradise if it so pleased God. Still, the exercise in permutation theory was a useful one, if only to remind us of the unfathomable riches God has made available to us on this earth. Music is thus a parable for the plentitude of His creation. In contemplating this science of sound, Mersenne continually reminds us, the pious listener is lead inexorably to greater devotion to God.

IV

It was indeed music's potential to serve as a virtual catechism of Christian doctrine that seemed to excite Mersenne most powerfully and may ultimately explain why this pious Minim was so powerfully drawn to music as a subject of research. The *Harmonie universelle* is filled with passages and long digressions in which Mersenne notes correspondences and analogies between music and the sacred. Music, he believed, offered the faithful vivid emblems of Christian doctrine that a skilled preacher could use to teach the faithful and convert the heretics. It is telling that one of the last major books of the *Harmonie universelle* is an essay entitled: 'Livre de l'utilité d l'harmonie & des autres parties des mathématiques' (Book on the Utility of Harmony and the Other Parts of Mathematics), in which Mersenne enumerates and summarizes many of the ways musical knowledge could be useful to men. (His ambitious agenda is clear from the very first proposition, in which he announces confidently, 'There is virtually no art, science or other discipline to which harmony and the preceding books may not be of service.')[29]

While music has a utility for virtually every profession – architecture, medicine, the military, politics – it was perhaps of greatest use to religion. First of all, Mersenne points out, music can be of practical help to hone a preacher's oratorical skills by teaching sensitivity to the pronunciation and stress of words, tone of voice, and the speed and style of delivery (4–9). But it can also help by offering endless numbers of topics and analogies by which doctrines of the faith may be vividly presented (20–8). We may learn of God's creative potency through the example of the generative fundamental; the unity of the Holy Trinity may be compared to the harmony of the perfect (major) triad; the path from sin to salvation is much like a dissonance resolving to a consonance; the duty to submit ourselves to the will of God may be likened to a string trembling in sympathetic resonance; the need for men to mediate justly sacred and secular authorities may be imagined as a harmonic or arithmetic proportion; the eight beatitudes can be likened to the eight modes of the church; and the love and grace of the blessed Virgin increased in geometric proportion from the time of her birth until her final assumption.[30]

Now Mersenne's use of analogies and images here certainly seems a far cry from the sober empiricist we have earlier observed. Whereas elsewhere we have seen Mersenne complaining that Galileo's experiments were undertaken without apparent rigour and verification, he is here seen content to report analogies that betray any possible rational grounding. His approach seems redolent of the Renaissance practice of emblematics, in which an author collects and reports (usually with little or no critical commentary) all possible correspondences, analogies, and signs relating to a given topic that may be culled from all available sources.[31] But while there is perhaps some truth in this accusation, I would like to see if there is not a deeper methodological agenda at play in Mersenne's madness.

Let us use as an example Mersenne's discussion of musical consonance – the music-theoretical topic to which he probably devoted more attention in his writings than any other. I will look mainly at the second book of his *Traité de l'harmonie universelle* of 1627, although similar discussions will be found in many of his later writings.[32] In the *Traité*, Mersenne analyses and explains in meticulous detail the various ratios of musical consonance in Book 1 of this treatise following classical discussions of musical canonics contained in the writings of Euclid and Bacchius. By Book 2, 'Livre second des paralleles de la musique,' he will begin to notice other places in which similar simple ratios and proportions seem to play a fundamental role and enumerate them in a series of 'theorems.'

As perhaps the most closely related to sounding musical consonance, Mersenne first turns to the temporal domain of music in Theorem 1: rhythms, metric feet, and versification. There he discovers that the same ratios governing consonance seem to govern the relation and disposition of rhythmic proportion and metrical feet, at least as understood within the dogmatic strictures of the Academy's *vers mesuré*. So the spondee, made up of two long syllables, is like the major third, made up of two perfect whole tones (e.g., C-D-E), while the Bacchean, made up of a short and two long syllables, is like the diatessaron, which contains a half-step plus two whole tones (e.g., E-F-G-A). If, however, the semitone occurs in the middle of the diatassaron (e.g., D-E-F-G), then the analogy is to a cretic foot, long-short-long; and if it is at the top of the tetrachord (e.g., C-D-E-F), it corresponds to a Palimbacchean foot, long-long-short. In this manner, Mersenne continues to itemize virtually every poetic foot and verse structure discussed in classical treatises of rhetoric and poetics, showing their correspondence with musical ratios (302–9).

But poetic feet are only the beginning. In the second theorem of the *Traité*, Mersenne now turns to other manifestations of musical consonance perceptible to the senses of taste, smell, and vision. Here the measurements of proportions and ratios are much less precise, more 'analogic' than empirical. Still, with the authority of the sixteenth-century humanist Girolamo Cardano as his guide, Mersenne argues that the various categories of taste groups (fatty, salty, sweet, sour, bitter, and such) can be combined in various proportions akin to musical ratios. So, for examples, sweetness is deemed by all to be the most pleasant of tastes and thus must correspond to the pure consonance of the octave. Anything with a fatty flavour – 'la saveur qu'on appelle *grasse*' – is comparable to the perfect fifth, since second to sweetness, it is the most pleasant of tastes. Using analogous reasoning, the perfect fourth must correspond to salt, since by itself it is disagreeable, especially in conjunction with anything sweet (just as the fourth added to the octave leads to discord). However when the fourth is combined with a fifth to make the octave, an agreeable sensation is aroused not unlike the combination of salt and fat. The major and minor thirds, which correspond to astringent and insipid tastes, respectively ('la saveur astringente et l'insipide'), while gentle to the tongue by themselves, mix most excellently with one another or in combination with anything sweet, but poorly with anything salty, just as thirds and octaves mix well, but not thirds and perfect fourths, creating a dissonant seventh.[33]

After some further culinary blending of his primary flavours in harmonic whole ratios, Mersenne turns to combinations of colours for further analogies of consonance (again drawing from Cardano). Colours are likened to both specific pitches of the gamut as well as to the seven primary consonances. Hence the lowest note of the Greater Perfect System, the *proslambanomenos*, is likened to the colour black, 'for it tends towards silence,' while the *nete hyperbolaion*, two octaves higher, represents white 'because of its acuteness and sharpness' (314).[34] Elsewhere Mersenne suggests that the octave represents the colour white and the perfect fifth represents green.[35] From colours he moves on to geometry, where a quick inventory of Euclid's *Elements of Geometry* shows that in virtually every chapter there are manifold correspondences between musical harmony and the proportions and ratios contained within the many geometric figures Euclid treats. But Mersenne reminds us that his breathless survey only touches on the possible analogies between music and geometry, 'for I should never be finished if it were necessary to relate all that geometry contains similar to music' (321).

It is worth stopping here for a moment to think about just what it is Mersenne is trying to accomplish with this motley accumulation of associations, analogies, and parallels that carry us from the ratio of the octave through the subjects of metrics, food, colour, and hexagons. As I have already noted, it is all too easy for a modern reader to dismiss this practice as a baleful remnant of Renaissance emblematics in which facile and specious correspondences are drawn with no empirical grounding. This was surely Doni's opinion when he gently chided his good friend concerning his uncritical use of such correspondences, advising him:

> I would also not use all of the analogies and symbols you do to matters of music. It seems to me that it would be better off to be content with a few, good examples that may serve for all the ones you can make. As it is now, there are some that are quite far flung [qui sont prises au loin] and of little

> real resemblance, such as [your comparison between] consonances and flavours that you adopt from Cardan.[36]

But Mersenne's analogic practice was not quite as fickle as Doni suggests. To begin with, the tradition of accumulating eclectic evidence and reports about any given topic was not uncommon among Jesuit scientists of Mersenne's day. (The writings of Athanasius Kircher on music serve as an ideal example here.)[37]

There was also a deeper pedagogical aim. By spinning out analogies, metaphors, and diverse arguments in ever greater concentric spirals, a reader would eventually be led to a firmer understanding and acceptance of the central argument around which these analogies circle. It was a technique of rhetorical *accumulatio* that Mersenne could have learned from his Jesuit teachers, too, in which one musters as many possible arguments as possible for a given proposition, less to prove it in any apodictic sense than to simply persuade (and perhaps overwhelm) the reader through cumulative iteration.[38] Whether Mersenne actually believed all of the individual correspondences he reported – and it is quite clear that he saw many of these as more metaphorical than empirical, more heuristic than apodictic – he obviously felt it relevant to collect as many varying views and ideas as possible in order to urge the reader towards acceptance of the greater truths to which they were pointing. In the examples we have cited regarding consonance, this truth was the ideal of harmonic order that God everywhere instilled in His creation – an order magnificently reflected in the ratios of musical consonances and made palpable to our senses through the hearing of music. Presumably, too, God instilled in all men a desire for this harmonic order, whether in the music we compose, the poetry we recite, the flavours we combine, or the colours by which we paint. Musical consonance simply embodies a universal principle of balance and order:

> As the beauty of the universe originates in the beautiful order observed between all its parts, and that of the face likewise from the comportment and relation of all the parts of which it is made, so too does the sweetness and beauty of music originate in the order observed in the consonances, and which serves as the principal matter of composition.[39]

This analogic style of argumentation is not quite the same thing as the practice of emblematics described briefly above. When Mersenne notes the marvellous correspondence between, say, the perfect major triad and the Holy Trinity, he is not saying that the resulting perfect triad *is* the Holy Trinity, that somehow signs of musical correspondences are hidden everywhere in nature waiting to be deciphered by those possessing the necessary wisdom and insight of ancient knowledge (*prisca scientia*). This was precisely the mistake of the Pantheists and naturalists such as Robert Fludd, who saw the physical world as itself brimming with divinatory presence and occult meanings.[40]

Mersenne's sense of correspondence was always more heuristic. The kinds of proportion and 'consonance' one could find within realms of taste, colours, or geometry were never meant to be understood literally as music. Rather, they were meant to illustrate by analogy a deeper truth about the desire for balance, proportion, and consonance in our lives, and the language of music theory was the ideal means by which to translate this wisdom most explicitly.[41]

As one final example, we might consider Mersenne's extended discussion of the unison in his book on consonance. It is telling that this single ratio of equality – a ratio that was not even accepted as a bona fide interval in traditional canonic theory – received the most attention of any interval in Mersenne's treatise.[42] Clearly it was not the practical value of the unison for composers that so interested Mersenne; rather it was its analogic value. The unison, or more specifically, the ratio of equality (1:1), suggested a host of vivid analogies in any number of disciplines: it represented equilibrium in mechanics, the calibration of bodily humours in medicine, the balance of rights in judicial prudence, and the equality of the holy Trinity for theologians. As the generator of all subsequent consonances, the unison enjoyed a special ontological status akin to the point in geometry, the number one in arithmetic, the prime virtue of love in theology, or indeed, as the divine Godhead in music from which all creation originates. (These latter arguments are almost entirely derived from Augustine.) Mersenne seemed sure that those who would read carefully his discussion of the unison would receive the most profound spiritual instruction:

> It is easy to draw great spiritual profit from this discourse, as more than any other instruction in the world, the unison may lead musicians to God. For all that produced the earth was made by the unison of the sun's rays and those of the other stars that unite with each plant since they awake nature and cause it to grow. When the body obeys the soul, it is by the movement of spirits that they are set in motion, just as the unison may set other strings into motion [through sympathetic vibration]. One may also easily notice

> how the movement of the heart sets the arteries into motion at the same time. If one reflects upon the knowledge of truth, one will have to confess that it is nothing but a unison made with understanding. And if one takes a step even higher, one will find that it is by force of the unison that God made all his creatures act, and that he turned us toward Him by the efficacious grace similar to that of a string whose vibrations are so powerful that they always shake our will without our ever being able to resist.[43]

In contemplating the many miraculous facets of the unison which remain unknown to practical musicians, the reader is given not only a small catechism of Christian thought, but a vivid lesson in the value of theoretical contemplation:

> Musicians, particularly teachers and composers, or those who lead and direct a concert, may take the preceding discourse [on the unison] as a chance to study by reason if they wish to cultivate the part of music in which God has engraved his image, and if they desire to escape the prison of the senses, whose shadows obscure so strongly the judgment that it almost loses its principle function, which is to judge according to equity and reason . . . Now musicians who will study by reason and use its light to dissipate the error of which they are predisposed, will receive a similar contentment from which they will have cause to lift themselves above all sorts of accidents and difficulties of the senses, and to contemplate the joy and inexpressible pleasure they will receive in heaven where they will be carried by the angels to play the harmonic archetype and to contemplate the infinite centre of the increated spirit, where all arguments come to an end, and where the eternal unison of man with angels, and of man and angels with God, and all the consonances will be encountered in all their sovereign perfection. (20–1)

V

It is this reconciliation of the spiritual universe of God with the corporeal world of man through the mediation of music theory that I believe is the ultimate animating force in Mersenne's *Harmonie universelle.* By showing how the mechanical world of material bodies in motion and contact obey precisely quantifiable laws, Mersenne believes we must be persuaded of the beneficent and rational plan of God. Music is not the *cause* of this order, to be sure (hence Mersenne's disapproval of Kepler, who seemed to believe that the whirling planets whose orbits he charted actually represented musical intervals or scales, or of Fludd, who believed the macrocosmos to be literally one grand monochord). But music *can* offer us a palpable sense of the harmonic order we see in the skies or experience in our ambient material world. It is a gift by God that allows us the smallest peak we are allowed into the magnificent and unfathomable design of His creation.

> Because when bodies make sound, they seem to resonate with us and say, listen to my voice and sound in order to understand my properties and nature. My creator gave me speech in order to teach you my properties and power, which you should use to give Him thanks. For He made us solely for your service and his glory.[44]

Never before, then, had music theory been called upon to fulfil such a momentous role, to assume such weighty epistemological and theological responsibilities. In the *Harmonie universelle*, Mersenne unfolds the science of music as a virtual *Gradus* of Christian salvation, one leading inexorably to the most profound moral truths. This is surely why Mersenne pursued the problem of the unison or the defining and ranking consonance with such impassioned urgency. It was not simply a question of sensual tastes. Rather, knowing that the unison was the cause and origin of consonance in music was no different than acknowledging God as the prime creator of the universe; knowing the division between consonance and dissonance was no less an ethical question for a musician than was knowing the difference between right and wrong, between Christian salvation and damnation.

> As a result of this, it can be said that the science of sounds comes closer to [the knowledge of God] than the other sciences, and that it is more suitable than they are for acquainting us with the author of the universe, insofar as it gives us greater knowledge of the properties of sensible things, making us ascend more quickly to the first cause – without which nothing can be known perfectly.[45]

Here was the ultimate virtue – the true utility – of harmony. And make no mistake about it: when Mersenne speaks of harmony, he does not mean musical harmony as a practical art and its many attendant virtues and cathartic powers. He is speaking of music *theory*, of 'la science des sons' – music decomposed to its most elemental parts and properties:

> Music is in God . . . for God has knowledge of all things at a sovereign degree of perfection; and if we knew the harmonic ratios that he has preserved in the fabric of the world, and in all its parts, this knowledge would delight us a thousand times more than any possible concert of music from the Hebrews, Greeks, Italians, French, or any other nation of the world.[46]

And elsewhere:

> Sounds can shed more light on philosophy than any other quality, which is why the science of music should not be neglected, even if all singing and playing were completely abolished and forbidden, as they are not the final end of music, as the practitioners believe, who misunderstand or are ignorant of the reason. In effect, there is not an honest man who would not rather have the knowledge of sounds and their proportions that we have introduced . . . than of all the songs and concerts that could be made following the rules of art.[47]

But let us do the favour of not misunderstanding Mersenne in his candid admissions. By elevating the truths of music theory over the mere practice of 'chants et concerts,' Mersenne is hardly advocating a return to some idealized ascetics of silent contemplation. Nothing could be further from the truth in picturing Mersenne as an unrepentant Platonist reflecting silently upon the sublime proportions of the heavenly spheres. On the contrary, it was the very acoustical phenomenon of sound about which Mersenne was most obsessed. For Mersenne's world was one that was absolutely drenched in noise. Never was there a listener who was more besotted by the sheer sensuality of sound, by the visceral, even carnal, experience of sonic stimulation of every sort.

Mersenne did not single-handedly discover this new sonic world of sensual sound, of course. The seventeenth century reverberated virtually everywhere with a new awareness of the musical acoustic. Just consider, as one example, how Dutch artists of the time began to depict the materiality of music in their many canvases with highly detailed still lives of musical instruments and paraphernalia as well as domestic scenes of sensual music making or raucous concerts. For the Dutch painters, music was not so much an abstraction of seemly proportions as 'pleasurable sound – a concrete, acoustical object of audible perception and consumption.'[48] This is not to say, of course, that the trope of music as divine harmonia ceased (we see perfectly well in Mersenne how both viewpoints may coexist). But certainly the new materiality recognized in music would prove the most consequential for the history of music theory and aesthetics. And no one did more to instil a sensitivity to this materiality than Marin Mersenne.

For any reader with the patience to wade through its hundreds of pages, the *Harmonie universelle* discloses a world of motley, cacophonous musical sounds produced from every imaginable source in every possible way; it reveals an unabashedly material, even violent, world of trembling strings and agitated membranes striking the tiny corpuscles of air and thereby sending undulations of sound waves hurling through space until they impact our eardrum, setting into chain reaction a stimulation of our nerves and disturbances of our bodily humours. It is this base, corporeal world of sound that Mersenne seems to take pleasure in submerging himself.

For the *Harmonie universelle* is ultimately a book *about sound*. Many critics have complained that there is too little about the practice of music, too few pages for one to learn anything really useful about composing in a mode, employing counterpoint, deciphering mensuration symbols, harmonizing a chant, on embellishing a melody. But this misunderstands Mersenne's intent. His was really not a book of *musica practica*. Indeed, it was not a book of *musica theorica*, either, at least in any traditional sense. It was a book, we might most accurately say, about *musique concrète*. What comes through powerfully and palpably to any listener of Mersenne's treatise is *noise*, the sheer physical impact of sound waves washing over one's ears.

Walter Ong has offered us the useful reminder that the early modern world of Mersenne was far more 'sound' oriented than those of us living in a visually dominated culture may realize. God's word – God's *logos* – Mersenne reminds us, was commanded to the prophets in sound (*Les questions theologiques*, 23). And it is through the sound of trumpets, he adds, that the triumphant return of our Saviour will be announced to the world. (Ever the empiricist, Mersenne calculates that these trumpet calls will take a bit more than ten hours to travel the full circumference of our earth!) For the pious, largely illiterate congregations to whom Mersenne's brothers would preach, this Word was heard, not seen. The voice was understood to have the most *effective*, more physically *penetrating* impact upon the body and soul, and hence was the ideal vehicle to inculcate Christian doctrines most potently in the soul of the listener.[49]

Consider the famous 'Livres des instruments' which conclude the *Harmonie universelle*. This was Mersenne's monumental contribution to organology, in which he inventories and describes in exhaustive detail every known musical instrument, present and historical.[50] But unlike his musicological predecessors Praetorius and Virdung, Mersenne was not content simply to compile descriptions, legends and pictures of instruments culled from contemporary reports or ancient sources. He wanted to know thoroughly how each instrument worked, how each *sounded.* Thus each musical instrument is subjected in the pages of the *Harmonie universelle* to minute analysis and experimentation; almost as in a laboratory experiment, each is pulled apart and dissected, so to speak, in order to reveal its inner components and configurations. When reassembled again, our band of instruments is then set into sonic animation.

It is amusing to peer over the shoulder of our curious Minim as he listens with alternating pleasure and astonishment to the colourful world of sounds he produces with his assortment of musical instruments, whether it is plucking strings and concentrating intently upon his beloved (if vexing) overtones, blowing through organ pipes in differing ways to see if contrasting vowel sounds might be produced by which words might be communicated, tapping bells and cymbals to measure their multiple fundamentals, comparing the sounds produced by varieties of strings on his viols and lutes (copper, brass, steel, silver, tin, lead, hemp, or animal gut), varying the tensions of these strings to determine the upper and lower limits of audibility, or testing minute variants in temperament and tunings on his *clavecin.*[51] True, not all of the musical experiments he proposes are realistic, as when he wondered if our voices could be carried through a one-inch tube up to the firmament and still be heard, or how high a given pitch would be produced if a six-pound string were weighted on one end by the whole earth (he calculated it would be forty-one octaves!).[52] Aside from these fanciful thought experiments, though, Mersenne's treatise is concerned very much with earthly sounds that we can hear and verify. On just about every page of his treatise, the *sound* of music sings out to the reader. In his 'Traité de la voix' from part one of the *Harmonie universelle,* alone, we see Mersenne trying out dozens of experiments with his own voice: how many differing vowel sounds can a voice produce? (Prop. 13) How loudly can one sing? (Prop. 16) Is it easier to move from a low pitch to a high pitch or vice versa? (Prop. 17) Is it possible to sing and whistle at the same time? (Prop. 22)

What a cacophonous world Mersenne must have lived in! What an absolute clangorous racket he must have created with his one-man band of musical experimentation! (We must wonder what his fellow Minims thought about the strange and jarring noises streaming day and night from their brother's cell that surely disturbed their contemplative hours.) For never was there anyone who wished to submerge himself so patently in the ambience of pure sound.

In a rare moment of self-reflection, Mersenne confessed to the almost irresistible attraction music held for him as a subject of study: 'There are those who turn to mathematics and are ravished by its numbers' he wrote in 1623:

> There are also those who value geometry just as much, and those who hold in high esteem the sciences of catoptrics or dioptrics, and yet others who value other sciences. I, however, devote myself above all to music, which can be clearly seen in my attempt to embrace its whole compass.[53]

In carrying out his own daily offices of acoustical experimentation, Mersenne never forgets for a single moment the Godly endowed, numerical order underlying the sounds he produces. This was a treatise, after all, entitled *Harmonie universelle.* But Mersenne does not wish to leave these harmonic truths (as did so many of his theoretical predecessors) as only abstractions, as the silent airy magnitudes of *musica mundana*; he strove, rather, to make their truths more sensible, more palpable in the corpuscular world of *musica instrumentalis.* For harmonic order was not something only to be apprehended abstractly by the mind; it was to be experienced corporeally through the senses, much as the Word of God was one that was most powerfully gained through the sensorium of hearing. In this way, music was perhaps the ideal 'experiment' in the nascent world of mechanical science – it offered a repeatable and testable *expérience* of sonic affect.

In her recent book, Kate van Orden has brilliantly allowed us to hear the sound world of late Renaissance France with new ears. It was a world full of terrible noise and often gruesome violence: deafening artillery, clanging swords, the crying of Protestant heretics as they were thrown into the Seine, and the thundering hoofs of charging cavalry.[54] In this noisy, tumultuous world of civil war and social unrest, music provided a kind of disciplinary order and regimentation. This was not the serene order of crystalline spheres, the contemplative chant of the monastery, or the idyllic pastoral of a court festival – although those were all there to be sure. Rather, it was a most corporeal, intrusive music disciplining the social body through bombastic military tattoos and drills, rowdy Te Deums for the King, the shouting of psalms by Huguenot martyrs as they burned at the stake, the stomping of Pyrrhic dancers, and exquisitely choreographed equestrian carousels.

Mersenne's project of musical mechanization is much a part of this most orderly, most regulated of corporeal worlds. (It is perhaps significant that in the penultimate book of the *Harmonie universelle,* Mersenne saw fit to include a lengthy proposition explaining 'the utility of harmony for engineers, for the military, for cannons, and for *gens de Guerre,* in which one may learn of the size and caliber of cannons.')[55] While never losing eye nor ear of the harmonic spheres whirling above our earth, Mersenne also never forgot that we are mere mortals living for a minuscule span of time on this material earth. It was the music and sounds of our material world that Father Mersenne showed us how to hear with new appreciation and reverence, sounds that turned out to be no less wondrous or magnificent than those dreamed of by our ancient forefathers. For in Mersenne's mechanics of sound, the music of the spheres has been yoked and brought crashing down to earth resoundingly; the airy magnitudes of Scipio's dream are now triumphantly performed in the material dance of moving, rigid bodies; the *harmonie universelle* of the ancients turns out to be the *terra sonorum* of the moderns.

NOTES

1 *Harmonie universelle contenant la théorie et la pratique de la musique* (Paris: S. Cramoisy, 1636–7), 'Livre premier de la nature & des proprietez du Son,' 1–84. Citations for the *Harmonie universelle* are notoriously problematic, not only because there are frequent printing errors in pagination and inconsistent chapter titles, but because numerous 'books' of the treatise were evidently published separately – and with individual numberings and paginations – and only later bound with other sections. One result is that scarcely any two copies of the work have identical orderings. (For background on the publishing history of the *Harmonie universelle,* see the useful introduction by François Lesure in the facsimile edition published by the Centre National de la Recherche scientifique in 1963, pp. v–viii.) To make citations as clear as possible in the present essay, I will simply refer to the treatise as *HU* followed by the opening title of the 'book' that is being referenced and use its internal pagination as closely as possible.

2 *HU,* 'Livre second des mouvemens de toutes sortes de corps,' 85–156; 'Livre troisiesme du mouvement, de la tension, de la force, de la pesanteur, & des autres proprietez des chordes Harmoniques, & des autres corps,' 157–228. Again and again, we might note, Mersenne returned in his text to advanced problems of physical mechanics and geometry – often in the midst of a

discussion of musical issues. Mersenne even saw fit to insert in the middle of the work a thirty-six-page compendium of mechanics by Gilles Personne de Roberval, a distinguished professor of mathematics at the Collège de France ('Traité de mechanique des poids soustenus par des puissances sur les plans inclinez à l'horizon . . . par G. Pers. De Roberval Professeur Royale dés mathematiques). Indeed, the final pages of the treatise end where it had begun – with a twenty-eight-page appendix containing miscellaneous observations on problems of mechanics that, for the most part, had already been discussed early in the treatise.

3 The relation between the two phenomena is closer than we might think. Galileo showed that the motion of a pendulum can be analysed as a kind of constrained weight in free fall (its period varying in proportion to the square root of its length). In turn, Mersenne was able to show (prior to Galileo's published demonstration) how the vibrating string could be analysed as a kind of pendulum (its oscillations likewise varying in proportion to the square root of its length). See Frederick V. Hinton, *Origins in Acoustics: The Science of Sound from Antiquity to the Age of Newton* (New Haven, CT: Yale University Press, 1978), 89–93. For the application of such theories to questions of affect, see the essay by Daniel Garber in this volume.

4 For an extensive history of the coincidence theory of consonance, see H.F. Cohen, *Quantifying Music: The Science of Music at the First Stage of the Scientific Revolution, 1580–1650* (Dordrecht: D. Reidel, 1984), esp. 75–97.

5 Peter Dear, *Mersenne and the Learning of the Schools* (Ithaca, NY: Cornell University Press, 1988), 139–41.

6 *HU*, 'Livre septiesme des instrumens de percussion,' 'Eloge de Jacques Mauduit excellent Musicien,' 63–9.

7 Penelope Gouk demonstrates that contemporaneous theorists of human physiology and psychology also relied heavily upon the models offered by music and music theory. See her essay in this volume.

8 Mersenne's complete correspondence is now available in a magnificent seventeen-volume set finished in 1988. See Paul Tannery et al., eds., *Correspondance du P. Marin Mersenne, religieux minime*, 17 vols. (Paris: PUF and CNRS, 1933–88). For the role of Mersenne as scientific 'secretary' in the early seventeenth century, see Richard Tuck, 'The Institutional Setting,' in *The Cambridge History of Seventeenth-Century Philosophy*, ed. Daniel Garber and Michael Ayers (Cambridge: Cambridge University Press, 1998).

9 *HU*, 'Livre troisiesme des mouvemens & du son des chordes,' 167. For the classic study of Mersenne as a scientist, see Robert Lenoble, *Mersenne ou la naissance du méchanisme* (Paris: Vrin, 1943). A.C. Crombie's comprehensive study of early modern science contains a most illuminating discussion of

Mersenne's scientific style, along with many helpful translations: *Styles of Scientific Thinking in the European Tradition*, vol. 2 (New York: Duckworth, 1994), 810–65. Much shorter and accessible is Crombie's entry, 'Marin Mersenne,' in *The Dictionary of Scientific Biography*, ed. C.G. Gillespie (New York: Scribner's, 1974). Peter Dear's indispensable study puts Mersenne's scientific agenda in broader intellectual perspective: Peter Dear, *Mersenne and the Learning of the Schools*. Studies that concentrate on Mersenne's acoustics are rare, but a helpful overview is found in F.V. Hunt, *Origins in Acoustics*, and Crombie, *Styles of Scientific Thinking*. Also worth mentioning is an older dissertation that is still of great value and insight: Frederick Bill Hyde, 'The Position of Marin Mersenne in the History of Music' (PhD diss., Yale University, 1954).

10 *HU*, 'Livre premier de la nature & des proprietez du Son,' 14, 38–44. For an abbreviated account of Mersenne's experiments to measure the speed of sound, see Hunt, *Origins in Acoustics*, 82–100. His inability to arrive at a consistent velocity for sound, it turns out, was due to the lack of a uniform and accurate instrument of time measurement. (He initially relied largely on counting his own heart pulses.) Recognizing the problem, Mersenne attempted to adapt Galileo's pendulum as a timing device, albeit with limited success. A pendulum clock would not be perfected until mid-century by Christiaan Huygens.

11 In a letter to Nicolas-Claude de Peiresc, one of his closest correspondents, Mersenne complained that Galileo clearly never verified his claims regarding the acceleration of bodies on an inclined plane through experiment, whereas he would repeat an experiment 'more than 30 times, and some ones more than 100 times, all in front of the most trustworthy witnesses, who have, without exception, all reached the same conclusions as me.' (Letter dated 17 September 1635, *Correspondance* V, #484). Also see Mersenne's correction of Galileo's numbers in the *HU*, 'Livre second du mouvement des corps,' 87.

12 *Dictionary of Scientific Bibliography*, s.v. 'Mersenne,' 318.

13 Just in the *Harmonie universelle* alone, the phenomena of overtones are mentioned in over a dozen separate passages. See Helmut Ludwig, *Marin Mersenne und seine Musiklehre* (Halle: Waisenhaus, 1935), 41fn5, for specific citations. For a general discussion of overtones and early vibrational theory in the seventeenth century, see Clifford Truesdell, 'The Rational Mechanics of Flexible or Elastic Bodies, 1638–1788,' in *Euleri Opera Omnia* (Leipzig: Teubner, etc., 1912–), series 2, vol. XI/2; and Sigalia Dostrovsky, 'Early Vibrational Theory: Physics and Music in the Seventeenth Century, ' *Archive for History of Exact Sciences* 14 (1975): 169–218. For Mersenne's contribution

to the understanding of overtones, with extensive translations, see Hyde, 'The Position of Marin Mersenne,' 190–245.

14 See his letter to Constantine Huygens, 12 January 1647, *Correspondance* XV, #1585.

15 *HU*, 'Traitez des instruments,' 210.

16 *Les questions theologiques, physiques, morales, et mathematiques* (Paris, 1634), 158.

17 Clifford Truesdell, 'The Rational Mechanics of Flexible or Elastic Bodies,' 28. Still, we should not overlook the tenacious hold such naturalist and numerological views continued to hold in the seventeenth century. The vibrating string – the very object upon which Mersenne seemed to ground his mechanistic philosophy in music – was also the phenomenon that naturalists such as Fludd cited as evidence for the occult nature of music. For many of these observers, the vibrating string seemed to convey as if by magic its vibrations through the air and set into sympathetic motion other objects, much as music itself could set into motion the fibres and humours of the body. See Penelope Gouk, *Music, Science and Natural Magic in Seventeenth-Century England* (New Haven, CT: Yale University Press, 1999), as well as her essay in this volume.

18 Mersenne's most impassioned polemic using arguments of science and music theory against scepticism came in his massive, 1,000-page treatise of 1625, *La vérité des sciences contre les septiques ou Pyrrhoniens*. Discussions on music may be found on 349–89 and 527–80. For the classic study of scepticism in early modern thought, see Richard Popkin, *The History of Skepticism from Erasmus to Spinoza* (Berkeley: University of California Press, 1979). Also see Richard Popkin, 'Father Mersenne's War against Pyrrhonism,' reprinted in *Essays on Early Modern Philosophers from Descartes and Hobbes to Newton and Leibniz*, ed. Vere Chappell (New York: Garland Press, 1992), vol. 2: 161–78.

19 *Questions harmoniques dans lesquelles sont contenuuës plusieurs choses remarquables pour la Physique, ou la Morale, et pour les autres sciences* (Paris, 1634; facsimile reprint, Stuttgart: Frommann, 1972). The *Questions harmoniques* was actually one of four treatises Mersenne published in 1634 that contained a large number of speculative problems concerning music theory, acoustics, and affect. (The others were *Questions inouyes ou recreation des scavans, Les questions theologiques, physiques, morales, et mathematiques* [cited above in n. 16] and *Les preludes de l'harmonie universelle.*) Quite likely the material in these books was all originally intended to be included in his forthcoming *Harmonie universelle.* But given their highly eclectic and speculative nature, Mersenne evidently decided to publish them separately.

20 For background on La Mothe Le Vayer, see Popkin, *The History of Skepticism*, 90–7. Here and elsewhere in this essay, I will be indicating most page citations within the text in parentheses. The work cited should be clear from

the context. If there are exceptions, page citations will appear in endnotes with the particular work indicated.

21 *Les questions theologiques, physiques, morales, et mathematiques*, 18.

22 Popkin, *The History of Skepticism*, 129–50. A good example of such delimited knowledge is Mersenne's discussion of Gilbert's magnet. Although he could not offer an explanation of its cause, it was quite possible to describe empirically the effects of the magnet and even to suggest obvious applications for surveying and navigation. *Les questions theologiques*, #27: 'Combien la pierre d'Aymant a-elle de proprietez?' (123).

23 *Questions harmoniques*, Question #5: 'A scavoir si la pratique de la Musique est preferable a la Theorie; et si l'on doit faire plus d'estast de celuy qui ne scait que composer, ou chanter, que de celuy qui ne scait que les raisons de la Musique' (226–51).

24 *Questions harmoniques*, 237–9.

25 *HU*, 'Livre premier des consonances,' 110.

26 *La verité des sciences*, 544: 'Dans lequel Il est traité des beaus airs, & des beaus chants, & montré s'il est possible de faire un chant sur un sujet donné, qui soit le plus beau de tous cues qui puissant ester faits sur le mesme sujet.' *Les preludes de l'harmonie universelle*, Question #5: 'Quelle doit estre la capacité, et la science d'un parfaict musicien.' Question #11: 'A sçavoir comme il faut composer les chansons, pout estre les plus excellenetes de toutes celles qui se puevent imaginer.' *HU*, 'Livre second des chants,' 103: 'Determiner s'il est possible de composer le meilleur chant de tous ceux qui se seuvent imaginer, & si estant composé il se peut chanter avec toute la perfection possible.' (Already in his *Quaestiones Celeberrimae in* Genesim, col. 1563–64, Mersenne asked what it would take to compose the most perfect music ('Quae requiruntur ut musicae perfecta vis restituatur'). Any attentive reader of Mersenne soon learns that he would constantly recycle questions and material from earlier writings, if with further elaborations or reflections.)

27 Mersenne's most extensive discussion of combinatorics is found in the *HU*, 'Livre second des chants,' 107–58.

28 *HU*, 'Livre des Chants,' 107. In his *La verité des sciences* of 1625, Mersenne attempted to be precise in his calculations. If there have been – according to Baron – 6,824 years since creation, and a year contains 8,766 hours, Mersenne determined that it would be impossible to sing all the permutations of a song containing only twelve tones assuming a leisurely rate of one song every forty seconds (553–4)!

29 *HU*, 'De l'utilité de l'harmonie & des autres parties des Mathematiques,' 1.

30 On the generative fundamental, see 'Livre premier des consonances,' 15; On the Holy Trinity and the harmonic triad, 'De l'utilité de l'harmonie,' 12,

16, and 'Livre quartriesme de la composition,' 204; on dissonance, 'Livre second des dissonances,' 122, 131; on sympathetic resonance, 'Livre premier des consonances,' 12; on harmonic proportions, see below note 41; on the eight modes, 'De l'utilité de l'harmonie,' 11; on the Virgin Mary and the geometric proportion, *Traité de l'harmonie universelle*, Book 2, Theorem 14 (cf. note 32 below).

31 On the Renaissance reading of emblems, see William B. Ashworth, 'Natural History and the Emblematic World View,' in *Reappraisals of the Scientific Revolution*, ed. David C. Lindberg and Robert S. Westman (Cambridge: Cambridge University Press, 1990). Many readers, of course, will naturally think of Foucault's Renaissance episteme of resemblance, to which the notion of emblems may be affiliated. But I am hesitant to enter too far into Foucault's theories in the present essay, which would demand a far more extensive exposé and critique than I am able to give here. In any case, for reasons I will hopefully make clear below, Mersenne's practice differs in important ways from Renaissance emblematics and, by extension, Foucault's episteme of resemblance.

32 The *Traité de l'harmonie universelle* (Paris, 1627; reprint edition, Paris: Fayard, 2003) was initially envisioned by Mersenne to be the beginning of his magnum opus on music. But the work contains only two of the promised sixteen 'books.' Clearly, he felt he needed more work on the project, which, of course, culminated in 1636 with the publication of the first volume of the *Harmonie universelle.*

33 *Traité de l'harmonie universelle* (reprint edition), 309–21. The work of Cardano from which Mersenne draws is *De Rerum Varietate*, Book 17 (1557). Cardano, I am quite sure, was a major source of musical lore for Mersenne in many of his other passages, although infrequently acknowledged. It would be a revealing project to study more thoroughly the many sources from which Mersenne drew for his musical writings.

34 Lest Mersenne be accused of too much consistency, we might note that in the *Harmonie universelle*, he changes his mind and suggests that the *proslambonomenos* ought to correspond to the colour yellow, since through Hebrew etymology, we know it to have been the primeval colour of the earth (*HU*, 'Livre second des chants,' 100).

35 *HU*, 'Livre premier des consonances,' 90.

36 Letter dated 8 November 1634; *Correspondance* IV, #391. Mersenne, we should note, acknowledged Doni's criticism in a letter he wrote back early the following year, explaining he included such examples only to solicit the thoughts of his reading public (letter dated 2 February 1635; *Correspondance* V, #405). He promised Doni to eliminate many of these analogies in his

forthcoming *Harmonie universelle* – a promise that, at least in regard to the analogy with taste, he kept. (Still, Mersenne could not refrain from at least touching on the analogy between consonances and colours, as we have noted in the previous two footnotes.)

37 William Ashworth has claimed that the eclectic method of Jesuit science in the seventeenth century – such as what Mersenne might have learned at La Flèche – was characterized by an emblematic approach, whereupon the observer would collect and report as many possible correspondences and associations of some given phenomenon as possible, usually with little discrimination or attempt at synthesis. See William Ashworth, 'Catholicism and Early Modern Science,' in *God and Nature: Historical Essays on the Encounter between Christianity and Science*, ed. David. C. Lindberg and Ronald L. Numbers (Berkeley: University of California Press, 1986), 155–6.

38 So for example, in the *Quaestiones Celeberrimae in Genesim*, Mersenne offers thirty-six arguments for the existence of God. Peter Dear calls these 'arguments of probability' (*Mersenne and the Learning of the Schools*, 29). I might add here another, related explanation for Mersenne's eclecticism. Paul Mueller has suggested that Mersenne's tendency to pile up endless numbers of examples in his arguments – many of them inconsistent with one another – reflects a tradition of textural criticism practised by the humanists to resolve differences among extant manuscript copies of ancient texts. By this method, one compiles all versions and variants of a text, juxtaposing them one against the other, in order to help evaluate and identify those that are authentic. See Paul R. Mueller, 'Marin Mersenne's *Questions Théologiques, physiques, morales, et mathématiques*: Agenda and Structure, with an Annotated Translation' (PhD diss., University of Chicago, 2006), 72. At least in the case of music, though, Mersenne never seems to insist that we choose from among the competing analogies he makes.

39 *HU*, 'Livre quatriesme de la composition de musique,' 197.

40 Fludd's macrocosm, Mersenne complained, used 'analogies and comparisons based only on imagination' (*Traité de l'harmonie universelle*, 392). His conclusion was damning: 'It must be concluded, then, that the universal harmony of Robert Fludd has no foundation other than his own imagination and that all books based on this foundation will have no truth other than that of symbolic analogy' (413).

41 Jean Bodin's oft-cited analogy between musical proportions and political states – repeated with evident approval by Mersenne – might likewise be seen as a kind of heuristic morality tale. Bodin had suggested that an aristocratic state is analogous to the geometric proportion, while a popular state

is like the arithmetic proportion, and a monarchy the harmonic proportion. Bodin saw music theory as ideally calibrating the kinds of tensions and balances any political state faces. In the same way, to the extent we can understand and mediate the various extremes between sacred and secular authorities which we find ourselves in life, we have the possibility of creating a more harmonious, just, and moral life. See Jean Bodin, *Les six livres de la république de J. Bodin Anguevin* (Paris, 1576), 727–59. For Mersenne's citation and discussion of Bodin, see his *La verité des sciences,* 419–31.

42 Pages 7–34 of the 'Livre premier des consonances' are devoted exclusively to that of the unison. In a tradition that may be dated back to the authority of Boethius, the unison was not accepted by most music theorists preceding Mersenne as a true interval, since it lacked the key-defining characteristic of an interval: a distinction between high and low sounds. (Boethius had written: 'Intervallum vero est soni acuti gravisque distantia.')

43 *HU,* 'Livre premier des consonances,' 22.

44 *Les questions théologiques,* 158–9.

45 *Les questions théologiques,*' 160–1.

46 *Traité de l'harmonie universelle,* 49.

47 *HU,* 'Livre premier des consonance,' 88.

48 Roy Sonnema, 'Musical Indulgences and Pleasurable Sound in Seventeenth-Century Dutch Art,' in *Art and Music in the Early Modern Period,* ed. Katherine A. McIver (Aldershot: Ashgate, 2003), 334. For more on the relationship between seventeenth-century Dutch music and art, see the essay by Richard Leppert in this volume.

49 Walter Ong, *The Presence of the Word: Some Prolegomena for Cultural and Religious History* (New Haven, CT: Yale University Press, 1967), esp. 179–91. Also see Gary Tomlinson, *Music in Renaissance Magic* (Chicago: University of Chicago Press, 1993), 58–60.

50 This is the only portion of the *Harmonie universelle* that has been translated into English. Marin Mersenne, *Harmonie universelle: The Books on Instruments,* trans. Roger E. Chapman (The Hague: M. Nijhoff, 1957).

51 On overtones, see 'Livre quatriesme des instruments,' 208; on sounding vowels with organ pipes, 'Livre sixiesme des orgues,' 380; on the sound of bells, 'Livre septiesme des instrumens de percussion,' 26–30; on varieties of strings, 'Livre troisiesme des instrumens à chordes,' 151–6; on the limits of audibility, 'Livre premier de la nature & des proprietez du son,' 72; on varieties of temperaments, 'Livre premier des instrumens,' 32 ff.

52 On the conveying of the voice to the firmament, see *Les questions theologiques,* Question 44(b): 'Quelle doit ester la force de la voix pour ester portée et

entenduë jusques à la Lune, au soleil, et au firmament, soit naturellement, ou par artifice'; on the frequency of a string weighted by the earth, see *HU*, 'Livre troisiesme des mouvemens & du son des chordes,' 186.

53 *Quaestiones celeberrimae in Genesim*, col. 1570. ('Sunt qui partem illam mathematicam, quae versatur in numeris, ita admirentur, qui geometriam tanti faciant, qui catoptricam et dioptricam in tanto pretio habeant ut caeteris scientiis illas facile anteponant – ego vero musicae primas tribuo, quippe quae reliquas ambitu suo complecti videtur.')

54 Kate van Orden, *Music, Discipline, and Arms in Early Modern France* (Chicago: University of Chicago Press, 2005). Van Orden comes to a similar conclusion in her close reading of Descartes's *Compendium musicae* of 1618. See 'Descartes on Musical Training and the Body,' in *Music, Sensation, and Sensuality*, ed. Linda Phyllis Austern (New York: Routledge, 2002), 17–38.

55 *HU*, 'Livre de l'utilité de l'harmonie,' 37–44. See also the 'Nouvelles observations physiques & mathematiques,' 23–4.

PART II

COLONIAL EXTENSIONS

chapter four

'Voluntary Subjection': France's Theory of Colonization/Culture in the Seventeenth Century

SARA E. MELZER

Colonization: A Love Story

One day a young Huron girl began to cry when a Frenchman briefly touched her hand to help guide her along a treacherous path in Quebec. Her friends, witness to this act, gasped in horror. Through her tears, the young girl reproached the Frenchman: 'I have washed my hands so often that it is impossible that anything can remain of the harm that [you] may have done me.' The girls had interpreted the Frenchman's touch to mean he had stolen her virginity from her. This story's narrator, Jesuit Father Paul Le Jeune, chuckled: 'Such innocence is most amusing.'[1]

This anecdote was typical of many stories found in the best-selling *relations de voyage,* reports that many French travellers to the New World wrote about their contact with the Amerindians. Church missionaries, state officials, and explorers wrote *relations* for the French reading public back home to convince them that the church and state's evangelizing/colonizing endeavour was making progress and was thus worthy of their support,financial and otherwise.[2] In this particular vignette, Jesuit missionary Paul Le Jeune was addressing those French readers familiar with Amerigo Vespucci's famous *Mundus Novus* (1503), a widely circulated letter which described the Amerindians' shocking, promiscuous sexuality that became a *topos* in France's travel literature.[3] The fact that some Huron girls experienced shame at having their hands touched dramatized how their hearts and souls were radically restructured by their contact with Catholic France since now they were imitating its morality. Never mind that the girls did not quite grasp the baffling new concept of virginity. Over time they would figure it out since 'mind is not lacking among the Savages of Canada, but education and instruction,' as the *Jesuit Relations* repeatedly noted (*JR*, V: 31–2). The girls' shame and their desire to imitate French, Catholic behaviour were 'structures of feeling' that the *relateurs* saw as signs of progress.[4] They would thus be suitable marriage partners for French men, since intermarriage was part of the colonial strategy in the New World.[5]

On the surface, this vignette and many others like it appear simply as innocent, charming stories, which explains, in part, why the *relations de voyage* were so popular both inside and outside the French court.[6] However, I will argue that these stories were not so innocent; they conveyed a covert theory of colonization. This theory was covert in the sense that France's colonial strategy was not developed explicitly as a theory but referred to only in occasional, sketchy snippets. Moreover, the evidence for this theory is not easily recognizable since it emerged indirectly through the imagined 'structures of feeling' that France's travel writers attributed to the American Indians. 'Structures of feeling' are, as Susan McClary has argued in her introductory essay in this volume, forms of human expression that have been below the threshold of awareness of most scholars. And yet, as I will show, they were pivotal to France's understanding of culture and colonization.

This essay's goal is to articulate a theory both of colonization and of French culture to show how, contrary to the dominant assumption in French studies, they were intimately bound together in the early modern era. The church and state wove them together because they used their culture as a key tool of colonization. The French sought to use the properties of their culture to alter the feelings of the colonized. For example, the fact that the Huron girls now supposedly felt shame at a man's touch, whereas previously they were shamelessly promiscuous, demonstrates that their contact with France's Catholic culture was altering their hearts and souls. This affective transformation indicated their desire and their capacity to become assimilated into Catholic France's community. Ultimately, the Amerindians would impose the bonds of colonization on themselves because of their longing to be like the French. Thus, since the French imagined colonizing the Amerindians' souls through Catholic France's culture, France's theory of colonization was also a theory of culture.

Before addressing the relation between culture and colonization, I would first like to define what I mean by culture and also by colonization. The term 'culture' existed in the seventeenth century, although it had a different meaning that referred to the cultivation of the earth, as in agriculture.[7] However, the act of cultivation began increasingly to refer to humans.[8] I thus understand the term 'culture' first as a process of cultivating the human as a plant and transplanting it into the 'garden' of Catholic France's civilized community. Culture thus had important work to perform – to transform and colonize the souls of outsiders to enable them to become insiders. I use 'culture' to refer to the social practices and material objects that both transformed outsiders and also defined the ideal of France's imagined, civilized community. These practices could be daily habits, beliefs, customs, or material objects such as food, clothing, or lodging, or they could refer to the arts and letters of an elite world – literature, music, painting, and so forth. These practices defined the ideals of France's ideal civilized world. Moreover, these practices restructured the feelings of outsiders, thus functioning as instruments of colonial expansion.

This notion of 'culture' differs significantly from our current twenty-first century understanding of the term. In our democratic, egalitarian society, we assume 'culture' is something that all societies have. As Webster's second unabridged dictionary defines the term, it refers to 'the concepts, habits, skills, art, instruments, institutions, etc. of a given people in a given period.' Such a modern definition does not hierarchically order the practices of different groups of people. Culture simply refers to their particularities and is not the exclusive property of an elite stratum. The seventeenth-century church and state would have been shocked by such a modern view since they thought that only some nations had culture and others did not. France had it, which was precisely why France had the right and the duty to help cultivate and civilize those who did not.

France's notion of colonization can often be difficult to recognize as colonization because it does not correspond to the standard model. When we think of colonization, we typically assume a colonizer who imposes its will on the colonized through military muscle. Acting contrary to the colonized's desires, the colonizer forces them to submit to a hateful, demeaning way of life. By contrast, the French mode of colonization presented itself as a kind of 'love story.' Seventeenth-century traveler Marc Lescarbot characterized this process as a 'voluntary subjection.' He wrote in his *Histoire de la Nouvelle France* (1609):

> The savages came from all around to see the manners of the Frenchmen, and lodged themselves willingly near them: they made Monsieur de Mons judge of their debates, which is a beginning of a *voluntary subjection*, from

> whence a hope may be conceived that these people will soon conform themselves to our manner of living. (my emphasis)[9]

This 'voluntary subjection' was predicated on France's dazzling cultural power, which was so magnetic that the Amerindians would voluntarily imitate Catholic and French ways of life to have what their chosen models had. Catholic French culture would act on the Amerindians' feelings, seducing them to voluntarily 'conform themselves to our manner of living.' Their 'voluntary subjection' appeared as a naturally occurring process resulting from the desire of those lower down on the barbarism-civilization evolutionary continuum to elevate themselves by imitating those on a higher rung. They would see France's king as their true master, for he would help them on their journey to civilization. Because this process was self-imposed and would supposedly lead to a self-improvement, or such was the theory, it did not look like a colonial relationship. It was a 'soft colonization' that was so soft that both the theory and the phenomenon itself were largely invisible.

Imitation, then, constituted the foundation of France's emerging colonial policy in the seventeenth century; imitation functioned as a covert form of colonization, thus buttressing what contemporary theorist Homi K. Bhabha would later observe about France's nineteenth- and twentieth-century colonial policy: 'mimicry emerges as one of the most elusive and effective strategies of colonial power and knowledge.'[10] In line with Bhabha's observation, I will examine the stories the *relateurs* told about the Amerindians' imitation of French, Catholic culture to illuminate the elusive nature of France's colonial strategy and show how it achieved its effects by camouflaging its dominating impulse. France's colonization of the Amerindians presented itself as a story about human emotions, relying in particular on the outsiders' supposed love/desire for France just as France felt love/charity towards outsiders. Needless to say, this theory of colonization and culture differed greatly from the historical reality of the colonial practices that took place on the ground on the opposite side of the Atlantic.[11]

In what follows, I will examine two very different kinds of texts from very different sources to explore France's theory of colonization/culture. The first source includes texts about France itself, which celebrated its language and culture. These texts were 'defences' of France's vernacular and its literary culture. As such, they participated in the overarching *Quarrel between the Ancients and the Moderns*, with the 'moderns' insisting on the independence of French from Latin and Greek, and also claiming the greatness of their nation's own literary production. The second were the anecdotes that the *relateurs* told about their encounters with the New World Indians. Neither set of sources, on the surface, appears to be about colonization. Nor do these sources appear to be connected. Yet, they were, which reflects the deceptive nature of France's colonial policy and of its hidden cultural agenda.[12]

It is problematic to speak of French culture during this time because to do so implies that the church and state had a precisely formulated notion of what that culture was and how it functioned. However, that was not the case; their culture was something that was in the process of being defined. I argue that France's understanding of its culture evolved in tandem with its colonizing endeavours, charged with responding to the dilemmas of its colonizing strategy. One task was to work on the feeling structures of the French readership back home to convince them that assimilation was both a desirable and viable strategy worthy of their support.

Shaping the feelings of France's literate elite, encouraging them to accept France's colonial strategy, was particularly important because the church and state adopted a rather unusual colonizing strategy: assimilation. Unlike the nineteenth-century state's version of assimilation which minimized contact between colonizer and colonized, the seventeenth-century church and state's ideal fostered an unusually high degree of contact. Their ideal promoted mixed communities, encouraging the two groups to live together, work together, pray together and even urged marriages, with the Native Americans made capable 'of being admitted into the common life of the French.'[13] Ultimately, they should all form 'a single people and a single blood,' as Louis XIV's minister, Colbert, wrote.[14] He instructed that dowries be offered to French–Native American couples as an incentive to marry and to remain in the French, Catholic community.[15] This French strategy contrasted with that of France's major contemporary, colonial competitors. Neither England, Holland, Spain, nor Portugal officially embraced such a policy in the New World but chose other approaches.[16] See, for example, Gary Tomlinson's 'Fear of Singing' and Olivia Bloechl's 'The Illicit Voice of Prophecy' in this volume for a discussion of the Spanish and British approaches.

France's distinctive assimilationist strategy was problematic in that it, more than other colonizing choices, risked blurring the 'us-them' boundaries. To fortify the boundaries, the church and state relied on the properties of their culture to help construct alternatives. The properties of French culture were charged with changing the feelings of the colonized, giving them a new, civilized set of emotions. The power of French culture would be so strong and alluring that the Native Americans would impose their own boundaries to identity with the Catholic, French side of the divide and reject their native culture. Moreover, the nation's cultural properties also had to alter the feelings of the French reading public and convince them that the civilized/savage boundaries would remain firm, protecting them from contamination. In sum, French culture had to acquire a force capable of assuming the crucial offensive and defensive functions that the military would more typically take on within a colonial context. It had to create new 'structures of feeling,' both within the colonized and the colonizer.

The French Language, Culture, and the *Gallic Hercules*

On the surface, the texts celebrating the greatness of France and its culture seem to be light years away from colonization. They did nevertheless articulate a covert theory of colonization. This theory emerged in the context of the Quarrel between the Ancients and the Moderns, understood in its largest sense, beginning in the early sixteenth century (or earlier) and extending to the eighteenth century. In this Quarrel, many French *lettrés* sought to defend the dignity and independence of the French language and culture from the stifling dominance of Latin and Roman culture.[17] Although France was at the height of its cultural power by the late seventeenth century, its writers and artists still felt overshadowed by ancient Rome and feared they were second-rate, just as many Romans feared they were second-rate compared to the Greeks.

For instance, Dominque Bouhours's best-selling *Entretiens d'Ariste et d'Eugène* (1671), an important voice in the Quarrel, defended the use of the French language against those who maintained that Latin, because it was the universal language, should be preferred over the vernacular. Bouhours claimed that French was fast becoming the new Latin – a universal language. But in boasting of its universalism, Bouhours was at the same time articulating a theory of colonization based on a 'voluntary subjection.' He fantasized a 'soft colonization' in which France was seducing and dominating the world through its arts and letters. France's cultural power acted like a magnet that compelled people everywhere to bang at its gates, clamoring to be part of France. Like moths to a flame, they were drawn by the light of France: 'all foreigners who have any spirit are proud to know the French language . . . there are hardly any countries in Europe where French is not understood.'[18] Bouhours expanded the dominion of French yet further, claiming that '[French] is in current use among the savages of America and among the most civilized nations of Asia.' The king of Persia, eager to promote commercial relations with France, insisted that 'the Persians study French with an incredible ardor. I suspect that the Chinese and Japanese also study it since there are French people among them . . . [I]f the French language is not yet the tongue of all people in the world, it seems to me that it deserves to be.' France's cultural imperialism was better than that of ancient Rome because when the peoples of the world learned Latin, they did so only *after* they were militarily conquered and only because they were forced to do so. France's cultural imperialism was superior, Bouhours boasted, because the peoples of the world spoke French voluntarily:

> It is something glorious for our nation . . . that the French language is in vogue in the capital of the Low Countries *before* French domination was established. The Latin language came after the Roman conquests but I do not see that it has ever preceded them. The nations that these conquerors had vanquished learned Latin in spite of themselves. Instead now those people who have not yet been subdued by France learn French *voluntarily*. (my emphasis)

Foreigners learned French willingly, 'almost as soon as their own, out of a secret instinct that warns them that despite themselves one day they will obey the King of France, accepting him as their legitimate master.' Once they learned French, they 'neglect their natural language entirely and pride themselves on never having learned it.' Bouhours imagined the day when 'all languages would be reduced to one.' Of course, that language would be French so that 'all people could communicate and understand each other in the way we do.'[19] French would provide the thought structures through which all peoples would understand themselves. French culture would dominate by insinuating itself into the souls and minds of the peoples the world over, acting on their feelings, restructuring their hearts so they would identify with the French and against their ancestral heritage.

In a similar vein, François Charpentier, a few years later, became engaged in the Battle of the Inscriptions, a huge controversy as part of the larger Quarrel between the Ancients and the Moderns that erupted over whether the inscriptions on monuments to the king should be written in French or in Latin. Charpentier, in his *Défense de la langue française pour l'inscription de l'Arc de Triomphe* (1676), argued they should be inscribed in the vernacular since French was becoming the new universal language. To praise its worth, Charpentier, like Bouhours, described the greatness of French by sketching out a theory of a 'voluntary subjection,' which he expressed by evoking the figure of the *Gallic Hercules*. This figure was a famous symbol of France's wise and effective governance, identified with French kingship ever since the beginning of the sixteenth century.[20] Many writers and artists used the *Gallic Hercules* to portray François I, Henri II, Henri IV, Louis XIII, and Louis XIV. The *Gallic Hercules*, before emerging in Charpentier's thought, had made one of its earliest appearances in Geofroy Tory's *Champ Fleury* (1529), which pictured a Hercules who led the people to civilization through the force of eloquence and culture, not brute force. His tongue had strings attached, very literally, because of his eloquence (see figure 4.1).[21] His words constituted delicate golden chains that were fastened to his tongue on one end and on the other hooked onto the ears of the men and women, and he thereby pulled them gently towards where he was heading – civilization. Because his chains were so delicate, the multitudes could have easily broken them, had they so wished. However, they did not, which was the key point. The multitudes, enchanted by Hercules' eloquence, followed of their own free will, voluntarily imposing chains upon themselves. This method of domination was akin to a 'voluntary subjection.' Tory used this argument to convince the state to value and to cultivate the power of the French language.

When Charpentier picked up on the *Gallic Hercules* image over a century after Geofroy Tory, he highlighted how France's cultural power would colonize the souls of outsiders. Its language and culture would stir up new feelings within them, inducing outsiders to voluntarily impose chains on themselves. Colonization would take place with the elegance and refinement that has come to be France's hallmark and thus not appear as an act of domination. France's arts and letters would 'bend their hearts by the charms of discourse,' Charpentier advised Louis XIV in 1676. Echoing Tory's words, Charpentier also insisted that Gallic Hercules' chains were voluntary. This heroic figure

> had several chains of gold and precious stones coming out of his mouth, by which he held on to an infinite number of people who were attached by their ears, so that they seemed to follow this Hero *of their own free will*, rather than by necessity since the chains were so light and *easy to break.* (my emphasis)[22]

Figure 4.1 ‘The Gallic Hercules.’ Printed in Geoffroy Tory, *Champ fleury* (Paris, 1529)
Courtesy of the British Library.

In short, seduced by France's dazzling arts and letters, people 'of their own free will' followed the *Gallic Hercules,* putting on their own chains. However, they did not view them as chains, but as helpful guides to lead them on the path to civilization. For Charpentier, the *Gallic Hercules* and its seductive eloquence were a 'symbol of the nation's genius'[23] since France could expand its empire without getting down and dirty by cultivating the resources of its culture to induce in others a 'voluntary subjection,' making this dynamic appear like a naturally occurring process.

However, this 'voluntary subjection' or 'soft colonization' was not as naturally occurring as Charpentier and Bouhours made it appear. The French state was behind the scene, pulling the strings to make such an effect seem natural. When the state founded a French Academy, it was, in part, with such a colonizing goal in mind. It sought to work on the hearts and minds of the people around the world, luring them into 'structures of feeling' that were 'voluntary chains.'

Nicolas Faret wrote a founding document for the French Academy in 1634 in which he described why such an Academy was necessary – to stimulate the desired effects of the French language on foreigners. 'Tempted by their love' for the French language, foreigners would 'conceive a secret desire to abolish theirs in order to speak only French,'[24] wrote Faret in his *Projet de l'Académie pour servir de préface à ses statuts.* Similarly, Paul Pellison's official *Histoire de l'Académie Française* (1652) argued that its goal was to make 'foreigners . . . fall in love with the language they have hitherto disdained.'[25] The fact that the Academy members used a language of love and desire suggests that they imagined that French culture could seep into the souls of people the world round so that they would volunteer, if not beg, to become French. The French Academy wanted France to become 'the master of hearts' of all the world, just as in Corneille's *Cinna* the Emperor Augustus realized that true power resided in rendering oneself the 'master of hearts' of those in his empire.

The French state developed its arts and culture as a self-conscious strategy with this imperialist agenda in mind. It began with seduction, creating a public culture so dazzling and prestigious that all subjects would imitate it, conferring prestige on those associated with it.[26] Louis XIV cultivated a 'build it and they will come' mentality – constructing Versailles, the largest single construction project undertaken in Europe since Roman times, as a magnetic force field. His development of culture, from extravagant festivals and spectacles, to theatrical events, ballet, opera, music, and poetry was to command the attention of foreigners worldwide.

Thus in 1663, Louis XIV founded the Petite Académie, whose goal was to fashion France's image. To create an aura of magic that would attract public attention, he founded more academies and cultural institutions than any other king in French history: L'Académie Royale de Peinture et de Sculpture (1648), L'Académie de Danse (1661), L'Académie Française de Rome (1666), L'Académie des Sciences (1666), L'Académie de Musique (1669), L'Académie Royale d'Architecture (1671).[27] In 1680, he established the Comédie-Française. Louis XIV furthered this notion of a dazzling, universal culture by transforming everyday activities into ritualized art forms. For example, France's haute cuisine originated as part of this impulse in the kitchens of Versailles. In addition, he promoted France's modes of dress, manners, and, of course, its language, as highly visible, supposedly imitable signs of France's superior civilization. To imitate them marked its participants as 'civilized.' Membership in this universalizable group would bind people together.

The texts I have examined thus far have only sketched out the bare outlines of how culture functioned as an instrument of colonization to shape the feeling structures of the colonized. In sum: French culture took the offensive without seeming to. France would colonize effortlessly with both arms tied behind its back, so to speak. The state self-consciously cultivated a culture that would lure outsiders into the French net, with the promise that France's fairy dust would rub off on them. Its Midas touch would transform outsiders into refined, civilized beings worthy of France. This process appeared as a 'civilizing mission' as opposed to a 'colonizing mission' because of its supposed voluntary nature.

In these texts, French culture remains at the centre, with colonization cast into the shadows at the periphery. I would now like to put on a wide-angle lens to bring the periphery into the picture and sharpen the focus to see the colonized up close and personal. To explore further the relation of culture to France's colonizing strategy, I now turn to the *relations de voyage* about the New World.

The *Relations de Voyage*

The *relations de voyage* offered a similar theory of colonization/culture, painting the New World Amerindians as imposing colonization on themselves as a natural outgrowth of their contact with Catholic France's culture. The spirit of the *Gallic Hercules* was behind the *relations*, dramatizing how a different kind of 'voluntary chain' seduced the American Indian into France's civilization. The 'voluntary subjection' emerged as a key notion that navigated the conflicting needs of France's offensive and defensive strategy. Assimilation had two contradictory goals. On the one hand, its offensive goal was expansion. The church and state sought to stretch the bounds of the community to include the *other*, even those who were as far out on the map of civilization as 'savages' from the New World. However, the Amerindians would only be included after they were Christianized, Frenchified, and civilized. France's assimilationist ideal was what we might call 'passing,' in which these 'savages' would pass as French Catholics and pass into the French, Catholic community.[28] On the other hand, the church and state's defensive goal was protection – to preserve the original identity and purity of that community from the *other* it was including. I would now like to examine how French culture allegedly functioned to induce in the colonized a 'voluntary subjection,' which worked to negotiate the contradictory goals of France's assimilation of the 'savage' *other*.

Colonization as the Art of Seduction

Seduction was the first step in the church and state's efforts to stimulate a 'voluntary subjection.' To colonize meant to seduce. The art of seduction constituted an offensive tactic to lure the Amerindians over towards the French. The nation's material culture were tools that set in motion an underlying dynamic of attraction and repulsion, causing the American Indians to be drawn into the French world and shun their own. For example, once the 'savages' had tasted French food and worn French clothes, there would be no turning back. They

> will become so accustomed to our food and our clothes, that they will have a horror of the Savages and their filth. We have seen this exemplified in all the children brought up among our French. They get so well acquainted with each other in their childish plays that they do not look at the Savages except to flee from them or mock them. (*JR*, IX: 106)

A magical aura seemed to surround French food, clothing, and lodging, as if they had cast a spell over the American Natives to bring them into the fold. At the most basic level, the Amerindians seemed to prefer the French world to their own:

> I know none amongst them who do not prefer in sickness the poorest house of the French to the richest Cabin of the Savages. When they find them-

> selves in comfortable beds, well fed, well lodged, well cared for, do you doubt that this miracle of charity will win their hearts? (*JR*, IX: 101)

The 'win[ning] of their hearts' meant that the Native Americans would correspondingly be repelled by their ancestral environment. The *relations'* stories presented the assimilationist ideal as emerging out of the American Natives' own desires for themselves since they were compelled by France's seemingly superior ways of life.

As evidence that French culture was having the desired effect on the Native Americans, the *relations* gave the colonized a voice through which they were the ones to articulate a theory of colonization in terms of their desires. With that voice, the Amerindians invited, indeed begged, the French to come to their land to serve as models for a civilized life. For example, according to explorer Samuel Champlain, a Huron chief in North America invited him and the French into their land to teach them to be like the French:

> If you would do us the favor to come live in our country and bring your wives and children, and when they are here we shall see how you serve this God who you adore and how you live with your wives and children, how you cultivate and plant the soil, how you obey your laws, how you take care of animals, and how you manufacture all that we see proceeding from your inventive skill.

If the Amerindians failed to understand French ways and could not imitate them successfully, Champlain continued, they would offer up their own children for adoption to French families: 'and if we cannot understand, you shall take our children who will be like your own.'[29] Similarly, the French newspaper, the *Mercure François,* offered an account of the French encounter with the Tupinamba in Brazil. Their chief supposedly welcomed the French into their land and expressed France's colonial ideal as their own: 'Our hope is that our children will learn the law of God and your arts and sciences. This hope makes us believe that in the future others will think us French.'[30]

That the colonized themselves articulated France's theory of 'voluntary subjection' suggests that they supposedly viewed the French as liberators, not colonizers. Champlain wrote that the Hurons' 'one wish and desire is to be fully instructed about what they ought to follow and avoid.'[31] According to Jesuit missionary Paul Le Jeune, the Native Americans in Canada were on bended knees, pleading with the French to free them from ignorance, 'asking help and uttering the word of that Macedonian to Saint Paul, *Transiens in Macedoniam adjuva nos;* "Come, help us, bring into our country the torch which has never yet illuminated it!"' (*JR*, VI: 25). And 'they are already tired of their miseries and are opening up their arms to us for assistance.' (*JR*, V: 32). Given the Native Americans' supposed pleas, how could the French church and state refuse their cries for help? The French church and state saw themselves as acting like saviours, responding with love and charity. 'It is a great pity to allow so many men to be lost and see them perish at our doors without succoring them, which can only be with the aid of kings, princes and ecclesiastics,' wrote Champlain.[32] Describing the French mission in Brazil, Capuchin Father Claude d'Abbeville observed that the French church and state acted 'not by force but by the cross and by love, which has so sweetly forced the Indians to give themselves and their country to the King of France.'[33] The oxymoronic phrase 'sweetly forced' echoed the voluntary chains of the *Gallic Hercules.* The Amerindians' supposed desires made their 'subjection' seem 'voluntary,' except that they would have not seen it as 'subjection' precisely because it was voluntary and emerged out of their desire to civilize themselves.

The Amerindians' 'voluntary subjection' constituted the primary ground upon which the church and state legitimated their claim to possess the New World. France was, of course, competing against other European nations to colonize the Americas. Her biggest rivals were Catholic Spain and Portugal, to whom Pope Alexander VI had originally given an official sanction to possess land in the New World and evangelize their inhabitants. To undercut the Spanish and Portuguese modes of evangelization and colonization, the French writers emphasized their violent tactics, highlighting the 'Black Legend.' By contrast, the French colonized with love and sweetness, stimulating a 'voluntary subjection,' which was proof that the French were more Catholic than her southern rivals. France, like England and Holland in particular, argued that mere 'discovery' did not entitle Spain or Portugal to the right of possession. France and its rivals grounded their respective claims for dominion on alternative grounds. As Patricia Seed has astutely argued, it was not clear what possession meant and on what ground it was legitimated.[34] France made its claim on the ground of consent. That consent was a 'voluntary subjection.' In France's 1613 mission in Brazil, Capuchin Father Claude d'Abbeville, French Admiral François Razilly, and Lieutenant General Raverdière planted the cross and the French coat of arms on Brazilian territory and explained to the gathered Indians what their symbolic action meant. D'Abbeville described the Tupis' reaction:

> The Indians were so attentive to this discourse that they made it seem that their *outside behavior was a sign of the emotion they felt in the inside*, assuring us that they were voluntarily and of their free will, receiving and embracing everything that we proposed. (my emphasis)[35]

D'Abbeville's narrative focused on the Amerindians' interiority, their supposed joy to be part of France. Their emotions implied their consent to 'put their land in the King's possession, and they avow they want to live and die with us, as the true and faithful servants of his Majesty.'[36] As Seed noted, 'no other Europeans so consistently sought the political permission of the natives in order to justify their own political authority.'[37] For D'Abbeville, the Amerindians willingly and voluntarily agreed to 'quit their bad way of life and principally to no longer eat human flesh' and that they would 'obey [France's] laws.'[38]

Because consent was vital to France's claim of dominion, French culture had to be endowed with strong seductive properties to make believable, *vraisemblable*, that the Amerindians were issuing their consent. It had to make believable that outsiders would want to become French and abandon their past ties and identities. If seduction was the first effect of France's dazzling cultural power, it then paved the way for the next stage in France's offensive task of colonization: transformation. The Amerindians had to be transformed from 'savages' into civilized French Catholics.

Culture/Colonization and the Transformation of the Soul

If the transformation of 'savages' responded to France's offensive needs of expansion, what was the nature of this transformation and towards what ideal was it turned? For the church, it meant conversion, a turn towards the Catholic faith and God.[39] However, the church often worked in tandem with the state since they had overlapping interests to expand their respective dominions over the New World, even though these two institutions often conflicted with each other. Even church officials believed that the Amerindians' religious conversion had to be accompanied by a similar cultural conversion: a 'frenchification.'[40] However, 'frenchification' was more problematic than its religious counterpart since it was not clear what Frenchness meant. Christianity was already much more clearly defined since it had been codified and embodied in a concrete set of practices, rituals, ceremonies, prayers, gestures, images, songs, beliefs, and so forth. The abstractness of Frenchness also needed to be defined in equivalent, concrete terms that responded to France's assimilationist needs.

Some defining properties of Frenchness emerged through the story about Attikamegou, a Huron baby living near Trois-Rivières in 1636. He was on his deathbed when his birth parents gave him to the Jesuits to see if they could cure him. No sooner did the Jesuit father pronounce some holy words than

> he opened his eyes, began to breathe, to stretch, and to move about in his little portable cradle. His mother . . . offered him the breast, which he could not take before; he took it now without difficulty, and before the Father departed from the Cabin he had entirely recovered . . . [T]hey were struck dumb with amazement. Now this little Christian is fine-looking and plump, the joy of his parents and the admiration of those who saw him in his sickness. (*JR*, IX: 13)

Impressed by the power of the Catholic faith, Attikamegou's parents gave him to the Jesuit priest: 'Do to him . . . all thou doest to the French children' (*JR*, IX: 14). The Jesuits renamed the baby François Olivier and gave him to a new set of adoptive parents, Sieur Olivier and Madame Hebout. His Huron birth father was grateful that these French people 'consented to do him this favor' (*JR*, IX: 14). The Jesuit father described a magical moment of transformation:

> They had swaddled this little Christian in the French fashion; its mother, holding it, said to her husband: 'I do not know what ails our little François Olivier; when he is dressed in the French way he laughs all the time, when he is dressed in our way he cries and grieves; when I hold him he is quite sad and mournful, and when a French woman holds him he acts as if he wants to jump all the time.' She wished by these words to show her satisfaction at seeing her son become French, as it were. (*JR*, IX: 16)

Le Jeune told this story from the Amerindian birth mother's supposed perspective. She observed that the baby's emotions had changed when he was 'dressed in the French way.' His new attire stimulated a magical transformation since he suddenly smiled and was happy, as opposed to his former sadness 'when he [was] dressed in the [savage] way.' His French godmother was like a fairy godmother who had sprinkled fairy dust over him. When his French godmother held him, the baby instinctively felt the difference and developed a new set of joyful emotions. What the French godmother did to produce this effect was not evident. But clearly she had a certain *je ne sais quoi* – an indefinable, ineffable something that produced a palpably visible change. And whatever that quality was, the birth mother did not have it.

'Frenchification' came to function like a religious conversion. French culture had to be endowed with the power to transform the soul and spirit, akin to the baptismal water into which one dipped a baby. In this way, the Amerindian could be born anew, with a new French heart and spirit. The state, seeking to compete with the church, saw its culture as working a magic analogous to religion. If conversion produced a new *Christian* heart, Frenchification would create a new *French* heart. Both were like heart transplants where the old was ripped out and replaced by a new improved version; both processes began by imitating outer signs of the heart, as when the non-believer imitated the outer signs and practices of the believer. Such was what Pascal recommended in his wager argument, putting forth a behaviouralist notion of conversion that featured imitation as a key to the transformational process. He advised the non-believer to imitate the outward gestures, the rituals and practices of the believer, even if at first they were simply empty signs. But by acting *as if* they believed, over time the non-believers' feelings would become aligned with their outer practices and induce faith.

The same would be true of a cultural transformation. It would begin by imitating the outer signs of Frenchness so that gradually one would be born anew, 'as if one became French.' Significantly, French culture took on magical qualities in the seventeenth century to enable the church and state to perform their transformative work. For example, festivals such as Louis XIV's Pleasures of the Enchanted Island created the illusion that French culture had special powers of enchantment. Magic was a major theme of seventeenth-century culture in part because it was at the hidden centre of France's colonial project, charged with transforming outsiders into insiders by creating new structures of feeling.[41]

In sum, France's needs for expansion pushed the church and state to define the elements of French culture to respond to the offensive needs of France's colonial strategy: to attract and transform outsiders. Because the Amerindians imitated French Catholics voluntarily, seeking to rid themselves of their old ways, their transformation was supposedly genuine. Their transformation meant that France could expand its boundaries without compromising its identity since the Amerindians, with their newly acquired 'insider' status, would feel the power of an 'us-them' boundary in their souls and thus reinforce that divide themselves against those on the outside. Because these boundaries were drawn in their hearts, they could be stretched to the ends of the earth.

Culture/Colonization and Protective Boundaries

If the seductive and transformative properties of French culture responded to the church and state's offensive needs to open and expand the community by including outsiders, the effects of French culture also met their defensive needs to protect the community's purity and identity. The *relations*' stories about the transformation of outsiders were also stories about boundaries. After France's culture lured the Amerindians over to the French side of the divide, it then restructured their hearts so they would not change the community itself. The properties of French culture worked to create boundaries out of the felt differences between the two worlds. The Native Americans were compelled towards the feelings that their contact with French culture stimulated in them and were allegedly repelled by the feelings they had when surrounded by their own kind. These feelings functioned as boundaries drawn in their hearts.

As French culture seduced these Amerindians and restructured their hearts, it also established borders to protect the newly expanded French community from being influenced by the outsiders it incorporated. However, these boundaries emerged in their souls, in an underlying attraction-repulsion dynamic that were the supposed effects of French culture, which created a natural 'us-them' divide. Even though the baby Attikamegou/François Olivier had not yet developed his rational faculties, he felt the difference instinctively, becoming happy when his adoptive French mother held him. Like Moses parting the Red Sea, French culture caused a parting of peoples, separating the civilized, Catholic, French side from the 'savage.' The divide was so strong that even a baby palpably felt the differences in his whole being. His changed feelings and behaviour indicated that the transformation in his soul was deeply rooted and the effects so positive that his birth mother was delighted to see her son 'become French.' Father Le Jeune observed that many young Amerindian children felt the effects of French culture: 'When [t]hese little girls are dressed in the French fashion, they care no more for the Savages than if they did not belong to their Nation' (*JR*, IX: 102–3). By turning towards the 'French fashion' and the French way of life, these girls correspondingly shunned their own former culture and their birth community.

Many stories about the Amerindians' transformation reinforced the image of a bounded Catholic, French community. The boundaries remained firm even in the wilderness, as the following story of Nanaskoumat dramatized. Nanaskoumat was a Huron, renamed François Xavier after his baptism. He went on a hunting trip for elk flesh with some French colonists and Jesuits just before Lent. He had prepared for the trip by bringing along some meat and smoked eel. The Jesuit Fathers had said nothing to him about Christian practices of abstaining from meat since they were lenient on the newly converted about this practice. Once they were in the woods, Nanaskoumat noticed that his French companions were not eating meat, even though they were weak with hunger. Imitating them, he thus refrained from eating meat. Father Le Jeune marveled at Nanaskoumat's restraint since his non-baptized family members who accompanied him were living it up, feasting on the meat from the tongue and upper lips of moose, an Amerindian delicacy hard to turn down. Nanaskoumat saw them 'eating the choicest morsels before his eyes' (*JR*, XVI: 81) and smelled the delicious odors waft past his nose. Father Le Jeune asked whether he wasn't tempted just to taste a little bit of the fine elk meat before him. Nanaskoumat replied that at the beginning of Lent he put his heart under the table, which is why his eyes did not even see the meat. He then added, 'Should we not suffer a little as well as the other Christians? We wish to please God, as well as you people' (*JR*, XVI: 80). Even in the wilderness, a divide between 'savage' and civilized Catholic, French behavior emerged. Le Jeune framed the story as a kind of tug of war between both worlds, with Nanaskoumat in the middle. He came out on the French, Catholic side. Father Le Jeune commented: 'Who would ever have thought that . . . such abstinence would be practiced by a Savage who formerly gorged himself with human flesh!' (*JR*, XVI: 80).

The 'savage-civilized' boundaries existed as structures of feeling inside the Amerindians' hearts. It meant the Amerindians would shun their past customs, beliefs, and practices, thus affirming the French assimilationist goal to 'wean [the Indians] from their native customs' (*JR*, IX: 102). Le Jeune reported that he overheard a conversation in which Nanaskoumat/François Xavier said to another Amerindian chief: 'Let us abandon our old ways to those which are taught us, and which are better than ours' (*JR*, XVI: 76). After another Amerindian, Negabamat, was baptized and renamed Estienne, he emerged from the baptismal sacred bath and said: 'It seems to me that I am different from what I was – that I have another life in me' (*JR*, XVI: 164). Completely transformed, he could no longer bear any connection with his old life. In a violent act of repudiation, he proclaimed, '[Let us] renounce all our follies, and trample under foot all our old customs' (*JR*, XVI: 166). The French goal to 'change . . . their Pagan and Barbarous life to one that is civilized and Christian' was apparently working (*JR*, X: 25).

Not only did French culture induce the right feelings in the colonized, but it also supposedly stimulated them to police the boundaries themselves. For example, Father Le Jeune described a young Huron girl who returned to visit her birth father after living with the French, having been brought up 'in the French way.' When she 'goes back to the Cabins of the Savages, her father, very happy to see his daughter well clothed and in very good condition, does not allow her to remain there long, sending her back to the house *where she belongs*' (*JR*, XI: 92–3, my emphasis). Her father, feeling the transformative effect of French culture on her soul as positive, understood that she no longer belonged on the 'savage' side of this divide. She was no longer his. He yielded to the thrust of civilization sweeping upward and sent his daughter back to the French side, as if that were her true place.

Once the American Indians had experienced the benefits of French Catholic life, they instinctively held their former life in horror, or so these narrators erroneously believed. The Amerindians did so because they had supposedly internalized the colonizer's values and perspective as their own and saw themselves through that borrowed lens. Frenchification meant not only to identify *with* the French, but also *against* their own ancestral heritage. Their 'voluntary subjection' made the French 'the judge of their debates,' and it stimulated them to lead their lives in light of internalized French, Catholic judgments, as Marc Lescarbot had wanted to think. As a result, the French did not need to impose physical restraints or boundaries since their culture was performing that same work. Identifying against themselves, the colonized would instinctively flee their past life and forget that they ever inhabited the wrong side of the divide. Such an interiorized patrol protected the community more forcefully than could any external law or military force.

In this essay, my argument about France's theory of culture/colonization has centred mostly on the projected structures of feeling within the colonized. By way of conclusion, I would like to emphasize that the *relateurs'* description of French culture/colonization was also addressed to France's reading public, centred on the colonizers' structures of feeling. As a result, the French *relations de voyages* cultivated the story form to captivate and entertain their readers. These stories were themselves an element of French culture, and they participated in, and constituted, part of the nation's colonizing strategy. In writing and circulating these stories in France, the *relateurs* enabled France's colonial strategy by seeking to restructure the feelings of the French readers to convince them that the Amerindians were good, docile colonial subjects, capable of inclusion in France's expanding community. Such stories worked to negotiate the contradictory offensive and defensive needs by convincing the French reading public that its culture possessed magical properties that would induce the Amerindians to engage in a 'voluntary subjection'; they created the illusion that its readers were safe because their community was strongly bounded. Catholic, French culture would seduce and transform the Amerindians so fully that they would not wish to alter the community's basic identity or fracture its supposed basic unity. While the community's boundaries would be stretched to include the *other*, they would snap back into place like rubber bands after the outsiders became insiders, thus reaffirming the original purity, identity, and unity of the community.

It is generally assumed that the colonizer influences the colonized. What is less evident, however, is the reverse – that the act of colonization affects the colonizer. I have sought to show how the process of colonization shaped the development of French culture, which emerged in tandem with and in response to the church and state's particular needs of colonizing the New World Amerindians. It should not be surprising that a colonizer would use its culture as an instrument of colonization. What is surprising here, however, is how the French church and state were able to weave their use of culture so subtly into their 'colonizing mission' that the connection between culture and colonization has remained obscured, even until today.

NOTES

1 *The Jesuit Relations and Allied Documents*, ed. Reuben Gold Thwaites (Cleveland: The Burrows Brothers, 1896), 22: 184. Henceforth all references to the *Jesuit Relations* will be from this edition, designated as *JR*, followed by the volume and page numbers and included in the body of the text.

2 While the church and state often conflicted, the dictum that politics makes strange bedfellows was in full swing in the Americas. These two institutions had overlapping, interdependent goals, which often pushed them into a joint evangelizing/colonizing/frenchifying/civilizing endeavour. See Peter A. Goddard, 'Two Kinds of Conversion ("Medieval" and "Modern") among the Hurons of New France,' in *Spiritual Conversion: The Christian Mission in the Colonial Americas*, ed. James Muldoon (Gainesville: University of Florida Press, 2004): 57–77, and 'Converting the "Sauvage": Jesuit and Montagnais

in Seventeenth-Century New France,' *Catholic Historical Review* 84 (1998): 219–239. For a general discussion of the inseparability of Catholicism and Frenchness in France, see Liah Greenfeld, *Nationalism: Five Roads to Modernity* (Cambridge, MA: Harvard University Press, 1992), 91–188.

3 'They live together without a king and without authorities, each man his own master. They take as many wives as they wish; a son may couple with mother, brother with sister, cousin with cousin, and in general men with women as they chance to meet.' Amerigo Vespucci, *Letters from a New World,* ed. Luciano Formisano, trans. David Jacobson (New York: Marsilio, 1992), 49–50.

4 For another example of this 'progress,' see also *JR,* XVI: 61–3.

5 For a discussion of this policy, see Sara E. Melzer, *Colonizer or Colonized: The Hidden Stories of Early Modern France* (Philadelphia: University of Pennsylvania Press, 2012); Melzer, 'L'histoire oubliée de la colonization française: universaliser la "Francité,"' *Dalhousie French Studies* (Autumn 2003): 133–48; Melzer, 'The Underside of France's Civilizing Mission: Assimilationist Politics in "New France,"' *Biblio* 17 (2001): 151–64; Gilles Havard and Cécile Vidal, *L'histoire de l'Amérique Française* (Paris: Flammarion, 2003). Cornelius J. Jaenen, *Friend and Foe: Aspects of French-Amerindian Cultural Contact in the Sixteenth and Seventeenth Centuries* (Toronto: McClelland and Stewart, 1976); Saliha Belmessous, 'Assimilation and Racialism in Seventeenth- and Eighteenth-Century French Colonial Policy,' *The American Historical Review* 110, no. 2 (April 2005): 322–49; and Guillaume Aubert, '"The Blood of France": Race and Purity of Blood in the French Atlantic World,' *The William and Mary Quarterly* 61, no. 3 (2004): 439–78.

6 See Melzer, *Colonizer or Colonized,* chap. 3.

7 Joan DeJean, *Ancients against Moderns: Culture Wars and the Making of a Fin de Siècle* (Chicago: University of Chicago Press, 1997); see especially chapter 4.

8 Melzer, *Colonizer or Colonized,* chap. 8.

9 Marc Lescarbot, *Histoire de la Nouvelle-France,* ed. W.L. Grant (Toronto: Champlain Society, 1907–14), 2: 509.

10 Homi K. Bhabha, 'Of Mimicry and Man,' in *The Location of Culture* (London: Routledge, 1994), 85.

11 Richard White, *The Middle Ground: Indians, Empires, and Republics in the Great Lakes Region, 1650–1815* (Cambridge: Cambridge University Press, 1991). Philippe Jacquin *Indiens blancs: Français et Indiens en Amérique du nord-est, XVIe-XVIIe siècles* (Montreal: Libre Expression, 1996).

12 For a more extensive discussion of this connection, see Melzer, *Colonizer or Colonized,* chapters 5–8.

13 Colbert to l'Abbé de Quéylus, 10 March 1671, in Colbert, *Lettres, mémoires et instructions de Colbert, publiés d'après les ordres de l'empereur,* ed. Pierre Clément (Paris: Imprimerie impériale, 1865), 3: 452.

14 Colbert to Talon, 5 April 1666 and 5 April 1667, *Rapport de l'Archiviste de la Province de Québec* (Quebec: Imprimerie de Sa Majesté le Roi, 1930–1), 45, 72; Colbert to Laval, 7 March 1668, *Rapport de l'Archiviste de la Province de Québec.* For discussions of this assimilation policy, see Jaenen, *Friend and Foe;* Havard and Vidal, *L'histoire de l'Amérique Française;* Belmessous, 'Etre français en Nouvelle-France: Identité française et identité coloniale aux dix-septième et dix-huitième siècles.' *French Historical Studies* 27, no 3. (Summer 2004): 507–40; Aubert, 'The Blood of France.' Leslie Tuttle, in *Conceiving the Old Regime. Pronatalism and the Politics of Reproduction in Early Modern France* (Oxford: Oxford University Press, 2010), has challenged the significance of this policy since few marriages were actually concluded. However, given that assimilation was the official ideal, regardless of its success, this ideal had an important symbolic force that shaped the dominant discourse about the nation's contact with the New World. See Melzer, *Colonizer or Colonized.*

15 H.R. and C.H. Laverdière Casgrain, eds., *Le journal des Jésuites* (Montreal, 1892), 312.

16 While the Portuguese encouraged mixed marriages in Asia, they did not do so in the New World. See Charles Boxer, *Race Relations in the Portuguese Colonial Empire: 1415–1825* (Oxford: Oxford University Press, 1963); Miguel Vale de Almeida, *An Earth-Colored Sea: 'Race,' Culture and the Politics of Identity in the Portuguese-Speaking World* (New York: Berghahn Books, 2004).

17 See Hubert Gillot, *La querelle des anciens et des modernes en France* (Geneva: Slatkine Reprints, 1968) and Terence Cave, "Ancients and Moderns: France," in *The Cambridge History of Literary Criticism,* ed. Glen P. Norton (Cambridge: Cambridge University Press, 1999), 417–25 for a long view of the Quarrel. See also Hélène Merlin-Kajman, *La langue est-elle fasciste? Langue, pouvoir, enseignement* (Paris: Seuil, 2003) ; Joan DeJean, *Ancients against Moderns.*

18 Dominique Bouhours, *Entretiens d'Ariste et d'Eugène* (Paris: Éditions Bossard, 1920), 36–7.

19 Ibid., 35–8.

20 Marc-René Jung, *Hercule dans la littérature française du XVIe siècle. De l'hercule courtois à l'hercule baroque* (Geneva: Droz, 1966); and Françoise Bardon, *Le portrait mythologique à la cour de France sous Henri IV et Louis XIII* (Paris: Picard, 1974), 49. See also Robert Hallowell, 'Ronsard and the Gallic Hercules Myth,' *Studies in the Renaissance* 9 (1962): 242–55. Joannes Annius of

Viterbo and Jean Lemaire de Belges saw the *Gallic Hercules* as the direct ancestor to the Pepin kings and Charlemagne.

21 Geoffroy Tory, *Champ Fleury* (Paris: Mouton, 1970).

22 François Charpentier, *Défense de la langue française pour l'inscription de l'Arc de Triomphe* (Paris: Claude Barbin, 1767), 228–9.

23 Ibid.

24 Nicolas Faret, *Projet de l'Académie, pour servir de préface à ses statuts* (Saint-Etienne: Université de Saint-Etienne, 1983), 44.

25 Paul Pellison, *Discours sur l'Académie Française, relation contenant l'histoire de l'Académie Française* (Paris: Thomas Joly, 1672), 468.

26 Jerah Johnson, 'Colonial New Orleans: A Fragment of the Eighteenth-Century French Ethos,' in *Creole New Orleans: Race and Americanization,* ed. Arnold R. Hirsch and Joseph Logsdon (Baton Rouge: Louisiana State University Press), 12–57.

27 See Peter Burke, *The Fabrication of Louis XIV* (New Haven, CT: Yale University Press, 1992); and Jean-Marie Apostolides, *Le roi machine: spectacle et politique au temps de Louis XIV* (Paris: Minuit, 1981).

28 Melzer, *Colonizer or Colonized,* chapter 4.

29 Champlain, *The Works of Samuel de Champlain,* ed. H.P. Biggar (Toronto: The Champlain Society, 1929), 3: 146.

30 *Mercure François,* vol. 3 (Paris: Estienne Richer, 1617), 171.

31 Champlain, *Works,* 147.

32 Ibid.

33 Claude D'Abbeville, *Histoire de la mission des Pères Capucins en L'Isle de Maragnan et terres circonvoisines* (Paris: Huby, 1614), 164.

34 Patricia Seed, *Ceremonies of Possession in Europe's Conquest of the New World 1492–1640* (Cambridge: Cambridge University Press, 1995).

35 D'Abbeville, *Histoire de la mission,* 88.

36 Ibid., 161.

37 Seed, *Ceremonies,* 62.

38 D'Abbeville, *Histoire de la mission,* 85.

39 Goddard, "Converting the 'sauvage.'"

40 For a study of the Frenchification process, see Melzer, 'L'histoire oubliée.' See also Saliha Belmessous, 'Être français en Nouvelle-France: identité française et identité coloniale aux dix-septième et dix-huitième siècles,' *French Historical Studies,* 27, no. 3 (Summer 2004): 507–40; and Jean Delanglez, *Frontenac and the Jesuits* (Chicago: Institute of Jesuit History, 1939), 35–65.

41 See Sara E. Melzer, 'Magic and the Conversion of "Outsiders" into "Insiders" in the French Empire,' in *The Meanings of Magic from the Bible to Buffalo Bill,* ed. Amy Wygant (Oxford: Berghahn Books, 2006), 178–210.

chapter five

Fear of Singing (Episodes from Early Latin America)

GARY TOMLINSON

> The zoo used to contain not just the animals, but also a music pavilion and, occasionally, exhibitions of exotic tribes, Samoans and Senegalese. But the only sound that penetrated to them from the distant pavilion was the sound of the kettledrum. Whether it be the memory of this, or simply the condensation of what has long been forgotten – even today, when I hear the kettledrum it brings back the memory of Tamasese, the tribal chief. And at the same time I recall that the heads of Tamasese's prisoners were used as drums, or perhaps they were the cauldrons in which the savages cooked human flesh. Is the drum the successor of human sacrifice or does it still sound the command to kill? In our music it resounds as an archaic survival. It is the legacy of violence in art, the violence which lies at the base of all art's order. While as a spiritualized activity art strips violence of its power, it continues to practice it. Freedom and domination commingle inseparably in art. Its integral form, the triumph of its autonomy, is what also casts a spell on the listener, leaves no one out and subjects everyone to its speechless performance. It is only necessary to listen to the humane Beethoven from outside, from a sufficiently great distance, and nothing remains but the terror aroused by Tamasese. But perhaps all humaneness does is to keep the consciousness of terror alive, the consciousness of all that can never be made good.[1]

It is difficult to tease apart, in this passage by Theodor Adorno, the layers of Euro-chauvinism and blinkered fantasy about others, of sad, ironic wisdom about Europe itself, even of vestigial hopefulness – almost as difficult, indeed, as it is to analyse our ambivalences in reading it today. Adorno's is a convoluted parable, at once celebrating the grand European fin de siècle at the expense of savages and pointing an accusing finger at Europe's own savagery.

If, on the one hand, the passage beckons us to contemplate it, it is not only because the brutality Adorno commemorated – his words come from 1951 – is with us still. It beckons also with its recognition that a familiar, comforting humaneness, the humaneness of Beethoven, is shadowed by atavistic terror. And it beckons, on a specifically musical level, in naming an art of hearing-at-a-distance that has been too rarely assayed by musicians and critics. (Musicologists have tended to hear only up close. When one of them, Susan McClary, heard Beethoven from an Adornian distance in the 1980s and said so in print, she was castigated for heterodoxy by other scholars and journalists.)

If also the passage repels with its apparatus of skull cauldrons and cannibalism – one more European fancy of others' savagery – it is because Adorno hesitated in the face of the proposition that humaneness might be found in equal measure in Beethoven and Tamasese. This diffidence is not unimportant. It allows formulations ostensibly like Adorno's to slide toward another vantage point from which music comes to seem equally the cipher of European refinement and others' barbarity. Music not our own becomes the fearsome, wild cry in the darkness: *the natives are restless tonight.*

It is not only Europeans, however, who are seized by fear at the sound of savage music. The essential richness of Adorno's *minimum moralium* lies in the role it accords Tamasese. Though he inspired terror in the child Adorno, the music in the parable casts him in the part of terrified listener, not musician. *He* heard the primal drum from the distance; it was not his own drum but its modern descendant that resounded from the pavilion where the acme of cultivated Europe, the symphony orchestra, played. Tamasese listened from a space Europe had fashioned, equivalent to the cages of the animals around him. Savagery is in the ear of the beholder.

Scenes and Songs of Apostasy

During the period of first contact between Europeans and Native Americans, the fear of others' singing, dancing, and playing of musical instruments was everywhere writ large. A sizeable anthology of citations reflecting this fact is easily culled from narratives of Latin American exploration and conquest – then doubled from accounts of European travels in Africa and Asia.[2] The incidents related in such accounts, I will argue, commemorate especially the powers of raised voices. In the travel narratives we do not often hear of instances where Indians or Europeans were frightened by exchanges of everyday speech, no matter how mutually incomprehensible these often were. Across huge cultural distances, that is, the burden of speech as communication was clear and unthreatening, even when what it said was neither the one nor the other. Heightened utterance, instead, showed a special capacity to threaten. In setting itself apart from normal talk it entered a realm expansive enough to embrace recitations, invocations, incantations, chants, song – and sometimes whispers, howls, and shrieks as well. The customary accompaniment of such utterance by musical instruments and extraordinary bodily movement and gesture only increased its distance from everyday speech.

This distance was ample enough to accommodate a whole metaphysics. The special qualities of song and its corollary forms of utterance were experienced, in a cognitive step that growing evidence suggests is hard-wired like the capacity for language itself, as a gaining of access to special realms not open to speech alone. In encounters of difference as dramatic as those between Europeans and Americans these realms loomed especially in the marshalling of song in organized, determinate rites. The real threat was not singing per se but what everyone involved knew to be conjured in its difference from speech. At the heart of ritual, the altered behaviour of voice and body constituted the unmistakable sign of a frightening, unassuageable otherness.

Throughout the Spanish colonies in America the missionaries charged with Christianizing the Indians paid implicit homage to the metaphysical powers of song, and this in two ways. First, they recognized it as a foremost element of the teaching they needed to bring to the Indians to convert them – as, in other words, a potent force in conveying their own metaphysics. Church schools throughout early Latin America placed teaching of singing (of Gregorian chant and church polyphony) alongside reading and writing as high priorities. The importance of music in celebrating Catholic services was everywhere recognized.

Second, the friars drew attention time and again to the insidious force of indigenous ceremony. Indeed, by the early seventeenth century a whole literature had sprung up concerned with the problematic persistence of such ceremony.[3] In it singing, drumming, and dancing were often enough named explicitly; more often still they were implicitly present, understood to be the medium of the drunken rites and orgies of the Natives. Everywhere in New Spain, it seemed, the Spaniards could rest assured that the old gods were truly dead only when they silenced the voices that invoked them. Conversely, where these voices were raised again (or raised still), the friars' deepest fears and most dogged efforts of cultural extermination were set in motion.

This literature concerning Native idolatry arose as a response of missionaries to an earlier, broad evolution in the dynamic of conversion. Across the first decades of colonization and evangelization the same course of this evolution was played out in different local situations throughout the Spanish colonies. It was linked to the consolidation of relations between colonizers and colonized and in particular to the contrasting, intermingled religious conceptions of these groups: the shifting efforts at conversion by the one, the complex of resistance and adaptation practised by the other.

On the Spanish side this evolution traced in general outline a course from initial optimism, to confidence that the process of evangelization was taking hold, to, finally, the crushing discovery of Native backsliding and persistent idolatry. Fernando Cervantes has recently analysed the ideological forces behind these shifts. For him the gathering pessimism in the mission of New Spain reflects religious currents imported from a Europe riven by Church schism and doctrinal re-evaluation. From the midst of this Reformation turmoil a new conception of the devil emerged. The maleficent devil of the late Middle Ages (signally, for Cervantes, the devil of the *Malleus maleficarum*, the infamous 'hammer' of witches first published in 1486) had posed a tractable evil, one that expressed itself in local, unsystematic offences and was finally impotent in the face of God and Church. The early modern devil that replaced this figure posed a direr threat. He ruled over a kind of counterfeit church, aping in his own rites the ceremonies of God and luring those he duped into a systematic idolatry and apostasy. This was the devil of the late-sixteenth-century witches' sabbath.

Increasingly across the sixteenth century, European observers of New World religious rites came to see in these the counterfeit church of Satan. A paganism that had in the first years of contact seemed a relatively innocent perversion, one that would be quickly eradicated through the sacred power of Christian sacraments, especially mass baptisms and communion, came more and more to seem the entrenched liturgy of the devil. Fray Bartolomé de las Casas, writing in the 1550s and '60s, found demons and devils aplenty in indigenous American deeds but explained them as the naturalistic products of a fallen human imagination. José de Acosta, writing a few decades later, saw behind all pagan religion the supernatural threat of an institutionalized, Satanic idolatry.[4]

The role of singing and related envoicings in these developments may appear at first glance to have been a peripheral one, but it was not. Heightened utterance had always resounded at the heart of Christian worship, a fact marked in Spanish evangelization by the importance accorded to the teaching of Christian song. In an analogous way, it resounded also in the rites of indigenous Americans. The Spanish observers could hardly have ignored or minimized the force of such song, familiar as it was from their own parallel religious experience. As they came increasingly to imagine indigenous ceremony as the diabolical mirror image of their own rites, the powers of its singing grew proportionately. The analogy itself between European and American systems of worship demanded an ever-clearer distinction of good singing (and ceremony) from bad. Ultimately, when ceremonies of song and dance thought to have been eradicated by the force of evangelization were found to be celebrated still in all their native force, the most basic doubts about evangelization arose among the missionaries. The ceremonies of the Natives, rediscovered by the Spaniards, led to the crash; Spanish disenchantment in the New World was a product of lingering indigenous enchantment. It grew from a song that could not be silenced.

The great evangelizer Bernardino de Sahagún left testimony as eloquent as any to this history as it unfolded in the valley of Mexico. It comes in an excursus in the *Florentine Codex* entitled *Relación del autor digna de ser notada*.[5] This miniature treatise of 1576 is a cry from the heart of the aged Franciscan, faced with the failure of the college for Indians he had helped to found four decades earlier at Tlatelolco and, worse still, the decline of the Christian mission in general. In a rambling exposition Sahagún attributed this decline to several causes: to the insidious moral effects of the mild Mexican climate (75, 77), to the repeated plagues that struck down so many (84–5), and of course to the licentious drunkenness of the Natives (75).

Sahagún's diagnosis, however, did not stop at these commonplaces. He went on to assign blame for the failure to the Spaniards themselves. He looked back with admiration to pre-Hispanic Mexica teaching practices in which children were educated in state schools away from their parents, seeing in them the proper antidote to the effects of climate and to natural tendencies toward licentiousness; he faulted the old system only for the pagan idolatry it embraced (77). He told how the early Franciscan initiative to educate the Indians had patterned itself after the old ways, raising the boys in the Franciscans' own houses. But this regimen, steeped in Christian tenderness, had not enforced the same rigours as the ancient one, so the students began to slide toward lascivious practices and had to be sent back to live with their parents (77–8). The Christian adaptation of the ancient ways collapsed, and no system of education remained that could steer the Natives away from immodesty and idolatry.

Beneath this sincere critique of Spanish methods lay one more level in Sahagún's diagnosis: a deep-rooted sense of betrayal by his Indian charges. The early optimism as to their capabilities in learning all they were taught – 'There is no art they do not have the capacity to learn and practice,' he proclaimed near the beginning of the *Relación* (74) – had disappeared, displaced over the years not so much by a changed sense of the Indians' abilities as by the imputation to them of an incorrigible deceitfulness.

The Indians, according to Sahagún, had managed to convince the Spaniards that the old idolatry was dead, when in reality it was still practised. He recounted how, with an aim similar to the first educational arrangements, married couples early on had been settled near the monasteries, so they could attend mass every day – 'a very good way to free them from the infection of idolatry and other evil practices which they could contract through association with their parents.' This practice lasted only a short time, however, since the young couples convinced the Franciscans 'that all idolatry, with all its ceremonies and rituals, was already so forgotten and abhorred that there was no reason to have this caution, since all were baptized and servants of the true God.' But in this the monks had been deceived, Sahagún now knew: 'And this was very false, as since then we have witnessed very clearly. Not even now do there cease to be many dregs of idolatry and drunkenness and many evil practices . . . Now it is almost hopeless to correct.' (79)

Meanwhile, the boys trained early on in Christian ways had once helped to root out the idolatry of their elders. Eventually they were stymied in their efforts by punishments they received from the other Indians. These at first were sometimes severe – some child informants were even killed by their parents, Sahagún reports. But now they were niggling, insidious, and doubly effective: 'They punish evilly, deceitfully, and slyly, keeping after [informants] in their private tasks, and inflicting other vexations on them which the sufferers neither can complain of nor are able to remedy' (81).

It is clear from these examples of Indian duplicity that it was most of all the pagan ceremonies, once thought to have been eradicated, that marked for Sahagún the Natives' betrayal. 'The idolatrous rituals which were held at night, and the orgies and celebrations which they secretly performed . . . in honor of the idols' had been brought to an end with the help of Native informants – or so it had seemed. Then the Spaniards eased their surveillance, 'because nothing which was worthy of punishment appeared publicly,' and the ceremonies sprang up again (80).

The ceremonies were marked above all by singing and dancing in honour of the old gods, and so they brought these acts to the heart of Sahagún's *Relación*. Song, indeed, is mentioned again and again in this miniature treatise. It plays the dual role we have already described, for there are two modes of singing: one the blazon of the Indians' capacity to adopt European ways, the other the sorry measure of Indian deceit and missionary failure.

Of the first Sahagún wrote frequently. Singing 'of plainsong and polyphony' (*de canto llano, de canto de organo*) and with it the playing of instruments figure in the list of disciplines the Indians are capable of mastering that begins the treatise; they come just before high academic pursuits of grammar, logic, rhetoric, astrology, and theology (74). After beginning thus, Sahagún called attention to instruction in Christian singing every time he referred to the educational efforts of the Franciscans: 'they . . . come of a morning to the schools to learn to read and write and sing'; 'there is no one in the schools . . . who correctly teaches reading and writing and singing nor the other musical things'; 'there we taught them to read and write and sing'; 'after we came to this land to implant the Faith, we assembled the boys in our houses . . . [and] began to teach them to read, write, and sing' (78–9, 82). The singing of the divine Catholic word, along with the reading and writing of the European alphabet, made up the core of Sahagún's educational program for the Indians – itself a striking testimony to the powers he heard in such song.

A different kind of singing, however, with powers originating elsewhere, intruded at the impassioned culmination of Sahagún's complaint. Nowadays, he writes, the Indians

> sing when they wish and celebrate their feasts as they wish and sing the ancient songs they were wont to sing in the days of their idolatry – not all of them but many of them. And no one understands what they say as their songs are very obscure. And if, after their conversion here, they sing some songs they have composed, which deal with the things of God and His saints, they are surrounded by many errors and heresies. And even in the dances and *areitos* many of their ancient superstitions and idolatrous rituals are practiced, especially where no one resides who understands them . . . This continues; every day it grows worse. (81)

These obscure, suspect *cantares* were diametrically opposed to the Catholic songs taught at the college of Tlatelolco. Their power to undermine Christian values stemmed not merely from the duplicity the Indians manifested in maintaining them but especially from the terrifying entity looming behind them. Sahagún made this diabolical presence amply clear in the brief introduction he provided to some Nahuatl 'demons' songs' whose words he transcribed (but did not translate) elsewhere in the *Florentine Codex*:

> It is a very ancient practice of our adversary, the devil, to seek hiding places in order to perform his works, consistent with the Holy Gospel which says, 'He who does evil detests the light' . . . Our enemy planted, in this land, a forest or a thorny thicket filled with very dense brambles, to perform his works therefrom . . . This forest or brambled thorny thicket is the songs which, in this land, he contrived to be prepared and utilized in his service and for his divine worship – his songs of praise, in the temples as well as beyond them. These songs contain so much guile that they say anything and proclaim that which he commands . . . And they are sung to him without anyone being able to understand what they are about except those who are natives and versed in this language, so that all he desires is sung with impunity – be it of war or peace, of praises to himself, or of scorn of Jesus Christ – without being understood by the rest.[6]

Here the *cantares* occupy a place analogous to Christian plainchant in a liturgy guided by and celebrating the devil; the imputing of institutional diabolism to the Indians described by Cervantes is stimulated in full force by Native song.

Singing was thus divided between the two sides of Sahagún's Manichaean cosmos. It could not pose itself as a neutral force, but conveyed either the word of God or the blandishments of Satan. No wonder it figured so centrally in Sahagún's gloomy and fearful complaint on the state of Mexico in 1576.[7]

The history Sahagún traced in the *Relación* was one of intense optimism – in the Indians' capacities and docile nature, in the Franciscans' effective conversion measures – giving way across several decades in the mid-1500s to equally intense disillusionment. The roles of singing in this history were central ones, both as educational cornerstone and, later, as revelation of diabolism and Native backsliding. We have little evidence with which to reconstruct the Indians' side of this history, but it is important to note that Sahagún's version of it was, in all likelihood, as much a product of his fond hopes as a reflection of reality – fond hopes for the early and thorough conversion of the Indians that cast later realizations in that much harsher a light. The history of indigenous worship, viewed from the Indians' side, probably entailed an unbroken practice of their ceremonies, more and more out of view of the Spaniards and involving selective adoption of Christian gestures, rather than any wholesale stoppage and later resurgence of them.[8] The combined history of colonizers and colonized, in this case, would have involved two trajectories: the continuous, gradually shifting performance of ancient rites in the midst of newly imported Christian practices on the part of the Mexica, and the overreaching optimism of the Franciscans at the start of their mission, doomed to selective blindness and final, angry collapse.

This kind of continuous, evolving indigenous perception of the sacred, with its adoption of and adaptation to Christian elements, has been described for the Yucatec Maya by Nancy Farriss. In its midst, she notes, indigenous sung ceremony survived and even thrived: 'Pre-Columbian songs and dances were incorporated into the Christian round of fiestas, and the great wooden drum, the *tunkul*, was still being used to accompany the dances, as well as summon people to mass, throughout the colonial period.'[9] In the sixteenth century the missionaries adopted a wavering, ambivalent stance toward the Native songs and dances. Often enough they praised them for the skill and synchrony they displayed, as when Diego de Landa, writing in the 1560s, described Maya dances that were 'very manly and worth seeing.'[10] In 1588, meanwhile, an 'ancient dance' was performed to applause in front of the visiting Franciscan Comissary:

> The Indians brought out to welcome him a strange device and it was: litter-like frames and upon them a tower round and narrow, in the manner of a pulpit, of more then two *varas* in height, covered from top to bottom with pieces of painted cotton, with two flags on top, one on each side. In this pulpit, visible from the waist up, was an Indian very well and nicely dressed, who with rattles of the country in one hand, and with a feather fan in the other, facing the Father Comissary, without ceasing made gestures and whistled to the beat of a *teponaztli* that another Indian near the litter was playing among many who sang to the same sound, making much noise and giving shrill whistles; six Indians carried this litter and tower on their shoulders, and even these also went dancing and singing, doing steps and the same dancing tricks as the others, to the sound of the same *teponaztli*.[11]

The darker side of Native ceremony was, however, never far from the friars' vigilant minds. The litter-dance performed for the Comissary calls to mind – and may have descended from – a pre-contact dance described by Landa:

> For the celebration of this festival, they made a great arch of wood in the court, filling it on the top and on the sides with firewood, leaving in it doors for going in and out. After this most of the men took bundles of sticks, long and very dry, tied together, and a singer, mounted on the top of the wood, sang and made a noise with one of their drums. All danced below him with great order and devotion, going in and out through the doors of that arch of wood.[12]

But while the Comissary enjoyed the performance of 1588, Landa, stepping back from his earlier praise of other Native dances, saw in this one a diabolical rite: It was part of an observance to ward off drought and famine that involved statues of demons made at the behest of Satan ('*Obligábales el demonio, para remedio de estas miserias, [a] hacer cuatro demonios*'). Suspicions like this one concerning Native song and dance were voiced early in the Yucatán. Though the mission there did not get underway until the mid-1540s, already by 1552 a judge sent from the *audiencia* of Guatemala was disturbed to find that the Native Maya chiefs still preached 'their rites and ancient ceremonies' in public gatherings and openly held feasts where 'dirty things of their pagan days' were sung to accompany drunken dancing.[13]

This wavering on Native performances is typical of missionaries throughout early Latin America. It bespeaks in the first place their pragmatic coming to grips with the ineradicable presence of Native song and dance. It also suggests that in optimistic moments they believed that Christian conversion could be achieved in a happy syncretism with Native cultural patterns dissociated from their original diabolism. Such moments, however, had their pessimistic counterpart: the gloomy, panicky realization that the connections of Native rituals to the devil could never be fully severed.

In the midst of the immense and uncertain labours of conversion in the Yucatán, it wanted only the right stimulus to arouse anguished pessimism similar to Sahagún's. This came, more dramatically than in Mexico, in May 1562, when idols and human skulls were discovered in a cave near the village of Mani. For complex reasons – involving power struggles between the friars, secular clergy, and lay settlers; the remoteness of the region from the centres of New Spanish authority, which lent its mission a special sense of frontier vulnerability; and the nature of the relics themselves, redolent of old patterns of human sacrifice – the effect of the discovery was electric. The response of the shocked Franciscans rose immediately to the level of hysteria and revealed through horrific deed the same anger at betrayal found in Sahagún's *Relación*.

The friars, led by Landa, resorted to torture. They rounded up thousands of Indians and coerced confessions of idolatry from them; over 150 died from the interrogation alone, others killed themselves at the approach of the friars rather than face the ordeal, and many more were left maimed and crippled.[14] Some of this testimony related practices that confirmed the Franciscans' worst fears: The surviving documents from several of the villages tell over and over again tales of the sacrifice of children, of their hearts torn still beating from their chests and offered to demonic idols, even of their crucifixion, before the very altars the Christians had built and consecrated, and sacrificial dumping in local *cenotes*.[15] How many of these blood-chilling incidents really occurred remains a matter of debate among historians. Some of them, at least, were probably the product of Franciscan suggestion and Indian eagerness to appease the torturers.[16]

The Yucatec crisis of 1562 had the effect of stiffening the local friars' resistance to Native ceremony of all sorts, but it was not explicitly linked, as was Sahagún's complaint, to song. This does not mean, however, that song and the fearsome, heightened utterance of which it is a primary manifestation had no role to play in the testimonies extracted form the Natives. Instead its role was an implicit one. Many of the accounts of human sacrifice relate also the invocations to Satan that accompanied the heart offerings:

> Antonio Pech and Diego Tzotz cut open the children with a knife and pulled out their hearts and gave them to the *ah-kin* [chief] Francisco Uicab. The said *ah-kin* held them up high and burned them and offered them to the idols that were there. And he said to the idols, speaking with them, 'Powerful Señor god, we offer you these hearts and we sacrifice to you these children so that you will give health to our governor,' speaking of the governor Juan Cocom.[17]

One of the testimonies also records words recited by a chief, officiating at a sacrifice, to a victim about to die. 'Strengthen yourself and console yourself,' he is reported to have pronounced, 'for we are doing you no evil; neither are we sending you to a bad place or to hell, but instead to the heavens and to glory in the customary way of our ancestors.' Inga Clendinnen has heard in these words the echoes of an outright song preserved elsewhere; it perhaps recalls in turn words sung in pre-contact days to captive warriors about to be sacrificed.[18]

If these roles of heightened utterance do not add up to the centrality Sahagún accorded *cantares* in his complaint about Native idolatry, the testimonies of 1562 nevertheless focused the Yucatec friars' attention with new clarity on Native rites that habitually involved singing, invocation, dancing, drumming, and drinking. It attuned them to their own fears of ritual song and its corollaries so that, after this watershed year, their watchfulness was redoubled, their Sahaguntine pessimism provoked. Singing as such was no doubt not their main concern as they hung up and whipped another Native to wrest from him unsettling confessions. But they knew that the heart of darkness they discovered in his words, so unimaginably different (as they thought) from their own behaviour, was entered into as effectively as any other way through special uses of voice.

The very decade of the 1560s that marked the collapse of the friars' confidence in the Yucatán saw, in the Viceroyalty of Peru, another crisis linked to indigenous ceremony and song. In Huamanga in the central Andes west of Cuzco, in 1564 or 1565, a Native movement was discovered that the clerical authorities would come to conceive as a full-fledged, millenarian revival of indigenous ceremony bent on destroying the Spaniards and their religion and restoring the old Inca ways. It travelled under the Quechua name *taki onqoy*, song-dance sickness; sometimes it was referred to also as *ayra*, a word whose meaning remains unclear but which probably likewise referred to singing and dancing.[19]

The most comprehensive account we have of the *taki onqoy* comes from Cristóbal de Molina's *Relación de las fábulas y ritos de los Incas*, written a few years after the events in 1574 or 1575. Molina reported the testimony of Luis de Olvera (or Olivera), a *padre* who, while serving in the parish of Parinacochas, was among the first Spaniards to discover the sect. Molina left no doubt that the movement aimed to revive the sacred sites or *huacas* of olden times and destroy the Spaniards in the bargain. The Indians

> believed that all the *huacas* of the realm, all those that the Christians had torn down and burned, were resurrected, and that they had formed two sides, the first joined with the *huaca* of Pachacamac, the other with the

> *huaca* Titicaca. [They believed] that all the *huacas* flew through the air, commanding [the Indians] to do battle against God and defeat him, [saying] that already his defeat was near; and that when the Marqués [Pizarro] entered this land, God had defeated the *huacas* and the Spaniards the Indians, but that now the world was overturning; and that God and the Spaniards would be left defeated this time, and all the Spaniards killed, and their cities flooded; and that the sea would rise and drown them so that no memory of them remained.[20]

The division of the revived *huacas* into two camps, allied to the major Andean sacred sites of Pachacamac (on the coast northwest of Cuzco) and the Island of the Sun in Lake Titicaca (to the southeast of Cuzco), conjures up the image of dual centres of sacred force arrayed on opposite sides of the primary area of diffusion of the *taki onqoy*, the area around Huamanga to the west and southwest of Cuzco. The detail lends an indigenous authenticity to Molina's report, since it seems to reflect the moiety organization that characterized not merely Inca rites and social organization but central Andean societies in general.[21]

According to Olvera and Molina, various practices marked the *taki onqoy*. Its preachers spread through the villages and countryside, proclaiming the return of the *huacas* and the need for the Indians to give them sustenance. While they fed the *huacas* with traditional offerings and celebrations, the Indians themselves had to turn away from all Spanish practices, avoiding the houses of the colonizers and even renouncing their Christian names. They needed also to abstain from sex and to fast, eating no salt, chilis, or corn – both practices recalling pre-contact purification rites.

One other development, however, was not so clearly anticipated in the ancient patterns: The *huacas*, the preachers said, 'no longer put themselves in the rocks and clouds and streams, but instead incorporated themselves now in the Indians and made them speak.'[22] The movement as a whole seems to have been, in other words, a possession cult, and the actions of its devotees involved sorts of behaviour typical of possessed individuals the world over:

> And thus it was that many Indians trembled and rolled around on the ground; others shouted taunts [*tiraban de pedradas*: hollered obscenities?] as if possessed by demons [*como endemoniados*], grimacing, and then fell silent. If they fearfully approached such a one and asked him what he had and what he felt, he responded that such-and-such a *huaca* had entered his

> body. Then they took him in their arms and carried him to a designated place where they made him a room with straw and blankets. Then they painted [his face] red, and the Indians entered to worship him. (80–1)

This burgeoning of ritualized spirit possession seems to place the *taki onqoy* among those sects I.M. Lewis has called 'peripheral' possession cults, 'thinly disguised protest movements' that arise in the midst of some more dominant religious authority and empower in some measure their practitioners. Certainly the desperate situation in the 1560s of the Indians in the area of Huamanga – they were increasingly victims of famine, disease, and the *encomenderos* who demanded ever larger commitments of labour and payments from them – rendered them ripe for such a development.[23]

At the same time, the *taki onqoy* answered to indigenous patterns that reached far beyond a local reaction to the hardship of the 1560s. In Cuzco and its environs, the Spaniards encountered a complex world of religious syncretisms involving three strands: the state religion of the Incas; local religious rites that predated and coexisted with Inca institutions; and the pan-Andean worship of a few major sacred sites and their *huacas*. In all likelihood the *taki onqoy* reflected patterns of some of the most important Inca celebrations, in particular the purification rite of Citua. To these patterns it added a rich mixture of local rites influenced in some measure, if only a reactionary one, by Christian importations and emphasizing, as revival movements in stressful periods often do, spirit possession. All this it combined with the larger, pan-Andean reliance on the *huacas* of Titicaca and Pachacamac.[24]

The village fortunate enough to have a man possessed by a *huaca* in its midst 'held fiestas for two or three days, dancing and drinking and staying up at night without sleep and invoking the *huaca* that he represented and said was in his body' (81). Molina presented these festivals as after-the-fact celebrations of possession already achieved, although modern interpreters have also seen them, in line with other, better-documented possession rituals, as trance-inducing exertions.[25] In either case, these festivals brought communal singing and dancing to the heart of the *taki onqoy*. They probably were the chief reason that Molina, in introducing Olvera's account, called the whole movement 'a kind of song' (*una manera de canto, el cual llamaban taquihongoy*; 78). Or perhaps he responded simply to the name *taki onqoy*, since *taki* was the primary Quechua word used in Inca times to denote singing, or even to the oracular pronouncements of the possessed *taki onqocs*. Whatever his reason, the remainder of the account in the *Relación* gives few hints as to the nature of this singing. Do we hear it dimly in the ritual that the *huaca*, speaking though its human medium, instructed its devotees to perform?

> Those possessed people demanded in the villages that, if someone had any remains of the burned *huacas* or some piece of stone from them, he should cover his head with a blanket in front of the village, and pour *chicha* on the stone and rub it with white maize flour, and then raise his voice, invoking the *huaca*, and lift himself up, with the stone in his hand, saying to the village: 'You see here your refuge, and you see here what it can do for you, giving you health, and children, and fertile fields; put it in its place, where it was in the time of the Inca.' And thus the sorcerers did, with many sacrifices. (82)

Here, as in the Yucatán, we find ourselves in the presence at least of a powerful invocation.

Aside from Molina's *Relación*, the chief sources giving extensive information about the *taki onqoy* are three *informaciones de servicios* concerning Cristóbal de Albornoz, recorded in 1570, 1577, and 1584. Albornoz had arrived in Cuzco in 1567. In his first years there, he had travelled to the parishes south and west of the city and taken an aggressive lead in the extirpation of the *taki onqoy* idolatry, uncovering and destroying hundreds of *huacas*. The *informaciones* later collected were, in effect, job recommendations – series of testimonials from influential Spaniards gathered at the instigation of Albornoz himself in hope of career advancement. They extolled his services to church and crown and were devised to be presented as formal testimony to the Council of the Indies.[26]

As witnesses to the *taki onqoy*, the *informaciones* are valuable chiefly in view of the scarcity of other accounts. (Admittedly they are valuable also because some of the testimony in them seems well informed: Molina and Olvera themselves appear among the witnesses.) In general, however, as sources on Indian practices they are more dubious and compromised than most Spanish writings. In the first place, their aim was not so much to report the doings of the Natives as to praise those of Albornoz. Moreover, they took the form of interrogations in which each testifier answered the same series of questions, with the result that the testimony often did little more than echo the wording of the question asked.

What makes the *informaciones* most suspect as accounts of Native practices is, however, something else: They trace, across the fourteen years of their production, an evolution of thinking about the *taki onqoy* that seems to have little to do with observation of indigenous practices on the ground outside Cuzco. This evolution instead seems to capture the growth of the Spaniards' own ideas about the movement, and thus it plots a course through a sacred imaginary more Spanish than Andean.[27] Along the way it reveals a crystallizing of the Europeans' fear of indigenous song around certain specific issues.

The testimony in the first *información* of 1570, recorded close to the heart of *taki onqoy* country in Huamanga, depicted the movement, with relative simplicity, as an apostasy in which converted Natives denied God and his sacraments (especially confession), turned away from his churches, and revived the old *huacas* and the ceremonies in their honour. It named some of the major *huacas* allied to the revival – Titicaca, Tiahuanuco, Pachacamac, Tambutoco, and a few others – and mentioned the belief that these had defeated the Christian god (64, 93). But there was no explicit (and scant implicit) sense in this testimony that the movement aimed to destroy all things Spanish or kill the Spaniards.

Only a few of the witnesses in this *información* departed from the wording offered in the question itself about the *taki onqoy*. One who did was Gerónimo Martín, a priest in one of the outlying *repartimientos* and an expert in Native language and affairs. He described the consequences the preachers foretold for those who did not worship the *huacas*: 'If they didn't adore the said *huacas* and do the said ceremonies and sacrifices preached to them, they would die, they would go about with their heads on the ground and feet in the air, others would turn into *guanacos*, deer, *vicuñas*, and other animals, and they would lapse into idiocy' (130). Another priest, Pedro Barriga Corro of Huamanga, introduced the name of one of the chief preachers of the sect, Juan Chono, reported bits of the speeches of the preachers, and affirmed that they spoke in their houses to the *huacas* and that 'the *huacas* responded to them' (147) in the fashion of oracles. All this seems to stay close to the kind of practices of indigenous worship we might expect to have lingered on throughout the Andes, especially in areas far from the newly established or ever-more-Hispanized cities. All this, moreover, reflects a Spanish reaction to such practices that is relatively temperate: another patch where the work of evangelization had not fully penetrated, another episode of Native backsliding to be chastised.

In the second *información*, recorded seven years later at Cuzco, the *taki onqoy* took on a different, more threatening profile. Here it resembled in most particulars the movement described in Molina's *Relación* – not surprisingly, since the most informative of the witnesses was Molina's source himself, Luis de Olvera. In contrast to the *taki onqoy* of the first *información*, now the movement came to seem murderous to the Spaniards. Now also, recalling the *Relación* but not the first *información*, the *taki onqoy* displayed the trappings of a possession cult. In wording similar at numerous points to his account that Molina had reproduced, Olvera told how the *huacas* invaded the bodies of the Indians, how those Indians trembled as they were possessed and spoke with the voice of the *huaca*, how their faces were painted, and how they were placed in closed spaces where they were worshiped (178). Most of this account of Olvera was echoed, almost verbatim, later on by another witness, Cristóbal Ximénez (191). Molina himself also testified, and for his part added to the details found in his *Relación*. He related now that the principal preachers of the apostasy were two men and a woman. They told the Indians, he added – fleshing out the mention in the *Relación* of *huacas* that flew through the air – 'that it was not God who gave them food, but one who flew through the air in a kind of basket' (181).

As it had in Molina's *Relación* two or three years earlier, the *taki onqoy* reflected here, ten years after the events, practices feared in Europe, especially the devil's possession of unwary souls – remember the phrase *como endemoniados* from the *Relación* – and the nocturnal flights of witches. The two nearly contemporary and closely related documents mark the second stage in a process that seems to constrain ever more narrowly Andean practices within a European imaginary.

The third and final stage in this description of the *taki onqoy* was reached in the last *información*, dictated in 1584, two full decades after the discovery of the movement. One new detail redolent again of European witchcraft emerged in these relatively short testimonies. Molina testified once more, naming among the leading preachers of the sect the same Juan Chono mentioned already in the first *información* (Molina called him Joan Chocne or Chocna). Molina added that Chono had told his Indian followers that he was accompanied by an invisible familiar: 'Don Joan Chocna said that he brought with him someone they could not see, who told him these things [he said], and that this one gave them their food and sustenance' (225).

But the major change in the portrayal of the *taki onqoy* came in the phrasing of the question about it. This offered wording, repeated in the answers of several of the witnesses, that cast the movement in a new, dimmer light:

> Item: whether they know that the said canon Cristóbal de Albornoz was the first who brought to light . . . the sect and apostasy called Taqui Ongo, in which the Indians, already baptized, gave themselves over to dancing

> and shaking, going round and round; and in that dance they invoked the devil [*ynbocaban al demonio*] and his *huacas* and idols, and in the dance they rejected and abjured the true faith of Jesus Christ and of all the teachings they had received from the Christians and priests that had come into this realm. (205)

From a grass-roots revival of *huacas,* to a demonic possession ritual, and finally to an orgiastic, Satanic rite: across the fourteen years of the *informaciones,* the questioners and witnesses transformed the *taki onqoy* into the round dance and chant of the witches' sabbath, conjuring the dark lord himself. Just as in Mexico and the Yucatán, Native ceremony in the Andes assumed a more and more explicit, diabolical form in the perfervid imaginations of Spaniards wearied by the rigours and setbacks of evangelization.

In this the *taki onqoy* took its place as an Andean variant of the larger evolution we have traced in Spanish views on Native song, dance, and ceremony. The Peruvian historian Juan Carlos Estenssoro Fuchs has discerned in the 1560s and 1570s the emergence of a new, uncompromising stance in the Andes toward indigenous ceremony and its *takis.* During the first decades of evangelization, optimistic, assimilationist models had prevailed. The Spaniards looked on as Native ceremonies were incorporated in Catholic services; festive dance songs called *hayllis* were sung in the cathedral of Cuzco, and Inti Raimi solstice ceremonies were transplanted into Corpus Christi processions. By the 1560s, however, views were strenuously divided. Some, especially among the Dominicans, continued to maintain that the answer to the problem of indigenous ceremony was to assimilate it to Christian practices while separating it absolutely from its original, diabolical associations; others, including the investigator of Andean religion Juan Polo de Ondegardo, urged a general extirpation. The arrival of Francisco de Toledo as the new Viceroy of Peru in late 1569, followed by the founding of a tribunal of the Inquisition in Lima in 1571, helped tilt the balance toward harsher measures. At the Third Ecclesiastical Council of Lima of 1583, Native celebrations in general were prohibited.[28]

It would be convenient to see this shift as a reaction to the alarm brought about by the discovery of the *taki onqoy.* But the change of views on this movement evident across the three *informaciones* of Albornoz and the fact that these documents span the very years from Toledo's arrival to the Third Council suggest that this is too easy an explanation. In place of its one-way causality, the evidence we have calls for a model of mutual evolution in which the *taki onqoy* aroused new suspicions regarding Native ceremony at the same time as it was transformed – produced, we might even say, in the form in which the scant documentation brings it to us – by a more and more pessimistic and fearful Spanish imagining of indigenous deed. What began in all probability as a local, peripheral possession cult, in the midst of indigenous hardship and Native *huaca* worship that had never lapsed, evolved into a diabolical sabbath. But the evolution seems to have taken place above all in the anxious minds of Spanish observers.

A New Form of Fear

The chronological coincidence of these three outbursts of Indian nativism and Spanish suspicion concerning it – in the valley of Mexico, the Yucatán, and the Andes – is almost exact: All three reflect experiences of the 1560s and 1570s. Together they reveal, at least, the widespread undermining of the missionaries' earlier confidence in the steady and unperturbed progress of evangelization of the Indians. At most, as I have suggested, their coincidence betokens a more general shift of the colonizers' and Indians' perceptions at this moment.[29]

On the part of the Indians, this shift probably had to do with a dawning awareness that the foreigners in their midst represented not a transient tremor but a permanent, seismic alteration of their cultural landscape. Undoubtedly, for both Indians and Europeans, the shift involved a deepening appreciation of the differences separating the two groups. In the fear the Spanish friars felt at the witnessing or even the mere reports of indigenous song and ceremony we sense recognition of the yawning gap that lay open between them and the Indians. In their moves to comprehend this song and ceremony within familiar structures of the European sacred imaginary we see their aggressive effort to close the gap.

European colonizers would repeat this dual move, recognizing and disavowing difference, in countless meetings with others over the next several centuries. In *Orientalism* Edward Said discerned something similar as a common thread in European encounters in Asia:

> What gives the immense number of encounters some unity . . . is . . . vacillation . . . Something patently foreign and distant acquires . . . a status more rather than less familiar. One tends to stop judging things either as completely novel or as completely well-known; a new median category emerges, a category that allows one to see new things . . . as versions of a

> previously known thing. In essence such a category is not so much a way of receiving new information as it is a method of controlling what seems to be a threat to some established view of things.

Homi Bhabha has taken Said's median category as the jumping-off point for an analysis of racial and sexual stereotypes in colonial societies. These, he argues, amount to something more complex than mere vicious misrepresentations promulgated by the colonizers. They exemplify a systematic pattern of ambivalence characteristic of colonial discourse in which a confronting of difference is countered by its masking and psychic accommodation. From this flux, this recognition and disavowal of difference, arise, in colonizers and colonized alike, kinds of subjectivization specific to colonial societies.

This subject-forming flux is related to for Bhabha, to the most basic interplay of self and other in which psyches take shape. He considers this both from Freudian and Lacanian perspectives, that is, as a function of early sexual differentiation reflected later in the fetish and of the mirror stage, the initial step of the self toward recognition of its identity and distinction from others. At this time the subject coalesces as a product of both alienation and identification: the child's recognition of sexual difference and fetishistic denial of it, the child's simultaneous separation from and desire for its image in the mirror. The stereotypes in colonial discourse incorporate a related tacking between aggression and pleasure, derision and desire, separation and narcissistic merger. They construct colonized and colonizer in relation to each other as at once radically other and wholly familiar (again, Said's median category), since they gesture toward difference but absorb it in the reactivation of a primal scene of wholeness and sameness.[30]

The two terms in this intersubjective relation – the sheer other and the utopic, undivided self – fix the poles of an incalculable, fearful difference and a desirous assimilation of it. These polar oppositions are however not distinct, dissociated subject positions. Instead they are bound together in the stereotype, hindering the more fluid interactions of differing subject positions of non-colonial societies. The stereotype remains unstable because the dynamic of difference and its effacement is continually disturbed by renewed assertions of difference. The play of different identities in colonial situations is in this way an exaggerated version of identity interactions in less confrontational circumstances.[31]

This theoretical model seems to capture, in general terms at least, the stage of colonial discourse reached in New Spain and Peru by the 1560s.

The revivals of indigenous ceremony and song perceived by the Spaniards in Mexico, the Yucatán, and the Andes were probably not organized uprisings at all, and perhaps not even revivals, but rather persistent local practices adapted and answering to the worsening hardship of Indian life in these decades. The Spaniards were brought to perceive them as murderous conspiracies and devil worship because of the collapse of the utopic visions of evangelization they had earlier entertained, a collapse needing only small shifts in Native practices for its onset and registered in the disenchantment, sense of betrayal, and anger of the missionaries. This perspective is not exclusive of other views, but rather coextensive with them: If the Spaniards' panicky reactions and harsh reprisals reflect the emergence of the new view of Native diabolism that Cervantes has analysed, they are also commensurate with the dissipation of a desired, illusory psychic ideal.

The collapse of Spanish confidence seems to have been new in its day. There is little trace, at any rate, of such widely dispersed and institutionalized fears in earlier decades of New World evangelization. They represent a crisis of the Christian mission in Spanish America about 1570 that seems to have entertained, for the first time, the prospect that the Indians might never be saved through conversion. The dawning of this possibility helps to explain the pessimism – despair, even – that spread through the mission in these years.

In giving palpable form to this new fear, the crisis assumes a broad, even epochal significance in the history of European colonialism. The idea of the failure of conversion must have challenged the friars' most basic presumptions concerning time and history. Johannes Fabian has described the sense of history involved in Europe's early modern global expansion as an incorporative, Christian temporal order that held out a future of salvation for all peoples – *eschatological time,* as we might call it, recognizing its teleological orientation toward an ultimate salvation. In Fabian's view this conception of time gradually ceded ground before the advance of a new, secular order. Secular time arrayed human history along a graded, evolutionary scale, effectively fragmenting it, since contemporary peoples could be located with ostensive scientific neutrality at different, disconnected points along it. 'Primitives' in a world increasingly controlled by Europeans came to be seen to be playing out their own, separate evolutions rather than awaiting, within a single temporal fold, the saving grace Europe brought. As Fabian put it, the 'pagan . . . always *already* marked for salvation' gave way to the 'savage . . . *not yet* ready for civilization.'[32]

Fabian located the advent of the new temporality in a generalized 'Enlightenment thought,' and undoubtedly the eighteenth century of Vico, Rousseau, and the rest is the moment of its first culmination. (Vico's model of independent providential histories for all societies provides an especially clear instance of the new temporal order conceived within an overarching Christianity.)[33] The true nascence of the new order, however, can be discerned two centuries earlier, in the late-sixteenth-century crisis of evangelization marked throughout the Spanish colonies. What was left in the wake of this disillusionment was certainly not a full-blown secular temporality; neither, of course, did it involve a wholesale decline of Christian tenets or any retreat of Christian missionaries. What was left instead was a new set of uncompromising imperatives guiding the mission, including new strictures aimed at indigenous expressive cultures. Left also was something less tractable but of far-reaching consequence: a tension between Europe's evangelizing efforts and a growing, unsettling awareness that irredeemable cultural difference might exist in the world. This was the impact on European mentalities, no doubt unsettling at deep levels, of the first decades of colonization.

At this time the fear of singing entered a new phase. Singing, chanting, and other raisings of the voice, along with their corollaries, dance and music-making, had a large role to play in opening out the new prospect of incorrigible difference. The heightened voices of the Indians were time and again heard by the Spaniards as a primary symptom of a dangerous, unassuageable otherness – heard, as I suggested above, as a locus of foreign metaphysical powers. Their special significance was redoubled by the extraordinary movements of Indian bodies, whether in organized, ritual dance or in the uncontrolled trembling of the possessed, and by the prosthetic extension of voice through the use of drums, trumpets, and other musical instruments.

Here the colonial dynamic of difference explored by Bhabha converges on the metaphysics of voice. Raised voices broach, in all societies and in ways recognizable across gaping cultural divides, an order of meaning distinct from that of normal speech. Singing, chanting, invocation, and so forth come to signify in part through their surplus over speech. Their effects cannot be pinned down and plotted through the signifying modes of the language they exceed, and this helps to explain why song traditions the world over exploit non-lexical words or vocables. In song, language itself is twisted by a torque of surplus vocalization away from its modes of meaning in speech.

Because of this generalized, non-speech significance, heightened vocalization conveys much of its meaning in the manner of a binary code, yielding only two possibilities: comforting, communal sameness or discomfiting otherness. In the confrontation of divergent identities characteristic of colonial society, then, discomfiture grows into threat. Amid perceptions of ungraspable difference of the kind that nurture the colonial stereotype, the always-audible gap between speech and raised voice widens, the mysteries of surplus signification are deepened, and the fear of singing burgeons.

There is this difference, however, between song and stereotype: The stereotype is a symptom of the psychic mechanism that moves to control threatening difference, and in this it shows a kinship to all the measures the friars took across the late sixteenth century to manage and limit Indian ceremony. Heightened voice, instead, is itself productive of the threat, inscrutable but bound to be heard and understood too well.

This difference signals once more the special place of ritual utterance and its many appurtenances in contact scenes and colonial societies. We may clarify it by comparison with another of the constitutive elements of Bhabha's colonial discourse. For him part of the apparatus producing colonial subjects is the colonizers' surveillance, which exercises a 'scopic' power over the colonized. This gaze effectively objectifies the colonial subject, at the same time offering an image in which is affirmed the wholeness of the viewer's identity; from this dynamic comes its power. But this specular construction of identity is, like the stereotype, easily undone. It depends on the colonized subject's consent in not gazing back. The gazing subject recognizes itself in a condition of continual risk that the objectified other might turn the tables. As long as the gaze is not returned, the colonizer's surveillance approaches the empowered condition of voyeurism.[34]

Listening to others sing does not hold out the promise of the control and empowerment of voyeurism; instead it offers the ambivalences of eavesdropping. Eavesdropping has in certain recent accounts been regarded as a kind of auditory voyeurism and thus assimilated to Lacanian theories of the gaze and its powers.[35] This can obscure important differences between the two phenomena. In eavesdropping there is no possibility of the unchallenging passivity on which the voyeur's power depends. The overheard necessarily assumes the form of a sonic intrusion from elsewhere. The confrontation that is possible in the returned gaze of the scopic dynamic here becomes inevitable. Where the gaze might operate to reassure and empower the viewer with illusory self-integration – with the narcissistic sense of undivided self and world without difference – the listener instead is always faced by an othering utterance. The eavesdropper, it is said, never hears good of himself. What is unsaid is that he *cannot* do so, if hearing good means attaining the comfort of a psychodynamic wholeness. Such solace, transiently profferred by the eye, is always out of earshot.

The colonial aural dynamic might then be conceived in relation to the Lacanian 'object voice' described by Mladen Dolar, a voice at once bearing plenitude of self-presence and the unassuageable otherness of the Real. For Dolar the musical voice poses this ambivalence in acute form, though at the same time he works to retain a force domesticating the voice's otherness in the 'aesthetic pleasure' music gives. By broadening his category beyond music to all heightened vocalization we come close to the otherness ever inhabiting voice – and to the special fears it has provoked in confrontational situations of encounter, conquest, and colonization.[36]

These fears, to turn the matter around, are nothing but a focusing of the peculiar force that voice exerts above and beyond its capacity to carry specific linguistic meaning. Gilles Deleuze and Felix Guattari, in their ontology highlighting instability and transformation rather than being and identity, recognize this special force. One name they give to transformation – of human subjects also – is deterritorialization; and among human acts music and the voice from which it springs are second to none in their power to deterritorialize. 'Perhaps,' they add, 'this trait explains the collective fascination exerted by music, and even the potentiality of [its] "fascist" danger . . .: music (drums, trumpets) draws people and armies into a race that can go all the way to the abyss (much more so than banners and flags, which are paintings . . .).'[37]

We have found our way back to the psychic violence of music – to Tamasese, the tribal chief on display in Adorno's recollected zoo, frightened by the rumble of the timpani from the distant orchestral pavilion. Perhaps, indeed, the back-and-forth convolutions we noted in Adorno's narrative are inescapable, reflecting the ambivalent dynamic of overheard sounds that cannot but undermine the construction of an empowered, stable self.

Spanish alarms at Indian apostasy in central Mexico, the Yucatán, and the Andes all were set off by the overhearing – direct or imagined through reports of the Indians themselves – of Native ceremony involving singing, invocation, and drumming. In these cases the integrated selves the Europeans had laboriously constructed in the face of dramatic difference, the stable subjectivities they achieved by objectification of the Indians, were undone by Indian actions. The Europeans' most primal fears of a world they could neither comprehend nor control were confirmed by the aggressive sonic excess of Indian ritual utterance. And was this not an inevitable confirmation, in conditions of exacerbated difference and through heightened voice, of a terror of transformation the Europeans had always already known?

In analysing yet another Latin American contact-moment, Michel de Certeau posed a related question in respect to the difference between writing and speech: 'Would it be too much to recognize already in the gap between what is seen and heard the distinction between two functionings of the savage world in relation to the [European] language that deals with it? Either as an *object* of a discourse that constructs schemes and pictures, or as a *distortion,* a rapture, but also a calling of this discourse?'[38] Writing, de Certeau argued, facilitated the fixing of Indians within European discourse, while speech threatened their escape from it. In a language itself almost rapturous, he celebrated the most basic absence – of living vocality – that haunts modern historiographic and ethnographic projects alike.

We need to take a step beyond de Certeau, calibrating more finely the gauge by which we measure this absence. Within the utterance that for him unsettled European discourse concerning the New World, we should discriminate speech from all its heightened alternatives. Speech remained a largely tractable force in the dynamic of seizure and escape; raised voices, instead, disrupted the European imaginary in which the colonizers struggled to locate the colonized. Song, especially, made good the Natives' flight, and in the space it opens a whole history of European colonialism might take shape.

NOTES

This essay presents a shortened version of chapter 6 of Gary Tomlinson, *The Singing of the New World: Indigenous Voice in the Era of European Contact* (Cambridge: Cambridge University Press, 2007).

1 Theodor Adorno, *Quasi una fantasia,* trans. Rodney Livingstone (London: Verso, 1992), 33–4.

2 For a sensitive consideration of accounts of musical encounters from southern Africa, see David Smith, 'Colonial Encounters through the Prism of Music,' *International Review of the Aesthetics and Sociology of Music* 33 (2002): 31–55.

3 For examples of this literature from Mexico, see Hernando Ruiz de Alarcón, *Treatise on the Heathen Superstitions That Today Live among the Indians Native to This New Spain, 1629*, trans. J. Richard Andrews and Ross Hassig (Norman: University of Oklahoma Press, 1984), and Jacinto de la Serna, *Tratado de las idolatrias, supersticiones, dioses, ritos, hechicerias y otras costumbres gentilicas de las razas aborigenes de Mexico*, ed. Don Francisco del Paso y Troncoso, 2nd ed., 2 vols. (Mexico: Ediciones Fuente Cultural, 1953); from Peru, Pablo Jose de Arriaga, *Extirpación de la idolatría del Pirú*, in *Cronicas peruanas de interés indígena*, ed. Francisco Esteve Barba (Madrid: Atlas, 1968), 191–277.

4 Fernando Cervantes, *The Devil in the New World: The Impact of Diabolism in New Spain* (New Haven, CT: Yale University Press, 1994), chap. 1. For an important musicological exploration of some similar issues in early European encounters with Native North Americans, see Olivia Bloechl, *Native American Song at the Frontiers of Early Modern Music* (Cambridge: Cambridge University Press, 2008), esp. chaps. 3–4; see also her essay in this volume.

5 For the passage see Fray Bernardino de Sahagún, *Florentine Codex: General History of the Things of New Spain*, ed. and trans. Arthur J.O. Anderson and Charles E. Dibble, 12 vols. (Santa Fe, NM: School of American Research and University of Utah Press, 1950–82), 1: 74–85; further page references will be given in the text.

6 Sahagún, *Florentine Codex*, 1: 58; trans. modified.

7 Writing also played a dual role in Sahagún's divided cosmos, if one seemingly less threatening than singing. He mentioned writing alongside singing each time he referred to the educational program for the Indians (see above); then, as in the case of singing, he turned to writing of a different sort near the end of the *Relación*: 'This people . . . communicated with one another by means of representations and paintings. And all their ancient customs and books they had about them were painted . . . in such a way that they knew and had records of the things their ancestors had done and had left in their annals . . . Most of these books and writings were burned when the other idolatrous things were destroyed. But many remained hidden, for we have seen them. And, even now, they are kept; through them we have understood their ancient customs' (82). It is probably revealing of the special force of performed song that Sahagún's reaction to the Native books seems so much more dispassionate – so much less caught up in a sense of betrayal – than his reaction to the singing of *cantares*.

8 For a description of the climate in which these Native ceremonies carried on and analysis of the deep differences with Christianity they manifested even as they adapted many of its traits, see Cervantes, *The Devil in the New World*, chap. 2.

For much more on the Nahuatl *cantares* and their cultural import see Gary Tomlinson, *The Singing of the New World: Indigenous Voice in the Era of European Contact* (Cambridge: Cambridge University Press, 2007), chap. 3.

9 Nancy M. Farriss, *Maya Society under Colonial Rule: The Collective Enterprise of Survival* (Princeton, NJ: Princeton University Press 1984), chaps. 10–11; for the quotation, 320; the *tunkul* mentioned by Farriss is the equivalent of the Mexican log-drum *teponaztli.*

10 *Landa's Relación de las cosas de Yucatan,* trans. Alfred M. Tozzer (Cambridge: Peabody Museum, 1941), 93; see Fray Diego de Landa, *Relación de las cosas de Yucatan,* ed. Angel Maria Garibay K. (Mexico: Porrua, 1966), 39.

11 Antonio de Ciudad Real, *Relación de las cosas que sucedieron al R. P. Comisario General Fray Alonso Ponce,* trans. by Inga Clendinnen in *Ambivalent Conquests: Maya and Spaniard in Yucatan, 1517–1570* (Cambridge: Cambridge University Press, 1987), 159–60

12 *Landa's Relación,* trans. Tozzer, 148–9; Landa, *Relación,* 69.

13 Quoted in Clendinnen, *Ambivalent Conquests,* 57–8.

14 See Clendinnen, *Ambivalent Conquests,* chap. 6, for a general account of the crisis; for the Indian deaths and suicides, 75–6.

15 Much of the documentation concerning the idolatry, including reports of testimony extracted under torture, is gathered in Frances V. Scholes and Eleanor B. Adams, *Don Diego Quijada, Alcalde Mayor de Yucatán, 1561–1565,* 2 vols. (Mexico: Porrua, 1938), 1: 24–232; see especially documents 12 and 13, 71–134.

16 See Clendinnen, *Ambivalent Conquests,* chaps. 8 and 12; Farriss, *Maya Society,* 291.

17 Scholes and Adams, *Don Diego Quijada,* 76–7; other examples on 88, 101, 115, 123, 127, and 155; for similar invocations not involving human sacrifice see 62–3.

18 For the speech to the victim, see Scholes and Adams, *Don Diego Quijada,* 106. The whole passage is translated in Clendinnen, *Ambivalent Conquests,* 195–200; on its similarities with the pre-contact song see 176–7; and for the words of the song itself, Alfredo Barrera Vázquez, *El libro de los cantares de Dzitbalché* (Mexico: Instituto Nacional de Antropología e Historia, 1965), 26.

19 For various interpretations of *ayra* see Ranulfo Cavero, *Los dioses vencidos: una lectura antropológica del Taki Onqoy* (Ayacucho, Peru: Universidad Nacional de San Cristóbal de Huamanga, 2001), 196–7, 199, 205; one of the most plausible connections of the word is to the *ayrihua,* a harvest song and dance mentioned by Pablo José de Arriaga in his *Extirpación de la idolatría del Pirú,* 213.

20 Cristóbal de Molina, *Fábulas y ritos de los Incas*, in *Las crónicas de los Molinas*, ed. Francisco A. Loayza (Lima: Domingo Miranda, 1943), second pagination, 5–84; see esp. 78–84; for this quotation, 79–80; further references in the text.

21 On these moieties see Tomlinson, *The Singing of the New World*, 136ff.; on the division of the *taki onqoy huacas* into two camps as a reflection of such moieties, Cavero, *Los dioses vencidos*, 180, and the literature cited there.

22 Molina, *Fábulas*, 80. *Huacas* lodged in rocks and streams are characteristic of Andean sacred practices, but *huacas* in clouds are not; Molina's *nubes* is probably either a mistake in his recounting of Olvera's information or in the transmission of the *Relación*. Olvera's own later testimony about the *taki onqoy* (see below) uses almost exactly the same wording but substitutes the more appropriate *árboles* (trees) for *nubes*. See Luis Millones, ed., *El retorno de las huacas: Estudios y documentos sobre el Taki Onqoy, siglo XVI* (Lima: Instituto de Estudios Peruanos, 1990), 178.

23 I.M. Lewis, *Ecstatic Religion: A Study of Shamanism and Spirit Possession*, 2nd ed. (London: Routledge, 1989), 27. For the situation of the Indians in these years, see Rafael Varón Gabai, 'El Taki Onqoy,' in Millones, ed., *El retorno de las huacas*, 380–405; for the 1560s as a particularly troubled time, Cavero, *Los dioses vencidos*, 134, and esp. Steve J. Stern, *Peru's Indian Peoples and the Challenge of Spanish Conquest: Huamanga to 1640* (Madison: University of Wisconsin Press, 1982), chaps. 2–3.

24 See Cavero, *Los dioses vencidos*, 36, 168, 191, 195ff; Stern, *Peru's Indian Peoples*, chap. 3.

25 For discussion of possession songs and dances, see Cavero, *Los dioses vencidos*, 182–6, 203–7.

26 The *Informaciones* collected by Cristóbal de Albornoz and related documents are gathered in *El retorno de las huacas*, ed. Millones, 41–308; further page references will be given in the text. For the date of Albornoz's arrival in Cuzco see Pedro M. Guibovich Pérez's introduction to *El retorno*, 'Nota preliminar al personaje histórico y los documentos,' 24–5.

27 Cavero, *Los dioses vencidos*, 24, has noted this shifting emphasis: 'Las distintas *Informaciones*, conforme va pasando el tiempo, se presentan más contaminadas con la percepción occidental y judeo cristiana.' On the general topic of Spanish interpretations of the Andean sacred imaginary in the sixteenth century see Sabine MacCormack, *Religion in the Andes: Vision and Imagination in Early Colonial Peru* (Princeton, NJ: Princeton University Press, 1991); for the *taki onqoy* in particular see 181–6.

28 Juan Carlos Estenssoro Fuchs, 'Los bailes de los indios y el proyecto colonial,' *Revista Andina* 10 (1992), 353–89; esp. 360–7. For Estenssoro's further discussion of this topic in an excellent general analysis of evangelization in

Peru, see Juan Carlos Estenssoro Fuchs, *Del paganismo a la santidad: la incorporación de los Indios del Perú al catolicismo, 1532–1750,* trans. Gabriela Ramos (Lima: Instituto Francés de Estudios Americanos, 2003), chap. 2.

29 The synchrony extends beyond Spanish to Portuguese America. In the Bahia region of Brazil the 1560s witnessed the rise of another messianic, nativist movement, which came to be called *Santidade.* Like the *taki onqoy* this movement prophesied an end to European rule and a deliverance of the Indians from disease and hardship. It involved rites, modelled in some features after Christian ceremony, in which 'the priests and congregation . . . intoned their prayers in a language nobody understood.' See John Hemming, *Red Gold: The Conquest of the Brazilian Indians, 1500–1760* (Cambridge, MA: Harvard University Press, 1978), 143, 156–8.

30 Homi K. Bhabha, 'The Other Question: Stereotype, Discrimination, and the Discourse of Colonialism,' in *The Location of Culture* (London: Routledge, 1994), 66–84; see esp. 73–84 and, for Said, 73.

31 Colonial identities, Bhabha writes, are 'played out – like all fantasies of originality and origination – in the face and space of the disruption and threat from the heterogeneity of other positions.' 'The Other Question,' 77.

32 Johannes Fabian, *Time and the Other: How Anthropology Makes Its Object* (New York: Columbia University Press, 1983), 26–7.

33 For this model, the important role of singing in it, and its eighteenth-century application to Mexican society see Gary Tomlinson, 'Vico's Songs: Detours at the Origins of (Ethno)Musicology,' *The Musical Quarterly* 83 (1999): 344–77.

34 See Bhabha, 'The Other Question,' 76–7. This Lacan-derived theory of the gaze, first brought into general cultural theory especially in film studies, has been extended to music by a number of scholars, with compelling results in the area of feminist and gender studies. See especially two writings by Lawrence Kramer: *Music as Cultural Practice, 1800–1900* (Berkeley: University of California Press, 1990), chap. 4 and esp. 111–12; and 'Culture and Musical Hermeneutics: The Salome Complex,' *Cambridge Opera Journal* 2 (1990): 269–94, esp. 272–3.

35 This is one implication of Kaja Silverman's consideration of the female voice in cinema; see *The Acoustic Mirror: The Female Voice in Psychoanalysis and Cinema* (Bloomington: Indiana University Press, 1988), 55–63. For an adaptation of these views to musicological ends, Rose Theresa, 'Spectacle and Enchantment: Envisioning Opera in Late Nineteenth-Century Paris' (PhD diss., University of Pennsylvania, 2000), esp. 235ff. and 389ff.

36 See Mladen Dolar, 'The Object Voice,' in *Gaze and Voice as Love Objects,* ed. Renata Salecl and Slavoj Zizek (Durham: Duke University Press, 1996), 7–31: 'There is . . . inside that narcissistic and auto-affective dimension of

the voice, something that threatens to disrupt it – the voice that affects one at the most intimate level, but which one cannot master and over which one has no power or control' (14); also 10, 16–28.

37 Gilles Deleuze and Felix Guattari, *A Thousand Plateaus: Capitalism and Schizophrenia,* trans. Brian Massumi (Minneapolis: University of Minnesota Press, 1987), 302.

38 Michel de Certeau, 'Ethno-Graphy: Speech, or the Space of the Other: Jean de Léry,' in *The Writing of History,* trans. Tom Conley (New York: Columbia University Press, 1988), 208–43 at 236.

chapter six

The Illicit Voice of Prophecy

OLIVIA BLOECHL

The 1634 Latin edition of John Smith's history of the Jamestown colony featured a series of elaborate engravings illustrating episodes from Smith's narrative, including one that showed several Powhatan priests singing and dancing around a fire in a state of trance (Figure 6.1). Smith had narrated this episode in the *Generall historie* (1624) as follows:

> Early in a morning a great fire was made in a long house, and a mat spread on the one side, as on the other; on the one they caused him to sit, and all the guard went out of the house, and presently came skipping in a great grim fellow, all painted over with coale, mingled with oyle; and many snakes and we[a]sels skins stuffed with mosse, and all their tayles tyed together, so as they met on the crowne of his head in a tassell; and round about the tassell was a coronet of feathers, the skins hanging round about his head, backe, and shoulders, and in a manner covered his face; with a hellish voyce and a rattle in his hand. With most strange gestures and passions he began his invocation, and environed the fire with a circle of meale; which done, three more such like devils came rushing in with the like antique tricks, painted halfe blacke, halfe red: but all their eyes were painted white, and some red stroakes like mutchato's, along their cheekes: round about him those fiends daunced a pretty while, and then came in three more as ugly as the rest; with red eyes, and white stroakes over their black faces; at last they all sat down right against him; three of them on the one hand of the chiefe priest, and three on the other. Then all with their rattles began a song, which ended, the chiefe priest layd downe five wheat cornes: then strayning his armes and hands with such violence that he sweat, and his veynes swelled, he began a short oration: at the conclusion they all gave

Figure 6.1 Several Powhatan priests singing and dancing around a fire. From John Smith, *The Generall Historie of Virginia, New-England, and the Summer Isles* (1624).

> a short groane; and then layd down three graines more. After that, began their song againe, and then another oration, ever laying downe so many cornes as before, till they had twice incirculed the fire; that done, they took a bunch of little stickes prepared for that purpose, continuing still their devotion, and at the end of every song and oration, they layd downe a sticke betwixt the divisions of corne.[1]

The ceremony Smith describes was part of a series of Powhatan rituals involving the captive Smith in the winter of 1607–8. In his study of Powhatan-English relations anthropologist Frederic Gleach has identified this as a redefinition ritual, which he argues was part of a protracted 'rite of passage "adopting" the English colony' and the colonists into the Powhatan confederacy.[2] If Gleach is correct, the priests' ritual song, oration, and dance may have been aimed at redefining the world to include Smith's people, transforming Smith into a subordinate *werowance* (chief) recognized by Powhatan and non-human *manito* peoples alike.

However, Smith interpreted the Pamunkey ceremony's purpose differently, as a rite of divination: 'Three dayes they used this Ceremony,' he wrote, 'the meaning whereof they told him, was to know if he intended them well or no.'[3] Smith may have misunderstood his captors' explanation, or their explanation may have been a deliberate oversimplification of sacred acts in the presence of someone who was not an initiate. Regardless, Smith's attribution of a divinatory function to a ceremony involving ecstatic song, oration, and dance would have indicated to European readers that an unknown and possibly diabolical spiritual force was active in the ceremony. This outsider's interpretation of the ceremony was amplified with the illustration in figure 6.1, which exaggerated the physical signs of ecstasy that Smith describes. The engraving shows the chief priest with his eyes rolled back in his head and his body in a radically askew dance position, both of which were visual conventions for representing extreme altered states. Faced with evidence of altered-state performance in Native American communities, European writers often reached for the explanations of diabolical possession or obsession. However, Smith's explanation aligned the Pamunkey ritual with the related, though metaphysically distinct, phenomenon of prophecy.

Prophecy, of which divination was one form, was an ambivalent category of religious experience for European Christians. While prophecy had biblical precedent, it was also associated with the oracles of pagan antiquity, which many canonic Christian writers from the patristic period onward suspected of diabolism. Moreover, a mere decade after the 1634 reprint of Smith's writings, England saw a dramatic resurgence of religious and political prophecy with the rise of the radical Dissenting sects during the Civil War (1642–9) and Interregnum (1649–60). The sects' resistance to religious orthodoxy and social norms earned them widespread derision, and among their most notorious practices was the ecstatic intoned or sung prophecy that they performed in communal worship, as well as in public squares, parish churches, and halls of government. Anglicans and more moderate recusants criticized what they perceived as the prophets' violation of an entrenched bodily and vocal decorum, and many even accused them of possession or madness, refusing the prophets' own explanations of their extraordinary orality and physicality. For this reason, hostile descriptions and visual depictions of Dissenting prophets commonly represent them with eccentric postures and eyes rolled back in their heads, as with the chief Powhatan priest in figure 6.1.[4] Figure 6.2 shows an early-eighteenth-century mezzotint by John Bowles, after Egbert van Heemskerck, that depicts a Quaker meeting presided over by a woman in the throes of religious ecstasy, as indicated by her rolled-back eyes and demonstrative gestures. Several audience members are shown in similarly altered states, especially the old woman seated at the bottom left of the print, who clenches her fists and casts her head and eyes backward in a frenzy as she listens.

The identification of the Powhatan priest's song and oration as prophecy in Smith's account and in the 1634 illustration drew the Pamunkey redefinition ceremony into an evolving European discourse on ecstatic vocality and its meanings. A rich critical vocabulary developed in England around mid-century for evaluating the charismatic preaching, singing, and prophesying that proliferated with the growth of radicalism during the Interregnum. Because prophets' preaching and singing were unauthorized by ecclesiastical institutions and were often heretical, they drew intense and usually hostile speculation as to their origins and

Figure 6.2 After Egbert van Heemskerck (1645–1704), *The Quakers Meeting.* Mezzotint – engraved by John Bowles. © Library of the Religious Society of Friends.

effects. Prophecy also reached toward extremes of oral expression, exposing the limits of the English social and religious order by violating its standards of vocal decorum. Worse, outsiders feared that the apparently unearthly source and transgressive potency of prophetic vocality could potentially induce change outside radical circles, by 'disordering' the bodies and worlds of even resistant listeners.

English travellers to North America had long represented Eastern Woodlands singing in ways that connected it to illicit forms of song familiar from their own societies, likening indigenous singers, for example, to Catholic priests, charlatans, or demoniacs. The close relationship between indicators of demonic possession and indicators of prophetic inspiration suggested the possibility that inspired singing by indigenous priests or healers was an instance of charismatic prophecy. Since English Protestant writers were largely unwilling to grant the benign or sacred nature of Eastern Woodlands song, signs of an altered state among its performers were normally attributed to diabolism, fakery, or delusion in the first half of the century. However, the resurgence of prophetic phenomena in English society at mid-century, and especially their hostile reception by Anglicans and Puritans, brought to the fore structural likenesses between the nature of the transgression attributed to the ecstatic singing of Dissenting prophets and Eastern Woodlands priests. Recognition of these structural connections occasionally surfaced in texts whose authors were critical of both Dissenting and Eastern Woodlands forms of inspiration. The Rhode Island colony's founder, Roger Williams, for example, attributed the resemblance he perceived between the Narragansetts and the colony's Quakers to their mutual diabolical inspiration, an explanation that, in the late seventeenth century, was patterned as much after controversial writings on English Dissenting prophecy as after possession discourse.

Such comparisons were never as common as others I have explored elsewhere (such as comparisons with demonic possession), but their existence confirms the transatlantic mobility of English discourses and ideologies of ecstatic song, which I consider here.[5] The inspired voice was an irresistible conundrum to seventeenth-century English on both sides of the Atlantic. Its discourse was based in native English ways of experiencing and thinking about ecstatic vocality, but I suggest that English representation of prophetic oration and song in the second half of the century was also subtly shaped by decades of colonial encounters with Algonquian and Iroquois ceremonial song. The travel literature made representations of inspired Algonquian and Iroquois singing available as a fund of negative examples for English religious polemic. However, English use of Native American ethnological examples also admitted a profound commonality between indigenous and European forms of ecstatic song, based on the possibility of their shared diabolism. Judging by their frequency of use, such comparisons were polemically effective as critique, but they inadvertently highlighted the vulnerability of the English to a resemblance with peoples whom they generally disdained after the Powhatan-English conflicts that commenced in 1622. If Quaker or Ranter prophecy seemed to embody a threatening power comparable or even identical to that perceived in Eastern Woodlands song, then English vocal behaviour needed careful monitoring for signs of an alien presence. The devil's influence was bad enough, but in the colonies perceptions of a diabolical presence manifest in English voices threatened the encroachment of savagery.

Prophetic Song in England and New England

Renowned for prophesying in spiritual songs and rhymed couplets 'from noon till night,' the Fifth Monarchist prophet Anna Trapnel is reported to have cried out before the spectators who thronged to her bedchamber: 'Thy servant is made a voice, a sound, it is a voice within a voice, another's voice, even thy voice through her.'[6] As with early modern English prophecy in general, Trapnel's prophecies are filled with imagery that identifies prophecy with the voice, particularly the ecstatic voice. 'Let true prophets,' she proclaimed, 'not go forth with the sound of their own minds, and their own carnal studies; but with the sound of thy spirit, and that is a right sound, and such will follow thee with timbrels, and with music.'[7] More potent perhaps than her imagery was the extraordinary presence of her entranced voice, singing religious and political prophecies hour after hour, before ministers, ex-members of Parliament, and members of the Council of State, the chief executive body following the execution of Charles I.[8] Trapnel was also known to vary the pitch of her voice to convey the theological significance of her words, for example, intoning references to Christ on a high pitch.[9]

A number of important studies of the Dissenting prophets have rightly emphasized the counter-hegemonic effects of their unorthodox behaviour and oration. However, most of these have overlooked the significance and efficacy of their ecstatic vocalization itself, not just their words. Struggles over religious and social issues in England commonly took the form of contested interpretations of song or other heightened vocal expression. For European listeners of this period, vocal performance communicated essential information about the identity and moral quality of performers and the social groups to which they belonged. The ecstatic humming, singing, howling, and sometimes barking or roaring of Dissenting prophets prompted shock and outrage from Anglican and Puritan quarters, because the prophets' transgression of vocal decorum symbolized and set into motion other kinds of transgressions. Critics of the prophets explained their vocal excesses variously as the product of imbalanced humours or the influence of the devil, as I discuss below; but regardless of the attributed cause, the ecstatic voice of prophecy signalled the presence of a non-rational force that had the power to alter the embodiment, and thus potentially the identity, of listeners.

Opponents of such latter-day prophets labelled them 'enthusiasts,' a term that censured those who claimed unmediated spiritual or philosophical inspiration.[10] Religious debates over enthusiasm had an ancient pedigree, but the Civil War period initiated the heyday of outraged responses to 'enthusiastical' sectarians. A relative freedom of religious expression at mid-century allowed the proliferation of radical spiritual and social movements, among them the Diggers, Seekers, Levellers, Ranters, Muggletonians, Quakers, and Fifth Monarchists.[11] Some of these, such as the Quakers, grew into religious denominations. Others were persecuted into non-existence or were absorbed by other sects. The Dissenting movements differed in many doctrinal and political particulars, but most had in common a dissatisfaction with the liturgy and ecclesiastical authority of the Church of England, and a persuasion that spiritual truth was available to the laity through direct revelation.

The latter belief, that immediate contact with the divine was available to the laity, was especially widespread and took many forms. Support for the congregational election of lay ministers was one manifestation, but a more arresting (to a modern reader) and equally characteristic feature of the radical sects was the phenomenon of lay prophecy. In its broadest sense, prophecy in the early modern period can be defined as 'any utterance produced by God through human agency,' a definition that potentially includes preaching and edifying.[12] However, the criterion for inclusion of writings surveyed here is ecstatic inspiration, with a special focus on ecstatic vocality. For the sake of convenience, and in agreement with prevailing definitions, I will refer to the ecstatic or inspired vocalization discussed here as prophecy.[13]

Prophets like Anna Trapnel manifested the divine through 'prayers and spiritual songs,' often uttered in a state of trance accompanied by prolonged fasting and other physical signs. *Cry of a Stone* states that Trapnel entered a state of trance while attending the examination of a Baptist or Fifth Monarchist preacher by the Council of State, at Whitehall:

> Waiting in a little room near the council, where was a fire, for Mr Powell's coming forth, then with a purpose to return home, she was beyond and besides her thoughts or intentions, having much trouble in her heart, and being seized upon by the Lord, she was carried forth in a spirit of prayer and singing.

While in this state, Trapnel took up residence at a tavern near Whitehall, where she continued to prophesy from her room for eleven or twelve days.[14]

At least some of those who witnessed Trapnel's prophesying possessed a nuanced awareness of different states of inspiration and sought to determine the source of the couplets that she sang for days at a time. Observers are reported to have asked Anna Trapnel of the prophecies at Whitehall, 'Was it only a spirit of faith that was upon you, or was it a Vision wrapping up your outward senses in trances, so that you had not your senses to see, nor hear, nor take notice of the People present?'[15] Although this query is rhetorically opportunistic in the context of Trapnel's autobiography, it is in keeping with the biblical injunction often repeated in the contemporary literature on Protestant prophecy, to 'try the spirits whether they are of God,' and given the intensity of the scrutiny drawn by prophetic performance, it is likely that those who witnessed Trapnel's inspired state would have asked like-minded questions.

Much of the available evidence regarding the reception of prophetic vocality was recorded by those hostile to the sects, but this writing is valuable inasmuch as it highlights the boundary-limits of English categories of song in this period. Hostile accounts of prophecy as it was practised by the Society of Friends was particularly copious, and it has been well documented by scholars.[16] Yet the prophets and their supporters had unprecedented access to the press, and they bore eloquent and copious witness to their own inspiration in the controversial pamphlet literature, as well as in their more intimate letters, journals, and exhortations. Most prophets understood inspiration as the result of an indwelling of a holy spirit, or the 'Inner Light,' as it was known among the Quakers. Physical signs of inspiration included trembling, fainting, and hearing voices or seeing visions, but spiritual manifestations also induced speaking or singing in a spiritual language, prophesying, humming, and singing spontaneous songs. The witness who recorded Anna Trapnel's prophecy at Whitehall noted, for example, that 'the effects of a spirit caught up in the visions of God did abundantly appear in the fixedness, and immovableness of her speech in prayer, but more especially in her songs.'[17] Martha Simmonds, who was briefly one of the leaders of the Quaker movement, is also said to have prophesied and sung at London meetings, in a sustained intoning that probably resembled the characteristic 'twang' of later Quaker delivery.[18] Indeed, 'singing in the Spirit' is a well-documented practice among early Friends. Thomas Holme described being moved to sing while he was imprisoned at Chester:

> A little before midnight, the power of the Lord came upon me, and sweet melody was within me. And about midnight I was compelled to sing; and the power was so great, it made all my fellow-prisoners amazed, and some were shaken, for the power was exceeding great. And I scarcely know whether I was in the body, yea or no.[19]

George Fox himself described a meeting of Friends at Munster in 1669 in which 'the power of the Lord was so great, that friends in the power and spirit of the Lord brake out into singing many together with an audible voice, making melody in their hearts.'[20]

As was the case with the other sects, Quaker attitudes toward singing in meetings were mixed. Many of the sects opposed singing psalms and other prescribed hymns or songs in services, arguing that these were mere form, without spiritual truth. George Fox explained the Quaker leadership's attitude toward psalm singing as follows:

> The singing of Psalms after their manner, we deny; for they sing David's tremblings, quakings and roarings, this they have turned into Meeter, as if we should see one of you lye roaring, crying, till your eyes should grow dim, and watering your Bed with your teares, and we should turne it into Meeter, and make a Rime of it, and take it, and goe among a company of ignorant People, and say, let us sing to the prayse and glory of God, O Lord I am not puft in minde, I have no scornful Eye, when they are puft in minds, and have scornful Eyes . . . [A]ll such practices we deny; but we will sing with the spirit, we will sing with grace, we will sing with understanding, Prayses, prayses unto the Lord God on high.[21]

An entry from 1648 in George Fox's *Journal* further articulates the difference that he perceived between the Anglican liturgy and the practice of singing in the spirit. Fox described his conviction that

> with and by this divine power and spirit of God . . . I was to bring them off from all the world's fellowships, and prayings and singings, which stood in forms without power; that their fellowships might be in the Holy Ghost, and in the eternal Spirit of God; that they might pray in the Holy Ghost, and sing in the Spirit, and with the grace, that comes by Jesus; making melody in their hearts to the Lord.[22]

Outside of communal worship, singing in the spirit became a tactic of resistance in the face of sustained harassment. Alexander Jaffray reported the astonishing effect that Friends' singing had on members of the town council at Aberdeen, where they were imprisoned:

> Though I was kept very empty a long time, yet at last the glorious power of God broke over the whole meeting, and upon me also, and ravished my heart – yea, did appear as a ray of divine glory, to the ravishing of my soul, and all the living ones in the meeting. So that some of those that were in the town-council above us confessed to some of our number with tears, that the breaking in of that power, even among them, made them say one to another, 'O, how astonishing it is, that our ministers should say, the Quakers have no psalms in their meetings; for such a heavenly sound we never heard in either old or new church.'[23]

Many Friends are also said to have preached, shouted, and sung spiritual songs in the streets. Margaret Newby, a widow from Hutton in Westmorland, recalled her own inspired singing while preaching with a female companion at Evesham:

> And I did speak amongst the people; and a Friend did hold me in her arms, the power of the Lord was so strong in me. And I cleared my conscience, and I was moved to sing. And Friends was much broken, and the heathen was much astonished. And one of them said that, if we were let alone, we would destroy the whole town.

Newby described being held in the stocks overnight by the mayor of Evesham and being whipped and sent into exile for their sung prophecy. Nevertheless, she wrote, 'we did not forebear, being both moved eternally by the Lord to sing in the stocks, each of us both legs in; and so remained till the tenth hour the next day.'[24]

Such punishment was not an uncommon response to Friends who preached and sang in the streets, denounced Anglican ministers, rejected key Anglican doctrines, and refused to observe social customs that recognized class differences. Friends' emphasis on lay inspiration as a source of spiritual truth contradicted the Protestant doctrine of the 'sufficiency of Scripture' and undermined clerical authority. Many Friends questioned conventional ideas about the Trinity and the nature of Heaven and Hell, and some claimed to be able to heal and work miracles, which went against the key anti-Catholic doctrine of the 'cessation of miracles.' Quakers resisted paying tithes, openly criticized the clergy, and called for the dissolution of the state church. Furthermore, Friends violated social and legal conventions by not doffing their hats when addressing superiors or attending services, by marrying only each other, without the spiritual and legal authority of the state church, and by refusing to take oaths.[25]

Quaker prophesying also challenged seventeenth-century norms of gendered vocal and bodily behaviour. As with other Dissenting sects, women initially outnumbered men as members of Quaker congregations, and they frequently prophesied in meetings, often in front of men.[26] Many women were also inspired to become itinerant preachers, who regularly preached, prophesied, and sang in the spirit in public places.[27] For those opposed to the sects (as well as many Dissenting men) women's preaching or prophetic oration was a clear violation of prescribed gender roles because it located verbal authority in a female body and voice.[28]

Men whose speech and song betrayed the inspiration of an unknown spiritual force were also censured in strongly misogynist terms for having 'degenerated' to the condition of women, since ecstatic expression contradicted the expectation that Englishmen's vocality should be rational, controlled, and properly authorized. The anonymous author of the broadside 'Quakers Ballad' of 1674, for example, compared the mixed-gender singing, prophesying, and preaching at Quaker meetings to the feminized vocality of a 'scold.'[29] Likewise, in an anti-Quaker tract printed four years later, an anonymous 'moderate Gentleman' complained to a male 'preaching Quaker' that the 'humming,' 'Whistling,' and 'inspir'd' preaching and prophesying heard at a Friends' meeting was comparable to the prophecies that the oracle at Delphi uttered while inspired by the god Apollo 'per pudenda,' which the author declined to translate 'for Modesty['s] sake.' Extending this vulvar imagery, the 'Gentleman' derides the male Quaker's prophecy as a kind of monstrous oral 'birth.' The Delphic oracles, he writes,

> as you are, were bodily possess'd by their spirit, disfigur'd by strange Convulsive Fits, raving and foaming, not knowing what they did, chang'd in

their Countenance, and horrid in their Aspects, when the throes of their Deity came upon them, were instantly deliver'd of the mysteries of their god, which when they were out, were usually as great mysteries, as they were before; such are all your ravings to me, and I believe to all men, that are not dazzl'd in their Understandings, and frighted from their little Witts.[30]

The comparison of Quaker men's ecstatic vocality with the vaginally inspired prophecy of the Delphic Pythia implied their own vulnerability to penetrative inspiration by a diabolical force, resulting in the false prophetic issue that the author derided.

Many of those who argued against Quaker practices did so out of a suspicion that a diabolical power was the true source of Friends' inspiration. Francis Higginson, who published one of the earliest anti-Quaker tracts, *A Brief Relation of the Irreligion of the Northern Quakers* (1653), argued that the vocal and physical manifestations of the spirit in Quaker meetings suggested satanic, not divine inspiration:

> While the agony of the fit is upon them their lips quiver, their flesh and joints tremble, their bellies swell as though blown up with wind, they foam at the mouth, and sometimes purge as if they had taken Physic. In this fit they continue sometimes an hour or two, sometimes longer, before they come to themselves again, and when it leaves them they roar out horribly with a voice greater than the voice of a man; The noise, those say that have hear it, is a very horrid fearful noise, and greater sometimes than any Bull can make.

The roaring and animal-like noises of Higginson's Quakers recalled the vocal eccentricities of the possessed. Higginson ruled out counterfeit, always a suspicion, arguing that 'it is an utter impossibility for any man, especially women, that never knew what belonged to Stage-playing, and young Children to feign such swounings, tremblings, palsie-motions, swelling, foaming, purging, such great horrid screechings, and roarings.' 'Surely,' he concluded, 'it must needs bee some black Art that works so turbulently on mens Spirits or bodies, and conjures them into such Surprizes.'[31]

If some critics of the Quaker prophets characterized their inspired vocality in terms usually reserved for demoniacs, others accused them of witchery that could cause possessed or obsessed behaviour in others. Still others resorted to medical explanations, especially melancholy, to explain the transgressive bodily deportment and vocalization that earned

Quakers such notoriety. Robert Burton was one of the first to introduce the discourse on melancholy into the religious debates with so-called enthusiasts.[32] An Anglican vicar and amateur physician, Burton grouped Catholics, Puritans, and radical Dissenters under the broad rubric of 'religious enthusiasts' and diagnosed melancholy as a secondary cause of what he believed to be their aberrant beliefs and behaviour. Burton followed ancient and contemporary precedent, however, in maintaining that the primary cause of melancholy and all other superstitious behaviour was the devil.[33] Burton's *Anatomy of Melancholy* was influential among Anglican critics of enthusiasm in the second half of the seventeenth century, and it helped to establish melancholy as a fixture of the enthusiasm debates. Despite the sustained influence of the trope of melancholy as the 'balneum diaboli,' or devil's balm, on anti-Quaker arguments, a tension soon emerged between medical and demonological accounts of enthusiasm, as the metaphysical bases for the medical understanding of melancholy began to change in the second half of the seventeenth century. Even toward the end of the century, most anti-enthusiasts still allowed for diabolism as a primary cause of enthusiasm, but by 1700 the frequency and prestige of demonological explanations for prophecy, or other 'melancholic' behaviours, had diminished.

In spite of decades of civic and ecclesiastical harassment, and accusations of heresy, gender disorder, hypersexuality, possession, and madness, inspired prophetic song remained an officially sanctioned practice among English Friends until the 1670s.[34] However, in the last decades of the century the Society of Friends itself increasingly discouraged what many Friends had come to regard as immoderate manifestations of the Spirit in song. The groaning, humming, and 'singing in the spirit' of early meetings thus gradually diminished, undoubtedly in response to the rationalist intellectual forces that also influenced their critics in the same period. The Society consolidated a centralized control over worship as it gradually became more formalized in the late seventeenth century. Predictably, controversy and even schisms arose in response, some of which centred on the question of oral manifestations of the spirit in worship. Of particular interest is the development of one or more schismatic sects known as the 'Singing Quakers,' whose existence is hinted at as early as 1655. In his treatise of that year, Francis Harris noted that the unity of the Quaker movement 'is not so great, as people imagine, For as to the shortnes of the time of their rise, and being, they have branched themselves into several sorts. As walking, singing, creeping, naked, and virgin-quakers, and in time they will break out, into as many sorts or orders as there are of Fryers.'[35] While Harris may have been exaggerating divisions within the community of English Friends for polemical effect, the Singing Quakers do appear to have gained notoriety in the late seventeenth and early eighteenth centuries, particularly in the American colonies.[36] In his *Essay for the Recording of Illustrious Providences* (1684), the Puritan Increase Mather denounced certain 'Singing Quakers' of Long Island, followers of Thomas Case who were known for their aggressive proselytizing. 'There was a young Woman,' Mather wrote, 'a Daughter of a Quaker among us, who was howled into their society . . . and quickly fell to railing on others, and then to raving.' As her fits continued, the Friends attending her heard 'a very doleful noise,' which they took to be an apparition. This sent the afflicted woman running, and they could not find her for some time. She was eventually recovered, however, and 'since, both that Woman and her Husband are railing Quakers, and do Hum and Revile as the rest of them.'[37] Mather concluded his account of the Singing Quakers pointedly, remarking that 'we may by this judge whose Servants the Singing Quakers are; and what Spirit doth powerfully breath in, and act those miserable and deluded Enthusiasts.'[38]

Other non-Quakers, aside from Puritans, objected to the practices of the Singing Quakers in New England, but some of the most powerful resistance to the Singing Quakers came from within the Society of Friends itself. Friends' objections to the Singing Quakers sometimes linked them to the anarchical English Civil War sect, the Ranters. Like the Quakers, the Ranters were accused, among other things, of inappropriate or ecstatic singing, especially as a form of protest. The Quakers were themselves often accused of being Ranters, and this connection persisted into the eighteenth century. In the 1650s groups of separatist Quakers, or Ranters, disturbed Friends' meetings in London, and in 1658 Bristol Friends experienced 'great trials' because of 'those that are called singers.'[39] From the 1670s, a group of Singing Quakers or Ranters interrupted meetings on Long Island. In a journal entry of 1675, William Edmundson denounced 'several who were gone from Truth, and turn'd Ranters,' and reported that Long Island Friends were troubled by these 'Men and Women who would come into Friends' Meetings, singing and dancing in a rude Manner, which was a great Exercise to Friends.'[40] In a letter to Thomas and Alice Curwen, the Friend Patience Story complained of the 'Ranting Spirits' who continued to disrupt meetings at Oyster Bay. 'We are, as it were, a Song among a wild Generation; and those Ranting Spirits are much as they were when ye were here; they come in the like manner Ranting, Roaring, Singing and Dancing into our Meetings.'[41] The English Friend Joan Vokins encountered Thomas Case and his followers at the Oyster Bay Half-Year's Meeting in 1681, where, she complained, 'Tho. Case, the grand Ranter, was bawling very loud.'[42] Singing Quakers also disrupted the New England Yearly Meeting in 1697 and were subsequently banned, as Dr Benjamin Bullivant remarked in a journal entry of that year. Friends came from two or three hundred miles to attend the yearly meeting at Newport, only to find their meetings disturbed by

> an ancient sort of Quakers called singing quakers, whome they keep out of theyr meeteing house, for by the sudden raptures of singing they fall into, & by theyr contradictive humor they give publique disturbance to ye Speaker & howbeit they are kept out of the house by persons who sitt at the door for that purpose, yet they faile not to crowd to the doore & under the windows, & ever now & then with an elevated Voice contradict the speaker, who notwithstanding holds on his discourse without replyeing . . . Indeed the quakers themselves did accknowledge to me, those singing quakers were of an older standing amongst them, but had fallen into Licentious practices which being against truth, they found in themselves a witnesse against them.[43]

Ecstatic singing had clearly fallen out of favour with the more moderate Society of Friends by the end of the century. Adherents to an older style of worship (and, perhaps, an older metaphysics) found themselves increasingly marginalized by the movement that had once nurtured them.

Prophecy at the Frontier

One of the most outspoken critics of Quakerism in late-seventeenth-century New England was Roger Williams, the founder of the Rhode Island colony who was himself a radical separatist. Williams initiated a public dispute with the Quakers in the summer of 1672, the same year that George Fox travelled to New England. He published his version of the debate as his last printed work, *George Fox Digg'd out of His Burrowes* (1676), and this received a reply in kind from George Fox, in *A New-England Fire-Brand Quenched* (1678). Williams's critique of Fox's theology employed arguments that, by the 1670s, had become fixtures of the anti-Quaker literature. Quakerism, for Williams, was comparable to Judaism, Islam, and Catholicism as an error among peoples who had received the law.[44] He accused the Quakers of being possessed by the devil and denounced their prophecies as 'the Spirit Breath or wind of the Devil.'[45] Williams also condemned 'their own un-Christian, Fantastical, absurd, and unprofitable way of Toning and Singing,' asking,

> What is their monstrous way of Singing and Toning and Humming many at once, as they often do and notoriously did at Portsmouth on Rhode Island this last year, when no man is edified, nor understands what they say, and it may be not themselves (and this under colour of singing in the Spirit) [,] what is it I say but rendring their Tongues which should be their Glory and the Glory of God, their scorn and Shame, and the holy Name of Gods holy Spirit contemptible also.[46]

In this last comment Williams drew on twenty years of hostile accounts of Quaker singing. It is not without irony that in so doing he echoed Friends' own denunciations of the Ranters and Singing Quakers from the same period.

Williams's critique departs in one significant way from previous attacks on the Quakers by explicitly comparing their customs and beliefs to those of Eastern Woodlands peoples. Williams's most significant work is his *Key into the Language of America* (1643), a description of the Narragansett language and way of life. In general, Williams regarded Native Americans as inhabiting a state of uncivilized barbarity, which was revealed in their nakedness and purported lack of religion. It is in this context that Williams compared George Fox's theology with that of 'these poor Natives of America,' and found it wanting.[47] Williams also compared the Quakers' refusal to observe customary greetings with the Indians' disregard for English behavioural norms.[48] And the Friends' reputed nakedness marked them, like the Indians, as irreligious brutes, for as Williams wrote of the Narragansetts, 'it is commonly known that as their garments hang loose about their Bodyes, so hangs their Religion about their Souls.'[49]

Despite his obvious contempt for Quaker and Narragansett worship and the ease with which he drew comparisons between the two groups, Williams never explicitly compared Friends' singing and humming with Narragansett ritual song. The closest he came to doing so was in *A Key into the Language of America*, where he described a healing ceremony in terms that recall hostile descriptions of Quaker meetings, not to mention earlier English accounts of Native American ceremonies. Of the Narragansett 'Powwaws,' he wrote,

> these Priests and Conjurers (like Simon Magus) doe bewitch the people, and not onely take their Money, but doe most certainly (by the help of the Divell) worke greate Cure . . . [Yet] the poore people commonly dye under their hands, for alas, they administer nothing but howle and roare, and hollow over them, and begin the song to the rest of the People about them, who all joyne (like a Quire) in Prayer to their Gods for them.[50]

Suggestive as they are, Williams's writings yield no explicit juxtaposition between Narragansett and Quaker ecstatic song. Such a juxtaposition would in any event have been uncharacteristic of the anti-Quaker literature: although writers describing Quaker and Native American ecstatic song borrowed from a common fund of images and ideas, most critics of Quakerism did not explicitly compare the two groups.

We find more explicit connections between Eastern Woodlands and English ecstatic song in the writings of a redeemed captive of the Narragansetts, Mary Rowlandson. In her captivity account, *The Sovereignty and Goodness of God,* Rowlandson described the Narragansetts, Nipmucs, and Wampanoags who attacked the town of Lancaster in February 1675, as 'a company of hell-hounds, roaring, singing, ranting and insulting, as if they would have torn our very hearts out.'[51] Although it had a broad range of meanings by 1682, in this context the word 'ranting' still recalled the ungoverned, irrational preaching practised by the Ranters at mid-century, and more recently in New England. Another such connection appears in an earlier anti-Quaker tract by the minister Jonathan Clapham, *A Full Discovery and Confutation of the Wicked and Damnable Doctrines of the Quakers* (1656). In a chapter on the miracles of Quaker prophets and preachers, Clapham devoted a paragraph to a 'pretended miracle at Norwich,' where a weaver was cured through a judicious use of cold water. The paragraph that follows concerns 'their quaking trances, visions, rapture, and Revelations.' In the margin beside this latter paragraph, Clapham remarked that 'the Pawwaw do greater cures then this upon the poor Indians, to confirm them in their worshipping of devils.'[52]

Published at mid-century, Clapham's marginal remark signals the extent to which the complex of ideas about Native American ecstatic singing, originally developed in the travel literature, had infiltrated English ideologies of religious and civil decorum. Clapham's text drew the Narragansett *powwaw*'s sung cures into an English Protestant discourse on ecstatic prophecy that, in 1656, was in the midst of an intense period of development. The absorption of Native American ceremonial song into this discourse lent polemical weight to Clapham's critique of Quaker prophecy, yet Clapham's gesture toward the colonies altered English controversial discourse on ecstasy in turn, by showing the relevance of colonial ideologies of song for domestic relations of difference. The supplemental presence of the ecstatic Indian voice in the margins of Clapham's anti-Quaker tract hints at the transatlantic mobility of European discourse that sought to determine the spiritual source and meanings of ecstasy.

The metaphysics and politics of the inspired voice were a central concern of English discourse on charismatic religiosity, whether it was Algonquian or English Dissenting inspired song that was at issue. Seventeenth-century European practitioners and critics of prophetic song lived in a world in which stories of inspired howling, wailing, humming, and singing circulated as signs of a powerful presence whose nature and agency were disputed, but whose existence itself was not normally questioned. Seventeenth-century Algonquian communities also valued 'visions, voices, and dreams,' as gifts from the spirit world, and songs performed in sacred ceremonial contexts were assumed to convey and execute spiritual power, as this was variously conceived by the nations whom the English encountered. Ecstatic or entranced song had different metaphysical foundations for seventeenth-century Eastern Woodlands and English peoples, but the English shared with their Algonquian contemporaries certain basic assumptions about the existence of non-human powers and the susceptibility of song to their influence. Rightly or wrongly, the English often recognized such power at work in indigenous song and were pressed to account for it in their own terms. I suspect that the hostility evident in most English accounts of Eastern Woodlands song is at least partly attributable to the challenge that its singularity presented to a Protestant metaphysics. Though the English characteristically subjected indigenous song to analysis that reconciled it to familiar metaphysical and moral categories, the persistence of such attempts in English travel writing suggests that they were not wholly successful. Like the cries of demoniacs or the prophetic song of Dissenting radicals, the ecstatic singing heard in many Algonquian rituals could convey a profoundly threatening surplus of vocal presence to English listeners.

The threat that English travellers and colonists heard in Algonquian singing was also rooted in the political problem of redefining English identity in an Eastern Woodlands context. Altered-state vocality presented this problem in microcosm. Spiritual inspiration and possession multiplied the being of an embodied self in ways that challenged the developing seventeenth-century ideal of a rational, unitary subject.[53]

Contemporary accounts describing two different voices issuing from the bodies of demoniacs illustrate this plurality, as does Anna Trapnel's self-described prophetic 'voice within a voice,' as cited above. However, the problem of a non-unitary identity had obsessed English travellers and migrants to North America from the first, and these larger political concerns also informed English writing on ecstatic vocality in the colonies. Widespread fear that the pale-skinned English would become 'tawny' from the effects of the American climate, or that proximity to Eastern Woodlands cultures and religions would alter English culture and religion haunted explorers and colonists throughout the seventeenth century, well before racial theories of European and Native American difference gained currency. 'We have [become] shamefully Indianized,' warned Cotton Mather in 1692, perceiving a dangerous prevalence of such supposedly 'Indian vices' as lying, laziness, indulgence of children, and a failure of patriarchal family governance.[54]

English fears of cultural hybridization or identity loss only intensified in response to the increasingly hostile relations between Algonquian communities and English colonists in the second half of the century. Strikingly, as the physical and cultural threat posed by surrounding indigenous peoples escalated with Metacom's (or King Philip's) War (1675–8) and King William's War (1688–99), colonists began to be obsessed or possessed by spirits who resembled Indians. Mercy Short, a redeemed captive from the Wabenaki raids of 1690, testified that the devil who obsessed and tormented her was 'of a Tawney, or an Indian colour,' and that he presided over 'Witch-meetings' of 'French Canadiens and Indian Sagamores' who sang chants from the Catholic office in their 'Idolatrous Devotions.'[55] And Mary Allen Toothmaker, who was tried for witchcraft at Salem, confessed that the devil had appeared to her 'in the shape of a Tawny man,' promising to protect her from the Wabenakis if she signed a pact on 'a piece of burch bark.'[56] English colonists captured in the conflicts of the late seventeenth century and later redeemed were also sometimes suspected of having been overly influenced by their contact with Algonquian society. They thus embodied the colonists' most profound anxiety concerning the blurring of boundaries between 'English' and 'Indian' identities. The suspicion focused on redeemed captives was encouraged by the captives' own narratives describing their daily life in Algonquian villages, which sometimes included their performance of Algonquian-style singing in ceremonial contexts. John Gyles, for example, described having been tortured and made to sing during his captivity among Cape Sable Mi'kmaqs in present-day Nova Scotia, in the autumn of 1689. Gyles and his fellow captives were apparently tortured in commemoration of the loss of Mi'kmaq people in the wars with the English. Gyles remarked that his captors thrust a tomahawk in his hand 'and order'd me get up and dance and sing Indian: which I perform'd with the greatest reluctance.' It is striking that, in an account of his own physical torment, what Gyles focused on was having been made to 'sing Indian,' which suggests an anxiety around the possibility of his assimilating into Mi'kmaq society of his own volition. To the Cape Sable Mi'kmaqs, however, Gyles's singing failed to seem 'Indian' enough. On the contrary, it reminded them of his Englishness, recalling to them the loved ones whom they had lost to war: 'Then those Cape Sable Indians came to me again like Bears bereaved of their Whelps, saying, Shall we who have lost Relations by the English, suffer an English Voice to be heard among us etc. Then they beat me again with the Axe.'[57]

From the perspective of the New English colonists, who persistently connected events in the sensible and supersensible worlds, the assaults on their physical and spiritual well-being by the devil and by neighbouring Algonquins were interconnected.[58] Mercy Short's captivity and her later obsession by the 'tawny' devil marked her body as a liminal site where two interrelated struggles played out: the conflict between the English and the Wabenakis, and the cosmic conflict between the Puritans' god and Algonquian *manitous,* non-human persons that the colonists misidentified as the Christian devil. Cotton Mather, who served as Short's interlocutor in the midst of her obsession, reported that in response to the devilish 'spectres' who 'howled' continually in her ears, 'Shee Shriek'd, shee Roar'd, shee Cry'd out, "This is worse than all the Rest! What? must I bee Banished from the Favour of God after all?"'[59] Her obsession compromised the bodily decorum expected of an English maidservant, drawing her perilously close to the ecstatic vocality of the century's shamans, demoniacs, and prophets. Worse, the devil's presence threatened to separate her from the 'Favour' of God, the very core of a Puritan's identity. If English Puritans were as susceptible as Wampanoags, Narragansetts, or Powhatans to the diabolical unreason of vocal ecstasy, what basis remained for differentiating them, especially in the colonies?

Ecstatic vocality was an important frontier in the struggle to define English and New English identities in the seventeenth century. Despite their many differences, the inspired singing of dissenting prophets and Algonquian priests mutually challenged England's self-identification as a rational, masculine, Protestant nation. For those hostile to the Dissenting sects, the other-worldly voices of 'enthusiastical' prophets presented the spectacle of a body – and, by extension, a body politic – split from itself, given over to the governance of a force other than reason. It is telling that Dissenting prophecy originated in a period of revolution when the Stuart monarchical order was already 'turned upside down,' in the words of historian Christopher Hill.[60] At a moment when the integrity of the English nation was threatened as never before, the inspired voices of radical prophets were perceived by many as a sign of the nation's monstrous disunity. Likewise, indigenous song in ceremonial contexts threatened to compromise the Englishness of the colonies, by splitting the colonists from their own English reason. Edward Winslow noted in the early years of the Plymouth Colony that a healing ceremony performed for the ailing Wampanoag *sachem* Massasoit upset the humoral balance of the English who were present: 'There were they in the midst of their charms for him, making such a hellish noise, as it distempered us that were well, and therefore unlike to ease him that was sick.'[61] The extremes of the New England climate, the colonists' proximity to non-Protestant cultures, and the powers of Algonquian priests and healers themselves conspired to alienate the colonists from their Englishness, creating the doubled colonial identity that the English feared. Algonquian priests' ecstatic prayers and sung cures were audible reminders that travellers and colonists were strangers in a land that remained largely un-Christianized and resolutely un-English.

For most English colonial observers, inspired song in Eastern Woodlands communities embodied an ungoverned force that some found comparable to the unruly prophesying of Protestant Dissenters. Such vocalization was suspected of having a diabolical cause, and for some New Englanders its performance gave audible form to the hostile forces occupying the boundaries of the colony, even the colony itself. It is perhaps significant that structural parallels between Dissenting and indigenous vocality seemed most compelling in the later decades of the seventeenth century: a period when political relations between New Englanders and neighbouring Algonquians grew more openly antagonistic, and when increasing numbers of non-Puritan Dissenters, especially Quakers, arrived in the colonies. In this environment the profound violation that many colonists heard in Native and Dissenting song alike came to emblematize the threat that their presence posed to the coherence and stability of New English society.

Gerard Croese's late critique of Quaker ecstatic worship, published in 1696, lacks the animal skins, rattles, and body paint of the priests in the account by John Smith quoted at the beginning of this chapter, but his terms are remarkably similar. 'When they are about contemplating Sacred things,' he wrote, 'that same very moment that the Spirit overtakes 'em, through the commotion of their Minds, and agitation of their Bodies, they presently fall a trembling, throwing themselves on the ground, oft-times froathing at the mouth, and scrieching with a horrible noise.'[62] In Croese's Quakers we hear, to be sure, the echo of European demoniacs and madmen, but the colonies' Algonquian singers are distantly audible as well.

NOTES

1 Philip L. Barbour, ed., *The Complete Works of Captain John Smith (1580–1631)*, 3 vols. (Chapel Hill: University of North Carolina Press, 1986), 2: 149–50. The Latin version of the episode in the 1634 volume concurs with the 1624 version cited here.

2 Following his capture Smith was granted an audience with the Powhatan war chief, Opechancanough, who took him to a succession of villages where he was the subject of several ceremonies, including this one, performed for three days at Pamunkey. Drawing analogies with the Lenape (Delaware) Big House (or *gamwing*) ceremony, Gleach argues that the ritual actions Smith described involved creating a mimetic 'map' or diagram of Tsenacommacah (Powhatan country), whose ritual use could effect change in the universe. In his reading, the circles of cornmeal represented the Powhatan homeland, the kernels of corn represented non-Powhatan, 'real' people and the boundaries of Powhatan lands, and the sticks placed between the circles represented the English. Frederic W. Gleach, *Powhatan's World and Colonial Virginia: A Conflict of Cultures* (Lincoln: University of Nebraska Press, 1997), 106–22.

3 Barbour, ed., *The Complete Works*, 2: 150

4 Harry Mount, 'Egbert van Heemskerck's *Quaker Meetings* Revisited,' *Journal of the Warburg and Courtauld Institutes* 56 (1993): 209–28.

5 See Olivia A. Bloechl, *Native American Song at the Frontiers of Early Modern Music* (Cambridge: Cambridge University Press, 2008).

6 Anna Trapnel, *The Cry of a Stone . . . Uttered in Prayers and Spiritual Songs, by an Inspiration Extraordinary, and Full of Wonder* (1654), ed. Hilary Hinds, Medieval and Renaissance Texts and Studies 220 (Tempe: Arizona Center for Medieval and Renaissance Studies, 2000), 4, 45.

7 Ibid., 48.

8 Ibid., Introduction.

9 Christine Trevett, *Quaker Women Prophets in England and Wales 1650–1700*, Studies in Women and Religion 41 (Lewiston, NY: Edwin Mellen Press, 2000), 40.

10 Major studies of early modern enthusiasm include Michael Heyd, '*Be Sober and Reasonable': The Critique of Enthusiasm in the Seventeenth and Early Eighteenth Centuries* (New York: E.J. Brill, 1995); Lawrence E. Klein and Anthony J. La Vopa, eds., *Enthusiasm and Enlightenment in Europe, 1650–1850* (San Marino, CA: Huntington Library, 1998); Ronald A. Knox, *Enthusiasm: A Chapter in the History of Religion with Special Reference to the XVII and XVIII Centuries* (New York: Oxford University Press, 1950); David S. Lovejoy, *Religious Enthusiasm in the New World: Heresy to Revolution* (Cambridge, MA: Harvard University Press, 1985); and Geoffrey Nuttall, *Studies in Christian Enthusiasm: Illustrated from Early Quakerism* (Wallingford, PA: Pendle Hill Publications, 1948).

11 General studies of mid-century radicalism include Frances D. Dow, *Radicalism in the English Revolution, 1640–1660* (Oxford: Basil Blackwell, 1985); Christopher Hill, *The World Turned Upside Down: Radical Ideas during the English Revolution* (New York: Viking Press, 1972); J.F. McGregor and Barry Reay, eds., *Radical Religion in the English Revolution* (New York: Oxford University Press, 1984); and Michael R. Watts, *The Dissenters: From the Reformation to the French Revolution* (Oxford: Clarendon Press, 1978).

12 Diane Purkiss, 'Producing the Voice, Consuming the Body: Women Prophets of the Seventeenth Century,' in *Women, Writing, History 1640–1740*, ed. Isobel Grundy and Susan Wiseman (London: Batsford, 1992), 139.

13 See Patricia Crawford, *Women and Religion in England 1500–1720* (London and New York: Routledge, 1993), 106; Trapnel, *Cry of a Stone*, xiii–xiv; Trevett, *Quaker Women Prophets*, 36; and Diane Watt, *Secretaries of God: Women Prophets in Late Medieval and Early Modern England* (Cambridge: D.S. Brewer, 1997), 3.

14 Trapnel, *Cry of a Stone*, 4; also xvii, 82–4n6.

15 Ibid., 16.

16 Anti-Quaker literature is catalogued in Joseph Smith, ed., *Bibliotheca Anti-Quakeriana* (London: Smith, 1873). Smith's catalogue is incomplete, but it remains valuable. Rosemary Moore has a taxonomy of anti-Quaker writings in *The Light in Their Consciences: Early Quakers in Britain, 1646–1666* (University Park: Pennsylvania State University Press, 2000), 88–97, 233.

17 Trapnel, *Cry of a Stone*, 16.

18 Friends' House Library, London, Caton MSS, vol. 3, 364–5. Cited in Crawford, *Women and Religion*, 174. On the Quaker 'twang,' see Kenneth L.

Carroll, 'Singing in the Spirit in Early Quakerism,' *Quaker History* 73, no. 1 (1984): 10–13.

19 Letter from Thomas Holme to Margaret Fell, 5 February 1654, Swarthmore MSS, 1.190. Cited in Nuttall, *Studies in Christian Enthusiasm*, 55–6.

20 George Fox, 'G.F. his travels into Ireland, in and out of Ireland, as followeth' (1669), Appendix I in George Fox, *The Journal*, ed. Nigel Smith (London: Penguin, 1998), 447–8.

21 George Fox and James Nayler, *Severall Papers: Some of Them Given Forth by George Fox, Others by James Nayler*, ed. A.P. ([London]: n.p., 1653), 5.

22 Fox, *The Journal*, ed. Smith, 35.

23 Alexander Jaffray, *Diary of Alexander Jaffray . . . with Memoirs of the Rise, Progress, and Persecution, of the People Called Quakers, in the North of Scotland*, ed. Robert Barclay (London: Harvey and Dalton, 1833), 513.

24 Letter from Margaret Newby, November 1655, Swarthmore MSS 1.359. Cited in Nuttall, *Studies in Christian Enthusiasm*, 56–7.

25 General studies of early Quakerism include T. Adrian Davies, *The Quakers in English Society, 1655–1725* (Oxford and New York: Clarendon Press, 2000); Phyllis Mack, *Visionary Women: Ecstatic Prophecy in Seventeenth-Century England* (Berkeley and Los Angeles: University of California Press, 1992); Moore, *The Light in Their Consciences*; Barry Reay, *The Quakers and the English Revolution* (New York: St Martin's Press, 1985); and Trevett, *Quaker Women Prophets.*

26 Crawford, *Women and Religion*, 189.

27 Studies of female Quaker prophets include Mack, *Visionary Women*; Trevett, *Quaker Women Prophets*; Christine Trevett, *Women and Quakerism in the Seventeenth Century* (York, UK: Sessions Book Trust, Ebor Press, 1991); and Watt, *Secretaries of God.*

28 Nearly two decades after the origins of the movement, Quaker leader Margaret Fell was compelled to argue in favour of women's public religious speech, in *Womens Speaking Justified, Proved, and Allowed of by the Scriptures* (London: s.n., 1666).

29 *The Quakers Ballad* (London: Printed for James Nayler [misattributed], 1674).

30 *Quakers, Mere Obbists: or a Letter to a Preaching Quaker, from a Moderate Gentleman* (London: Printed for the Author, 1678).

31 Francis Higginson, *A Brief Relation of the Irreligion of the Northern Quakers* (London: Printed by T.R., 1653), 15, 16.

32 Heyd, '*Be Sober and Reasonable,*' 64–71.

33 Robert Burton, *The Anatomy of Melancholy*, 6 vols., ed. Thomas C. Faulkner, Nicolas K. Kiessling, and Rhonda L. Blair (Oxford: Clarendon Press, 1989–2000), 1: 428.

34 Moore, *The Light in Their Consciences*, 152–3.

35 Harris, *Some Queries Proposed to the Consideration of the Grand Proposers of Queries the Quakers* (London: Printed for Henry Fletcher, 1655), 28.

36 On Quakers in the English colonies, see Lovejoy, *Religious Enthusiasm*, and Arthur J. Worrall, *Quakers in the Colonial Northeast* (Hanover, NH, and London: University Press of New England, 1980). On the Singing Quakers, in particular, see Carroll, 'Singing in the Spirit,' 11–13; Lovejoy, *Religious Enthusiasm*, 140–3; Richard Cullen Rath, *How Early America Sounded* (Ithaca, NY: Cornell University Press, 2003), 127–44; and Worrall, *Quakers in the Colonial Northeast*, 65–6.

37 Increase Mather, An Essay for the Recording of *Illustrious Providences* (Boston: Samuel Green for Joseph Browning, 1684), 344–5.

38 Ibid., 356.

39 Carroll, 'Singing in the Spirit,' 9.

40 William Edmundson, *A Journal of the Life, Travels, Sufferings, and Labour of Love in the Work of the Ministry of William Edmundson* (Dublin: Printed by Samuel Fairbrother, 1715), 105.

41 Letter from Patience Story to Thomas and Alice Curwen, 10 August 1675, in Anne Martindell, *A Relation of the Labour, Travail and Suffering of That Faithful Servant of the Lord Alice Curwen* ([London]: s.n, 1680), 40. Lovejoy misattributes this observation to Alice Curwen.

42 Joan Vokins, *God's Mighty Power Magnified* (London: Printed for Thomas Northcott, 1691), 35. See Worrall, *Quakers in the Colonial Northeast*, 66

43 Benjamin Bullivant, 'A Journall with Observations on My Travail from Boston in N.E. to N.Y. New-Jersies & Philadelphia in Pensilvania (1697),' in Wayne Andrews, 'A Glance at New York in 1697: The Travel Diary of Dr. Benjamin Bullivant,' *The New York Historical Society Quarterly* 40 (1956): 59.

44 See Roger Williams, *George Fox Digg'd out of His Burrowes* (1676), in *The Complete Writings of Roger Williams*, ed. J. Lewis Diman (New York: Russell and Russell, 1963), 5: 258–9.

45 Ibid., 5: 29, 45, 144.

46 Ibid., 5: 212, 5: 134–5.

47 Ibid., 224.

48 Ibid., 211, 309.

49 Ibid., 258; also 28, 62, 241–2, and 310.

50 Roger Williams, *A Key into the Language of America* (1643), ed. Howard M. Chapin, 5th ed. (Rhode Island and Providence Plantations Tercentenary Committee, 1936), 198.

51 Mary Rowlandson, *The Sovereignty and Goodness of God*, 2nd ed. (Cambridge: Printed by Samuel Green, 1682), 5.

52 Jonathan Clapham, *A Full Discovery and Confutation of the Wicked and Damnable Doctrines of the Quakers* (London: Printed by T.R. and E.M., 1656), 46.

53 See Judith Becker, 'Listening Selves and Spirit Possession,' *World of Music* 42, no. 2 (2000): 25–50; and Mary Keller, *The Hammer and the Flute: Women, Power, and Spirit Possession* (Baltimore, MD: Johns Hopkins University Press, 2002).

54 Quoted in Ronald Takaki, 'The *Tempest* in the Wilderness: The Racialization of Savagery,' *Journal of American History* 79, no. 3, *Discovering America: A Special Issue* (1992): 909–10.

55 Cotton Mather, 'A Brand Pluck'd out of the Burning,' in *Narratives of the Witchcraft Cases, 1648–1706*, ed. George Lincoln Burr (New York: Scribner and Sons, 1914), 261, 281–3. Many of the Wabenakis were Catholic converts or were allied with the French.

56 Cited in Mary Beth Norton, *In the Devil's Snare: The Salem Witchcraft Crisis of 1692* (New York: Alfred A. Knopf, 2002), 239–40.

57 John Gyles, *Memoirs of Odd Adventures, Strange Deliverances, etc. in the Captivity of John Gyles* (Boston: Printed by S. Kneeland and T. Green, 1736), 12–13.

58 Norton, *In the Devil's Snare.*

59 Mather, *A Brand Pluck'd out of the Burning*, 277.

60 Hill, *The World Turned Upside Down.*

61 Edward Winslow, 'Good News from New England' (1624), in *Chronicles of the Pilgrim Fathers*, ed. John Masefield (New York: E.P. Dutton, 1910), 307–8.

62 Gerard Croese, *The General History of the Quakers* (London: Printed for John Dunton, 1696), 5.

PART III

THE POLITICS OF OPERA

chapter seven

Daphne's Dilemma: Desire as Metamorphosis in Early Modern Opera

WENDY HELLER

In his marvellously erotic novel *Leucippe and Cleitophon,* the Greek novelist Achilles Tatius offered a highly eroticized retelling of the invention of Pan's pipes. He describes the goat-god's fruitless pursuit of the lovely Syrinx – a chase 'inspired by love.' Just at the moment in which he, 'close on her heels,' is about to grasp the nymph by the hair, Pan realizes that he holds only a clump of reeds. 'In a passion,' Achilles Tatius writes, Pan 'cuts away the reeds, thinking that they were hiding his beloved from him.' After searching for her in vain, and realizing that she had actually been transformed into the reeds, he fears that he might have been responsible for cutting the very object of his desire. But what is most interesting here is the way in which the nymph's transformation initiates yet another metamorphosis – that of Pan's groans and kisses into music:

> So he collected the fragments of reed as though they had been the maiden's limbs and put them together as though to form a single body: and then, holding the pieces in his hands, kissed them, as though they had been her wounds. As he put his lips to them he groaned from love, and breathed down upon the reeds while he kissed them; and his breath, pouring down through the holes in them, gave musical notes, and the pan-pipes found its voice. (Achilles Tatius, 8.6.7–11)[1]

In this etiological meditation on the nature of music, desire, frustration, and the death of the nymph lead to the invention of sound and the birth of an artist whose music would provide the sonic dimension for the Arcadian imagination.

This provocative tale of music and metamorphosis is best known from Ovid's *Metamorphoses* (1.689–712), where it appears embedded, almost like a brief and whimsical echo, in the story of Apollo and Daphne *(Met.* 1.452–567).[2] It follows a narrative pattern similar to many of the tales in that poem: a young nymph, sworn to chastity in the service of the goddess Diana, is pursued by a god such as Apollo or demi-god like Pan. She attempts to deny her favours to the pursuer – sometimes successfully, sometimes not – and is transformed from something human into something less than human, losing not only her female body but also her powers of speech in the process. Sometimes the metamorphosis allows the nymph to preserve her chastity. This is the fate shared by numerous Ovidian heroines: Daphne, pursued by Apollo, is transformed into the tree; Lotis, chased by Priapus, becomes the bush that bears her name (*Met.* 9.345–9); Arethusa, desired by the river-god Alpheus, assumes the form of a sacred-forest spring (*Met.* 5.572–641). In other instances, the metamorphoses are the aftermath of rape or vigorous seduction. The nymph Calisto (*Met.* 2.466–95), for example, is turned into a bear by a vengeful Juno, while Jove (*Met.* 1.610–21) transforms his lover Io into a remarkably fetching cow. In another and similar tale, Apollo's desire for the nymph Leucothoe (*Met.* 4.190–273) and disdain for Clytië initiates a veritable chain of metamorphoses. Apollo rapes (or possibly seduces?) Leucothoe after having assumed the guise of her mother.[3] When a jealous Clytië informs Leucothoe's father of her daughter's loss of chastity, the father has his daughter buried alive. Apollo then sprinkles nectar on her grave while expressing his grief, transforming her into an aromatic frankincense bush (*Met.* 4.249–55); Clytië, wasting away from unrequited love, turns into a sunflower (*Met.* 4.256–70). In all of these cases, Ovid contrives for the human consciousness to continue operating, even as the physical body is no longer capable of forming words, creating in this intermediary moment a kind of grotesquerie.[4]

I have recounted all of these tales of women's metamorphoses at length to illustrate not only the common elements in this narrative pattern but to demonstrate as well the potency that it achieves through repetition and variation. The notion of metamorphosis, which becomes less and less improbable with each iteration, is further reinforced by the ironic tone of the narrator and the skill with which he deftly controls the reader's gaze. At the same time, the stories recounted in the *Metamorphoses* are also about origins – of the plants, flowers, trees, and stars.[5] Thus, each of the mythic creatures whose physical forms are altered over the course of the poem becomes a new entity, while at the same time retaining some element of its original form: the hardness of Daphne's heart is preserved in the laurel tree; Leucothoe's sweet aroma wafts from the frankincense bush; Hyacinth's beauty is retained in the flower for which he is named; and the cool spring evokes Arethusa's purity. Sometimes the transformation is merely a metaphor taken a bit too far – Ovid's purpose, as Leonard Barkan so elegantly describes, is 'to make flesh of metaphors,' and he notes the 'variety of logical, pseudo-logical, or illogical connections that might be made between the original and the transformed object.'[6] Yet embedded within many of these etiological meditations is a predominant precipitating factor: desire. It is physical desire that triggers a chain of events that leads first to a transformation and second to a loss of humanity, until the relationship between the subject and newly formed object of desire must ultimately be reconfigured.

This is precisely what happens in the tale of Pan and Syrinx. In Ovid's version, Pan, after his initial disappointment, becomes in fact quite delighted with his new musical toy. He is, as Ovid explains, 'touched by this wonder and charmed by the sweet tones,' and he exclaims: 'This union, at least, shall I have with thee' (*Met.* 1.710). But in the lengthy, more theatrical version told by Achilles Tatius with which this essay began, the emphasis is on the inherent eroticism of the actual metamorphosis and its aftermath. Pan does not merely blow upon the reeds. He tries to reverse the process that his uncontrolled desire initiated: he reassembles the reeds into human form, as if they were Syrinx's legs, and then kisses what remains of her body. It is this erotic act – Pan's breath flowing through the reeds – that creates sound. Desire, frustration, and the death of the nymph lead to the invention of music and the birth of an artist. It is certainly true that the reader might share in Pan's delight with the discovery of his pipes. Music – like the plants, stars, and trees – is, after all, one of the greatest of all creations. Nevertheless, there is still something unsettling, even disturbing, about this narrative, since it self-consciously resists the happy ending and conventional union of lovers that is part and parcel of comedy. Syrinx, like her sister Daphne, is all but erased from the story, becoming merely an extension of Pan's artistic will. At the end we are left only with the lone beast, a curious meshing of artistry and autoeroticism, and the suspicion that the living Syrinx has been discarded: she has outlived her usefulness for Pan, except as the source of his musical inspiration.

This essay is concerned with some of the ways in which these Ovidian narratives served a special role in the expression of gender ideologies on the operatic stage, a space in which transformations of all sorts comprised a very peculiar 'structure of feelings' in early modern Venice. I am particularly interested in the gendered implications of these metamorphoses as musical theatre: how composers, librettists, and producers staged not only the transformations themselves but also the aftermaths; how these 'fleshy metaphors' – to paraphrase Barkan – were expressed in sight and sound, particularly in those instances in which the newly formed entities lost the power of speech, which – in an operatic context – results in a silencing of a (usually female) protagonist. In so doing, these operatic transformations eloquently convey notions about sexuality and the body that would otherwise be difficult or impossible to express without music. I focus on the operatic treatment of Pan's counterpart and sometimes competitor in love, music, and loss: the sun god Apollo. After briefly considering Apollo's representation in what is often regarded as the first opera libretto, Rinuccini's *La Dafne* (from which Marco da Gagliano's 1608 setting survives in its entirely), I turn to two operas produced in mid-seventeenth-century Venice: *Gli amori di Apollo e di Dafne* (1640), with music by Francesco Cavalli and libretto by Busenello, and *Gli amori di Apollo e di Leucotoe* (1663), with music by Giovanni Battista Volpe (known as Rovettino) and libretto by Aurelio Aureli.[7]

By considering mid-Seicento operas, I look well beyond the conventional view in opera historiography that Ovid's primary significance for seventeenth-century opera is limited to the self-conscious humanistic leanings of the earliest practitioners, who were drawn to musically inclined mythological characters as a means of justifying sung drama.[8] Indeed, tales based loosely on the *Metamorphoses* – in particular those involving musicians such as Apollo and Daphne or Orpheus and Euridice – were readily annexed by pastoral drama as part of the impetus to turn spoken drama into sung entertainment, ostensibly in imitation of Greek drama.[9] A languishing shepherd or hard-hearted nymph may well be inspired to burst into song occasionally, but, as Nino Pirrotta and others have argued, it is an Orpheus or Apollo who had access to the music of the spheres and could more plausibly sing rather than speak.[10]

But while this explanation may help us to understand the aesthetics and mechanisms of early opera, as well as the relationship between set pieces (aria) and enhanced speech *(recitar cantando)*, it scarcely takes full account of the evocative value of Ovidian myths for Renaissance readers and viewers, their malleability within any number of cultural contexts, and the sheer delight that sixteenth- and seventeenth-century artists, sculptors, and poets took in a playful brand of eclecticism. Mid-seventeenth-century Italian opera, particularly the Venetian model – with its often self-conscious rejection of Aristotelian unities and its embrace of contrast, variety, and complexity of plot – represents a quite special and arguably different moment in the humanist project. These operas and the brand of humanism that they absorb, I propose, might be best understood beyond their narrow constraints of opera historiography: they are evidence of a prevailing desire to gaze upon the images of the ancients and attach onto them narratives that collapsed the past with the present; they are also part of an impulse – even a compulsion – to submerge completely into a reinvented ancient world saturated with both vibrant visual images as well as movement and sound.

Moreover, the whole notion of metamorphosis might be linked to Seicento opera in a fundamental way, presenting librettists and composers with attractive opportunities to indulge in special musical and dramatic effects. They therefore not only placed these shape-shifting figures on the stage early on in the history of opera – Apollo, Daphne, Pan, Leucothoe, Clytië, Arethusa, Jupiter, Callisto, and Echo to name but a few – but also took special delight in dramatizing the sorts of deceptions and disguises that were part of Carnival's expressive vocabulary as well as exploiting the resulting emotional shifts that the transformations necessarily engendered. In addition to turning women into plants, stars, rivers, or musical instruments, opera – even when shunning the world of myth – transformed actors into singers, masters into servants, women into men.[11] The castrato, too, represented a rather special sort of transformation – one that confounded normal associations between gender and vocal register.[12] Even the rage for mad scenes that took Venice by storm in the 1640s might be understood in the context of metamorphoses. For the hero of Cavalli's *Egisto* (1644), for example, a schizophrenic break brought on by a vengeful Venus and a hard-hearted lover causes him take on a series of new identities with breathtaking rapidity: first he imagines that he is Orpheus, then Jove, and finally Cupid – providing, at the same time, a subtle satirical commentary on the genre itself.[13] We might go further and imagine opera itself as a potent transformative potion: the joining of poetry, art, and music provided a unique way through which the imagined ancient world, captured in frozen images by artists or described by poets, could be transformed into something that could delight both eye and ear simultaneously.[14]

Early modern thinking about gender and sexuality played no small part in the interpretation of these tales of metamorphoses, and indeed they seem to have inspired many of opera's most novel reinventions of Ovid. A world inhabited solely by humans placed a limit on the number and types of narratives available to express the tensions created by unsatisfied lust and stubborn chastity – usually, but not always, mapped onto the conflict between male desire and female restraint. The early moderns therefore seem to have been particularly attracted by the imaginative possibilities provided by the Arcadian realm, one in which the gods held sway and bodily form could be more transient, in which singing was one of many unusual behaviours that might be adopted.[15] It is difficult to imagine a better – and safer – place to experiment with the consequences of desire's fluid identities than in a primitive universe, quite divorced from normal civilization, where violence was often part of an elaborate game in which both sexes participated with equal pleasure. Arcadia, as portrayed with the often-ironic power of the point of view taken by Ovid's narrator, represented the ideal realm in which to indulge in fantasies and suppressed desires, to experiment with notions of female presence or absence, silence or eloquence, resistance or acquiescence. Where else, for example, could a nymph such as Daphne face the cruel dilemma of either accepting the unwanted love of a god or preserving her chastity through eternity by allowing herself to be changed into the form of a laurel tree?

Was it because of shared concerns with verisimilitude or pure coincidence that the tale of Daphne and Apollo played such a prominent role in early opera, not only in the northern Italian courts of Florence and Mantua, but also in the commercial opera theatres in Venice?[16] Self-consciousness about the nature of opera – and its similarity to pastoral dramas, such as Guarini's *Il pastor fido* – may well have been part of the inspiration for Ottavio Rinuccini's libretto for *La Dafne* (1598), first set by Jacopo Peri, from which only fragments survive.[17] The libretto was sufficiently well regarded that Marco da Gagliano's version, which was set to a revised and somewhat expanded version of the libretto, was performed at the Gonzaga court in Mantua in 1608 – just months after the premiere of Monteverdi's and Rinuccini's *Arianna*. It was also printed in an edition dedicated to Vincenzo Gonzaga that included detailed performance instructions.[18] In Venice, where opera became a commercial enterprise, Apollo and Daphne were the central protagonists in one of the earliest examples of the genre refashioned as carnival entertainment for the most Serene Republic. Francesco Cavalli's *Gli amori di Apollo di Dafne* was written only three years after the premiere of public opera in Venice. It is Cavalli's second contribution to the genre, as well as the first libretto penned by Giovanni Francesco Busenello, best known today as the author of the libretto to Monteverdi's *L'incoronazione di Poppea*.

Given Busenello's well-known association with the infamous Venetian Accademia degli Incogniti, it is not surprising that *Gli amori di Apollo e di Dafne* reflects at least some part of the libertine and even heterodox approach to conventional morality – and ambivalence about women – that infuses so many other works of the period.[19]

Let us briefly consider the primary source material from which both Rinuccini and Busenello drew their inspiration. Ovid's rendition of the tale of Apollo and Daphne, as noted above, appears in the first book of *Metamorphoses*, prior to Mercury's telling of the tale of Pan and Syrinx. Apollo, who boasts about his triumph over the Python, incurs the wrath of Cupid. Cupid takes his revenge by sending forth two darts, one of which kindles love for Daphne in Apollo; the other hardens Daphne's heart to the entire notion of love, leading her to reject all suitors and yearn for perpetual virginity. Apollo assumes the sometimes comic role of an unrequited lover, pursuing Daphne with the fierceness of a dog – though here the narrator proffers his opinion: 'The winds bared her limbs, the opposing breezes set her garments a flutter as she ran, and a light air flung her locks streaming behind her. Her beauty was enhanced by flight' (*Met.* 1.525–35). Daphne speaks only a few words: she begs her father to change or destroy the beauty that has been the cause of her trouble. Ovid provides the reader with a vivid description of how the chase was abruptly halted by Daphne's transformation:

> Scarce had she thus prayed when a down-dragging numbness seized her limbs, and her soft sides were begirt with thin bark. Her hair was changed to leaves, her arms to branches. Her feet, but not so swift, grew fast in sluggish roots, and her head was not but a tree's top. Her gleaming beauty alone remained. (*Met.* 1.548–52)[20]

Like Pan, delighted with this new version of Syrinx as a set of pipes, Apollo, too, falls in love with his Daphne in her new form; he feels her heart beating through the wood and kisses her trunk. The god is unfazed by the fact that the wood recoils from his touch, since he has never paid much attention to Daphne's resistance anyway, and he consoles himself by declaring that the leaves of the laurel tree will serve as an ornament for his lyre and as a garland to welcome the heroes of Rome. Here, the structures of feeling in early modern Italy with regard to masculine desire are manifest in the ease with which Apollo accepts the new physicality of Daphne, an object of desire without the female body or the power to sing. In fact, it seems almost natural, as if no other possibility existed, when Daphne's beautiful hair, the long legs Apollo so admired, and the heart that she hardened in resisting the desires of the gods are transformed into the beloved laurel tree. Lest we be too horrified by the brutality of Apollo's pursuit of Daphne, the veiled detachment of the narrator allows us, as Mary Barnard has observed, to appreciate both the comic and grotesque elements of the situation.[21] How could a god such as Apollo behave like a lowly satyr? How could a woman actually turn into a tree before our eyes? And how could Apollo so calmly accept the transformation?

In fashioning his libretto, Rinuccini must certainly have looked to Ovid as an authority for his work; he underlines the Roman author's centrality by having him actually sing in the prologue: 'I am he who on the learned lute sang of the passions of the celestial gods, and of the metamorphoses of their appearances, so sweetly, that the world still admires me.'[22] This Ovid, however, was also well aware of his Florentine audience, offering praise to his patrons and explaining that the fable will serve as a cautionary tale about underestimating love in all its guises.[23] The opera, in fact, unfolds in an episodic style that owes much to Ovid.[24] Rinuccini follows Ovid's model by prefacing the tale of Apollo and Daphne with a presentation of Apollo's victory over the Python, a scene that might have been familiar to Rinuccini – and some members of the Florentine audience – from the third intermedi of *La Pellegrina* from 1589.[25] His boasting inspires Amor's vengeance, a position that Venere (Venus) heartily supports. Apollo's heroism notwithstanding, Dafne resists the god's advances with the now familiar consequences. However, as in both Greek tragedy and early opera – our most familiar example being Monteverdi's *Orfeo* – the metamorphosis happens offstage; the audience experiences the transformation only through the expressive narration of the Nunzio (renamed Tirsi in da Gagliano's 1608 version). Tirsi's monologue captures much of the horror and fascination of Ovid's tale: curiously, the narrator claims he could not hear Dafne's tearful appeal to the heavens with her hands outstretched as her legs turn into tree trunks nor her utterance of a mournful sound, because she was too far away. Rinuccini, in fact, captures the often ironic omniscience of Ovidian narrators, heightening the audience's sensitivity to inaudible noises: how, we might ask, could he have known that she uttered a sound if he could not hear it?

For our purposes, however, one of the most critical moments in the dramatization of this myth has to do not only with the monstrous transformation, but also with how both Apollo and his shepherd companions express themselves musically in its aftermath. Does Apollo lament the loss of his love, or, like Pan, does he find consolation in music? And how do Apollo's fellow Arcadians experience this event? Notably, in the version of Rinuccini's libretto set by Marco da Gagliano, the shepherds respond to the news of Dafne's transformation by singing a lengthy strophic lament ('Ahi dura, ahi ria novella!'), which arguably heightens the sense of tragedy associated with the event; this element is not a feature of Ovid's text.[26]

But perhaps of greater interest is the fact that da Gagliano's preface to his 1608 version, with its detailed performance instructions, provides us with some vital clues as to how he wanted the audience to witness or, more precisely, to *hear* Apollo's reaction to Dafne's transformation. Apollo, da Gagliano emphasizes, must sing the lament with 'the greatest emotion possible; with all that, the singer should have regard for increasing it, where the words demand it the most.'[27] He goes on to add that Apollo should 'wind the laurel branch over which he will have been lamenting, around his head, crowning himself with it' when he sings of her branches being a garland for Roman heroes – in the verse 'faran ghirlanda le tue fronde, e i rami' [your fronds and branches will make a garland].[28] More striking yet is the musical effect that da Gagliano specifies for this moment: 'It is necessary to make it appear to the auditorium that from Apollo's lyre comes a more than ordinary melody. So let there be placed four string players (*da braccio* or *da gamba* matters little) in one of the exits close by, in a position where they are unseen by the audience watching Apollo, and as he plays his bow on the lyre, they should play.'[29] Apollo may lament the loss of Dafne, he might be overcome with feelings of remorse and loss, but he is nevertheless able to recover sufficiently to wrap himself in her garlands and sing with heightened expressivity over Dafne's apparent demise. Moreover, Apollo goes beyond mere recovery: he is even able to play the lyre with supernatural powers. Therefore, Dafne's metamorphosis has a transformative effect on the art form itself; Apollo's loss is music's gain: Dafne the woman is no more; in her place Apollo now has the sonic capabilities of four musicians.[30] Framed by two victories – the triumph over the python and the transformation of passion to art – Apollo emerges not only unscathed, but greater and more gifted for the experience.

Three decades later, in 1640 and in the Republic of Venice, Busenello and Cavalli presented this tale in an entirely different manner.[31] Some of this difference is a result of changes in the genre from a court entertainment to a commercial enterprise. In Venice, opera did not glorify a particular court or family, nor was it used to celebrate dynastic events; instead it was supported by a complex financial and artistic infrastructure – made up of Venetian nobles, musicians, and artisans, and interested foreign patrons, who through their collaborative efforts created a new style of opera suitable for a carnival entertainment that exhibited Venetian liberties to the rest of Europe.[32] Not surprisingly, they were structured differently. Venetian operas were typically arranged in three acts, used a large cast of characters, and employed numerous set changes and multiple plot strands. They thus not only refused to adhere to Aristotelian dramatic principles, but also designed their operas for audiences that were more heterogeneous and – as some have argued—conceivably less discriminating in their tastes than their exclusively aristocratic predecessors. Indeed, this is not a work that commentators have considered seriously in terms of its use of ancient sources, perhaps following Pirrotta's notion that mythological topics in early Venetian opera were primarily inspired by concerns with verisimilitude.

Busenello may read Ovid rather differently than Rinuccini, but his use of Ovid is no less sensitive and perceptive, and probably more so. While Rinuccini may have actually presented Ovid as a character in his prologue, Busenello's libretto is arguably more faithful to Ovid's original – not through a slavish imitation of Ovid's text and narrative, but through his emulation of the narrative style of the *Metamorphoses*, weaving together disparate tales in a manner that defies logic and chronology, requiring the viewer to consider both individual narrative strands and also their relationship to one another.[33] It may well be this sort of fidelity to an ancient author to which Busenello refers in his preface to the 1656 published version of the libretto. After summarizing the tale of Daphne's transformation for the reader, he notes that 'the other episodes in the present drama are woven together in a way you will see, and if by chance some genius would have considered the unity of the fable divided by the duplicity of loves, that is Apollo and Daphne, Tithonus and Aurora; Cephalus and Procris, he should take pleasure in recognizing that this weaving together does not unmake the unity, but adorns it.' He also reassures the reader that a similar strategy had been used by Guarini in *Il pastor fido*, adding further that 'the stingy, narrow minds have corrupted the world, because while they endeavour to wear ancient clothing, they render their garments absurd with modern usage, and this is verified in a maxim by the Divine Petrarch, "everyone should be content with what they know."'[34] For Busenello, it would seem, a constricted approach to antiquity – one in which a narrow view of unity predominated – was all too common in modern times.[35] This is more than a conventional apology; it is a manifesto for a new aesthetic.

All the myths that Busenello interweaves in this opera, in fact, have one thing in common: they involve desire in its various guises. Busenello combines the story of Apollo and Daphne with two others involving female sexual longing: first, the frustration of the goddess Aurora with her immortal but impotent husband (*Homeric Hymn to Aphrodite,* 218–38)[36] and her abduction of the beautiful Cephalus; second, the despair of Procris abandoned by Cephalus (*Met.* 7.661–865). In Busenello's version, however, Procris's lament is inspired by Cephalus's obvious delight at being abducted and the fact that he enjoys Aurora's favours with such pleasure. Thus, a myth that is ostensibly concerned with female resistance to love is ornamented by a series of tales in which desire (and its consequences) is presented in every possible guise. The ultimate culprit here is Love, urged on by the often vengeful Venus.

Considered together, the three myths present a quite vivid (and somewhat ironic) picture of a sexually volatile world of passion and desire, albeit one in which both men and women participate equally and fully. But *Gli Amori di Apollo e di Dafne* also deals explicitly with music and musicians; this is an opera in which the close relationship between desire and self-expression – implicit in the Pan and Syrinx tale – is put into play. Apollo may be the legendary musician, associated with the harmony of the spheres; he will certainly assert that power at the end of the opera – particularly after Dafne has lost her voice and become a laurel tree. But in act 1, scene 4, it is the music of Dafne, her nymphs, and the shepherds that is being celebrated. Dafne is given no fewer than three discrete arias in this scene: first, she vows never to give into love ('O più d'ogni richezza') and then celebrates her liberty while accompanying herself on the lyre ('Libertade gradita'), both arias leading to a *ballo* sung by the nymphs and shepherds. The scene culminates with Dafne's stunning and virtuosic prayer to music, 'Musica dolce, musica tu sei.'

The aria is remarkable from a number of perspectives. After the previous simpler strophic arias in triple metre and the homophonic choral dance, the duple-metre 'Musica dolce,' with its free, improvisatory style and elaborate ornamentation, takes the listener into an entirely different sonic world, one in which earthly pleasures are a reflection of heavenly delights, one in which the music of the spheres is given full reign. From a stylistic point of view, this is perhaps somewhat unexpected; in subsequent Venetian repertoire such displays of virtuosity would usually be reserved for the deities and most often tucked away in an allegorical prologue, where such demonstrations of power and eloquence are the property of the gods. Cavalli creates for Dafne an aria in which the beauty of music is clearly manifest.

Example 7.1 Francesco Cavalli, *Gli amori di Apollo e di Dafne*, act 1, scene 4: 'Musica dolce, musica tu sei' (I-Vnm IV 404 [=9928]).

Note, for example, the care with which Cavalli sets the phrase 'musica dolce' in mm. 1–5: the sweetness of her entrance at the third on the sustained 'mu-,' the three-fold repetition of 'dolce,' on the off beat, each with increasing dissonance, and the untethered, ethereal quality achieved by the sustained E in the bass mm. 4–5. The extraordinary melisma on the word 'celeste' (mm. 10–12) seems to suggest that Dafne not only understands but even has access to the celestial music that Apollo habitually commands. Yet she is also particularly sensitive to the music of the Arcadian forests – the sonic nuances of Ovid's world in which the earthly and heavenly commingle. In this context the use of the *forte/piano* opposition on the first two beats of m. 13 to create the echo effect goes beyond mere convention. Are we perhaps to understand this as a reference to another familiar Arcadian sound – the cries of Echo – the nymph who would be transformed from female body into pure voice because of her passion for Narcissus? Regardless, as she goes on to demonstrate with the next luscious melisma, the forests themselves reverberate with the pure, wordless sound of heavenly music, which is itself an imitation of that most precious utterance of both man and the gods – laughter. In this one luscious moment, Cavalli and Busenello thus endow Daphne – not Apollo – with the Orphic voice and access to the music of spheres.[37] Later, when she is silenced, that power will be apparent elsewhere.

The significance of Daphne's musical prowess is made vividly apparent by Busenello's ironic twist at the opera's conclusion. First, we should consider the transformation itself. Unlike in Rinuccini's *La Dafne*, in *Gli amori di Apollo e di Dafne* the transformation is actually shown on stage. Dafne's father Peneo (Peneus) grants her request, and she becomes a laurel tree in front of Apollo's eyes – and ours as well. That Busenello and Cavalli should focus the viewer's attention on the actual metamorphoses, of course, is by no means surprising. This, after all, is the age of theatrical baroque sculpture, the age of Bernini.[38]

Bernini's sculpture of Apollo and Daphne (figure 7.1) creates a sense of both motion and stasis, one that heightens the viewers' awareness of the physical consequences of the metamorphoses in an unabashedly dramatic fashion. This masterpiece captures the abruptness with which Daphne's movement is halted as her legs turn into the trunk of the tree: her outstretched arms so readily become branches, her fingers become twigs, her hair becomes leaves. Apollo, too, seems to be in flight, managing to touch her at last, albeit just at the moment in which she hovers between a human and non-human state. One of the most striking elements of the sculpture is its implicit sound. Indeed, if a piece of sculpture can be said to make noise, Bernini has accomplished this with true operatic drama. Daphne's mouth is open in the shape of an 'Oh,' and she seems to be uttering a cry – perhaps the one that Rinuccini's Tirsi could not quite hear. Regardless of whether Busenello or Cavalli actually knew Bernini's statue, their presentation of the metamorphoses seems to

Figure 7.1 Gian Lorenzi Bernini, *Apollo and Daphne.* Detail of heads. Galleria Borghese, Rome. Scala / Art Resource, NY.

owe much to his sense of movement and gesture, one that creates a feeling of desire barely evident in Rinuccini's libretto. Busenello and Cavalli make the physical and aural consequences of metamorphoses palpable on both the visual and aural planes.

The metamorphosis occurs in act 3, scene 2, as Dafne, determined to save her chastity, asks her father Peneo for aid. He finds only one solution – he will transform her into a plant, a laurel tree that will always retain its leaves. Dafne, for her part, gladly accepts and declares that rather than losing her virginity (apparently a fate worse than death) she would even gladly be transformed into a stone.[39] In a passage of dignified recitative, Peneo transforms his daughter with apparent foreknowledge of the significance of the laurel: he imagines his watery self to be both a mirror that will forever reflect the image of his transformed daughter and a river of tears that he will always shed over her fate – a vision that reminds us of the loss of Dafne's voice that had echoed through the forest.

Example 7.2 Cavalli, *Gli amori di Apollo e di Dafne:* excerpt from conclusion of act 3, scene 2 and opening of subsequent scene.

In this striking example, Cavalli places the unusual *quadro* sign on the word 'pianto.' This unexpected chromatic intrusion of the B-natural in the context of a cadence on F not only expresses Peneo's sorrow, but also sets up a system change from flat to natural that acts as a musical metaphor for Dafne's metamorphosis.

Apollo, not surprisingly, reacts to the transformation with shock. His cry, 'Ohimé che miro,' is marked with the introduction of an A-major sonority, an anguished cry in his upper register, and a chromatic upper neighbouring tone in the bass.[40] This begins what for him is a complex

25
- - ri Ba - ciar le fo - glie all' a - do -
31
ra - - - ta pian - ta, ba - ciar le fo -
37
glie all' a - do - ra - - - - - - - ta pian -
43
ta. Sgor - ghi - no sgor - ghi-no ho

Example 7.3a,b. Cavalli, *Gli amori di Apollo e di Dafne*, act 3, scene 3: excerpt from 'Misero, Apollo' and melisma at conclusion of his monologue.

psychological process, one in which he is not lamenting the death of a beloved in any conventional sense, but rather only the loss of his beloved's body, his 'fire' now transformed into wood. The lament that follows can be understood as Apollo's attempt to assimilate this new knowledge about Dafne, both to mourn her and to contain and rechannel his overwhelming desire, for which there is no longer any possibility of physical satisfaction or release.[41]

In this section, Cavalli introduces a number of brilliant musical touches that portray Apollo's frustration with and ultimate acceptance of his reconfigured relationship with his now-transformed object of desire. One is the repeating harmonic pattern imprinted on each strophe of his lament: four statements of the descending tetrachord from a to e provide the underpinning for Apollo's struggling ascent from e to a, marked by half-step motion and dissonant F-sharps and G-sharps. The difference between Apollo's desire and Dafne's earlier pleasure could not be more apparent. Where her voice echoed freely through the woods, Apollo is trapped – at least at the outset of each strophe – in the obsessive world of the ostinato bass. Notably, he does not completely give in to the obsessiveness of grief: by m. 16 the ground-bass pattern is relinquished in favour of diatonic movement by steps and fifths, with a more stable quasi-tonal harmonic motion, as Apollo imagines himself changed into wind so that he might caress her leaves (strophe 1), or seeing his bitter tears as providing her with water (2). By the fourth strophe, Apollo discards the lament entirely; when Giove fails to respond to his plea – that he find someone else to take over his job as the sun so that he might enjoy Dafne's shade – Apollo takes on an entirely different vocal strategy: with an extravagant melisma (example 7.3b), he imagines the way in which his divinity will provide a fertile garden for his beloved in which they are joined in sweet union. Notably, in Apollo's fantasy about this idyllic garden, it is the sun god whose virtuosity is celebrated. Male desire trumps female autonomy, and Dafne, the laurel tree, remains a passive and silent recipient of the god's love.

We will recall that the story ends at that point in Rinuccini's *La Dafne*. As described by da Gagliano, Apollo laments, receives consolation from the lamenting shepherds and nymphs, and then drapes himself in the laurel branches with amplified sound. But in *Gli Amori di Apollo e di Dafne*, the brilliant melding of mythic fragments inspires the arrival of unexpected guests. First Amor appears to mock Apollo's loss and gloat over his triumph. Then Pane (Pan), having made his entrance several hundred lines earlier (at least as far as Ovid is concerned), suddenly appears in the wrong myth to console Apollo over the loss of Dafne, even while she is hovering between a human and inhuman state.

Pane asks Apollo what is troubling him, and after an anguished explanation, he offers a solution. He describes his similar pursuit of Syrinx, who, as mentioned earlier, also begged to be transformed from woman into a plant under identical circumstances. Presenting the results – the famed pipes – to Apollo, Pane explains that they are 'harmonious memories' of his lost love. Apollo, he advises, should sublimate in a similar fashion and take comfort by removing branches and leaves from the tree, using them to crown his head and his lyre.[42]

Although Apollo considers this to be a reasonable plan, when he actually tries to cut down the branches, Dafne – who has not yet entirely crossed over into the arboreal world (and must have patiently been listening to all of this discussion about her fate) – cries out in protest. How, she asks, could he be so cruel to an innocent nymph? Not only was Apollo an enemy of her honour when she was a woman, Dafne exclaims, but he continues her assault on her even though she is now a plant.[43] Cavalli and Busenello thus pointedly call attention to that curious moment in the metamorphoses in which, as Leonard Barkan describes it, human consciousness albeit briefly is maintained even as the physical body is lost. The fact that Dafne herself is aware of the process makes this moment even more poignant. As she bids a final farewell to Apollo, she sings: 'Quest'arbore non può più lungamente organizar parole' [This tree cannot much longer organize words].

The arrival of a sympathetic Pane is a brilliant dramatic stroke by Busenello: he could have found no better way to call our attention to the parallels between these two tales, implicit in Ovid's text. Since overwhelming passion had the same effect on Syrinx, transforming her into the beloved vibrating body, Pane suggest that Apollo follow his example – and use the laurel wreathes to decorate his lyre – thus implying that Dafne, too, could bring Apollo similar pleasure by serving as an ornament to his artistic endeavours. Although Apollo does not actually turn Dafne into an instrument – though his physical assault on the branches is certainly suggestive – the implication is much the same: her body is there to glorify his own music making.

In an operatic context, this has quite astounding consequences. Dafne, as a young virgin, had enjoyed her innate link to the music of the spheres; in this act of presumption or assumption of male prerogative, the power of music that had brought her and her maidens such delight is transferred from the female to its rightful place in the male sphere – not an unfamiliar tactic in the Venetian Republic.[44] Moreover, Pane and Apollo join to celebrate their newfound expressive power and the eternal memories of their lost loves Dafne and Siringe (Syrinx). This is not the conventional love duet that will conclude so many subsequent operas – as, for example, in the infamous duet that consummates the love between Nerone and Poppea at the end of Monteverdi's opera. Rather, what we have here is an unholy alliance between the heavenly Apollo and the earthly Pane: two figures whose differences in physical appearance, habits, and sensibilities are matched by the utter incompatibility of their music making. Compare, for example, the contrasting representations of Pan and Apollo in a mid-sixteenth-century print by Giorgio Ghisi (figure 7.2).

In the duet with which the opera *Gli amori di Apollo e di Dafne* concludes, Pane and Apollo sing together with surprising stylistic uniformity: 'Yes, yes, let them live together eternally, the love-filled lights of our flames. Let their beauty be eternal for those who nourish such blessed passion. May heaven never tire of their sounds.' Tim Carter refers to Pane's appearance as making possible an 'apotheotic conclusion,' attempting, perhaps, to understand Cavalli's and Busenello's work as a descendant of Monteverdi's *Orfeo*.[45] But despite the praise for Dafne and Siringe, there is something more earthbound and conspiratorial about

Figure 7.2 Giorgio Ghisi, after Francesco Primaticcio, *Apollo, Pan, and a Putto Blowing a Horn,* 1560s. Engraving (29.8 × 16.5 cm). The Elisha Whittelsey Collection, The Metropolitan Museum of Art, New York, NY, USA / Art Resource, NY.

Example 7.4 Cavalli, *Gli amori di Apollo e di Dafne*, act 3, scene 4: final duet, excerpt.

their musings on their lost women. Apollo has learned well his lesson from the goat-god, and even takes the lead, singing with a simplicity of expression that seems more to do with Pane's primitive urges than with Apollo's supposedly celestial leanings.

In this newly reassembled vision of antiquity, the composer offers a Pane and an Apollo who not only transcend their profound differences – physical, social and aesthetic – but even join forces in producing music. This combination of earthly and heavenly – of the Dionysian and Apollonian – would become central to the peculiar aesthetic of Venetian opera. The fact that *Gli amori di Apollo e di Dafne* was written so early in the history of the Venetian opera suggests that the concept of a woman turning into an instrument might also have served as a metaphor for opera itself. The desires of Pane and Apollo for Dafne and Siringe are sublimated and transformed into sublime music making – in other words, the pleasures of opera.

The stories of Daphne and Syrinx tell us much about the inspirational power of frustrated desire. Another opera dealing with opera, written nearly twenty-five years later, provides us with a metamorphosis in which Apollo actually gets the girl – but is unable to keep her. The opera is *Gli amori di Apollo e di Leucotoe*, presented at the Teatro SS Giovanni e Paolo in 1663.[46] The composer was Giovanni Battista Volpe, also known as Riveting, and the libretto was written by Aurelio Aureli, one of the most inventive librettists of the period.[47] The story, to which I alluded earlier, concerns Apollo's deflowering of the nymph Leucothoe, who is buried alive by her own father after hearing of his daughter's lack of chastity from the jealous Clytiē. Leucothoe is transformed into a frankincense bush, while Clytiē becomes a sunflower.

As is the case with other Venetian operatic treatments of Ovidian rapes – *La Calisto* being the primary example – Leucotoe does not make any attempt to resist Apollo's affections – if indeed it was necessary for him to disguise himself as Leucothoe's mother to gain access to the nymph, this must have happened at an earlier point in the narrative. When she first appears in the opera, Leucotoe is already deeply in love with Apollo and awakens early, before the sunrise, so that she might await his arrival in the garden outside her bed chamber. Thus, in Aureli and Volpe's interpretation of the tale the culprit does not focus on a woman's chastity or resistance to love, but rather on another popular female sin: jealousy. The opera opens with Climene, Apollo's wife, railing against her husband's philandering, and she sends her sons Orfeo (Orpheus), Fetonte (Phaeton), and Escuplapio (Esculapius) down to earth to thwart their father's desires.[48] The invented subplot introduces the young Eritreo (Eritreus) presumably the son of Perseo (Perseus) and Andromeda, who is also in love with Leucotoe and who – in another moment of metamorphosis – will lose his wits over the loss of his beloved.

Example 7.5 Giovanni Battista Volpe, *Gli amori di Apollo e Leucotoe*, act 3, scene 17: 'Diffondete miei ragi' (I-Vnm, Cod. It IV 386 [=9910]).

What is particularly interesting, however, is the way in which Aureli and Volpe manage to craft a satisfactory *lieto fine* that nonetheless allows for a somewhat faithful rendition of the myths – that is, two of the central female characters turn into plants. First, Clitia (Clytië) tells Leucotoe's father of his daughter's transgression; he brutally condemns her to be buried alive, despite her eloquent and touching protestations.[49] Apollo comes upon her only after she's been buried: once again he is frustrated by the realization that his beloved is enclosed in a tomb that is unworthy of her.[50] In this instance, however, he does not lament – after all, he's already consummated the relationship. Instead, in Volpe and Aureli's opera, it his singing that actually triggers the metamorphosis. The aria in which this occurs is curious in many respects: through-composed, with an unambiguously cheerful affect that is scarcely funereal, composed of short motives in the opening phrases, and building to a virtuosic conclusion in which Apollo's musical ability enacts the metaphor of the aroma of the frankincense bush.

Desire here becomes the tool of metamorphosis, and (despite the arguably sombre tone of the dramatic situation – that is, the entombment of the central female character) there is no attempt to suggest that Apollo suffers over his loss. Moreover, in the following scene, as Clitia attempts to renew her affair with Apollo, she, too, will lose her body. Her concluding recitative traces her self-aware moment of transformation – both musically and dramatically: what violent force, she asks, causes my tears to become petals, and transforms me into a sunflower? How could mortal pleasures so quickly pass away and come to an end?[51] Bemoaning the cruel vengeance of Apollo, she recognizes that she, now transformed into a flower, will always follow his beautiful light.

None of this, however, seems to negate the happy ending. Eritreo the heroic son of Perseo and Andromeda, regains his senses and is consoled for his lost love through the good graces of Giove, who declares him to be a virtuous hero. Climene and Apollo are rejoined as husband and wife, and they rejoice in their newfound marital bliss with Oceano (Oceanus) and Theti (Thetys) and a chorus of Nereids.

In this instance, the metamorphosis triggered by desire removes the disruptive female elements and allows for marital fidelity and heroism. From a twenty-first-century perspective, this is the most convenient (if brutal) of all plot devices – what better way to dispose of a pair of former mistresses than to turn them to plants? The jealous wife is placated, the purity of marriage is undisturbed, and – as a bonus – even the environmental cause is served, through the creation of new and beautiful species of flora. Of course conventional early modern gender narratives are built into the stories – male action contrasts with female passivity; chastity is cruel; resistance is futile; and female silence is – predictably – the consequence of either good or bad behaviour. And nowhere is this given more vivid representation than in an opera in which several of the primary female characters aren't actually capable of participating in the *lieto fine*.

Example 7.6 Volpe, *Gli amori di Apollo e Leucotoe*, act 3, scene 17: 'O qual violente.'

However, there is a more profound implication in all of these operatic adaptations of Ovid's *Metamorphoses.* In each of these stories, the lover is forced to do without the physical presence of the beloved – usually the female body – but, as we have noted, he is always left with the proverbial 'something to remember her by.' It could be a fragrance (here worshipful devotion), a face surrounded by petals, the sound of vibrating reeds, or the willowy limbs encased in wood. Through repetition and juxtaposition we are reminded again and again that desire – regardless of the barely suppressed violence – has a certain procreative power that merits celebration.

These myths provided opera in seventeenth-century Venice with an opportunity to use a fictional universe to explore a notion of sexuality somewhat free of moral constraints, one that – from an often ironic male-centred viewpoint – regards desire as the source of all artistic and procreative inspiration. In this case, we could push Barkan's formulation further and say that the metaphors are not *made* flesh – if anything they represent the unmaking or unmasking of flesh, as the woman who becomes an object, as a creation of the poet's or musician's imagination, is always separated from her original bodily context, much like the branches of the laurel tree. It is only on the operatic stage, however, that these metaphors could be made audible. Opera allows us both to see and to hear the metamorphoses; we hear the disembodied echo of Dafne's voice and her struggle to speak; we hear Clitia's despair as she grows petals, and we experience Apollo's pain and subsequent self-consolation. We also recognize something that Pan certainly discovered as he tried with such futility to put Syrinx's body back together – that feelings could give birth to music.

NOTES

I would like to dedicate this essay to the memory of composer, musician, and friend, Daniel Pinkham (1923–2006).

1 *Achilles Tatius*, trans. S. Gaselee, The Loeb Classical Library (London: William Heinemann; New York: G.P. Putnam's Sons, 1917). Achilles Tatius (second century AD) is best known for *Leucippe and Clitophon*, a novel that is particularly notable for its narrative, digressions, fantasies, theatricality, and use of ekphrasis. The first complete Latin translation was published in Venice in 1544, vernacular treatments appeared in Italy shortly thereafter, and the book continued to be reprinted well into the seventeenth century. See, for example, *Achille Tatio Alessandrino, De gli Amorosi Avvenimenti di Leucippe, & di Clitophonte Gia dal Greco tradotti, nella nostra lingua Italiana* (Venice: Battista Bonfadino, 1607). The passage cited above appears on 107. Achilles Tatius's

theatrical treatment of myth may well have provided inspiration for artists in the sixteenth and seventeenth centuries, supplementing Ovid and mythographies. Donald Stone, Jr, 'The Source of Titian's Rape of Europa,' *Art Bulletin* 54, no. 1 (1972): 47–9, for instance, proposes that the description of Europa's rape in Achilles Tatius (rather than Ovid) was the primary literary inspiration for Titian's painting on the subject.

2 As noted above, the story of Pan and Syrinx actually forms part of Ovid's tale of Giove's love for the nymph Io, whom he transforms into a cow to avoid Juno's jealousy. Juno, who inevitably discovers her husband's infidelities, demands the cow as a gift and leaves her captive under Argus's one hundred watchful eyes. Mercury tells this beguiling story to Argus in order to put him to sleep and thus gain Io's freedom.

3 On this point, see Michaela Janan, '"There Beneath the Roman Ruine Where the Purple Flowers Grow": Ovid's Minyeides and the Feminine Imagination,' *American Journal of Philology* 115, no. 3 (1994): 427–48.

4 '[W]hen she [Io] attempted to voice her complaints, she only mooed. She would start with fear at the sound, and was filled with terror at her own voice' (*Met.* 1.635–7). Ovid provides a detailed description of Callisto's struggle to communicate: 'And when the girl stretched out her arms in prayer for mercy, her arms began to grow rough with black shaggy hair; her hands changed into feet tipped with sharp claws; and her lips, which but not Jove had just praised, were changed to broad, ugly jaws; and that she might not move him with entreating prayers, her power of speech was taken from her, and only a harsh terrifying growl came hoarsely from her throat. Still her human feelings remained, though she was now a bear' (*Met.* 2.477–85). Leonard Barkan, *The Gods Made Flesh: Metamorphosis and the Pursuit of Paganism* (New Haven: Yale University Press, 1986), describes this moment of transition from the human to the beastly as an apparent 'interpenetration of identities' (24).

5 This is a central point made by Barkan in *The Gods Made Flesh,* chapter 1.

6 Barkan, *Gods Made Flesh,* 23.

7 *Gli amori di Apollo e di Dafne* was presented at the Teatro S Cassiano in Venice in 1640. For a facsimile of the score and libretto, see Pier Francesco Cavalli, *Gli amori d'Apollo e di Dafne,* introduced by Howard Mayer Brown, vol. 1: *Italian Opera, 1640–1770* (New York: Garland Publishing, 1978). *Gli amori di Apollo e di Leucotoe,* with music by Giovanni Battista Volpe (1620–91), was presented at the Teatro SS Giovanni e Paolo in 1663.

8 There is an extensive bibliography on the 'birth' of opera, humanism, and myth. For the documents associated with early opera, see Claude Palisca, *The Florentine Camerata: Documentary Studies and Translations* (New Haven, CT: Yale University Press, 1989); 'The Florentine Camerata: A Reappraisal,' *Studi*

Musicali 1 (1972): 203–36; on early opera and humanism, see Barbara Russano Hanning, *Of Poetry and Music's Power: Humanism and the Creation of Opera,* Studies in Musicology 13 (Ann Arbor: UMI Press, 1980); Gary Tomlinson, 'Music and the Claims of Text: Monteverdi, Rinuccini, and Marino,' *Critical Inquiry* 8 (1982): 565–89; Howard Mayer Brown, 'How Opera Began: An Introduction to Jacopo Peri's *Euridice* (1600),' in *The Late Italian Renaissance, 1525–1630,* ed. Eric Cochrane (New York: Harper and Row, 1970), 401–44. The notion of a humanistic birth of opera has also been influential in critical assessments of the genre, most notably that by Joseph Kerman, *Opera as Drama* (Berkeley: University of California Press, 1956). For Kerman, in fact, much of baroque opera is part of the 'dark ages' and thus apparently impervious to the light of humanism. Much of the work on Ovid in early opera has focused on Monteverdi's *Orfeo.* See, for example, Frederick Sternfeld, 'The Birth of Opera: Ovid, Poliziano, and the *Lieto Fine,*' *Analecta Musicologica* 19, no. 1979 (1979): 30–51; Nino Pirrotta, 'Monteverdi and the Problems of Opera,' *Music and Culture in Italy from the Middle Ages and the Baroque* (Cambridge, MA: Harvard University Press, 1984), 235–53; John Whenham, *Claudio Monteverdi, Orfeo,* ed. John Whenham (Cambridge: Cambridge University Press, 1986). One of the few studies of the use of Ovid in the later Seicento is Ellen Rosand, ' L'ovidio trasformato,' in *Orfeo by Aureli and Sartorio, Venice 1673,* ed. Ellen Rosand, Drammaturgia musical veneta 6 (Milan: Ricordi, 1983).

9 Nino Pirrotta, in his foundational studies of early opera, emphasized the extent to which the use of mythological characters – particularly those known as gifted musicians, such as Apollo or Orpheus – provided a justification for song, even within the pastoral world in which a greater licence for poetic and musical self-expression was already implicit. See Pirrotta, 'Early Opera and Aria,' *Music and Theatre from Polizano to Monteverdi,* trans. Karen Eales (Cambridge: Cambridge University Press, 1982), esp. 262–4.

10 In Pirrotta's view, in fact, the continued self-consciousness about verisimilitude was also a factor in the popularity of mythological themes during the first decades of Venetian opera, including works such as Cavalli's *Gli amori di Apollo e di Dafne*: 'One must conclude that, as had been the case for the audience of *Arianna* thirty years ago, the Venetian public was not fully prepared for the novelty of *recitar cantando* as the normal means of expression for human beings; accordingly, it was only natural for the librettists to select themes that either could be developed on a double level, one of which at least would allow the composer a freer hand and compensate for the restraint to which he was obliged when handling human characters' ('Early Opera,' 272). Although Pirrotta, of course, never states explicitly that this is the *only* significance of mythological themes in early opera, it is a prevailing

attitude, I would suggest, that has prevented scholars from considering the broader implications of Ovidian themes in early opera. See Wendy Heller, 'Il canto degli dei: opera, verosimiglianza, and mitologia nel primo Seicento,' *Atti del Convegno internazionale 'Musicologia fra due Continenti: l'eredità di Nino Pirrotta,'* ed. Franco Piperno and Fabrizio della Seta (Florence: Olschki, 2010), 127–39

11 A striking example is Ovid's Iphis (*Met.* 9.666–781), an opera heroine brought to the Venetian stage in 1672: Nicolò Minato, *Iphide Greci* (Venice: Bertani, 1671). Born a woman, disguised as boy by her mother, Iphis manages – at just the right moment – to grow the necessary equipment that all but reverses the ritual of castration. Of note is the fact that the music also went through its own sort of metamorphosis: each act was composed by a different composer: Do-menico Partenio (act 1); Domenico Freschi (act 2); Antonio Sartorio (act 3).

12 On the castrato in seventeenth-century Venice, see Wendy Heller, 'The Castrato as Man: Trajectories from the Seventeenth Century,' *British Journal for Eighteenth-Century Studies* 28, no. 3 (2006): 307–21.

13 Giovanni Faustini, *Egisto* (Venice: Surian, 1644).

14 This is the topic of my forthcoming study, *Animating Ovid: Opera and the Metamorphosis of Antiquity in Early Modern Italy.*

15 On Arcadia and Pan, see also Philippe Borgeaud, *The Cult of Pan in Ancient Greece,* trans. Kathleen Atlass and James Redfield (Chicago: Chicago University Press, 1988), 4–5; for the operatic implications of the Arcadian realm in Cavalli's *La Calisto,* see Wendy Heller, *Emblems of Eloquence: Opera and Women's Voices in Seventeenth-Century Venice* (Berkeley: University of California Press, 2003), 178–81.

16 Barbara Hanning views Rinuccini's *La Dafne* as a central text in her hypothesis that Rinuccini's librettos present a 'coherent program that grew out of Renaissance humanistic theories about the power and function of art,' and she attributes this very specific allegorical intent to both Ovid and Rinuccini. See 'Letter from Barbara Russano Hanning,' *Journal of the American Musicological Society* 29, no. 3 (1976): 501–3; see also Hanning, 'Glorious Apollo: Poetic and Political Themes in the First Opera,' *Renaissance Quarterly* 32 (1979): 485–513.

17 Rinuccini and Peri's setting of *La Dafne* was first performed at the Palazzo Corsi for carnival in 1597–8, repeated at the Palazzo Pitti a year later before for Cardinals Monte and Montalto, and was performed again the following year at the Palazzo Corsi. On sources and dating for *La Dafne,* see Oscar G. Sonneck, '"Dafne," The First Opera: A Chronological Study,' *Sammelbände der Internationalen Musikgesellschaft* 15, no. 1 (October-December 1913): 102–10; W.V. Porter, 'Peri and Corsi's *Dafne*: Some New Discoveries and

Observations,' *Journal of the American Musicological Society* 13 (1965): 170–96; F.W. Sternfeld: 'The First Printed Opera Libretto,' *Music & Letters* 49 (1978): 121–38. On Peri's setting, see also Tim Carter, 'Jacopo Peri,' *Music & Letters* 61, no. 2 (1980): 121–35.

18 Angelo Solerti, *Gli albori del melodramma* (Hildesheim: Georg Olms Verlag, 1969), 2: 64–105, includes Rinuccini's libretto for *La Dafne*, along with Marco da Gagliano's preface for the 1608 performance in Mantua. The facsimile of the score is printed as *La Dafne di Marco da Gagliano* (Florence: Cristoforo Marescotti, 1608; repr. *Biblioteca Musica Bononiensis* 4, no. 4 (Bologna: Forni, 1970).

19 On the Accademia degli Incogniti and their views on gender, see Heller, *Emblems of Eloquence*, chapter 2.

20 Translated by Franz Justus Miller, revised by G.P. Goold, The Loeb Classical Library (Cambridge: Harvard University Press, 1977).

21 On the notion of grotesquerie and comedy in the myth, see Mary E. Barnard, *The Myth of Apollo and Daphne from Ovid to Quevodo: Love, Agon, and the Grotesque* (Durham, NC: Duke University Press, 1987), 9–11, 19–37.

22 Rinuccini, *La Dafne*, lines 5–11. 'Quel mi son io, che su la dotta lira / Cantai le fiamme de' celesti amanti, E i trasformati lorvari sembianti / Soavi sì, ch'il mondo ancor m'ammira.' On the prologues in early opera, see Jette Barnholdt Hansen, 'From Invention to Interpretation: The Prologues of the First Court Operas Where Oral and Written Cultures Meet,' *Journal of Musicology* 20 (2003): 556–96.

23 Rinuccini and his audiences would have known this Ovidian tale from countless visual representations, which decorated their homes and public spaces, as well as translations and literary commentaries, which provided readers with a host of competing interpretative possibilities for understanding this tale. See, for example, Mary Barnard, *The Myth of Apollo*; Ann Moss, *Latin Commentaries on Ovid from the Renaissance* (Signal Mountain, TN: Summertown Texts for the Library of Renaissance Humanism, 1998); Claudia Cieri Via, *L'arte delle metamorfosi: decorazioni mitologiche nel cinquecento* (Rome: Lithos editrice, 2003).

24 For debates about *La Dafne*, and in particular about the viability of its dramatic structure, see Barbara Russano Hanning, 'Apologia pro Ottavio Rinuccini,' *Journal of the American Musicological Society* 26 (1973): 240–62; Gary A. Tomlinson, 'Ancora su Ottavio Rinuccini,' *Journal of the American Musicological Society* 28 (1975): 351–6; and 'Letter from Barbara Russano Hanning,' 501–3. Tomlinson, who sees *Arianna* (1608) as the perfect realization of Rinuccini's skills as dramatist, is particularly critical of the first version of *La Dafne*, finding that there is 'little attempt to unify the two elements of the plot' (i.e., Apollo's triumph over the python and his pursuit

of Daphne). He finds fault as well with the relatively little importance accorded Daphne in the libretto, viewing it as a 'hodgepodge of dramatic elements' (Tomlinson, 'Ancora su Ottavio Rinuccini,' 354). From the strict point of view of dramatic structure, Tomlinson might indeed be right; however, this way of thinking about the opera fails to account for the fact that Ovid's text neither aspires to nor succeeds in being unified or dramatically coherent. For further response to Tomlinson and a detailed account of the possible significance of the Apollo iconography for the Medici, see Hanning, 'Glorious Apollo.'

25 See D.P. Walker and J. Jacquot, *Les Fêtes de Florence (1589): Musique des intermèdes de 'La Pellegrina'* (Paris, 1963), xxiii–lviii.

26 For Gary Tomlinson, 'Ancora su Ottavio Rinuccini,' 355, these extra strophes enhance the dramatic structure and balance of Rinuccini's original libretto, as well as demonstrate the poet's evolution as a dramatist between the composition of *La Dafne* and *Arianna.* Ovid does present us occasionally with the laments of shepherds and Arcadian creatures, most strikingly, perhaps, in his rendition of the Marsyas and Apollo story, when it is Apollo's flaying of Marsyas that inspires such sorrow.

27 Marco da Gagliano, Al lettore: 'La scena di pianto d'Apollo, che segue, vuol esser cantata co' l maggior affetto che sia possibile; con tutto ciò, abbia riguardo il cantore d'accresserolo dove maggiormente lo ricercano le parole.' Solerti, *Gli Albori,* 2: 72.

28 'Quando pronunzia il verso '*Faran ghirlando le sue fronde e i rami,*' avvolgasi quel ramuscello d'alloro, sopra il quale si sarà lamentato, intorno al testa, incoronandosene. . .'

29 '. . . è necessario far apparire al teatro che dalla lira d'Apollo esca melodia più che ordinaria, però pongansi quattro sonatori di viola (a braccio o gamba poco rilieva) in una delle strade più vicina, in luogo dove non veduti dal popolo veggano Apollo. . .'

30 Hanning reminds us that this is why Rinuccini would not have been so concerned with making Daphne a dramatically vibrant character: 'Despite the title of the work, then, the characterization of Daphne clearly remained less important to Rinuccini than her transformation and subsequent immortalization. In fact, the pathos of her fate is inconsequential compared to Apollo's exaltation of her metamorphosed state' (449). While Hanning, in 1979, was not particularly attentive to the gendered implications here, her analysis reminds us of the fate of the female body in this enterprise: 'For Ovid and Rinuccini the dénouement of the myth is thus symbolic of the power of art which, if it cannot possess natural body, can still triumph in immortalizing it' (449). Indeed, as Hanning emphasizes, it is not surprising

that the Medici would have been drawn to the allegorical significance of the Apollo tale.

31 On Cavalli, *Gli amori di Apollo e di Dafne,* see Wendy Heller, 'Venice and Arcadia,' *Musica e Storia* 12 (2004): 21–34; Tim Carter, 'Mask and Illusion: Italian Opera after 1637,' in *The Cambridge Guide to Seventeenth-Century Music,* ed. Tim Carter and John Butt (Cambridge: Cambridge University Press, 2005), 249–59.

32 On the financial structures of Venetian opera, see Beth Elise Glixon and Jonathan Glixon, *Inventing the Business of Opera: The Impresario and His World in Seventeenth-Century Venice* (Oxford University Press: Oxford and New York, 2006).

33 See Andrew Zissos and Ingo Gildenhard, 'Problem of Time in Metamorphoses 2,' in *Ovidan Transformations: Essays on the Metamorphoses and Its Reception,* ed. Alessandro Barchiesi, Philip Hardie, and Stephen Hinds (Cambridge: Cambridge Philological Society, 1999), 31–47.

34 Busenello, *Gli amori di Apollo e di Dafne* (Venice: Giuliani, 1656).

35 'Gl'ingegni Stitici hanno corrotto al Mondo, perche mentre si studia di portar l'abito antico, si rendono le vesti ridicole all'usanza moderna. Ogn'uno abbonda nel senso, & io abbondana nel mio, e trovo in me verificata la massima del nostro Divino Petrarco, *Ogn'un del suo saper par che s'appaghi.'* The passage from Petrarch is taken from his *Trionfa della fama,* 3.96.

36 Aurora, known as one of the most rapacious of all the goddesses, fell in love with Tithonus, a mortal. She then asked Zeus if he would grant Tithonus immortal life; he did so, but allowed him to age first. 'So while he enjoyed the sweet flower of life he lived rapturously with golden-throned Eos, Erigeneia (early-born), by the streams of Okeanos, at the ends of the earth; but when the first grey hairs began to ripple from his comely head and noble chin, Lady Eos stayed away from his bed, though she cherished him in her house, nourished him with food and ambrosia and gave him rich clothing. But when loathsome old age pressed full upon him, and he could not move nor lift his limbs, this seemed to her in her heart the best counsel: she laid him in a room and put to the shining doors. There he babbles endlessly, and no more has strength at all, such as once he had in his supple limbs' (*Homeric Hymn 5 to Aphrodite,* 218).

37 In his discussion *of Gli amori di Apollo e di Dafne* in the *Cambridge History of Seventeenth-Century Music,* Tim Carter notes that Cavalli provides us with a 'glorious musical display of Dafne's voice' (258), then comments that 'it does almost nothing to project any drama, save allowing a character to state her position several times over.' This is an example in which an adherence to a rigid aesthetic criterion – one that insists upon dramatic realism above

other parameters – limits our understanding of opera's encounters with the ancient world. Thus, while Carter correctly observes the fact that the opera is saturated with references to music and song, he still sees this in terms of the notion of verisimilitude. 'It helps, of course, that here the characters are gods and nymphs living in an Age of Gold; this has been the justification for music in the very first operas, not the least of those based on the Orpheus myth' (259).

38 On the role of Bernini in theatrical and artistic endeavours, see Frederick Hammond, *Music and Spectacle in Baroque Rome: Barberini Patronage under Urban VIII* (New Haven, CT: Yale University Press, 1994); *Gian Lorenzo Bernini: registra del barocco*, ed. Maria Grazia Bernadini and Maurizio Fagiolo dell'Arco (Milan: Skira, 1999); Maurizio Faigolo dell'Arco, *Novità sul registra del barocco: Berniniana* (Milan: Skira, 1999). See also Wendy Heller, 'A Musical Metamorphosis: Ovid, Bernini and Handel's Apollo e Dafne,' *Handel Jahrbuch* (2008), 35–63.

39 Busenello, *Gli amori di Apollo e di Dafne*, act 3, scene 2: 'Vada la vita mia, com'à te piace, / Per salvar l'honestate, / Se non basta in un'a bore, in un sasso, / Trasformarmi a tuo senno. / Vada perigrinando / Per mille varie esser mio, / Pria, che cader dal virginal decoro / Delle grand'alme singolar tesoro.'

40 Busenello, *Gli amori di Apollo e di Dafne*, act 3, scene 3: 'Ohimé, che miro? Ohimé dunque; in alloro / Ti cangi, o Dafne, e mentre in rami, e in frondi, / Le belle membra oltredivine ascondi, / Povero tronco chiude il mio tesoro. / Qual senso humano, ò qual celeste ingegno / A' si profondo arcano arrivò mai? /Veggo d'un viso arboreggiare i rai / Trovo il mio foco trasformato in legno.'

41 For a transcription of the entire lament, see Rosand, *Opera in Seventeenth-Century Venice* (Berkeley and Los Angeles: University of California Press, 1991), 628–34.

42 Busenello, *Gli amori di Apollo e di Dafne*, act 3, scene 4 : 'Prendi tu di quei rami / E te ne fa corona al biondo crine; / Coronane la cetra, e ti consola, / Che ne fronzuti, e immortali allori / La memoria vivrà d'eterni amori.'

43 Busenello, *Gli amori di Apollo e di Dafne*, act 3, scene 4 : 'Ohimé dunque si crudo / Contro ninfa innocente / Stendi la man feroce? / Questi sono gli amori / O insidioso Apollo, / Nemico del mio onor mentre fui donna / Frattor de' rami miei, mentro son pianta.'

44 On this point, see Heller, 'Tacitus: Incognito: Opera as History in L'incoronazione di Poppea,' *Journal of the American Musicological Society* 52 (1999): 39–96.

45 Carter, 'Mask and Illusion,' 253.

46 For the score, see I-Vnm, Cod. It IV 386 (= 9910); the libretto is published as Aurelio Aureli, *Gli amori di Apollo e di Leucotoe* (Nicolini: Venice, 1663).

47 On Aureli's librettos, see Wendy Heller, 'Poppea's Legacy: The Julio-Claudians on the Venetian Stage,' *Journal of Interdisciplinary History* 36, no. 3 (Winter 2005): 279–302, and 'The Beloved's Image: Handel's *Admeto* and the Statue of Alcestis,' *Journal of the American Musicological Society* 58, no. 3 (2005): 559–637.

48 The libretto only includes Apollo's son Phaeton (Fetonte); in the score, however, the inclusion of Orpheus (Orfeo) and Esculapius (Esculapio), representing music and medicine respectively, provided Volpe with an opportunity to write an elaborate trio at the end of act 1, scene 2.

49 For a transcription and discussion of Leucotoe's lament, see Rosand, *Opera in Seventeenth-Century Venice*, 380–1; 665–7.

50 Aureli, *Gli amori di Apollo e di Leucotoe*, act 3, scene 16: 'Diffondete miei raggi in terra i lumi, / Mia bella estinta il tuo sepolcro indoro / Chiuso in povero tronco il mio thesoro / Produr vedrassi incenso grato a Numi. / Sorgi o pianti gradita, e o odor Sabeo. / Spirarmi in seno ò vaga mia deffonta / Mentra Apollo per te mesto tramonta / Splende al tuo Funeral lume Febreo. [Spread light, my rays, over the earth, / your guilded tomb, my dead beauty / My treasure enclosed in a poor trunk, I would see bring forth an aroma pleasing to the Gods,/ Rise, oh welcome plant, and exhale a Sabean / aroma into my breast, / O lovely deceased one /While, for you, Apollo sadly sets the sun, / Phoebus shines for your funeral.]

51 Aurelio Aureli, *Gli amori di Apollo e di Leucotoe*, act 3, scene 17: 'Qual forza violente / Mi trahe sottera, e come in un momente/ le mie piante infelicie / Qui diventan radici? / In Elitroppio mi trasformo? Ahi lasso! / In piacer de mortali / Così presto quaggiu termina, e passa? / O vendette d'Apollo, o crudo Nume? Gel di morte divien l'ardor d'Amore? / Anco cangiata in fiore / Seguirà Clitia ogn'ora il tuo bel lume.

chapter eight

A Viceroy behind the Scenes: Opera, Production, Politics, and Financing in 1680s Naples

LOUISE K. STEIN

Undeterred by the centuries-old Black Legend that 'equated Spain with the Inquisition, religious bigotry, and the bloody persecution of Protestants and Jews,'[1] scholars in recent decades have worked insightfully to understand the relationships among power, authority, religion, nobility, and musical expression in early modern Spain and its extensive dominions. A number of early modern Spanish rulers and aristocrats were ardent connoisseurs, collectors, or patrons of music, art, and theatre – individuals with taste, passion, and personality, rather than faceless bureaucrats or prudish zealots. The question I hope to begin to address in this essay concerns the extent to which their choices and actions as patrons were shaped by personal or private concerns, rather than the broadly political, 'official' motivations that scholars have tended to take for granted when studying seventeenth-century music and society. In particular, my inquiry concerns the extent to which operas performed both publicly and in private were flexible structures of feeling designed for personal expression and affective projection, rather than political assertion or sovereign displays of authority. I also suggest ways in which opera might constitute or work within structures created to explore the affective world of patrons and producers, rather than the composer's thoughts, attitudes, temperament, or biography.

Opera under the Spanish viceroys in late seventeenth-century Naples presents an inviting case study in the intersection of private and public or personal and governmental motivations. The viceroys were at once mere agents of an absent sovereign and hands-on absolute rulers themselves; each controlled and was controlled by some portion of the vast bureaucracy of the Spanish monarchy; and each served in Naples for only a limited period, such that each short reign might constitute a circumscribed moment in the history of patronage and production. Toward the end of the Hapsburg epoch, just before most of Europe became engulfed in the War of the Spanish Succession, Spanish diplomats and colonial rulers enjoyed considerable prosperity and freedom to construct their own opulent courts far from Madrid.

Late seventeenth-century Naples also constitutes a critical locus for the development of enduring musical forms, theatrical conventions, and institutions. The vital contribution of the Spanish viceroys has not been fully understood, in part because their limitations as colonial rulers presiding over a hybrid culture (at once Neapolitan, Spanish, and Italian) cannot be adequately accommodated within the standard paradigms for the study of opera production developed for more homogeneous seventeenth-century courts and cities.[2] Naples was a densely populated city with a busy calendar of public and private festivities (religious and secular), where the viceroys had long used entertainments, processions, and performances as vehicles for the kind of ubiquitous propaganda upon which early modern sovereigns everywhere depended. When opera was integrated into public and private life in this, Europe's most densely populated, city, it became one of several kinds of theatrical performance already sponsored by various agents and in a variety of locations.[3] The intersection of private and public in the final decades of Spanish Hapsburg rule (roughly, 1650–1708) – how private patrons were instrumental in funding and shaping private and public performances, and how the preferences of individual patrons (for singers, topics, and aria styles, for example) were accommodated by the developing systems of production – has not been sufficiently recognized.[4] Scholars sometimes have generalized about the politics of opera in Naples without knowing securely, for instance, how qualities such as 'public' and 'private' were defined, or how local circumstances and the personal inclinations of one or another sponsor might have conditioned specific productions.

Naples presents an additional challenge because opera production there was not an exclusively 'Italian' phenomenon. True, opera was financed and supported by private individuals among the Neapolitan nobility, but also by members of the 'Spanish families' in Naples who owed allegiance to the Spanish crown and, principally, by Spanish viceroys who came to Naples with little or no prior experience of Italian music, Italian opera, Italian singers, Italian musical conventions, or Italian models of production. Yet they supported Italian opera and its performers, and they renovated, reconstructed, or enhanced the spaces for opera. Given the 'foreignness' of opera as a genre to these Spanish aristocrats and the unfamiliarity of the musical language of mid-century Italian opera to most of them (and perhaps to a good part of the Neapolitan audience as well, at least in the first years), it is hard to imagine that the genre only served as an instrument of simple propaganda conveying hegemonic narratives of empire.

Spanish patrons at home and abroad supported many genres of musical-theatrical spectacle, and, indeed, for Spaniards, opera was but one among several types of lavish theatrical entertainment. Most important, fully sung opera was an exceptional genre in the Spanish context; at the royal court in Madrid it was cultivated selectively in the seventeenth century for celebrations of monarchy (royal birthdays and weddings, for example), but it was not the genre of choice for public festivities or broadly political statements of the sort that the genre of the *serenata* offered the ruling families, ambassadors, and influential cardinals in Rome and Naples in the late seventeenth century. Because Spanish viceroys and ambassadors carried their culture with them to their Italian postings, it may prove useful to question whether opera in Naples was produced exclusively in accordance with Italian models, and whether its inspiration, social function, and affective potential were as limited as has generally been supposed.

The first aristocratic producer of opera in the Hispanic context, the producer of both the first extant Spanish operas at the royal court in Madrid and the first operas composed by Alessandro Scarlatti for Naples, was anything but a faceless bureaucrat. This Spanish aristocrat, Gaspar de Haro y Guzmán (figure 8.1, Portrait of Carpio) was known as the marquis de Heliche (also Liche, Eliche, Licce) in Madrid and as marquis del Carpio in Italy.[5] He was the son of Luis Méndez de Haro, the *valido* or first minister to King Philip IV who played a decisive role in European politics as principal representative of the Spanish crown in the negotiations toward the Peace of the Pyrenees and the marriage of Louis XIV to María Teresa of Spain. Gaspar de Haro y Guzmán (born 1 June 1629) not only inherited wealth and a substantial art collection from his father at a relatively young age, but became the 'foremost private collector' of paintings in Europe in his time, if only for the quantity of paintings he possessed.[6] At his death in 1687 in Naples, his collection contained more than 3,000 works, 1,200 of them in his Spanish palaces and about 1,800 more in Naples.[7] Beyond collecting art and antiquities, he was a patron of contemporary artists (Diego Velázquez, Carlo Maratta, and

Figure 8.1 Jacques Blondeau, *Gaspar de Haro y Guzmán*, engraving, 1682. Madrid, Biblioteca Nacional de España.

Luca Giordano were among the painters he supported) and a producer of plays, operas, semi-operas, musical theatre, and all manner of fiestas and entertainments.[8]

Among the Spanish viceroys, the marquis de Heliche y del Carpio (hereafter simply 'Carpio') was unique because he was an experienced producer of musical theatre in Madrid long before he was sent to Italy as Spanish ambassador to the Holy See (1677–82) and then viceroy of Naples (1683–7). Because Italian opera was not performed in Madrid in his lifetime, Carpio had no chance to experience it until he arrived in Italy in 1677, but his early experience in Madrid surely was fundamental to his understanding of operas as 'structures of feeling' later in 1680s Naples. His activity as a producer of Spanish musical plays began at a crucial moment in the 1650s, just after the reopening of Madrid's public theatres and the renovation of court plays that anticipated the arrival of a new young queen, Mariana de Austria. Carpio held a number of court appointments, but his early responsibilities were not designed to advance his career along the paths of power that we generally imagine as appropriate for a male aristocrat (toward an advantageous military command, for example). Rather, his duties at court placed him in close emotional and physical proximity to the king and his family. At age fourteen (in 1643) Carpio was appointed Royal Huntsman to Philip IV, in charge of the king's beloved hunting parties, whose outdoor exercise was deemed necessary for the king's physical health and virility, and thus essential to the well-being of the entire monarchy. In addition, two years later Carpio began to serve as companion to the child-prince Baltasar Carlos (who died suddenly in 1646). From an early age, then, Carpio was entrusted with duties both familial and intimate – responsibilities whose success depended on his personal energy, organizational talent, and capacity for empathy.[9] He was valued for his affective contributions and sensitivity; in particular, Philip IV long remembered his kindness to the young prince Baltasar Carlos and the reciprocal affection the prince showed Carpio.[10]

In the 1650s, Carpio's purview broadened when he took on the responsibilities of Alcaide or Governor of the Buen Retiro, Pardo, and Zarzuela palaces in place of his father, who was burdened by affairs of state and had no interest in theatrical production. Invested with this new authority over the royal pleasure palaces and performance spaces, Carpio began to produce plays with music to entertain Philip IV and his young queen. In assigning the duties of alcaide to his son, Luis de Haro clearly recognized his son's aesthetic sensibility, understood where his talent lay, and how he might advance his career at court. Carpio directed the renovation and redecoration of the Coliseo theatre of the Buen Retiro palace,[11] and his knowledge of contemporary art and artists served him well as he supervised the stage architects, painters, and designers he recruited from Italy for the Spanish king's service.[12] At the Buen Retiro, Carpio mounted productions of mythological semi-operas in 1652 and 1653, in addition to sponsoring the royal hunting parties, banquets, and performances slightly later at the pastoral retreat in the wooded outskirts of Madrid known as the Palacio de la Zarzuela. In 1657 he produced the first examples in the partly sung burlesque and generally pastoral genre of the zarzuela. It was surely Carpio who put together the creative team of Pedro Calderón de la Barca, poet and court dramatist, and Juan Hidalgo, virtuoso harpist and composer, for the royal operas, semi-operas, and zarzuelas of the period (1650–62).[13] In spite of the fact that he was working within the Spanish court's creaky old administrative apparatus, burdened with all manner of bureaucratic baggage and ancient protocols, Carpio forced open the way for the creation of a Spanish kind of opera, and designed the new genres of the zarzuela and the semi-opera long before his own journey to Italy. Indeed, as I hope to demonstrate, the skill and taste that distinguished Carpio's early hands-on experience as a producer of Spanish entertainments at Madrid served him well when he ruled Naples and produced Italian opera there in the 1680s.

It was during Carpio's tenure in Madrid that the Spanish genres (mythological semi-operas, pastoral zarzuelas, and two fully sung operas) developed the strikingly unique performance conventions that would distinguish Spanish musical theatre well into the eighteenth century.[14] In the Madrid productions, singing roles were assigned with particular attention to the gender and vocal timbre of the performers. All of the serious singing roles in the zarzuelas, semi-operas, and operas (whether male or female characters) were taken by singer-actresses. The top singers had high voices (the tessitura of the principal roles in the opera scores tends to hover at the upper part of the range longer than what is typical of most Italian roles of the mid-seventeenth century, even after the required transposition of the high clefs to sounding pitch) but enough histrionic ability to perform second-tier spoken roles in the standard comedias for the public theatres. Castrati seem not to have sung onstage in Spanish court productions (though the royal chapel included them), and men did not sing serious roles onstage, except when they formed part of a verisimilar, anonymous ensemble of 'músicos' singing courtly ensemble songs within the play. One of the large machine plays with music that Carpio prepared in 1655 was said to exhibit twenty-four singing women on each of its fantastic stage machines, while the burlesque that he presented later in the same year showcased seventy.[15] The casts of the two operas Carpio produced in 1660–61 call for eleven to fifteen female singers and only one or two men in comic or special roles.[16]

In order to stage the musical plays, Carpio used his position early on to bring the best actress-singers in Spain to Madrid for the court productions. One of his commands forced all of them to desert their regular companies and congregate in Madrid to work under his orders.[17] Thus, exercising his personal preference for female voices and feminine display, Carpio converted his personal inclination into law. Carpio's productions both promoted women and exhibited them for the pleasure of the court. He arranged for the actress-singers to wear only the best in dresses and jewellery, made sure they were ferried to and from rehearsals and performances by royal coachmen, and protected them from overwork and indecent exposure before men of anything but the highest class. True, the actress-singers were exploited as objects on display for the royal enjoyment, but, in another sense, his patronage ennobled them because it provided an opportunity for low-born women to enjoy at least the illusion of power onstage – a chance they enjoyed in much smaller numbers, if at all, elsewhere in Europe.

It should not surprise us that the musical plays featured and favoured a display of feminine talent that far exceeded that of other European patrons, given his preferences. The musical-theatrical works that Carpio staged for Philip IV contained scenes that can be associated as well with flagrantly erotic paintings in his own or the royal collection. His art collections contained a significantly larger number of paintings on profane and mythological subjects than other Spanish collections, with an especially large number of paintings with female nudes.[18] He owned various paintings by Juan Bautista Martínez del Mazo that were copies of Titian's *Poesie* (the famously prized group of erotic mythological paintings in the Alcázar that Carpio knew first-hand from an early age). Displayed at the heart of the Alcázar palace in the king's private chambers, the Titian *Poesie* and other paintings of female nudes were enjoyed by aristocratic viewers precisely because they were pointedly erotic – though they were covered with a cloth when a lady or the queen passed through.[19] For a wall in his own palace (the Palacio de la Moncloa in Madrid, destroyed in 1936) Carpio commissioned a frescoed copy of José Ribera's passionate *Venus Lamenting the Death of Adonis*, in which a Venus with hair let down and bared breasts flies to the side of her mortally wounded lover.[20] By 1651, when he was only twenty-two years old, his collection of about 350 master paintings included Diego Velázquez's *Venus at the Mirror* or *Venus and Cupid* (the *Rokeby Venus* now in the National Gallery in London) – the only extant painting of a completely nude female by a Spanish seventeenth-century painter and the first Spanish painting on this theme.[21] It is likely that Carpio commissioned or obtained this undeniably erotic masterpiece in roughly the same years as he began to explore the erotic potential of musical theatre as court entertainment.[22]

Carpio's peers recognized his ability to appreciate and cultivate the erotic as a patron, collector, and producer, but his contemporaries also remarked on the intensity of his amorous and sexual relationships with women of lower social status.[23] The diarist Barrionuevo ascribed the frequent seizures and bouts of ill health that he suffered as a young man in Madrid to the fact that he was 'bewitched' by these women.[24] Insinuations about his tendency to become intimate with non-aristocratic women followed him even later in life.[25] When serving in Rome as Spanish ambassador, a particularly nasty cardinal accused him (without basis) of harbouring a 'donna di mala vita' in the embassy itself.[26] Unguarded displays were unusual in Spanish gentlemen, though his generosity and gallantry toward women were much admired. While Carpio's promotion of women as actresses, singers, and artists is unprecedented in the Hispanic context, as far as I know, his sexual involvement with actresses was to be expected of a Spanish aristocrat in seventeenth-century Madrid. It was the intensity of Carpio's liaisons that drew attention, not the mere fact that he pursued extramarital affairs.

Carpio's passionate nature fascinated his contemporaries in Italy as well, but many kinds of evidence reveal his very steady hand and the degree to which he was admired and respected. During his years in Italy, he not only collected paintings of women, but supported female artists, even using his position as viceroy to found an informal academy of female painters in Naples.[27] Women of all sorts liked him, in spite of his very ugly face. The famously devout Queen Christina of Sweden admired him, though they attended the same events only during a brief period in his Roman residence, given her political alliance with the French.[28] Aristocratic ladies sought his company in Rome, and he spent weeks, literally, paying them farewell visits prior to leaving Rome at the end of 1682.[29] The gentleness he displayed toward the child-prince Baltasar Carlos; the tenderness he expressed for his wife, daughters, and favourite niece; his popularity with the Roman ladies are all clues to his extraordinary personal sensitivity – an important quality in a hands-on opera director, in any age.

Carpio's passionate nature and gift for artistic appreciation were, most likely, inseparable from his appreciation of women in the flesh, on the stage, and on canvas. Carpio promoted works of an exquisite lyricism that moved the 'affections' of his audience. His tendency to express himself without inhibition and his support of feminine intelligence placed him at the forefront of what Dewald has underlined as a movement toward 'affective individualism' among the European nobility,[30] though Carpio's modern biographers have insisted on censuring the man while valuing his record as a patron.[31]

However personal his involvement in them, Carpio's theatrical productions were not merely personal. A Spanish aristocrat had two primary duties – to the monarchy and to his family. In an absolutist system sustained by a hereditary monarchy, the question of the royal succession was most important – a king needed to produce heirs, especially male heirs, to perpetuate his dynasty. Likewise, members of the aristocracy were expected to perpetuate the system by producing heirs to carry on their traditions, accumulate wealth, and serve the monarchy in hereditary positions. Without heirs who would survive to adulthood, a family faded from the scene. The primary responsibility of each male aristocrat was to '*crear sucesión*,' both in the physical sense and as a service to the monarchy. This may explain why the stimulating and fertile extramarital escapades of King Philip IV himself were not a source of more censure and embarrassment (he sired and recognized at least two bastard offspring), and why every instance of a missed menstrual period for the queen was publicly announced and joyously celebrated as a sign of possible royal pregnancy. Men like Carpio reported their wives' missed menstrual periods in letters to other men in their families, though Spanish culture reserved a special place for noble women, who passed their days in the protective custody of groups that excluded men. The higher the social position, the more remote and cloistered their lives. By reserving passionate physicality for their encounters with lower-class women or professionals, Spanish aristocrats protected their wives from anything close to violence in the sexual act, thus reserving their wives' slender bodies and sexual energies for, it was hoped, the supremely important act of procreation. Erotic paintings and theatre provided a kind of refined titillation for aristocratic audiences – an incitement to productive action – especially because both noblemen and women were in attendance at court productions. Ideally, the king and his vassals would be sexually productive, even in old age. Procreative activity was essential to the perpetuation of the ruling class and its hierarchy, and Spanish aristocrats valued erotic stimulation. Thus erotic art, theatre, and music held political value because they were as 'good' for kings and aristocrats as they were potentially dangerous to the uneducated.

When a young and vital Carpio organized the king's hunts and diversions, he took on the all-important job of providing an exhausted monarch with healthy, relaxing pleasures and stimulating entertainment, just at a time when the security of the Spanish royal succession was endangered. Philip IV's first wife, Isabel, had died suddenly in 1644, and his only son from that marriage died in 1646 at the age of four. Philip remarried in 1648, taking his niece, Mariana of Austria, as his bride (she was then only thirteen). Beginning with her entry into Madrid in 1649, the court was transformed in an effort to keep her cheerful – the poor young thing was married to a depressed old man, and, after all, in her womb and in her propensity for sexual activity (or lack of it) lay the future of the kingdom. Mariana and Philip eventually produced one male heir who lived past his childhood – Carlos II, born in 1661. But in light of the high infant mortality rate among the royal babies, much of the entertainment that Carpio produced at court between 1650 and 1662 surely was meant to inspire the royal couple or to celebrate their procreative success (however temporary). Operas and musical plays were only performed for events that had some dynastic importance – royal births and their anniversaries, celebrations of the queen's pregnancies, the name days of the royal family, and, finally, the celebration of dynastic weddings.

The marquis del Carpio was invested with the power to entertain, and this was a weighty responsibility. What's more, he was *chosen* to carry out this important service precisely because of his good taste and his obvious affinity for things erotic. In other words, he was not awarded his court position in spite of his temperament and his appetite for women and extravagance, but precisely because of them. Carpio was famously 'without scruples' when it came to collecting, trading, or talking about nude paintings, and he was neither boastful nor ashamed of his strong sexual appetite.[32] The disgrace that he suffered in Madrid in 1662 – his trial, temporary exile, and imprisonment – must have seemed a cruel mockery of his passion and sensitivity as the king's theatrical producer, whether or not he actually committed the crimes of which he was accused (he may well have been framed).[33]

The marquis del Carpio's love affair with Italian opera began when he took up residence in Naples as the Spanish viceroy more than twenty years later, in 1683. Though Naples by this time had a varied thirty-year history of public and private opera, Carpio's intervention changed the way operas looked, sounded, and were produced in Naples, setting a new high standard that was to distinguish Neapolitan opera decades after his death. Even before Carpio's arrival there, the organization of productions in Naples (such as it was) owed a great deal to the Spanish procedures introduced by the viceroys.[34] Indeed, beginning in late 1660, in conformity with what Carpio had organized in Madrid, the Count of Peñaranda (Gaspar de Bracamonte y Guzmán) instituted the practice of offering operas at the Palazzo Reale for the royal birthdays (that of the Queen Mother of Spain 22 December, and of Charles II on 6 November after 1661).[35] This created a short Advent season with productions celebrating the same occasions that the Spanish court in Madrid honoured annually with musical plays. In Naples, as in Madrid, opera was linked to dynastic events that the viceroy commemorated in homage to his sovereign.

The system that financed opera in Naples (though it can hardly be called a 'system') also had a Spanish flavour – one that did not adhere exclusively to the nearest Italian precedents. Opera in Rome was sustained almost entirely by private patronage and produced in aristocratic palaces with sporadic seasons in commercial theatres. In Venice opera flourished thanks to a combination of income from ticket sales and box rentals, supported by the private and ostensibly non-governmental backing of wealthy families with civic pride and an appetite for social status. But the financing of operas in Naples under some of the viceroys reflects Spanish court practice.

In the 1670s and later – for instance, during Carpio's time – most of the operas were financed thanks to the viceroy's access to royal funds, though his private funds were most likely also deployed as necessary. Support from the viceroys facilitated both palace productions for the invited nobility and public, commercial opera. The general practice was to stage operas in a temporary theatre erected in the Sala Grande at the Palazzo Reale and, subsequently, at the public Teatro di San Bartolomeo.[36] Opera libretti printed in Naples in the 1670s and 1680s bear dedications to the viceroy in power.[37] To some extent, the viceroys subsidized the carnival operas at the public Teatro di San Bartolomeo, though carnival was also the period each year that provided the impresario, musicians, and singers their best income. The schedule in Naples projected two operas in the late autumn, with the December opera sometimes appearing in the public theatre in January, followed by another opera or two during carnival. An additional summer opera with a smaller cast in June or early July was sometimes offered. In Carpio's reign, each opera was first performed privately for the viceroy and the nobility at the Palazzo Reale, and then at the Teatro di San Bartolomeo for a substantial run of public performances. The income from ticket sales and the rental of boxes could not wholly cover the full production cost, so the impresarios always had problems paying the singers and meeting their contractual obligations to the Florentine financiers who appear to have put forward the start-up money for each season. Subventions from the viceroy not only allowed the public opera productions to continue, but also brought the Neapolitan practice closer to the integration of court and commercial financing that the viceroys expected, based on what they knew from Madrid.

Although the Palazzo Reale in Naples did not have a permanent theatre during the late seventeenth century, performances in a dismountable theatre set up in the Sala Grande were often opened to the public. Here again, in Naples the viceroys emulated the practice of their Spanish sovereigns, who opened the italianate Coliseo theatre of the Buen Retiro palace to the public, sometimes for a period of weeks at a time.[38] The temporary theatre in the Sala Grande surely also reminded them of the temporary theatre often erected quickly or on short notice by a team of engineers and carpenters in the Salón Dorado of the Alcázar palace in Madrid.[39] The fact that some of the Italian operas produced at the San Bartolomeo reused sets and costumes paid for by the viceroy for palace performances suggests that performances with full staging took place in both the palace and the Teatro di San Bartolomeo (i.e., that duplicate sets were built). But there is also evidence that the sets were moved from the temporary stage in the palace to the permanent stage of the San Bartolomeo theatre, though it is unclear whether both venues were equipped with the same kinds of stage machinery. The temporary theatre apparently had the mechanisms necessary for the elaborate visual spectacle called for in the libretti and for which the court productions were famous, especially during Carpio's reign. In any case, the viceroys drew upon a Spanish royal precedent when they moved whole productions from one theatre to another in Naples.

In Naples the justifications for the use of official funds in support of public opera were the same ones put forth in Madrid on behalf of the *corrales*: theatrical performances provided a controlled distraction and entertainment for the citizenry, while displaying the power, good intentions, and generosity of the sovereign (or viceroy), and honouring the monarchy. But public theatre in Naples (as in Madrid) also supported charities. Since Philip II's royal decree of 1583, a portion of the profits from the rental of boxes in the Teatro di San Bartolomeo was given to the Ospedale degli Incurabili (the lunatic asylum or hospital for the mentally ill). The Santa Casa degl'Incurabili, responsible in part for the erection of the San Bartolomeo in 1621 as a venue for spoken theatre, held the monopoly on public commercial theatre, thanks to a reinforcement of the *jus repraesentandi* decree by Philip IV; the order's permission was required before anyone could sell tickets to a staged entertainment in Naples.[40] But commercial performances did not preclude private ones, and the impresarios were still obliged to and supported by the viceroy. The performers in the 1657–9 operas at the Teatro di San Bartolomeo, for example, collected into a company known as the Accademia degli Armonici, were bound in a commercial relationship with the impresario Gregorio delle Chiave; but their 1658 contract required them to perform at the San Bartolomeo and the Palazzo Reale when requested by the Viceroy.[41]

Because few documents survive, it is difficult to know just how much of the funding was provided by each viceroy's personal accounts and how much from royal funds. Some official funding for opera in Naples undoubtedly came from the Cuenta de Gastos Secretos assigned to each Viceroy but regulated from Madrid, given that money for other public spectacles sponsored by the viceroy came mostly from this account. Certain expenses incurred in the course of producing public events could be paid from the fund for Gastos Públicos, but the two accounts were not to be commingled. To facilitate the hiring of singers and purchase of materials before a given season, money was loaned by financial agents to the impresarios – but it may be that money from the viceroy actually sustained this 'loan,' as funding from the viceroy could be transferred and deposited in the bank accounts of financial agents, in one or more of the public banks. The very few extant payment records pertaining to opera performance in Carpio's reign do not include the stipulation 'per servizio di Sua Eccelenza,' which accompanies the payments from Scarlatti's bank account to the musicians who played in the 1686 *serenata*.[42] But there is one payment issued from the account of the financial agents Guidetti and Gondi to the castrato Matteo Sassano 'as ordered by His Excellency the marquis del Carpio, Viceroy,' to pay for Matteucio's performances in the three operas of the previous season.[43] If, as this might indicate, the financing of Carpio's opera productions resembled that for his 1686 *serenata*, then his operas drew on money provided through the Gastos Secretos, but dispersed by independent financial agents (Guidetti and Gondi) who were not part of the governmental bureaucracy.[44]

The Neapolitan viceroys had access to a stream of royal funding because musical theatre was deemed politically beneficial to the monarchy and a source of solace for its subjects.[45] Public and semi-private festivities (the overtly political *serenatas*, the seaside spectacles and bullfights the viceroy offered at Posilippo, the operas performed during carnival at the Teatro San Bartolomeo, and the expensive private productions for the nobility at the Palazzo Reale) were justified as politically expedient. That the crown sanctioned and encouraged the presentation of operas on royal birthdays is made absolutely clear in letters from the king to the viceroy in which the king begs for fiscal restraint in a time of budget crises, but grants that 'fiestas are indispensable for celebration of my birthday and for the diversion of the populace.'[46] Given the support offered by the viceroys to the San Bartolomeo productions, both the operas produced publicly and those given privately at the palace were financed by 'public' funds and in the service of the monarchy. Indeed, the best-known notarial document concerning the finances of Carpio's first opera season makes it clear that the musicians were paid for their work in both venues, 'having performed in the San Bartolomeo Theater and the Royal Palace in the Royal Festivities of the past season of the year 1683.'[47] In this sense, the Neapolitan situation presents a relationship between court and public theatres that bears considerable resemblance to what the viceroys were familiar with from Madrid.

The fact that the court at Naples had no traditional administrative mechanism for assuring the presence of a resident operatic troupe, together with the status of professional opera singers in Italy, created difficulties for the viceroys (within the Spanish system) that other, independent rulers at Italian courts probably did not face. For example, soon after assuming power in Naples in September 1675, Carpio's predecessor, the marquis de los Vélez, began to organize an opera at the Palazzo Reale and ordered three singers from the royal chapel to perform in it 'just for this one time,' in spite of the prohibition preventing chapel singers from performing in the theatres.[48] The singers served the viceroy and did not wish to ignore his orders, but they were male professional singers dedicated to the performance of sacred music and prohibited from working with members of a lowly acting company. It is likely that de los Vélez felt that he was justified within Spanish precedent, since musicians in the Spanish royal chapel (mostly not singers, but continuo players such as the harpist Juan Hidalgo and the keyboard player Francisco Clavijo, for example) were often called upon or commanded to perform in royal theatrical productions in Madrid (for which they were remunerated with an 'ayuda de costa').

Even if the three castrati from the royal chapel performed in the November 1675 opera for the king's birthday, viceroy de los Vélez learned quickly that an opera season could not be mounted with the forces already at court. In preparation for carnival 1676, he paid the travel expenses and a subsidy to bring a complete opera troupe of 'Istrioni Musici, chiamati col nome generale di febi Armonici' from Rome, as had several previous viceroys.[49] Prior to Carpio's reorganization of operatic production in Naples (and his bold appointment of first-rate opera singers to the royal chapel), every season in Naples presented a set of practical difficulties for viceroys conditioned by the Madrid experience. In Madrid, theatrical production at court was facilitated by the two resident acting companies that remained in Madrid nearly all year, thanks to the income from their almost-daily performances of spoken plays at the commercial theatres. The female singers who graced the court stages there were members of these resident troupes, not independent, high-salaried castrati. In Naples, Italian operas required specialist singers who did not depend on spoken theatre for their livelihood. Thus, de los Vélez and other viceroys before Carpio often were forced to hire and import troupes from outside Naples to stage even the operas expected for the royal birthdays in November and December.

This practice of one-off, private organization for individual seasons and performances was perfectly in keeping with the patronage patterns for the Neapolitan aristocracy (both for opera and for other kinds of legitimate theatre), to judge by the number of references to private performances at noble *palazzi* in the yearly sets of *avvisi.* But it was cumbersome to Spanish viceroys more accustomed to a system in which resident performers of low social status presented themselves at a moment's notice to follow orders at court. Further, the Spanish precedent allowed the public to attend performances staged at court theatres in Madrid, and the royal household routinely subsidized productions in the commercial theatres. When Viceroy de los Vélez opened some performances of *Il Teodosio* at the Palazzo Reale in Naples in November 1676 to a paying public,[50] he was surely following this precedent, though the opera was given again at the palace and subsequently at the commercial San Bartolomeo theatre as well during carnival 1677.[51] The viceroy subsidized the performances with personal funds ('a proprie spese') and reimbursed the singers for the original cost of their costumes for the November 1676 performance at the Palazzo Reale.[52] The costumes were most likely used again when *Il Teodosio* was performed at the public theatre in carnival 1677. In like manner, when *Alessandro Magno in Sidone* (Marc'Antonio Ziani) was staged for the king's birthday in November 1679 at the Palazzo Reale, and then also produced at the San Bartolomeo ('nel pubblico Teatro'),[53] the commercial production was heavily subsidized by de los Vélez, given that the San Bartolomeo staging borrowed costumes and sets originally used for the palace performances. In Madrid, this kind of subsidy was altogether routine. In Naples, de los Vélez's personal investment was beyond the ordinary, as he seems also to have paid the living expenses of the acting troupe well beyond the dates of the opera season in order to retain the singers in Naples.

Spanish viceroys with no previous experience as patrons or connoisseurs of Italian opera established Italian opera as a regular feature of both court and civic culture in Naples. Their practice in Naples (shared productions and shared publics between court and public theatres) was clearly shaped by their experience of the royal court in Madrid, where a busy schedule of comedia performances in the public theatres known as *corrales* continued alongside a regular but expandable schedule of spectacle plays (semi-opera, zarzuela, opera, and comedia) at court on special occasions. The crown subsidized theatrical troupes and productions in order to assure that the king was supplied with appropriate entertainments performed elegantly by the most talented companies. By attempting to apply this same benevolently selfish sponsorship to Italian opera in Naples, viceroys such as the Count of Oñate and the marquis de los Vélez sustained both court opera and the public, commercial opera theatre, reducing the financial risk of commercial production.

Some of the Spanish viceroys who preceded the marquis del Carpio exploited the political utility of private and public productions, though most of them invested more vigorously in visually magnificent, monumental urban projects (such as the architectural rehabilitation and redesign of the city). Earlier viceroys did not work as hands-on producers, and the operas they financed were not tailor-made to the Neapolitan situation in artistic or political terms. Operas in Naples before Carpio's time were mainly revivals of Venetian operas, brought by the troupe known as the Febiarmonici. Since the singers and most of the instrumentalists for these operas before 1683 came from outside Naples, this enforced a very clear separation between the 'king's musicians' in the royal chapel and assorted others who performed in the theatre. Viceroys such as the

Count of Oñate and the marquis de los Vélez, then, exercised little or no control over the content and performance values of the operas they supported financially.

The marquis del Carpio displayed his public face principally through the operas. His decisive intervention in Naples was fuelled by both his personal preferences and his Spanish experience. Although his generosity as a patron of musical theatre and the enormous expenditures he released for public festivities in Naples invited criticism on more than one occasion,[54] his genius as a producer enhanced his popularity as a viceroy. He did not simply pick an opera or a libretto off the very full shelf of libretti that circulated in Italy in the 1680s, but instead chose the stories and supervised the writing or revision of the libretti and the set designs when his health allowed him to do so. Three of the Alessandro Scarlatti operas for Naples were, in fact, based on Spanish plays that Carpio had commissioned in Madrid years earlier. The libretti to *L'Aldimiro o vero Favor per favore,* produced in Naples for the king's birthday in November 1683, and *La Psiche,* for the queen mother's birthday in December 1683, are both based on plays by Calderón that Carpio had also produced just the previous year in the Spanish embassy in Rome (as well as long before that in Madrid, in the case of the Psyche play). As I have explained elsewhere, Carpio's motivation for mounting these non-operatic Spanish plays in Rome was both personal and political, and he considered the resulting productions successful and politically astute in part because they were 'showy' and caused quite a stir.[55]

The operatic version of *L'Aldimiro o vero Favor per favore,* with libretto by De Totis and music by Alessandro Scarlatti, was the first opera produced by Carpio and his team in Naples. It is a reworking of Calderón's *Fineza con fineza,* a play first staged in Vienna in 1671 as a birthday present for the empress Margarita (daughter of Philip IV) but not performed publicly in Madrid until December 1682, as far as is known. Carpio presented the Calderón play in the Spanish embassy in Rome in early 1682 as a birthday treat for his niece, Lorenza de la Cerda (residing in Rome as wife of Filippo Colonna). He seems to have chosen this play for Lorenza's birthday because of its especially royal lineage, and it may be that its presentation in Madrid in December 1682, with the sponsorship of the Duke of Medinaceli (Lorenza's father and Carpio's father-in-law from his first marriage) and only months after Carpio's private staging in Rome, was somehow prompted by Carpio's Roman production.[56]

Another Calderón play, *Ni amor se libra de amor,* an erotically charged musical play about Cupid and Psyche, was the basis for Carpio's next opera in Naples, *La Psiche, ovvero Amore innamorato* (Naples, 1683) by Alessandro Scarlatti with libretto by De Totis. The mythological story of Cupid and Psyche seems to have held special significance for Carpio, and *Ni amor se libra de amor* had been his last triumph at the Spanish court when it was first performed 19 January 1662 in Madrid,[57] just a month before his arrest. The play also served as the source for two of Carpio's productions in Rome in 1681 and 1682,[58] where its central story offered an allegory of Carpio's personal fidelity to the crown. In both Spanish play and Italian libretto, the character of Cupido/Amore (a god smitten with a mortal) seems a clear projection of the marquis del Carpio himself – the generous lover touched and disarmed by extreme feminine beauty, who protects and lavishes his wealth on a woman of lower status as he hides his own true visage.

The De Totis/Scarlatti *La Psiche* follows the Calderón play with some adjustments. In the opera Cupid is '*un mostro d'amor*'; Psyche is forbidden to see his face, which Psyche and her sisters in the operatic version suspect may be disfigured. Like this Cupid, Carpio was ugly of face but famously generous (in the play and the opera Cupid bestows on Psyche a vast palace and every luxury then imaginable). Carpio suffered throughout his life from ill health, most especially a crippling gout, severe enough during his time in Italy to require long periods of bed-ridden confinement. He was a loving vassal of the monarchy but his reputation was deformed or defaced, so to speak, by the 1662 accusation of treason and the resulting scandal. Moreover, like Cupid, who is unable to dwell with Psyche in the light of day but may visit her only in the dark, Carpio was banished from proximity to his sovereign and his reflected glory – he was, in this sense also, deformed or crippled. Through his Portuguese exile and subsequent postings in Italy, he was separated from his wife and prevented from fathering a sufficient family of legitimate heirs, though he was famous as a lover, in spite of his most obvious disability – his very unattractive face.[59] It may well be that through the role of Amore and the passionate arias of the Scarlatti opera, Carpio projected himself as – in Calderón's words – the '*amante perfecto,*' '*sabio, solo, solícito, y secreto*' (wise, alone, discreet, and secret) for beautiful Psyche: 'a monster of love and devotion to his sovereigns.'[60]

Carpio supervised the preparation of a third opera, *Il Fetonte*, the libretto of which was based on another Calderón play, to commemorate the king's birthday in November 1685. It is hardly surprising that this opera also developed a mythological story that held special significance in his personal history. In a letter of 16 October 1685 to his friend and brother-in-law, the duke of Pastrana in Madrid (also a patron of musical theatre), Carpio wrote:

> The play that is to be performed for the His Majesty's birthday will be given just as this letter reaches the post, and it has given us a lot of trouble, especially the task of adjusting it, because it is *Faetón* translated from the one that was done there, with lots of machines, and with the best musicians in all of Italy, an expensive enhancement, and the stage with not be undeserving of the play. This is all I can tell you about it for now.[61]

The '*Faetón* translated' was the libretto to *Il Fetonte* (1685), written at Carpio's request, most probably by Giuseppe Domenico De Totis.[62] Carpio's comments reveal his deeply personal responsibility for this production, which cost his team – 'us' – a lot of trouble. Moreover, he describes the libretto as a 'translation' of a play performed in Madrid with elaborate machines and stage effects that had to be 'adjusted' ('*el ajustarlo*') or adapted for Naples. The fine Italian musicians, the 'best in all Italy,' are an expensive enhancement ('*un encarezimiento*'), but Carpio is confident that the staging this time will do them justice.

Carpio's personal entanglement with the Spanish play that served as the model for *Il Fetonte* makes his choice of story for the opera in 1685 especially significant. The libretto is modelled on Pedro Calderón de la Barca's *El Faetonte*, or *El hijo del sol, Faetón*, first performed at court in Madrid in 1661 or 1662, most likely the last court spectacle play that Carpio readied for production before his exile.[63] Indeed, the marquis's political disgrace in Madrid was related directly to his work on this play. When gunpowder was discovered beneath the sets for *El Faetón* on 14 February 1662, Carpio fell under suspicion. As the story goes, his passionate identification with the staging was such that he plotted to blow up the stage rather than see credit for the ingenious machines assigned to his rival.

Calderón's play adapts the myth of Phaethon's ill-fated ride in the chariot of the sun, emphasizing the dangers of youthful impetuousness and erotic vulnerability. The rivalry between Faetón and his half-brother, Epafo, might portray Heliche's rivalry with his cousin (Medina de las Torres), whose lineage allowed him to usurp Carpio's position as alcaide at the Buen Retiro.[64] In the third act of the Neapolitan libretto for Scarlatti's *Il Fetonte* (based on the Calderón text), the title character is impulsive, obsessed, and frenzied. As he strives to prove himself superior to his fraternal rival, he sings impassioned arias challenging destiny and death, but plunges violently to earth when he loses control of the chariot of the sun. Like Carpio, Fetonte lands in exile far from home, a victim of his uncontrolled ambition, passion, and familial jealousy. Carpio's choice of the Phaethon story and Calderón's play as the basis for one of Scarlatti's first operas for Naples may have been motivated by his self-projection, rather than by any larger political plan. Though the occasion was both public and innately political (the celebration of the king's birthday), the opera's content seems to have been dictated by private concerns. And it cannot be coincidental that the machine for '*el carro del Sol*' was brought into a public fiesta yet again in August 1685, in the festivities Carpio organized at Posillipo in honour of Queen María Luisa's name day.

As he explained, for *Il Fetonte,* Carpio brought 'the best musicians that all of Italy has to offer' to Naples. Further, Carpio changed the system of production in Naples by forming a hand-picked resident company for the operas. Again, this is perfectly in keeping with his personal precedent – he liked to have his performers close at hand, and in Madrid he created a production team by gathering the necessary talent around him. Most of the artists he brought to Naples had worked for him in some capacity in Rome during his years as Spanish ambassador.

The composer Alessandro Scarlatti came to Naples permanently thanks to Carpio's patronage, but it may be that Carpio began to count himself among Scarlatti's patrons even in Rome, though Scarlatti wore the title of musician to Queen Christina of Sweden.[65] Scarlatti was a rising star, but his sudden installation as maestro of the Neapolitan royal chapel was unprecedented, especially since a more experienced Neapolitan, Francesco Provenzale, was next in line for the post when the aged Venetian maestro, Pietro Andrea Ziani, died as expected in February 1684. Although Ziani held the position until his death, Provenzale had served actively in his place as '*maestro onorario*' to cover for Ziani's many absences. Carpio's appointment of Alessandro Scarlatti as maestro, in spite of Provenzale's legitimate claim, must have been expected by the Cappellano Maggiore, who wrote to Carpio on 9 February 1684 in Spanish, warning him in the clearest of terms against appointing a non-Neapolitan over the heads of proven musicians who already served faithfully in the chapel.[66] Scarlatti's installation is a vivid example of the audacity with which Carpio institutionalized his personal taste as law.

Carpio also hand-picked other artists and performers for his productions. Filippo Schor, who had designed ephemeral architecture for Carpio and others in Rome, most famously the displays for the 1681 *serenata* in the Piazza di Spagna, was brought to Naples as '*Regio Ingegnere*' to design the stage machines and scenes, and appointed to the production team with

Nicola Vaccaro and Francesco della Torre, the impresario of the Teatro di San Bartolomeo.[67] The poet Giuseppe Domenico De Totis, who provided the text for Carpio's public *serenata* in the Piazza di Spagna in Rome in 1681, became Carpio's resident Italian dramatist in Naples. It can hardly be coincidental that De Totis's first opera libretto for Naples (*L'Aldimiro*) was presented within months of Carpio's arrival and was the first libretto ever commissioned especially and solely for Naples (with the possible exception of the much earlier *Veremonda* [Cavalli] of 1652–3, which actually may have been composed for a Venetian premiere). Carpio financed the first productions of at least four of De Totis's eight libretti.

Moreover, Carpio seems to have chosen the singers for his Neapolitan operas. Again, during his years in Rome he had heard the best castrati of the moment sing at the Spanish church of San Giacomo degli Spagnoli. 'Paoluccio,' the soprano castrato Paolo Pompeo Besci (also Beschi), had served the Spanish church in Rome and as principal soloist in Carpio's 1681 *serenata.* Though Paoluccio also named Queen Christina as his primary patron (in libretti he is '*musico della Maestà della Regina di Svezia*'), he was not only contracted for productions in Naples, but also instantly awarded a nicely paid position in the Neapolitan royal chapel, thanks to Carpio's intervention.

The famous castrato Siface (Giovanni Francesco Grossi) sang in Carpio's operas of the 1683–4 season as well, on personal loan to Carpio from the Duke of Modena. Siface's hiring illustrates the degree of Carpio's personal involvement in planning the operas. He surely had heard Siface in Rome, when the singer sang in the cappella at San Giacomo degli Spagnoli in 1677. In 1683 Siface was brought to Naples to sing Amore in Scarlatti's *La Psiche* (planned for the queen mother's birthday in December 1683, but actually performed in January 1684) and then Mitridate in Scarlatti's *Il Pompeo* at Naples during carnival 1684 (originally a tenor role in the premiere at the theatre in the Colonna palace in Rome, January 1683, but revised for Naples). Carpio obtained Siface's services with the assistance of his friend and highly placed intermediary, Cardinal Barberini, but Carpio himself wrote to Siface's principal sponsor and employer, the duke of Modena, first to secure the singer's presence in Naples and then to prolong his stay after carnival until the close of April 1684. By the end of April, Siface was on his way back to Modena, with Carpio's letter of safe passage in his pocket, together with an effusive letter of gratitude from Carpio to the duke. As is well known, Siface's meteoric career brought him enough well-remunerated performances in the north (Florence, Venice, Reggio, Modena, Bologna, and so on) between

1681 and 1687 that he did not return to Carpio's Naples, where opera production and repertory were so personally controlled by the viceroy.[68]

Although an extant contract indicates that singers for the Teatro di San Bartolomeo were recruited with funding put forward by the financial agents Guidetti and Gondi, it is likely that Carpio also wrote personally and used aristocratic intermediaries to borrow singers from other nobles, at least for the first operas he produced. In the cast for *Il Pompeo*, for example, Michele Fregiotti belonged to the prince of Palestrina (a close acquaintance of Carpio's); Giovanni Hercole belonged to the musical establishment of Contestabile Lorenzo Onofrio Colonna (whom Carpio knew well, though the two were often at odds); and both Scarlatti and Paoluccio still belonged in some sense to Queen Christina.

Carpio seems also to have been instrumental in launching or sustaining the careers of some singers. He was among the first to recognize the talent of the young Niccolino Grimaldi, who made his debut at the age of twelve as a soprano in the summer 1685 production of Provenzale's *La Stellidaura vendicante*, and in the following year received the highest payment among the singers for his performance in the Scarlatti *serenata* '*L'Olimpo in Mergellina*' in Naples. Nicolini was soon in demand throughout Italy and was later among the first Italian singers to conquer the London stage (his triumphs included the title role in Handel's *Rinaldo* in 1711).

The career of soprano Giulia Francesca Zuffi seems to have prospered with Carpio's patronage. It may be that Zuffi was recommended to Carpio by the Spanish ambassador in Venice, and there is at least some possibility that Carpio heard her sing there if he visited the city during the opera season of 1678. Both Giulia Zuffi and Siface sang in Carlo Pallavicino's *Il Vespasiano* for the opening of the new Teatro San Giovanni Grisostomo in Venice in 1678. But whereas Siface's career included performances in many different cities, Zuffi seems temporarily absent from Naples after her debut there, only to return for Carpio's productions. She performed there in 1679 and 1680, and again in Scarlatti's *L'Aldimiro* and *La Psiche*, in the revival of Scarlatti's *Il Pompeo*, as well as in the Neapolitan adaptations of Legrenzi's *Il Giustino*, Pallavicino's *Il Galieno*, and Severo De Luca's *Epaminonda*.[69] In short, it appears that Carpio attempted to recreate in Naples something like the closely knit resident team that had worked for him in Madrid, though here his principal singers included expensive star castrati in addition to dependable leading ladies. True, Carpio did what any discerning patron would do – he hired the best musicians available – but, once in Naples, singers, designer, librettist, and composer were, quite literally, at his beck and call.

As I have noted, the De Totis libretti for Scarlatti's *L'Aldimiro*, *La Psiche*, and *Il Fetonte* were based on Calderón plays and 'adjusted' for Neapolitan opera production. Extending this notion of translation and recomposition, it may be that visual and musical features of Carpio's operas were also brought into line with his particular style and taste. Like his Madrid productions, his Naples operas began with elaborately staged allegorical prologues in praise of the Spanish sovereigns. Some of them even reproduced visual effects and machines he had tested earlier in Madrid. The prologue to *Il Giustino* (1684), for instance, opens with precisely the same allegory and stage machines (a huge automaton of Atlas sustaining the globe) that had opened the *loa* to Calderón's semi-opera *Fortunas de Andrómeda y Perseo* in Madrid nearly thirty years earlier (figures 8.2 and 8.3).

Figure 8.2 Baccio del Bianco, drawing with dedication scene, shows the curtain being raised as the *loa* begins, from the 1653 production of *Fortunas de Andrómeda y Perseo* (text by Calderón de la Barca). Courtesy Houghton Library, Harvard University.

The central plots of the Naples operas (including the revivals on ostensibly heroic themes 'arranged' for Naples, such as *Il Pompeo* or *Il Giustino*) unfold much in the manner of Spanish plays – they include one or two comic *gracioso* characters with silly scenes, and love scenes and cape-and-sword intrigues dominate. Even the operas about ancient Roman historical figures manage to call forth fantastic, elaborate scenic effects of the sort that were Carpio's trademark.[70] *Il Nerone* includes a tiny opera-within-an-opera in which erotic mythological episodes about the amorous adventures of the goddesses Venus and Diana ('Gli amore di Venere, e di Marte, di Cintia, et di Endimione') are elaborately staged, revisiting the complex, burlesque mythology of one of those Madrid musical plays from the 1650s that featured female singers draped on stage machines.[71] It may be that Carpio chose to mount this production because the libretto called for some of the effects he was proudest of.

The question of how his Spanish patron's musical taste might have affected the work of Alessandro Scarlatti, Carpio's principal Italian

Figure 8.3 Baccio del Bianco, drawing of set from the *loa,* with Atlante holding the globe on his shoulders and dancers as signs of the zodiac being lowered to the stage on clouds, from the 1653 production of *Fortunas de Andrómeda y Perseo* (text by Calderón de la Barca). Courtesy of Houghton Library, Harvard University.

opera composer in Naples, is difficult to answer. Whereas the Italian visual artists and architects who served Carpio in Rome and Naples naturally shared a general technical and stylistic inheritance with the artists Carpio had brought to Madrid in his youth (artists who had trained or practised in Florence, Rome, or Bologna), Italian opera composers in the seventeenth century had little in common with their Spanish counterparts. Composers working in Rome and Naples in the 1680s knew some Spanish bass patterns and dance tunes (the *folía* and the *chacona*, for instance), but the *coplas* and *estribillos* of Spanish theatre songs were not intrinsic to their musical training or heritage.[72] The compositional norms and techniques of 1680s Naples do not find models in the unpublished music of the operas and semi-operas by Hidalgo that Carpio had produced more than two decades earlier in Madrid, though Alessandro Scarlatti most likely heard some of Hidalgo's music before he moved to Naples, thanks to Carpio's activites in Rome.[73] Because he was such a discerning patron, accustomed to exerting his personal taste, it is unlikely that Carpio hired Scarlatti merely because he was becoming famous. It is worth asking how Scarlatti's music might have served Carpio's needs.

Scarlatti's music for all three of the operas whose libretti were 'translations' from Calderón has survived at least partially.[74] These operas are defined by their arias, such that each opera unleashes a torrent of short arias, each devoted to a single affect or poetic idea and fashioned around a principal motive. It may be that Carpio felt at home with this kind of music. It could be argued that these early Neapolitan operas by Scarlatti contain more aria texts in strophic form than was typical of Italian operas elsewhere in the 1680s. And there are a great many short, passionate arias (some of them strophic), with very little in the way of bel canto 'spinning out,' but with a concentrated musical focus on an affectively charged primary motive and its repetition. This description of short, spare, focused pieces also fits the songs and *tonadas* that the Spanish composer Juan Hidalgo had provided years earlier for Carpio's Madrid productions. In both Hidalgo's scores and these early Scarlatti operas for Naples, recitative is employed only sparingly (mostly for dramatic soliloquys), and the thoughts, feelings, and reactions of characters are conveyed in rhetorically compact but powerfully affective airs, many of them quite declamatory.

The music that Scarlatti composed for Carpio's productions, like Hidalgo's music, is without 'purely musical' challenge or complexity. It wears its heart on its sleeve. Each aria delivers a miniature bombshell of passion. It may be that Scarlatti responded to the taste of his patron, the marquis del Carpio, but it could also be argued that Carpio hired Scarlatti precisely because his music was so pointedly and openly passionate. The peculiarly compact and 'simple' features of Scarlatti's early Neapolitan arias have been accepted as merely the immature efforts of a composer whose true style only blossomed later, in his 'mature' baroque arias. But the affective intensity and stylistic and formal consistency of Scarlatti's arias in the 1680s smack of deliberation and focus, rather than mere immaturity, not to mention that the longer and more 'mature' arias were composed for other patrons and in changed political and artistic circumstances. I suspect that Scarlatti's arias for Carpio may have been shaped by the latter's preferences.

This viceroy's personal attention distinguished him among patrons and producers of opera. In Carpio's hierarchy of aesthetic and genre, opera and operatic music (rare in the Hispanic context) were distinguished precisely by affective intensity and an erotic overloading of passion. The music of opera in Carpio's Madrid and Naples was endowed with an especially focused and passionate musical language with a narrow range of affects. The operas were intensely personal for their patron, but they were also central to his plan for ennobling cultural life in Naples to reflect well on the crown, thereby displaying his fidelity and encouragement to his sovereigns. Carpio was not concerned to remind Neapolitans of Spanish 'power' (which he took for granted), but to demonstrate optimism in the monarchy and his own noble generosity. Once his ideas about musical theatre were adapted for Italian singers, including castrati, and generalized Italian conventions of performance, the eroticism that had been so prominent in Carpio's Madrid shows was tempered in the Neapolitan operas.

But in Carpio's politics, 'guitars and fables' were still principal weapons and tools of diplomacy. Scarlatti's first operas for the Palazzo Reale in Naples were an important contribution toward the creation of a social life for the Neapolitan nobility centred on the viceroy, while the public operas Carpio produced at the Teatro di San Bartolomeo represented the vitality and generosity of the monarch and his viceroy. Carpio spent public funds lavishly to produce amorous, personal stories (even Spanish mythological plays translated into Italian opera libretti), with elaborate staging, and casts again dominated by beautiful high voices. They sang powerfully about erotic longing and dynastic continuance, love of family, loyalty to the crown, and the primacy of love and beauty. In Madrid and Naples, Carpio's productions were emblems of his fidelity to his sovereign, coloured by his personal experience and audibly displaying his preference for non-discursive, passionate music and elaborate staging. In Naples, as in Madrid, he enlisted the erotic potential of musical theatre not merely for the fun of it, but to serve his king and encourage a healthy dynastic succession. In his personal life and in his political life, the need to '*crear sucesión*' was ever in his thoughts. Plays and operas provided especially strong structures of feeling, and, when he produced them, Carpio was offering the gift of himself to his sovereign, in 'Vida, hacienda, y, sobre todo, la sucesión de los hijos.'

NOTES

1 Richard Kagan, 'From Noah to Moses: The Genesis of Historical Scholarship on Spain in the United States,' in *Spain in America: The Origins of Hispanism in the United States*, ed. Richard Kagan (Urbana and Chicago: University of Illinois Press, 2002), 22. The term 'Black Legend' comes from Julián Juderías, *La leyenda negra: estudios acerca del concepto de España en el extranjero* (Madrid: Tipografía de la Revista de Archivos, Bibliotecas y Museos, 1914). See also Charles Gibson, ed., *The Black Legend: Anti-Spanish Attitudes in the Old World and the New* (New York: Alfred E. Knopf, 1971), and, especially, Ricardo García Carcel, *La leyenda negra: historia y opinion* (Madrid: Alianza Editorial, 1992). Concerning the Black Legend and the historiography of Spanish music, see especially Judith Etzion, 'Spanish Music as Perceived in Western Music Historiography: A Case of the Black Legend?' *International Review of Aesthetics and Sociology of Music* 29 (1998): 93–120; Begoña Lolo, 'El sentido de la historicidad en música: España versus Europa,' *Anuario del Departamento de Historia y Teoría del Arte* (Madrid: Universidad Autónoma) 4 (1992): 359–65; and my 'Before the Latin Tinge: Spanish Music and the "Spanish Idiom" in the United States, 1778–1940,' in Kagan, ed., *Spain in America*, 193–245.

2 Lorenzo Bianconi's insightful study of the Neapolitan situation is fundamental to all subsequent work; see 'Funktionen des Operntheaters in Neapel bis 1700 und die Rolle Alessandro Scarlattis,' in *Colloquium Alessandro Scarlatti, Würzburg 1975* (Tutzing: Schneider, 1979), 13–111; and the pioneering case studies offered by Bianconi and Thomas Walker over three decades ago in 'Dalla 'Finta Pazza' alla "Veremonda": Storie di febiarmonici,' *Rivista italiana di musicologia* 10 (1975): 379–454. The most useful paradigms concerning opera production outside Naples have been drawn from the well-studied earliest operas in Florence and Mantua, as well as the operas produced in Rome and Venice in the mid-century.

3 Essential documents are brought together in Ulisse Prota-Giurleo, *I teatri di Napoli nel secolo XVII*, ed. Giorgio Mancini [et al.], 3 vols. (Naples: Il Quartiere Edizioni, 2002); new light has been shed by Dinko Fabris in 'Nápoles y España en la ópera Napolitana del siglo XVII,' *La ópera en España e Hispanoamérica*, ed. Emilio Casares and Álvaro Torrente (Madrid: ICCMU, 2001), 117–30, and Fabris, *Music in Seventeenth-Century Naples: Francesco Provenzale (1624–1704)* (Aldershot: Ashgate, 2007).

4 For a case study of the production of private operas in Naples in light of public political concerns, see my 'Opera and the Spanish Family: Private and Public Opera in Naples in the 1680s,' in *España y Nápoles: coleccionismo y mecenazgo artístico de los virreyes en el siglo XVII*, ed. José Luis Colomer (Madrid: Centro de Estudios Europa Hispánica, 2009, 223–43.

5 An early biography is included in Joseph Antonio Álvarez y Baena, *Hijos de Madrid*, 4 vols. (Madrid, 1789–91), 2: 298–301. The standard modern biography is Gregorio de Andrés, *El marqués de Liche, bibliófilo y coleccionista de arte* (Madrid: Artes Gráficas Municipales, 1975), which is based on a narrow selection of Spanish sources and does not consider Carpio's time in Italy; some Italian sources were brought to light in Maria Elena Ghelli, 'Il viceré Marchese del Carpio (1683–1687),' *Archivio Storico per le province napoletane* 58 (1933): 280–318; 59 (1934): 257–82.

6 Carpio's activities as patron and collector in Italy are introduced in Frances Haskell, *Patrons and Painters: A Study in the Relations between Italian Art and Society in the Age of the Baroque*, rev. ed. (New Haven and London: Yale University Press, 1980), 190–2; see also Beatrice Cacciotti, 'La collezione del VII Marchese del Carpio tra Roma e Madrid,' *Bolletino d'Arte* 86–7 (1994) [anno LXXIX, serie VI]: 133–96; the most detailed study to date of his activity as a collector in Spain is included in Marcus B. Burke and Peter Cherry, *Collections of Paintings in Madrid 1601–1755*, 2 vols. (Los Angeles: Provenance Index of the Getty Information Institute, 1997); see also Rosa López Torrijos, 'Coleccionismo en la época de Velázquez: El marqués de Heliche,' in *Velázquez y el arte de su tiempo* (Madrid: Alpuerto, 1991), 27–36; Fernando Marías, 'Don Gaspar de Haro, marqués del Carpio, coleccionista de dibujos,' in *Arte y Diplomacia de la Monarquía Hispánica en el siglo XVII*, ed. José Luis Colomer (Madrid: Fernando Villaverde, 2003), 209–19; Jorge Fernández-Santos Ortiz-Iribas, 'Un lote de pinturas de la colección del Marqués del Carpio adjudicadas al Duque de Tursi,' *Reales Sitios* 155 (2003): 42–7; Fernando Checa Cremades, 'El Marqués del Carpio (1629–1687) y la pintura veneciana del Renacimiento. Negociaciones de Antonio Saurer,' *Anales de Historia del Arte* 14 (2004): 193–212; Leticia de Frutos Sastre, 'El arte de la posibilidad: Carpio y el coleccionismo de pintura en Venecia,' *Reales Sitios* 162 (2004): 54–71;

and María Jesús Muñoz González, 'La Capilla Real del Alcázar y un altar de pórfido,' *Reales Sitios* 164 (2005): 50–69.

7 Burke and Cherry, *Collections of Paintings in Madrid*, 157.

8 Aspects of Carpio's musical patronage are considered in Thomas E. Griffin, 'Nuove fonti per la storia della musica a Napoli durante il regno del marchese del Carpio (1683–1687),' *Rivista Italiana di Musicologia* 16 (1981): 207–28; my 'Opera and the Spanish Political Agenda,' *Acta Musicologica* 63 (1991): 126–67; my '"De la *contera* del mundo": las navegaciones de la ópera entre dos mundos y varias culturas,' in *La ópera en España e Hispanoamérica*, 2 vols., ed. Emilio Casares and Álvaro Torrente (Madrid: ICCMU, 2001), 1: 79–94; my 'Three Paintings, a Double Lyre, Opera, and Eliche's Venus: Velázquez and Music at the Royal Court in Madrid,' in *Cambridge Companion to Diego Velázquez*, ed. Suzanne Stratton-Pruitt (Cambridge and New York: Cambridge University Press, 2001), 170–93, 226–35; and my 'Opera and the Spanish Family.'

9 Gaspar de Haro y Guzmán was made Caballero de la Orden de Alcantara on 21 November 1646 and recognized from that date with the title Marquis de Heliche; on 28 December 1648 he was sworn in as Gentilhombre de Cámara; on 23 January 1654, he became Montero Mayor; from 27 September 1642, he served the post of Alcaide of the Pardo palace, in place of his father; subsequently, on 6 December 1648, he was assigned the Buen Retiro palace as well. His father reaffirmed Gaspar's governance of the Buen Retiro in August 1654. After his father's death, the king removed Gaspar from the governance of the Buen Retiro but affirmed him as alcaide of the Pardo and Zarzuela palaces, 'con su sitio y bosque, a pesar de pertecener a la Alcaydía del Buen Retiro, de que es propietario el Duque de S. Lucar.'

10 'Fue muy favorecido del Príncipe Baltasar Carlos en sus tiernos años y este favor fue con suma aprobación de su padre, Felipe IV,' according to the unsigned contemporary biography (probably by Juan Vélez de León, one of Carpio's secretaries); Madrid, Biblioteca Nacional de España [BNE] MS 18722/56, fol 204.

11 Whether or not Carpio actually designed the Coliseo, contemporary and later observers assumed he had done so; when Cardinal Savo Millini arrived in Madrid as papal nuncio (1677), he noted that this 'bellissimo teatro da comedie' was made according to Heliche's orders (Palma, Biblioteca de la Fundación Bartolomé March [BFBM], Papeles de Savo Millini 6/3/347, 'Memorie sopra la Nunziatura').

12 Numerous documents in Archivo General de Simancas [AGS], Tribunal Mayor de Cuentas, Legajo 3766, in the years 1653–61, name the marquis de Heliche (Carpio) as 'superintendente' and illustrate his close management

of the Italian artists who worked on the Coliseo and its productions (including Baccio del Bianco, Francesco Rizzi, and Angelo Nardi, to name a few). David García Cueto, *La estancia española de los pintores Boloñeses Agotino Mitelli y Angelo Michele Colonna, 1658–1662* (Granada: Universidad de Granada, 2005), 186–202, provides a detailed account. My thanks to Shirley Whittaker and to David Grarcía Cueto for sharing with me many suggestions about Carpio's relationship with Italian artists.

13 My *Songs of Mortals: Dialogues of the Gods: Music and Theatre in Seventeenth-Century Spain* (Oxford: Clarendon Press, 1993) offers a detailed account of the Spanish genres and the collaboration of Pedro Calderón de la Barca and Juan Hidalgo. The dramatist Francisco de Bances Candamo, writing in Madrid around 1690, named Carpio as the first to organize plays with elaborate scenic effects: 'fue el primero que mandó delinear mutaciones, y finger máquinas y apariencias' (Francisco Bances Candamo, *Theatro de los Theatros de los passados y presentes siglos,* ed. Duncan Moir [London: Tamesis, 1970], 29, 42). Emilio Cotarelo y Mori understood Carpio's important position as theatrical producer of musical plays (*Actores famosos del siglo XVII: Sebastián de Prado y su mujer Bernarda Ramírez* [Madrid: Tipografía de la Revista de archivos, bibliotecas y museos, 1916], 83 and passim), as did Norman D. Shergold in *A History of the Spanish Stage from Medieval Times until the End of the Seventeenth Century* (Oxford: Clarendon Press, 1967), 328–9. María Teresa Chaves Montoya, *El espectáculo teatral en la corte de Felipe IV* (Madrid: Ayuntamiento de Madrid, 2004), considers the Italian stage designers and painters but overlooks Carpio's leadership.

14 Concerning these conventions, see my *Songs of Mortals,* and the several essays cited in these notes.

15 As reported in Jerónimo de Barrionuevo, *Avisos (1654–1658),* 2 vols., ed. Antonio Paz y Meliá (Madrid: Atlas, 1969), 1: 121, 153.

16 Leaving aside the brief ensembles for peasants and soldiers, *La púrpura de la rosa* calls for fifteen female solo roles (eleven if nymphs also double as allegorical figures) and only two male singers – a baritone for the allegorical figure Desengaño, and a tenor for Chato, the comic rustic or *gracioso. Celos aun del aire matan* offers ten solo roles for women and only one male role (again, a comic tenor, the *gracioso* Rústico). See my *Songs of Mortals* and my edition of Tomás de Torrejón y Velasco/Juan Hidalgo, *La púrpura de la rosa* (Madrid: Ediciones Autor/ICCMU, 1999).

17 Carpio's recruitment of actress-singers for the court productions is documented beginning in 1657; see the anonymous 'Relación de las fiestas del felice parto de la Reyna . . .' (BNE MS 18660/12, fol. 5v), a satire portraying Carpio as a pimp and his actresses as prostitutes. Barrionuevo, *Avisos,* 2:

74–5, 149; Cotarelo, *Actores famosos,* 104–7; *Genealogía, origen y noticias de los comediantes de España* [BNE, MS 12917 and MS 12918], ed. N.D. Shergold and J.E. Varey (London: Tamesis, 1985), 419–20; and Cristóbal Pérez Pastor, *Documentos para la biografía de D. Pedro Calderón de la Barca* (Madrid: Real Academia de la Historia, 1905), 248.

18 Burke notes that Carpio's collection was 'notably profane' even during his Madrid years, with 'only about 20 percent' of the works treating sacred topics. Burke and Cherry, *Collections of Paintings in Madrid,* 464.

19 Concerning Philip IV's collections of nude paintings, Javier Portús has noted (p. 43) 'the greatest art-loving monarch that Spain has ever known decorated the walls of the most intimate and personal room of his palace with paintings by Titian which represented mythological scenes or other subjects which included nudes,' but 'this is not the only occasion within the context of Spanish culture of this period where we find an association between the siesta and looking at nudes'; see Portús, *The Sala Reservada and the Nude in the Prado Museum* (Madrid: Museo del Prado, 2002), 13–65. On the other hand, Portús also points out that Rubens's resplendently nude Andromeda was displayed in the Salón Nuevo of the Alcázar, a central room where many public functions took place; see Steven N. Orso, *Philip IV and the Decoration of the Alcázar of Madrid* (Princeton: Princeton University Press, 1986).

20 Rosa López Torrijos, *La mitología en la pintura española del Siglo de Oro* (Madrid: Cátedra, 1985), 80–2, 420. The fresco may have copied the painting attributed to Ribera and now held in the Cleveland Museum of Art; not surprisingly, the stage direction for Venus's arrival onstage in the analogous scene of Calderón's *La púrpura de la rosa* is in keeping with Ribera's depiction.

21 The Venus painting was included in an inventory of Carpio's holdings drawn up 1 June 1651 in Madrid. A later inventory of 1677 notes that in the Madrid palace known as the Jardín de San Joaquín it hung on the ceiling of a gallery with other pictures that included female nudes – a depiction of the chaste Susana before the elders, a Danae 'with the shower of gold in a landscape naked lying on a red cloth,' and a canvas of sleeping Apollo 'with the nine Muses around him playing musical instruments.' See Duncan Bull and Enriqueta Harris, 'The Companion of Velázquez's Rokeby Venus and a Source for Goya's Naked Maja,' *The Burlington Magazine* 128 (1986): 643–4. Francis Haskell has written: 'la Venus del espejo ha tenido una reputación extraña: quienes la conocieron más de cerca – el marqués del Carpio, los Alba, Godoy, Morritt – estaban convencidos (y sin duda encantados) de que era indecente y sólo apta para ser vista por unos pocos escogidos; y hay que

admitir que, en el contexto de sus épocas, tales supuestos eran razonables.' Francis Haskell, 'La *Venus del espejo*,' in *Velázquez* (Barcelona: Galaxia Gutenberg, Amigos del Museo del Prado, 1999), 235; likewise Fernando Marías, in *Velázquez: Pintor y criado del rey* (Madrid: Nerea, 1999), 169–73, comments on the painting's overt sensuality and suggests a number of sources for its erotic imagery.

22 Concerning seventeenth-century musical eroticism, see my 'Eros, Erato, Terpsíchore and the Hearing of Music in Early Modern Spain,' *Musical Quarterly* 82 (1998): 654–77; '"Al seducir el oído . . .," delicias y convenciones del teatro musical cortesano,' in *El teatro cortesano en la España de los Austrias,* ed. José María Díez Borque, Cuadernos de Teatro Clásico 10 (Madrid, 1998), 169–89; and 'Three Paintings, a Double Lyre, Opera, and Eliche's Venus.'

23 For example, in a letter of 13 March 1661 from the Duke of Montalto to his brother, 'El marqués de Eliche havia dado en gustar de una comedianteja hansela desterrado, y se halla con perturbación de ánimo, enojándose a ratos con su padre, sintiéndose del Rey, y destemplándose con todos.' Madrid, Archivo Histórico Nacional [AHN], Estado, Libro 104.

24 Barrionuevo reported that Carpio seemed to be 'hechizado' (bewitched or hexed) by women; see *Avisos* 1: 65, 71, 120.

25 Carpio's biographer considered his appetite for women of inferior social class a kind of tragic flaw: 'Fue solo de reparar que gustó demasiado el marqués de mujeres, pero estas de baja esfera, que no las facilitava la autoridad, sino su dinero, como lo hiciera otro qualquiera.' BNE, MS 18722/56, fol. 204.

26 Reported in a letter of 27 May 1677 from Savo Millini in Madrid (BFBM, Papeles de Savo Millini, vol. 34/1, fol. 187v). Millini was among those cardinals who recognized Carpio's strength of character but worked to discredit him in the hope of seeing him recalled from Rome and the ambassadorship. A few years later, Carpio was unjustly accused of allowing 'escandalosos excesos' and 'gente de mala vida' to flourish in the Spanish embassy's jurisdiction (BFBM, Embajada de Roma, Tomo 59, letter of 30 July 1682). On Carpio's brilliant defence of diplomatic immunity and the *quartiere spagnolo,* see Alessandra Anselmi, 'El marqués del Carpio y el barrio de la Embajada de España en Roma (1677–1683),' in *La Monarquía de las Naciones: Patria, nación y naturaleza en la Monarquía de España,* ed. Antonio Álvarez-Ossorio Alvariño and Bernardo J. García García (Madrid: Fundación Carlos de Amberes, 2004), 563–95.

27 Burke and Cherry, *Collections of Paintings in Madrid,* 166.

28 There are scattered references to Queen Christina in some of the correspondence; a letter of 28 September 1681 from Carpio to Madrid mentions his relationship with Christina (BNE, MS 7946, fol. 542); and in a later letter dated 11 April 1682, from Carpio in Rome to the marquis de los Vélez in Naples, Carpio sends greetings from Christina and Cardinal Azzolino 'as the Queen ordered him to do in her name' (Palma, BFBM, Embajada de Roma, Tomo 61). In a letter of 25 July 1687, the marquis de Cogolludo (then Spanish ambassador in Rome) writes that he has presented Queen Christina with a letter from Carpio and that she spoke of him with 'grande veneración de su persona' (BFBM, MS B81-A-02, fol. 21v). Rosa López Torrijos, 'Coleccionismo en la época de Velázquez: El marqués de Heliche,' *Velázquez y el arte de su tiempo* (Madrid: Alpuerto, 1991), 36, suggests that the marquis attended sessions of Queen Christina's academy in Rome.

29 Carpio wrote to the Spanish ambassador in Venice, Antonio de Mendoza y Caamaño de Sotomayor, marquis de Villagarcía, that his last weeks in Rome were devoted principally to visits with the Roman ladies ('visitas de despedida'); Villagarcía, in his reply and in other letters, refers to Carpio's extreme 'galantería' (AHN, Estado, Libro 198, letters of December 1682).

30 See Jonathan Dewald, *The European Nobility, 1400–1800* (New York: Cambridge University Press, 1996), 168–76.

31 Making much of Barrionuevo's diary, the short biography by the late Gregorio de Andrés, *El marqués de Liche,* legitimized a negatively tinged portrait of Carpio as a spoiled playboy whose lasciviousness brought him well-deserved punishment through ill health. Art historian Marcus Burke has registered his disapproval of Carpio as a 'notorious womanizer' who indulged in 'scandalous liaisons' even while married to an internationally celebrated beauty. Supporting these morally contingent judgments with accusations of 'mental instability,' Burke concludes that Carpio 'either had an unbalanced mind or was suffering from venereal disease.' For Burke, then, Carpio's libertine tendencies reveal deep neuroses or a sexually twisted mind. Burke and Andrés (neither of whom worked with Carpio's letters or the Italian documents about him) censure Carpio for his 'unbounded sexual appetite' and consider his 'artistic interests' to be his only redeeming trait. See Burke and Cherry, *Collections of Paintings in Madrid,* 462–4.

32 In letters between the marquis de Villagarcía in Venice and Juan Gaspar Enríquez de Cabrera, almirante de Castilla (Carpio's father-in-law) in Madrid, Carpio is mentioned with reverence for his lack of scruples in such matters (AHN, Estado, Libro 197, letters of February 1683). In *Imagen y propaganda: capítulos de historia cultural del reinado de Felipe II* (Madrid: Akal, 1998), 206,

Fernando Bouza relates that the almirante admired that Carpio 'no escrupulizaba los desnudos más atrevidos.'

33 As revealed in transcripts of his trial, when Carpio's father died in 1661, the position of governor of the Buen Retiro passed to the Duke of Medina de las Torres, a cousin who inherited the title of Duke of San Lucar upon Luis de Haro's death. Suddenly betrayed by his lineage, Carpio refused to relinquish the keys to the royal theatres, ostensibly to prevent his cousin from claiming credit for the ingenious stage machines for Calderón's *Faetón o el hijo del sol.* It was rumoured that Carpio planned to blow up the stage machines and scenery awaiting rehearsals in the Coliseo theatre. When a trail of gunpowder was discovered, he was accused of treason – had the fuse been lighted during the production, the king and queen would have been blown to bits by the explosion, since they were then in residence at the Buen Retiro palace. Cleared finally of this charge, he was eventually sentenced to exile and served a short prison term and exile for attempting to poison a witness. The record of the trial is preserved in legal documents (BNE, MS 6751, fol. 110 and BNE MS 2280, 'Papeles del Buen Retiro,' 'Causa contra el marqués de Heliche'). After his arrest, Heliche was held in the Castillo de la Alameda de Osuna with only two servants to look after him, until he was overtaken by a severe illness and almost died. The king intervened and Heliche was moved to house arrest within the palace of another noble. For the crime of conspiracy to murder a potential witness (his own Turkish slave), he was fined 10,000 ducats and sentenced to two years' imprisonment in a closed castle and eight years of exile. See the summary in Andrés, *El marqués de Liche,* 18–24, and Burke and Cherry, *Collections of Paintings in Madrid,* 463.

34 According to Dinko Fabris, 'Los virreyes intentaron uno tras otro imponer en la ciudad usos y tradiciones españolas'; see his review of *El robo de Proserpina y sentencia de Júpiter,* ed. Luis Antonio González Marín, in *Revista de musicología* 19 (1996): 423.

35 For details of Neapolitan productions before the 1680s, see Bianconi, 'Funktionen des Operntheaters in Neapel'; Bianconi and Walker, 'Dalla "Finta Pazza" alla "Veremonda" '; and Fabris, *Music in Seventeenth-Century Naples,* 154–61.

36 In addition to the 'Pallonetto di Palazzo' used during count Oñate's time, other rooms in the Palazzo Reale hosted theatrical performances on occasion, including the 'Salone Grande' or 'Sala grande,' the 'Sala del duca d'Alba,' and the 'Salone dei Viceré,' but it does not appear that any of these rooms housed a permanent theatre; Pier Luigi Ciapparelli, 'I luoghi del teatro a Napoli nel seicento: le sale "private," ' *La musica a Napoli durante il*

seicento, ed. Domenico Antonio D'Alessandro and Agostino Ziino (Rome: Edizioni Torre d'Orfeo, 1987), 384–92.

37 The information concerning dedicatees for a long list of libretti is included in Bianconi, 'Funktionen des Operntheaters in Neapel,' 45–111.

38 On this point, see J.E. Varey and N.D. Shergold, *Teatros y comedias en Madrid: 1666–1687* (London: Tamesis, 1974), 35–8; N.D. Shergold and J.E. Varey, *Representaciones palaciegas 1603–1699* (London: Tamesis, 1982), 37–8; and José María Díaz Borque, 'Espacios del Teatro Cortesano,' in *Teatro cortesano en la España de los Austrias*, ed. José María Díaz Borque, *Cuadernos de Teatro Clásico* 10 (1998): 132–4.

39 Noted in Lorenzo Bianconi and Thomas Walker, 'Production, Consumption, and Political Function of Seventeenth-Century Italian Opera,' *Early Music History* 4 (1984): 260–1. Concerning the Salón Dorado, see J.E. Varey, 'L'auditoire du Salón dorado de l'Alcázar de Madrid au XVIIe siècle,' in *Dramaturgie et Société*, 2 vols., ed. Jean Jacquot (Paris: CNRS, 1968) 1, 77–91; and the introduction to Juan Vélez de Guevara, *Los cellos hacen estrellas*, ed. J.E. Varey and N.D. Shergold (London: Tamesis, 1970), lv–lxxi. Fernando Checa provides a list of documents about 'arming' and 'disarming' the temporary theatre for the Salón Dorado; see *El Real Alcázar de Madrid: Dos Siglos de Arquitectura y Coleccionismo en la Corte de los Reyes de España*, ed. Fernando Checa Cremades (Madrid: Nerea, 1994), 35.

40 Bianconi and Walker, 'Production, Consumption,' 265; Dinko Fabris, 'Music in Seventeenth-Century Naples: The Case of Francesco Provenzale' (PhD diss., Royal Holloway, University of London, 2002), 60; eighteenth-century documents that include copies of the language from the original 1583 decree of Philip II, along with subsequent decrees or consultations of 1646, 1670, and 1685, are included in 'Appendice IV' of Francesco Cotticelli and Paologiovanni Maione, *Le Istituzioni Musicali a Napoli durante il Viceregno Austriaco (1707–1734)* (Naples, 1993), 145–75.

41 'nel Reale Palazzo quando fussero chiamati da S.E.' Prota-Giurleo, *I teatri di Napoli*, 3: 28.

42 For 'L'Olimpo in Mergellina,' a serenata performed probably by 'a hundred musicians among the voices and instrumentalists,' organized by the marquis del Carpio in August 1686, for example, financial agents deposited money destined for public spectacles into Scarlatti's bank account at the Banco di San Giacomo, and then the bank paid the musicians and singers directly from his account. A typical entry from the account books at the Banco di San Giacomo with a musician's payment for work in the serenata reads: 'Ad Alessandro Scarlatti, ducati cinque, et per esso ad D. Mattia Barella per haver sonato alle prove e serenate fatta ad Posillipo li 25 agosto per servizio

di Sua Eccelenza.' See my '"Una música de noche, que llaman aquí serenata": Spanish Patrons and the *Serenata* in Rome and Naples,' in *La serenata tra Seicento e Settecento: musica, poesia, scenotecnica,* Atti del Convegno Internazionale di Studi, ed. Nicolò Maccavino (Reggio Calabria: Laruffa Editore, 2007), vol. 2 [at press], for an analysis of payments to musicians who performed in this *serenata.* A list of the payments has appeared as an appendix in Paologiovane Maione, 'Il mondo musicale seicentesco e le sue istituzioni: la Cappella Reale di Napoli (1650–1700),' in *Francesco Cavalli. La Circolazione dell'Opera Veneziana nel Seicento,* ed. Dinko Fabris (Naples: Turchini Edizioni, 2005), 332–9.

43 'd'ordine di questo Eccmo. Marchese del Carpio, Viceré'; Archivio storico dell'Istituto – Fondazione Banco di Napoli, Banco di San Giacomo, Giornale di Cassa, Matricula 456 (26 February 1687), 234. This payment is noted in Mauro Amato, 'Le antologie di arie e cantate tardo-seicentesche alla Biblioteca del Conservatorio "S. Pietro a Majella" di Napoli,' 2 vols. (Dottorato di Ricerca-VII Ciclo, Cremona, Scuola di Paleografia e Filologia Musicale, 1997), 1: 116.

44 Although the account books for the '*Cuenta de Gastos Secretos*' in Carpio's time seem not to be extant, letters and copies of letters in Naples, Archivio di Stato [ASN], Regia Camera della Sommaria, Segretaria, Regale, Carte Reali, at least clarify the nature of this fund. For example, in copies of letters from 1685, Carpio is asked to reduce from 90 to 24 ducados per year the amount he expects to draw on from the gastos secretos, 'incluyéndose el de las fiestas reales y de carnestolendas, y poniéndose per gasto público lo que se pagava de sueldos, ayudas de costa, y limosnas a oficiales y a otro género de personas' (Naples, Archivio di Stato [ASN], Regia Camera della Sommaria, Segretaria Regale, Carte Reali, Busta 10, fol, 205). This argument about what should be paid through '*gastos secretos*' versus the fund for '*gastos públicos*' continued for some years. Carpio and his successors in Naples requested more money through the '*gastos secretos,*' with the support of the Collateral Council.

45 According to letters from the king (19 June 1689), even in difficult financial circumstances the royal fiestas were indispensable: the *comedias* and fiestas were to be supported through funds in the *gastos secretos* account as usual, 'y el ser inexcusables estas fiestas en celebridad de mis años y para divertimiento público' in spite of the fact that 'el estado de mi real hacienda obliga a escusar qualquier gasto superfluo por mínimo que sea maiormente . . . en estos tiempos devia limitarse, y no estenderse para comedias' (ASN, Regia Camera della Sommaria, Segretaria Regale, Carte Reali, Busta 11, fol. 251–251v).

46 Ibid., letter of 19 June 1689.

47 'li quali hanno rappresentato nel Teatro di S. Bartolomeo e Regio Palazzo nelli Festini Reali nella passata Stagione del passato anno 1683.' This document dated 6 December 1684 (Naples, Archivio di Stato [Pizzo Falcone], Notai del XVII sec., Geronimo de Roma, prot. 1214, n. 24, c. 872) is transcribed in Guido Olivieri, 'Per una storia della tradizione violinistica napoletana del '700,' in *Fonti d'archivio per la storia della musica e dello spettacolo a Napoli tra XVI e XVIII secolo,* ed. Paologiovane Maione (Naples: Editoriale Scientifica, 2001), 245–6.

48 Concerning this prohibition and its repeated enforcement under other viceroys, see Maione, 'Il mondo musicale,' 321–3.

49 'S.E. [los Vélez] ha fatto venire da Roma,' Bianconi and Walker, 'Dalla "Finta Pazza" alla "Veremonda,"' 387; Prota-Giurleo, *I teatri di Napoli,* 3: 272.

50 Prota-Giurleo, *I teatri di Napoli,* 3: 96 and 277: 'la notte in Palazzo li Musici della Cappella Regia rappresentorno il Teodosio in musica, ove concorse Nobiltà infinita Napoletana e Spagnola e anche molta gente Civile del Popolo a goderla.'

51 Bianconi, 'Funktionen des Operntheaters,' 67.

52 Prota-Giurleo, *I teatri di Napoli,* 3: 277

53 Fuidoro, *Giornale,* quoted in Prota-Giurleo, *I teatri di Napoli,* 3: 109.

54 As pointed out in Thomas Griffin, 'The Late Baroque Serenata in Rome and Naples: A Documentary Study with Emphasis on Alessandro Scarlatti' (PhD diss., UCLA, 1983), Carpio's fiestas in Naples were particularly lavish. After the celebration of the queen's name day in 1686, a Venetian, Antonio Maria Vincenti, criticized Carpio's extravagance in a report to the Venetian senate (27 August 1686): 'e che si consumò in inutili passatempi gran summe di danaro, e versè l'applicazione del Signor Vicerè ad'inventar nuovi trattenimenti, e feste per consumarne dell'altri più tosto che all'estintione de debiti immensi della Camera, et de crediti di tanti miserabili, che languiscono nelle indigenze, et esclamano [reclamano?] senza frutto' (Venice, Archivio di Stato, Dispacci degli ambasciatori al senato, Napoli, Filza 97).

55 Fearing that the French ambassador, d'Estrées, was planning a public affront, Carpio decided not to frequent public places during the busy carnival season and instead organized plays to be performed at the Palazzo di Spagna for his niece, the princess of Paliano, and the 'Roman ladies.' In letters of 24 and 31 January 1682, he explains that his intention is to be 'purposefully showy (the plays are '*vistosas*') and to keep up all appearances of maintaining myself with some degree of dignity' (Madrid, AHN, Estado, Libro 198, letter of 24 January 1682 to the Spanish ambassador in Venice, marquis de Villagarcía). See my 'Opera and the Spanish Family,' 7–8.

56 If so, this was not the only time that Carpio's activity in Italy affected the performance of plays in Madrid. In 1686 the marquis de Astorga in Madrid wrote to the marquis de Villagarcía in Venice: 'From here I can tell you that Their Majesties are well; and that the name-day and birthday of the King our Lord . . . was celebrated in the usual way, and with a spectacular machine play ('comedia de gran teatro') in the Coliseo of the [Buen] Retiro, sent by the marquis del Carpio' [BNE, MS 7951, fol, 303–4]. The play performed at the Buen Retiro for the king's birthday in November 1686 at the Coliseo, *El juicio de París* 'con loa, saynetes y fin de fiesta' has not been identified. See J.E. Varey and N.D. Shergold, *Teatros y comedias en Madrid: 1666–1687* (London: Tamesis, 1974), 159 and 191; and N.D. Shergold and J.E. Varey, *Representaciones palaciegas 1603–1699* (London: Tamesis, 1982), 173–4.

57 *Ni amor se libra de amor*, published in Calderón's *Tercera parte de comedias* . . . (Madrid, 1664), was revived in 1679, 1687, and 1693. For an insightful comparison of the De Totis *Psiche* libretto with the Calderón text, see Nancy D'Antuono, 'Il teatro in musica: tra fonti spagnole e commedia dell'arte,' in *Atti del Convegno Commedia dell'arte e il teatro in musica*, ed. Alessandro Lattanzi and Paologiovane Maione (Naples: Editoriale Scientifica, 2003), 213–34. Concerning the musical aspects of the Calderón play, see my *Songs of Mortals*, 171, 178, 270–2, 320, 348, and passim.

58 Among the mythological paintings in Carpio's collections, quite a number treated the story of Cupid and Psyche, the sleeping Cupid, and the scene in which Psyche approaches the sleeping Cupid holding a lamp or candle (see the inventories transcribed in Burke and Cherry, *Collections of Paintings in Madrid*).

59 In the printed *Relation de l'état et gouvernement d'Espagne*, a visiting Frenchman who met Carpio [Heliche] in Madrid in 1659 wrote: 'Le marquis de Liche son aisné, qui est Grand, comme je viens de dire, vit plus à la Françoise, qu'aucon Seigneur d'Espagne . . . luy ayant toujours une espèce de Cour le matin à son lever, où il se laisse voir, encore qu'il soit des plus laids hommes du monde a mais droit & bien fort dans le taille'; BNE 2/6030, pp. 37–8, bound with Antoine de Brunel, *Voyage d'Espagne* (Cologne, 1667).

60 In the words of the printed description of his 1681 Roman serenata, 'porque quien examinare las acciones deste gran Príncipe [Carpio] hallará a todas luces, que es un Monstruo de amor y de fineza.' *Applauso festivo alla sacra real maestà di Maria Luigia Regina delle Spagne. Serenata a 3 voci. Disposta da Giuseppe Fede. In ossequio dell'Eccellentissimo Signor Marchese dal Carpio Ambasciator . . . Cantata in Roma la sera di S. Luigi nella Piazza di Spagna* (Rome: N. Angelo Tinassi, 1681) [Rome, Biblioteca Apostolica Vaticana [BAV],

RG.ArteArch.IV.1 (21), no. 19, fol. 160, a large-sized commemorative printing most likely paid for by Carpio himself. Other exemplars are in BAV, Chigi Misc. IV 2236, fols. 118–21, and BAV, Barb. Lat. 3878, fols. 44–7v].

61 'La comedia que se haze para los años de Su Magestad se Representará en partiendo este correo, que nos ha embarazado mucho, y también el ajustarlo que es Faetón traducido de la que se hizo allí, con gran máquina, y con los mejores músicos de toda Ytalia, un encarezimiento, y el teatro no deslucirá la fiesta. Esto es cuanto puedo dezirte de por ahora' (Toledo, Archivo Histórico Nacional [AHN-Nobleza], Sección Nobleza, Osuna Cartas, Leg. 38/1).

62 *Il Fetonte, Melodramma* . . . di Filippo Schor e Nicola Vaccaro, Naples, Giovanni Francesco Paci, 1685 (RBC, Comm. 316/4). The *protesta* in the 1690 libretto to the Scarlatti/De Totis *La Rosmene* includes a statement to the effect that the libretti to *L'Idalma, Tutto il mal non vien per nuocere, La Psiche, Il Fetonte,* and *L'Aldimiro* are all by the same poet; as first noted in Alfred Lorenz, *Alessandro Scarlatti's Jugendoper*, 2 vols. (Augsburg: Filser Verlag, 1927), 1: 106; and Gordon F. Crain, 'The Operas of Bernardo Pasquini,' 2 vols. (PhD diss., Yale University, 1965), 1: 123.

63 A first-rate analysis of the libretto in relation to the Calderón play is offered in Nancy L. D'Antuono, 'Calderón a la italiana: *El hijo del sol, Faetón* en la corte virreinal de Nápoles en 1685,' in *El texto puesto en escena. Estudios sobre la comedia del siglo de oro en honor a Everett W. Hesse*, ed. Barbara Mujica and Anita K. Stoll (London: Tamesis, 2000), 22–32. The date of the Madrid premiere of *El Faetonte* is accepted by some scholars as 1 March 1661, and by others as 14 February 1662, as summarized in the introduction to *El Faetonte. Fábula escénica*, ed. Rafael Maestre (Madrid: Comunidad de Madrid, 1996), 1–2, 14–15, and explained in Chaves Montoya, *El espectáculo teatral en la corte de Felipe IV*, 292–9.

64 In the analysis of Margaret Rich Greer, *The Play of Power: Mythological Court Dramas of Calderón de la Barca* (Princeton: Princeton University Press, 1991),105–17, the play is understood as Calderón's 'lesson' to Philip IV concerning the ambitions of his bastard son, Juan José de Austria; but Greer did not take into account Carpio, who commissioned it. Carpio and other influential aristocrats were strong supporters of don Juan José because they feared that Carlos II would be an unfit sovereign and unlikely to produce heirs.

65 Documents to this effect will be presented in my forthcoming study; Prota-Giurleo seems also to have gathered evidence of Carpio's early relationship with Scarlatti; he stated that the Duke of Maddaloni met the composer for the first time thanks to Carpio and heard 'in casa dell'Ambasciatore [in

Roma] ad una recita della sua recente composizione *Gli equivoci nel sembiante.*' Ulisse Prota-Giurleo, 'Breve storia del Teatro di Corte e della musica a Napoli nei secoli XVII–XVIII,' in *Il teatro di corte del Palazzo Reale di Napoli* (Naples, 1952), 33.

66 The now-lost document dated 9 February 1684 containing the letter from the *cappellano maggiore* (ASN, Mandatorum, 285, f. 125) is transcribed in Proto-Giurleo, *I teatri di Napoli,* 3: 137–8, 329–30; and Fabris, 'Music in Seventeenth-Century Naples,' doc. 193, II, 347.

67 Concerning Filippo Schor, see Alba Cappellieri, 'Filippo e Cristoforo Schor, "Regi Architetti e Ingegneri" alla Corte di Napoli,' *Capolavori in Festa. Effimero barocco a Largo di Palazzo (1683–1759)* (Naples: Electa, 1997), 73–8.

68 A fuller study of the marquis del Carpio and his singers in Spain and Italy is forthcoming in my monograph, *Spaniards at the Opera.*

69 Sergio Durante, 'Zuffi, Giulia Francesca,' Grove Music Online, ed. Laura Macy, http://www.grovemusic.com.proxy.lib.umich.edu (accessed 1 June 2007); and Proto-Giurleo, *I teatri di Napoli,* 3: passim.

70 In his analysis of Scarlatti's early work, Grout made the perceptive observation that the Roman score for *Il Pompeo,* Scarlatti's first *dramma per musica,* lacks the 'pastoral episodes and, more importantly, the comic characters and scenes – which however will come in as soon as we get to Naples.' Donald J. Grout, *Alessandro Scarlatti: An Introduction to His Operas* (Berkeley and Los Angeles: University of California Press, 1979), 37. Of course, Grout assumed that the composer himself chose the subjects for his operas and did not consider Carpio's intervention as motivating the change of libretto type and the incorporation of these features.

71 The fables of Psyche and Cupid and Endymion and Diana are entwined in Antonio de Solís's *Triunfos de Amor y Fortuna,* which called for a large cast of mythological gods and pastoral characters mixed with allegorical figures when Carpio produced it in February 1658 in Madrid to celebrate the birth of Prince Philip Prosper. Carpio recruited forty-two actress-singers from all over Spain for this production, which showcased numerous complicated stage effects within the framework of nine principal scenic transformations. He also issued a special luxury *suelta de lujo* edition of the text, whose title page credits his work as producer (see BNE, T-24111). See my *Songs of Mortals,* 282–5, concerning the music and the cast; and Chaves Montoya, *El espectáculo teatral en la corte de Felipe IV,* 265–76, for a description of the visual effects.

72 For musical evidence of the extent to which Italian composers, even in Naples, misunderstood the Spanish style, or, at the least, handled it with extreme clumsiness, see *El robo de Proserpina y sentencia de Júpiter* (Naples, 1678),

an opera commissioned by the marquis de los Vélez with Spanish text by Manuel García Bustamente and music attributed loosely to Filippo Coppola, then maestro of the Cappella Reale in Naples. See the modern edition, *El robo de Proserpina y sentencia de Júpiter*, ed. Luis Antonio González Marín (Barcelona: CSIC, 1996), and especially the editor's commentary (p. 33) to the effect that 'Ese *estilo español* no era ni más ni menos que la imitación de los usos convencionales en el teatro musical hispano . . . y sobre todo lo más característico de dicho estilo era la utilización de formas estróficas (las series de coplas) y de estribillos.' The review by Jack Sage in *Il Saggiatore musicale* 5 (1998): 156, is useful; Dinko Fabris's review in *Revista de musicología* 19 (1996): 421–6, offers contrary conclusions concerning the nationality of the composer and musical styles in the opera.

73 It may be that Scarlatti witnessed or was involved in the performances of Calderón plays with Spanish music that Carpio produced in Rome in 1682; people of all social levels ('gente de todas esferas') and at least one prominent Italian musician attended them. A production of the Calderón-Hidalgo opera *Celos aun del aire matan* was sponsored by the Prince of Piombino, Giovanni Battista Ludovisi, in Naples in 1682, and it is likely that Carpio had Hidalgo's score for this opera with him in Rome (see my 'Opera and the Spanish Family').

74 A full score for *L'Aldimiro* is preserved as an unattributed manuscript (Ms 141) listed in John A. Emerson, *Catalog of Pre-1900 Vocal Manuscripts in the Music Library, University of California at Berkeley* (Berkeley: University of California Press, 1988); the manuscript was identified as Scarlatti's opera by John Roberts in 1996. I thank Professor Roberts for his generous help with unpublished material for this opera. Arias from *L'Aldimiro* are extant in several collections; an aria from *Il Fetonte* survives in Nc 33.4.367 I, and arias from *La Psiche* in Nc 33.3.4, Nc 33.4.5, and Nc 33.5.37; a scene from *La Psiche* (erroneously identified as a cantata) is in *4 Cantate Inedite*, ed. G. Tintori (Milan: Ricordi, 1958), 35–41. The arias in Naples are identified in Mauro Amato, 'Le antologie di arie e cantate tardo-seicentesche alla Biblioteca del Conservatorio "S. Pietro a Majella" di Napoli,' 2 vols. (Dottorato di Ricerca-VII Ciclo, Cremona, Scuola di Paleografia e Filologia Musicale, 1997); see also Teresa M. Gialdroni, 'Bibliografia della cantata da camera italiana (1620–1740 ca.),' *Le Fonti Musicali in Italia* 4 (1990): 31–131. I thank Dr Amato for his invaluable guidance and many astute suggestions.

PART IV

BAROQUE BODIES

chapter nine

Crashaw and the Metaphysical Shudder; Or, How to Do Things with Tears

RICHARD RAMBUSS

William Ian Miller's absorbing, though in places erotically blinkered, book *The Anatomy of Disgust* details with gusto 'the interpretively rich universe of the disgusting.'[1] In doing so, Miller finds biological and social life to be rich with revulsion, with so many things making the case for being vilest of all. As one would expect, excrement, blood, gore, pus, and rot in turn all come to the fore of Miller's visceral phenomenology of what turns the stomach and how. But other leading candidates emerge here as well. Miller recalls, for instance, the beginning of Julia Kristeva's book on rejected and abjected objects, *Powers of Horror,* which memorably exemplifies the disgusting as the layer of sticky skin that forms on heated milk.[2] Perhaps yet more loathsome than this milk membrane is Miller's own 'life soup,' his unsavoury name for the seethingly fertile, fetid ooze that is the disgusting run-off from the processes of decomposition to which all organic material (including us) is fated (18; 40–1). But elsewhere Miller contemplates that it might be something as trifling as hair, hair out of place – say, in or near one's mouth – that is 'the universal disgust substance.' On this account, he reminds us of the Clarence Thomas confirmation hearings and the pubic hair on that Coke can: an image 'branded on our consciousness,' leaving 'Thomas himself,' Miller remarks, 'forever polluted and trivialized because of it' (54–5). Then again, one finds Miller repeatedly invoking 'the horror of semen' (105), which he introduces into the discussion as 'perhaps the most powerfully contaminating emission' of the body and to which he accords nearly alchemical powers 'to feminize and humiliate' whatever comes in contact with it (19). Later in the book, Miller has grown more decided: 'I am of the view,' he asserts, 'that semen is of all sex-linked disgust substances the most revolting to *men.*' 'Men,' he adds, 'can never quite believe that women aren't as revolted by semen as men feel they should be' (103–4). Indeed, speculates Miller, 'it just may be that the durability of misogyny owes much to *male* disgust for semen' (20; emphasis in the original). I suppose Miller has not rubbed shoulders with many gay men, or even watched much heterosexual male pornography, in which nearly every scene perfunctorily climaxes in the so-called 'money shot': a spectacularized display, served up for the male viewer's delectation, of external ejaculation as documentary proof of both parties' pleasure.[3]

There is, however, some refuge for us from all this revulsion, inasmuch as Miller isolates a few things that 'seem almost incapable of eliciting disgust.' 'Is snow polluting anywhere? Are stones?' he asks. 'And how low,' he posits, guardedly venturing back to the domain of the corporeal, 'are the odds that tears will be?' (16). The eyes, Miller later expounds, are 'the only orifice from which a non-disgusting secretion flows: tears, which owe their privileged position to their source, their clarity, their liquidity, their non-adhering nature, their lack of odor, and their clean taste' (90). Yet one wonders whether this taxonomist of disgust would have been moved to wager otherwise about even the crystalline teardrop in view of one of English literature's most famous tear texts (and here I come to my subject): Richard Crashaw's 'The Weeper' and the remarkably aversive body of criticism that this seventeenth-century metaphysical poet, and this poem of his in particular, have accrued in modern criticism.

'The Weeper' herself is, of course, that exemplar of Christian penance, Mary Magdalene, one of Christianity's first female converts and most famous saints, a figure in whom there has recently been a renaissance of cultural interest. Mary Magdalene's current celebrity is principally due to her pivotal role in Dan Brown's religio-conspiracy thriller, *The Da Vinci Code*, first a huge blockbuster novel and then a high-grossing Hollywood film. The Magdalene was also an attractive subject for devotional expression throughout the English Renaissance. The sixteenth-century English Jesuit priest and poet Robert Southwell wrote two poems on her: 'Mary Magdalens Blushe and 'Marie Magdalens Complaint at Christs Death.' Southwell also composed a highly wrought, melodramatic prose meditation titled *Mary Magdalens Funeral Tears,* which went through numerous early modern editions. But this kind of Magdaliana is not only a recusant expression of devotion. Anglicans such as George Herbert, Andrew Marvell, and Henry Vaughan, among others, also contributed verse on Mary Magdalene to the period's literature of tears.[4] Yet it is Crashaw – first a

Church of England poet-priest and then a Roman Catholic convert—who opens the floodgates in 'The Weeper,' with its stanzaic strings of remarkable metaphysical conceits on Mary's spectacularly unstopped eyes:

> Hail, sister springs!
> Parents of silver-footed rills!
> Ever bubbling things!
> Thawing crystal! snowy hills,
> Still spending, never spent! I mean
> Thy fair eyes, sweet Magdalene! (st. 1)[5]

'The Weeper' appears in all three volumes of Crashaw's English verse: the 1646 *Steps to the Temple*, the substantially expanded 1648 *Steps to the Temple*, and *Carmen Deo Nostro*, published posthumously in 1652 in Paris. Whether by Crashaw's design or his printer's, this poem opens both editions of *Steps to the Temple*, thereby serving as the first of its 'Steps for happy souls to climb heaven by,' as the anonymous prefatory 'Letter to the Reader' introduces the devotional verse that follows.

Crashaw was an inveterate reviser and amplifier, and the version of 'The Weeper' that appears in the second edition of *Steps* comes with nine new stanzas. Among them is one that has turned out to be the single most notorious passage in all of this poet's work, which is saying something, given that Crashaw's extravagances are, as one critic says, 'all but proverbial.'[6] Indeed, that passage ranks among the most infamous in English Renaissance poetry. It comes at stanza nineteen, which asks us to conceive of the Magdalene's tears as at once pooling and setting into motion as 'Two walking baths; two weeping motions; / Portable, and compendious oceans.' Remarkably, Crashaw envisions each eye as its own little ocean. Just one ocean – much less a mere river – of tears apparently isn't of enough effect here! What is more, these sister seas are mobile, ambulatory; they can follow the Saviour, we're told, 'where'er he strays.' Am I alone, I wonder every time I read this poem, in imagining that Jesus himself may be rather embarrassed by this emotional outpouring, that the Saviour's 'straying' hints at even his desire to get away from the Weeper?[7]

Whatever the divine response might have been to Mary's mode of contritional bodily comportment, the influential Victorian man of letters Edmund Gosse's verdict on Crashaw's *poetic* comportment in this instance was decidedly not favourable. 'These are,' he judges, 'the worst lines in Crashaw. They are perhaps the worst in all English poetry.'[8] (This is reason enough, in my book, for taking note of Crashaw.) Beginning with Gosse, criticism of 'The Weeper' becomes an exercise in hyperbole, much like the poem itself, which is typically regarded by critics to be at once utterly eccentric and tellingly representative. That is, 'The Weeper' is treated as both a singular, almost unbearably grotesque poetic anomaly and, at the same time, the signal instantiation of Crashavian poetics, or even of metaphysical poetry more generally, with its propensity for 'enormous and disgusting hyperboles' and 'far-fetched' conceits. These terms of censure come from Samuel Johnson's 'Life' of Crashaw's Cambridge friend Abraham Cowley, with its mostly disapproving account of a metaphysical 'race of writers' whose penchant for amplification, carps Johnson, 'had no limits.'[9] I will return to Johnson on the metaphysicals later. Here I want now to continue with Gosse and his precendential handling of 'The Weeper' as a work that is simultaneously idiosyncratic and indicative. For, having just designated the poem's nineteenth stanza as the height of literary excess and tastelessness, Gosse then insists that the lines 'must not be omitted here, since they indicate to us the principal danger to which not only [Crashaw] but most of his compeers were liable' (174–5). Indeed, 'The Weeper' long (though now no longer) had the curious distinction of being both Crashaw's most reviled and most anthologized poem.[10]

The tale of how Crashaw came to acquire his reputation as the author of the canon's worst verse makes for lively reading in the history of taste, literary and religious. It also exemplifies the usefulness of what's bad, of what's set out to be marginal or even to be rightfully scorned. For where would aesthetics be without disdain? In a 1939 monograph, Austin Warren declares that Crashaw is capable of metaphors 'repugnant to normal taste.'[11] Writing twenty years later, Ruth Wallerstein likewise concedes in her own monograph on Crashaw that he can be at times no less than 'the very model of bad taste in poetry.'[12] The contemporary poet Alice Fulton updates that estimation in an essay that sees Crashaw's poems as 'models of camp,' 'stupendous examples of ecstatic high seriousness that crashes unwittingly into banal low comedy.'[13] Fulton's 'textbook example' (her term) of that tendency? What else but 'his poem on the tears of Mary Magdalen,' which 'finds the pilgrim,' Fulton quotes, '"follow'd by two faithfull fountaines; / Two walking baths; two weeping motions; / Portable, and compendious oceans"'? Fulton touches upon 'the grotesque sensibility of Crashaw' (193) by way of comparison to another seventeenth-century English poet and the actual subject of her essay – Margaret Cavendish – in whom Fulton discerns a 'Crashaw-like campiness' (213).

Janel Mueller also treats Crashaw in a comparative context in an essay on gender and the metaphysicals. But unlike Fulton, Mueller is not amused by our poet, whom she sets forth as 'an idiosyncratic extreme in the adoption of Continental modes of sensibility.'[14] For Mueller, Donne is everything – English, Protestant, masculine, and decidedly heterosexual – that Crashaw is not.[15] William Kerrigan likewise smirks that 'Donne, thankfully, was not Crashaw.'[16] My sense, however, is that Crashaw has more in common – devotionally, poetically – with Donne and his compeers than most modern critics care to admit. The baroquely ornamented surfaces of Crashaw's verse and his capacity to out-Marino Marino, the great sixteenth-century Italian mannerist, allows for criticism to regard similar, if more occasional, expression in Donne, Herbert, Cowley, and even the young Milton as less beholden to Continental poetics than they may indeed be. It is worth noting in this respect that Johnson's foundational account of a metaphysical school (which neglects to mention Crashaw himself) recognizes Donne et al. as 'borrowers' of Marino, and this to their detriment.[17]

Let me now turn to one objection in particular that shows up just about everywhere in 'Weeper' criticism, such as it is. That objection is incisively expressed by Austin Warren, who complains that 'From his poem, Crashaw has excluded the story, the character, the psychology, and the moral.' 'Mary,' Warren thus concludes, 'has no part in her poem; it should be called not "The Weeper," but "Tears"' (127). ('The Tear,' by the way, is the title of another of Crashaw's several Magdalene poems, one that follows directly on the heels of 'The Weeper' in *Steps to the Temple,* though Crashaw probably wrote it before he wrote 'The Weeper.') Warren has a point here. Over the course of its thirty-one stanzas, 'The Weeper' offers no narrative of Mary Magdalene's conversion, of who she is or how she entered into the state of extreme, world-altering feeling that here has so consumed her.

> Not, so long she lived,
> Shall thy tomb report of thee;
> But, so long she grieved,
> Thus must we date thy memory.
> Others by moments, months, and years
> Measure their ages; thou, by tears. (st. 26)

In contrast to the Magdalene's status as an icon of the contemplative life, Crashaw's 'The Weeper' is notable as a lyric poem about contrition without any evocation, much less excavation, of the subjective experience of contrition. I call the poem a rendering of contrition, but in fact we hardly know why Crashaw's Magdalene weeps so much. Are hers simply tears of sorrow? Of shame? Or also of spiritual relief? 'Excess of joy weeps,' Blake famously says.[18] Might Mary's sobs then be an expression of happiness, of pleasure too? Even of ecstasy? Crashaw's poem about them is 186 lines long, but it does not say.

'We recognize in crying,' Tom Lutz writes in his engrossing book on the subject, 'a surplus of feeling over thinking, and an overwhelming of

Figure 9.1 Icon of the contemplative life. Titian, *The Penitent Magdalene* (1555–65); oil on canvas, 106.7 × 93 cm. Courtesy of The J. Paul Getty Museum, Los Angeles.

our powers of articulation by the gestural language of tears.'[19] Crashaw's tour de force tear text renders acute affect absent psychology. Here the lachrymosity is all surface special effects. The eye is supposed to be our window to the soul. Miller remarks the eye's privileged status as the only bodily orifice that opens 'not to muck and slime but instead to the spiritual inside' (90). But in this case that portal is completely flooded, blocking our access inside. 'My words are my tears,' intones Samuel Beckett. Lutz responds that 'for many of us the opposite is equally true. Tears are a kind of language, a primary, and often primal form of communication' (24). Likewise for Crashaw's Weeper, to whom the poem attributes no words or thoughts, only tears and more tears: tears 'still spending, never spent.' Not one, but two oceans of tears, which, notwithstanding Miller's inclination to grant this one bodily excretion his sole categorical exemption from the disgust response, have repelled readers in their sheer excess.

'Leave nothing of myself in me,' Crashaw intones at the conclusion of the ecstatic coda that he appends to the revised 1652 version of 'The Flaming Heart,' the third work in a remarkable four-poem sequence on mystical experiences of Teresa of Avila, the other female patron saint of his verse. This is one of few interjections of personal prayer in Crashaw's entire devotional corpus. Tellingly, it is a cri de coeur for the extinguishment of the self, for the sacrificial forfeiture of the poet's own voice to the living text (*la Vida*) of the saint:

> Leave nothing of my self in me.
> Let me so read thy life, that I
> Unto all life of mine may die. (ll. 106–8)

This desired evacuation of voice and selfhood, combined with the absence of the kind of introspection that is a hallmark of the period's devotional verse, may be among the chief reasons why interest in Crashaw's work has waned so dramatically over the past several decades of subjectivity-centred, Protestant-oriented critical enterprise.

Perhaps we can look to the recent renewal of interest in early modern English Roman Catholic culture to help rectify this situation. That said, I am surprised that Crashaw – who cultivated a coterie of female Catholic patrons (most notably Queen Henrietta Maria) and whose poetry evinces such enthusiasm for female saints and female conversion – does not figure more prominently in Frances Dolan's *Whores of Babylon*, her illuminative cultural history of the gendering of Catholicism in seventeenth-century England.[20] When, if ever, the new scholarship on Catholicism comes to embrace Crashaw within its purview, it needs first to recognize, however, that the poet was not always already the Roman Catholic convert that Barbara Kiefer Lewalski's cursory mention of his work in her canon-reshaping *Protestant Poetics* makes him out to be. Crashaw warrants next to no place in a study of English Protestant devotional literature, Lewalski influentially determines here, because he 'writes out of a very different aesthetics emanating from Trent and the continental Counter Reformation, which stresses sensory stimulation and church ritual (*rather than scripture*) as means to devotion and mystic transcendence.'[21] One of the problems with Lewalski's view is that we do not know precisely when Crashaw – whose first book of English poetry, *Steps to the Temple*, is so titled to draw comparison to George Herbert's *The Temple* – actually converted to Roman Catholicism. I'd venture that Crashaw never would have done so, never would have departed what he calls in his sole extant letter his 'little contentful kingdom' of Peterhouse, the Cambridge college of which he was a fellow, and Little St Mary's, the church adjacent to the college, where he was a curate, for the Continent (first Leyden, then Paris, then Rome, and finally Loreto), if the High-Church sacramentalism he espoused had remained a devotional option in England in the 1640s.[22] What is likely is that much of Crashaw's poetry – including 'The Weeper' and the Teresa poems – came to him, at least in its initial form, while he was still a High-Church Anglican. Consequently, his extravagances of expression cannot be so readily cordoned off as merely Counter-Reformational, Continental, baroque, foreign. Rather than thus marginalizing Crashaw, we might instead ask what seventeenth-century English devotional writing looks like when Crashaw is restored to the mix.

With respect to that endeavour, Ramie Targoff's book *Common Prayer* usefully notes that the preface to *Steps to the Temple* heralds Crashaw as 'Herbert's second, but equal.'[23] Although Targoff does not move from this observation to a reading of Crashaw, her work on poetry and liturgy – on poetry *as* liturgy – would, I think, afford us an especially elucidative vantage onto his poetic devotional project. Targoff effectively puts to rest that enduring, but fairly useless, antithesis (operative in Lewalski and others) that has conventionally associated Roman Catholicism with group ritual, on the one hand, and Reformed Christianity, on the other, with private, personal devotion, while coding the former as artificial, formulaic and the latter as sincere. Targoff reads more closely into the introspective involutions in the works of great Protestant poets such as Donne and Herbert to reveal the lineaments of liturgical language and method that shape these thrillingly pressurized devotional subjectivities.

Yet Crashaw may be the most profoundly liturgical of all seventeenth-century English poets. Here we might begin with the fact that so much of his poetry is presented under the generic heading of the hymn. Many of them are original compositions; for example, 'In the Holy Nativity of Our Lord God: A Hymn Sung as by the Shepherds,' or the 'Hymn for the Circumcision Day of Our Lord,' or 'A Hymn to the Name and Honor of the Admirable Saint Teresa.' Others are Crashaw's own Englishings of classic Latin Church hymns, such as the 'Stabat Mater Dolorosa' and the 'Dies Irae.' Indeed, Crashaw's final volume of poetry, *Carmen Deo Nostro* (posthumously published in Paris for a European as well an English readership) proffers itself as a kind of hymnal, as songs for *our* God, the *Nostro* of its Latin title signalling that this poet's devotions are conceived as collective devotions, transnational ones at that. Throughout his writing, Crashaw expressed a devotional cosmopolitanism that values ecstatic religious experience over national or doctrinal difference. In his 'Apology' for his Teresa hymns, he thus exclaims: 'What soul soe'er, in any language, can / Speak heav'n like hers is my soul's country-man. / O 'tis not Spanish, but 'tis heav'n she speaks!' (ll. 21–3). *Carmen* also offers an 'Office of the Holy Cross' – perhaps the volume's fullest melding of liturgy and poetry – which provides versified ritual prayers and hymns for each hour of the day. Crashaw's Office probably draws upon the Sarum Primers, which remained in regular use at Little Gidding, the High-Church Anglican religious community established by Herbert's friend Nicholas Ferrar. We know that during his years at Cambridge Crashaw was a regular participant in the daily offices and nightly vigils that structured devotional life there, which he depicts in the poem 'Description of a Religious House and Condition of Life,' itself an influence on T.S. Eliot's 'Little Gidding' in *Four Quartets.*

Not that Crashaw's verse ignores scripture for liturgy and ritual. His very first volume of poetry, *Epigrammatum Sacrorum Liber* (Cambridge, 1634), is composed of Latin epigrams that work witty turns on scriptural texts, texts principally from the Gospels and Acts of the Apostles. Crashaw's New Testament focus distinguishes him from the contemporary Jesuit poets – Biderman, Remond, and Bettinus – who are typically cited as his chief models. They are as likely to write about saints or latter-day Catholic martyrs as they are to poeticize a scriptural text or subject.[24]

In contrast, Crashaw's book of sacred epigrams departs from the Bible only once in 'Upon the Powder Day' – Guy Fawkes Day – which Crashaw, according to Anglican custom, marks as a kind of national holy day: 'How fit our well-ranked fasts do follow, / All mischief comes after *All Hallow.*'[25] Crashaw's own English renderings of these poems appear as a group under the title 'Divine Epigrams' in both editions of *Steps to the Temple.* Most of them come with headings that identify the specific New Testament passages from which they derive. Lewalski's disqualification of Crashaw on the grounds that his poetics are not biblically oriented is thus hardly warranted. Nor does it seem right to me always to set scripture and liturgy in opposition, especially in an Anglican context. Crashaw does diverge from Donne, Herbert, Vaughan, and Milton inasmuch as he seldom presents his poetry as personal, as arising from individual experience or concentrated, inward-coiling reflection. But Targoff's work has shown that self-expression and ritual expression need not always be posed against each other. In view of this important insight, we might reopen Crashaw's poetry to parse the devotional subjectivity effects that are particularly attendant upon sacrament and ritual, especially when, as is the case here, the lyricist has abandoned himself to common prayer and hymn.

But that question is matter enough for another essay. In the remaining pages of this one, I want to return to the recurrent complaint that in Crashaw's poetry there is too much of the gross material world and not enough of the transcendently spiritual, or at least the intriguingly psychological. I would frame this impression in different terms by saying that Crashaw is an Incarnational artist, that his variety of metaphysical wit is premised on the tenet that the Christian Saviour is at once wholly God and wholly man – human like us in every respect, save for sin. Crashaw says as much about his own poetics in his 'Hymn to the Name Above Every Name,' which heralds the Incarnation as authorizing 'New similes to nature' (l. 96), a new order of natural/supernatural similitude rendered in literary trope and conceit.

Crashaw's poetry is an at once ecstatic and intellectual contemplation of Incarnational theology. Here matters of the soul appear as spectacles of the body. In 'The Weeper,' Mary Magdalene's contrition is, as we have seen, drained of interiority and stylized into a series of somatic and natural emblems. Indeed, the penitent herself – body and soul – is all but dissolved into a gushing superfluity of ingenious literary conceits on incessant weeping. Consider stanzas 4 and 5:

Upwards thou dost weep.
Heav'n's bosom drinks the gentle stream.
Where th' milky rivers creep,
Thine floats above; and is the cream.
Waters above th' heav'ns, what they be
We're taught best by thy tears and thee.

Every morn from hence
A brisk cherub something sips
Whose sacred influence
Adds sweetness to his sweetest lips.
Then to his music. And his song
Tastes of this breakfast all day long.

Instead of allowing them to splash onto the soggy ground, Crashaw floats the Magdalene's tears heavenward, so high heavenward that they are absorbed and re-concocted into a confluence of celestial rivers. There (as if the conceit had not already been stretched enough), the perpetual river of tears clots into cream – a literal Milky Way – so as daily to feed 'a brisk cherub.' And as if that weren't enough, the poet makes it so that this angel's dulcet 'song / Tastes of this breakfast all day long.' A milky hiccup amid the angelic hallelujah. How's that for triggering a 'metaphysical shudder'?[26] And if this still were not enough, Crashaw has another go at the conceit in his lush, if not always luscious, poem 'Music's Duel,' the opening work in *The Delights of the Muses*, the title given to the selection of his secular and occasional verse that is appended to *Steps to the Temple*. In 'The Weeper,' a single cherub sips. In 'Music's Duel,' a whole choir of them chugs: 'sweet-lipped angel-imps, . . . swill their throats / In cream of morning Helicon, and then / Prefer soft anthems to the ears of men, / To woo them from their beds' (ll. 76–9).

Crashaw's 'The Weeper' keeps ringing changes on Mary Magdalene's hyper-metamorphic eyes and tears. The tears that will turn first to cream in stanzas 4 and 5 and then to saltwater baths in stanza 19 begin as bubbling, crystalline runoff from melting snowy hills in stanza 1. The poem then rockets skyward in stanza 2, reconcocting Mary's tears as seed for stars (''Tis seed-time still with thee / And stars thou sow'st . . .'). By stanza 7 her tears have solidified into gemstones, 'proudest pearls' fit for a queen (figure 9.2). In stanza 10, they turn liquid again, but now as an effluvium so thick that it 'creeps' – not rolls, but 'creeps'; that's Crashaw's word for

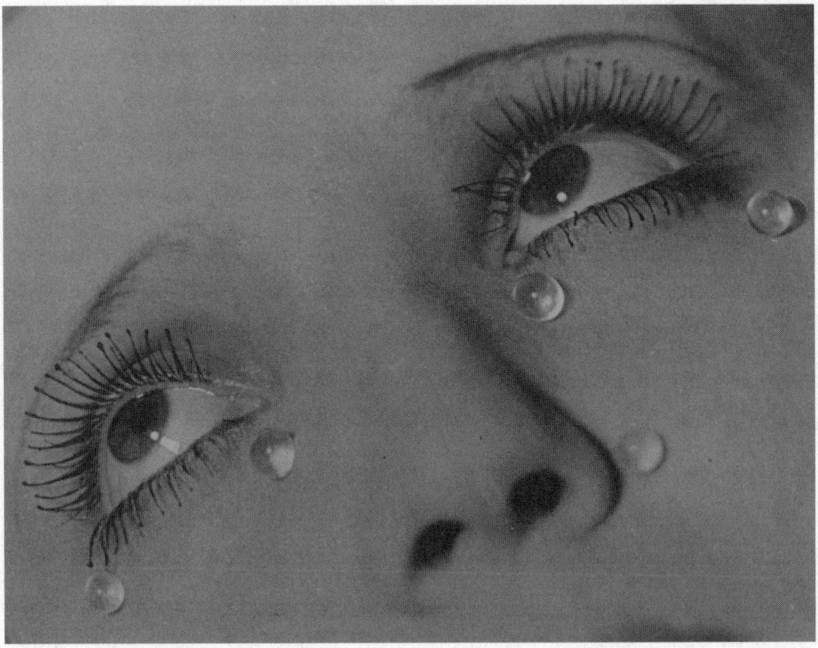

Figure 9.2 'Then, and only then, she wears / Her proudest pearls; I mean, thy tears' (Crashaw, 'The Weeper,' lines 41–2). Man Ray, *Les Larmes (Tears)* (1930–3); gelatin silver print, 22.9 × 29.8 cm. Courtesy of The J. Paul Getty Museum, Los Angeles.

the motion – down Mary's cheeks. Two stanzas later these same tears are bottled as water for God that turns into wine for his angels – a heavenly re-enactment of the miracle at Cana. From here it's tears into molten silver coinage in stanza 21; alchemical elixir in stanza 25; and sweat (perfume) extracted from roasted roses in stanza 27 – among many other things. 'The Weeper's' concluding stanzas depart from this liquefacient string of conceits for an image even stranger:

> Say, ye bright brothers,
> The fugitive sons of those fair eyes,
> Your fruitful mothers!
> What make you here? what hopes can 'tice
> You to be born? what cause can borrow
> You from those nests of noble sorrow? (st. 28)

The poem's final anthropomorphic turn is a return to the familial figure of the first line. The 'silver sisters' of Mary Magdalene's eyes are here delivered of their offspring, a shining band of brothers, who, no sooner born, swiftly make for the poem's ultimate object:

> Whither away so fast?
> For sure the sordid earth
> Your sweetness cannot taste,
> Nor does the dust deserve your birth.
> Sweet, whither haste you then? O say
> Why you trip so fast away? (st. 29)

In answer to the thrice-repeated question, Mary Magdalene's tears are granted the voice the saint herself otherwise lacks:

> We go not to seek,
> The darlings of Aurora's bed,
> The rose's modest cheek,
> Nor the violet's humble head.
> Though the field's eyes too weepers be
> Because they want such tears as we.
>
> Much less mean we to trace
> The fortune of inferior gems,
> Preferred to some proud face
> Or perched upon feared diadems.
> Crowned heads are toys. We go to meet
> A worthy object, our Lord's feet. (st. 30–1)

In yet one more metamorphic movement, the Magdalene's tears turn towards the Lord's feet – and turn again (as they have ever been) into feet, into a poem. Tears as words as feet: that is, the rhythmic measures of verse. 'Does thy song lull the air? / Thy falling tears keep faithful time. / . . . / Still at each sigh, that is, each stop, / A bead, that is, a tear, does drop' (st. 24).[27]

'The point,' thus recognizes Mario Praz, 'was to say the most marvellous things possible on Mary Magdalene's tears, and Crashaw has collected in upwards of thirty stanzas a great part of what in such a subject seemed poetical to his contemporaries, for whom wit and poetry were synonymous.'[28] I have lately been thinking that my past work on Crashaw may have underplayed the intellectual qualities of his poetry in its relish for the poetry's visceral, protean physicality. In Crashaw's time, the term 'conceit' – which shares the same root with 'conception' – served as a synonym for thought or idea. An alternate title for this essay might hence be 'Crashaw's Intellectual Poetry': that is, 'How to Do Things with Tears.'[29] Of course, to recognize the opulence and amplification of Crashaw's poetry as an intellectual, even academic, performance (and pleasure) is not to say that it is not also devout. This is a literary practice of piety and intellect.

To my mind, one of the more interesting things that has been said about 'The Weeper' comes in a short, tart 1925 essay by Kathleen M. Lea simply titled, appropriately enough, 'Conceits.' There she descries Crashaw's poem as 'beyond disgust.'[30] What, we might pause to ask, is *beyond* disgust? I have little doubt that Lea is here simply deploying the phrase in a hyperbole of dismissal and censure. Critics talk that way all the time about Crashaw. But let us think seriously for a moment about what might lie through and past disgust. 'To feel disgust,' Miller declares, 'is human and humanizing' (11). Indeed, the great virtue of Miller's book is its gripping ability to make disgust feel so pivotal, as it relentlessly, if queasily, demonstrates how our notions of personhood, privacy, rank, virtue, democracy, even love in turn are involved with the matter of revulsion. 'Love,' Miller argues, 'bears a complex and possibly necessary relation to disgust' (xi). 'Love often manifests itself,' he continues, 'by its special stances toward the disgusting and by special undertakings either to lower one's sensitivity to disgust . . . or, as in sex, to find in the disgusting itself a source of pleasure' (140–1).

What is true with respect to disgust for the various species of human devotion (parental, domestic, erotic, etc.) may also be true for that other, or not so other, form of devotion: namely, religious devotion. Here Georges Bataille, as I have written elsewhere, may still be our best guide theoretically.[31] *Erotism: Death and Sensuality*, Bataille's foray through the cross-circuits of religion and eroticism, especially in their most amplified, world-altering registers, activates a host of aversive devotional affects, including embarrassment, abjection, nausea, and disgust. Hold in check the dark, neo-Sadean tones of Bataille's celebration of taboo, sacrifice, and subjective dissolution, and we have something akin to the luminous ten pages that Susan Stewart devotes to Crashaw in *Poetry and the Fate of the Senses.* What Bataille expresses as nausea, Stewart figures as baroque vertigo. She finds that Crashaw's stretched conceits and extravagant transpositions and reversals 'twist, torque, and turn the reader about and summon the mind to heavenly aspirations in the ways bodies careen through Baroque architecture.'[32] In treating Crashaw as a baroque artist rather than a metaphysical poet, Stewart follows in the footsteps of T.S. Eliot, who hails Crashaw as 'more baroque than the baroque.'[33] (What would *that* look like?) Elsewhere Eliot remarks what a strange thing it is that this should be so, that 'the finest baroque poetry should have been written by an Englishman in English.'[34]

I suggested earlier that the perception that Crashaw's poetry and devotion lack depth, that it is all style and decorated surface, may be responsible for the contemporary waning of interest in him. As if anticipating such an outcome, Wallerstein, all the way back in the 1930s, looks to salvage his reputation by relating 'the story of Crashaw's life and inner growth,' by locating a vein of developing, deepening devotional inwardness in his work that exists at a remove from its otherwise 'grotesque physicality.'[35] What this critic wants is an interiorized Crashaw: a poetry of depth. Perhaps now, however, may be the time to take up precisely the opposite approach: that is, to embrace Crashaw as the (devotional) poet of surfaces, forms, decoration, sensations, ritual texts, and objects. In 'The Weeper' he blazons Mary Magdalene's eyes as 'Ever bubbling things' (l. 3). 'What bright soft thing is this?' he begins his other Magdalene poem, 'The Tear.'Among the notable aspects of both 'The Tear' and 'The Weeper' as devotional poetry is their trenchant thing-ness. Here, in line with Crashaw's Incarnational poetics – an aesthetic principle for him as much as it is a doctrine – religious sentiment is an expressive matter of the body that provides matter for more matter, for more things: stars, seed, cream, pearls, dew, balsam, flowers, drinking water, wine, April showers, oceans, bath waters, money, perfume, mothers and sons, and so on and on.

Perhaps the greatest virtue of Crashaw's poetry is how it exposes, if only implicitly, what poor theological grounds Christianity ultimately makes for dualism. Christianity's God-Man effects humanity's redemption as much by what he allows to be done to his body – which is, among other things, bathed by penitential tears, defiled, wounded, slain, before resurrected as his eternal habitation – as by any operation of his spirit. And in Crashaw's poetry the most intimate access that we have to Jesus comes by way of the body, more specifically through an orifice or wound in *his* body, as in the epigram 'I Am the Door': 'And now th'art set wide ope. The spear's sad art, / Lo! hath unlocked thee at the very heart' (ll. 1–2). Or in 'To the Name above Every Name,' where the ancient martyrs' wounds become the 'purple doors' through which Christ comes in and takes possession of them (ll. 216–17). Once rendered permeable, the sacred bodies in Crashaw verse – whether Jesus' or the martyrs' or Mary Magdalene's or Teresa's – typically open onto yet more objects, such as the 'book of loves' written by and in the wounds of the crucified Christ in 'Sancta Maria Dolorum' (st. 6), or the drops of blood shed by the newly circumcised Infant Jesus that turn into adorning rubies in his 'New Year's Day' poem (ll. 13–16).

Crashaw does not provide the kind of world of interiors that we expect coming to the period's verse via Donne and Herbert. What he does offer is a seriously sensationalist poetry, a poetry in which, as Eliot rightly recognizes, the intellectual resources of metaphysical wit are called upon to 'stimulate, to over-stimulate, feeling lest it should flag.'[36] Indeed, Crashaw, for Eliot, is both a baroque poet and a metaphysical one, as we see from his 1926 Clark Lectures at Trinity College, Cambridge, which he titles 'On the Metaphysical Poetry of the Seventeenth Century with Special Reference to Donne, Crashaw and Cowley.' My question is: if Eliot could have his Donne *and* have his Crashaw too – that is, an English devotional wordscape of depths and surfaces, of subjects and objects – why now can't we?

NOTES

This piece has benefited from its presentation to the 'Renaissances' workshop at Stanford (thanks especially to Stephen Orgel and Jennifer Summit) and to the European Studies Seminar at Emory (special thanks to Deborah Elise White, my astute commentator in that forum). I also want to acknowledge what an inspiration Ramie Targoff has been to me. And thanks yet again to Chuck O'Boyle: here for what comes first, not to say all that follows.

1 William Ian Miller, *The Anatomy of Disgust* (Cambridge: Harvard University Press, 1997), xii.
2 Ibid., 63–4; the reference is to Julia Kristeva, *Powers of Horror: An Essay on Abjection*, trans. Leon S. Roudiez (New York: Columbia University Press, 1982), 2–3.
3 See Linda Williams's now classic study, *Hard Core: Power, Pleasure, and the 'Frenzy of the Visible,'* Expanded Paperback Edition (Berkeley: University of California Press, 1999), 72–3, 93–4, 100–1.
4 On the literature of tears 'which flooded Europe during the sixteenth and seventeenth centuries,' see Louis L. Martz, *The Poetry of Meditation* (New

Haven, CT: Yale University Press, 1954), 199–203. But see also Richard Strier's important corrective, 'Herbert and Tears,' *ELH* 46 (1979): 221–47. Strier, principally through a virtuosic reading of Herbert's 'Marie Magdalene,' elaborates crucial differences between Reformation and Roman Catholic notions of contrition and penance, differences that go unremarked in Martz's argument about the Counter-Reformation textures of seventeenth-century English religious poetry.

5 All citations of Crashaw's poetry are, unless otherwise noted, according to *Carmen Deo Nostro* (Paris, 1652). I have silently modernized Crashaw's spellings.

6 John Peter, 'Crashaw and 'The Weeper,'' *Scrutiny* 19 (1953): 258.

7 My reading here of 'The Weeper' draws upon and extends the brief consideration of the poem and its critical reception that I offer in an earlier essay, 'Sacred Subjects and the Aversive Metaphysical Conceit: Crashaw, Serrano, Ofili,' *ELH* 71 (2004): 497–530. See, in particular, 500–3.

8 Edmund Gosse, 'Richard Crashaw,' *Seventeenth Century Studies* (London: William Heinemann, 1914), 174. (Gosse's chapter on Crashaw is reprinted from *Cornhill Magazine* 47 [1883]: 424–38). He later adds: 'Crashaw, however, possesses style, or he would not deserve the eminent place he holds among our poets' (175).

9 See *Johnson's Lives of the Poets*, ed. J.P. Hardy (Oxford: Clarendon Press, 1971), 11–19.

10 The first work of literary criticism about Crashaw comes from the hand of Alexander Pope in the form of a 1710 letter to Henry Cromwell that accompanies a gift copy of Crashaw's poems. The only work that Pope treats here at any length is 'The Weeper.' He judges five stanzas of it 'sublimely dull' and another seven to be 'soft and pleasing,' while the rest 'might have been spared, being either but Repetitions, or very trivial and mean.' As is the case in so much subsequent Crashaw criticism, Pope deems 'The Weeper' exemplary of the poet's body of work, which, like this poem, tends to be a 'Mixture of tender gentle Thoughts and suitable Expressions, of forc'd and inextricable Conceits, and of needless fillers-up to the rest.' Pope nonetheless recommends Crashaw as 'one of those whose works may just deserve reading' – provided that readers 'skim off the Froth, and use the Clear underneath.' Pope is even said to have rated Crashaw a better poet than Herbert. See Pope's letter to Henry Cromwell, 17 December 1710, in *The Correspondence of Alexander Pope*, 5 vols., ed. George Sherburn (Oxford: Clarendon Press, 1956), 1: 109–11. See also Spence's *Anecdotes, Observations, and Characters, of Books and Men Collected from the Conversation of Mr Pope* (London: W.H. Carpenter, 1820), 22, which records Pope's assessment that 'Herbert

is lower than Crashaw, Sir John Beaumont higher, and Donne, a good deal so' (22).

11 Austin Warren, *Richard Crashaw: A Study in Baroque Sensibility* (Ann Arbor: University of Michigan Press, 1957), 88.

12 Ruth C. Wallerstein, *Richard Crashaw: A Study in Style and Poetic Development* (Madison: University of Wisconsin Press, 1959), 112.

13 Alice Fulton, 'Unordinary Passions: Margaret Cavendish, the Duchess of Newcastle,' in *Green Thoughts, Green Shades: Essays by Contemporary Poets on the Early Modern Lyric,* ed. Jonathan F.S. Post (Berkeley: University of California Press, 2002), 212–13.

14 Janel Mueller, 'Women among the Metaphysicals: A Case, Mostly, of Being Donne For,' *Modern Philology* 87 (1989): 144.

15 'Using tactics the opposite of Donne's, Crashaw attempts to reconfigure intense subjectivity and sexualized love. While Donne always keeps his male speaker and his female subject distinct, Crashaw merges them to produce a hybrid consciousness, a supersensibility that must remain a merely imaginary ideal deprived of physical realization' (ibid., 151). Hence Crashaw, Mueller concludes, 'finally corroborates far more than he defies the generalization that Donne was the last English poet of the metaphysics of heterosexual love' (144).

16 William Kerrigan, 'The Fearful Accommodations of John Donne,' in *John Donne and the Seventeenth-Century Metaphysical Poets,*' ed. Harold Bloom (New York: Chelsea House, 1986), 41.

17 Johnson, 'Life of Cowley,' 14.

18 Blake, *The Marriage of Heaven and Hell,* 'Proverbs of Hell,' l. 26, facsimile edition, ed. Sir Geoffrey Keynes (Oxford: Oxford University Press, 1975), xviii.

19 Tom Lutz, *Crying: The Natural and Cultural History of Tears* (New York: Norton, 1999), 21. Lutz begins his study by noting both that weeping is a human universal and that weeping is exclusively human (17).

20 Frances E. Dolan, *Whores of Babylon: Catholicism, Gender and Seventeenth-Century Print Culture* (Ithaca, NY: Cornell University Press, 1999). Whereas Dolan at least makes a few passing references to Crashaw, Raymond D. Tumbleson surprisingly has nothing to say about him in *Catholicism in the English Protestant Imagination: Nationalism, Religion, and Literature 1600–1745* (Cambridge: Cambridge University Press, 1998). In contrast, Alison Shell offers an insightful discussion of 'the deracination of Crashaw within English literary history' in her *Catholicism, Controversy and the English Literary Imagination, 1558–1660* (Cambridge: Cambridge University Press, 1999), 97.

21 Barbara Kiefer Lewalski, *Protestant Poetics and the Seventeenth-Century Religious Lyric* (Princeton: Princeton University Press, 1979), 12; my emphasis.

22 Anthony à Wood's brief entry on the poet in his 1689 history of Oxford University suggests that Crashaw would never have 'changed religion' at all, apart from his 'infallible foresight that the Church of England would be quite ruined by the unlimited fury of the Presbyterians.' See Wood, 'Fasti Oxonienses,' in *Athenae Oxonienses* (London, 1692), vol. 2, col. 688. Even Gosse concurs: 'If the civil war had never broken out, it is probable that Crashaw would never have left the Anglican communion' ('Richard Crashaw,' 428). Crashaw's letter is reproduced in *the Poems English, Latin and Greek of Richard Crashaw*, 2nd ed., ed. L.C. Martin (Oxford: Clarendon Press, 1957), xxvii–xxxi. See xxix for the passage I here cite.

23 Ramie Targoff, *Common Prayer: The Language of Public Devotion in Early Modern England* (Chicago: University of Chicago Press, 2001), 96.

24 See Warren, *Richard Crashaw*, 81.

25 I have cited Crashaw's own English rendering of his Latin original as republished in the 1646 *Steps to the Temple.*

26 Judah Stampfer, *John Donne and the Metaphysical Gesture* (New York: Funk and Wagnalls, 1970), chapter 1.

27 I am indebted to Deborah Elise White for this line of reading.

28 Mario Praz, 'Crashaw and the Baroque,' in *The Flaming Heart* (New York: Norton, 1973), 226.

29 Here I am borrowing the title of Allen Grossman's *How to Do Things With Tears: A Book of Poems* (New York: New Directions, 2001), which is itself, of course, troping upon J.L. Austin's classic, *How to Do Things with Words* (Oxford: Clarendon Press, 1962).

30 Kathleen M. Lea, 'Conceits,' *Modern Language Review* 20 (1925): 403.

31 See Rambuss, 'Sacred Subjects,' 519–20.

32 Susan Stewart, *Poetry and the Fate of the Senses* (Chicago: University of Chicago Press, 2002), 185.

33 T.S. Eliot, *The Varieties of Metaphysical Poetry*, ed. Ronald Schuchard (San Diego: Harcourt Brace, 1996), 178.

34 T.S. Eliot, 'Devotional Poets of the Seventeenth Century: Donne, Herbert, Crashaw,' *The Listener*, 26 March 1930, 553.

35 Wallerstein, *Richard Crashaw*, 15.

36 Eliot, *The Varieties of Metaphysical Poetry*, 169.

chapter ten

'Law's Bloody Inflictions': Judicial Wounding and Resistance in Seventeenth-Century England

SARAH COVINGTON

In the annals of punishment, the brutalization of James Naylor, the self-proclaimed Quaker messiah, was particularly notorious. Charged by parliament in 1656 with 'horrid blasphemy' (among other offences, he rode into Bristol on a donkey, singing hosannas with his palm-wielding followers), the incendiary preacher-Christ and troublesome colleague of George Fox was ordered to the pillory, to be whipped at every cross street along the way. Accounts vary as to the extent and nature of Naylor's sufferings during his grim procession, with one witness describing three stripes on his back, 'no bigger than a pin's head,' and another writer claiming that 'there was no skin left between his shoulders and his hips. It was no mock punishment.' After further lashings, as well as being trod on by horses so that 'the print of the nails were seen on his feet,' Naylor arrived at the place of punishment, and there the disparity between accounts ends. Standing before the crowd, wearing a paper hat that proclaimed, evocatively, 'This is the King of the Jews,' Naylor was then bound with cords while a red hot iron, 'about the bigness of a quill,' was bored through his tongue. There followed a procedure in which a handkerchief was placed over his eyes, and the iron put to his forehead 'til it smoked,' as a B, for blasphemer, was inscribed. Spared the fate of execution, he was then set free, having faced his punishment with 'astonishing and heart-melting patience.' One of his followers proceeded to lick the wound on Naylor's forehead, but in the days that followed his acolytes soon melted away, and the false messiah, robbed of an ultimate martyrdom, departed back to prison, and to an obscure and disappointed life in the four years left to him.[1]

In the last three decades, the symbolic meaning of the kind of punishment suffered by Naylor has received a by-now saturated attention, propelled by interest in ritual, violence, the carnivalesque, discourses of power, and the body. Meriting equal attention, however, has been the purely theatrical aspect of punishment, which was designed for the edification of a crowd that could, depending upon one's interpretation, erupt in spontaneous displays of the carnivalesque or become subsumed under the formality and ritual scripted by the majestic force of the state.[2] Whether the drama was manifested in last dying speeches or in the literary depictions and responses constructed after the death of figures such as Charles I, executions were embedded in the theatrical imagination of early modern England as much as any performance to be found on the stage. As Molly Smith has written, the theatrical and the punitive, the stage and the scaffold, were 'communal worlds,'[3] and it is not surprising that one could therefore slide imperceptibly into another, at the same time that important distinctions remained. In the production of punishment, in what Foucault once termed the theatre of power,[4] the executioner thus performed his role; the preachers performed theirs; and in the centre of it all stood the malefactor himself (or herself), whose dramatic function was to depart the world with correct bearing and gesture, pleading forgiveness before the God and nation that he or she had so grievously offended.[5]

The victim of the scaffold or pillory, however, was not always the passive object on which the state's law and justice were inscribed. As this essay will attempt to demonstrate, through their bodies – primarily their voices and gestures – criminals could express subversive agency as well as myriad subjective capabilities from a point of otherwise extreme penal abjection; last dying speeches, for example, were one mode of defiance, as were gestures that were directed to crowd supporters or that resisted the literal and symbolic containments of officials. But the mortal or lesser wounds that were central to early modern punishment could also, in and of themselves, generate their own kind of performative and bodily speech, taking on a life of their own in their shapes and placements on the body, their profane bloodiness, their larger transcendent authority, their posthumous existence, and perhaps above all their catalytic role in transforming identity.

Though a kind of redemption was expected to take place through the act of public punishment – the traitor pleading forgiveness before God, or the thief formally repudiating his ways – the mark of guilt, in the form of a branding to the forehead or a whip's stripe, could constitute, on the one hand, a permanent insignia of sin and identity; as the sociologist Erving Goffman once wrote, such stigma constituted a socially defining force that penetrated an individual to the very core of his being.[6] From the perspective of the state, wounds in the form of severed hands or branded faces were intended not only to deter others (and the offenders themselves) from committing further crimes, but also to claim and define the criminal in a kind of act of state ownership – to forever contain, or imprison, the bearer in fleshly desecration. But the transformations that judicial wounds effected could swing the other way as well, with criminals or religious figures, and in Charles I even the king himself, embracing them as elevating rather than debasing, liberating rather then delimiting of identity. The means by which this was to occur thus rested with the offenders themselves, who often seized such wounding debasements as badges not only of resistance but even of victory against the state and its injustices, thereby utilizing their damaged bodies to rally others to their cause.

On the stage of judicial injuries, bodily wounds in this sense inspired not one but two performances, running counter to each other. On the one hand was the official performance, scripted by the state's representatives, who sought to cut into the sealed body in a manner that resonated with symbolic, punitive meaning; in a world in which the law was still lacking the kind of policing and other enforcing machinery of a later age, such formal gestures of projection were important. At the same time, however, the very wounds inflicted could be transformed in an act of agency, when a convicted individual claimed his or her injuries as tokens of an empowered identity, revealing not bodily abjection but, on the contrary, badges of an *imitatio Christi*: tokens of a final, defiant stand against the world. Both performances were ultimately framed and directed toward an audience; but the crowd could be ambiguous, as it sought to view the official script as it was precisely delineated,[7] or as its sympathies turned in favour of the victim who was best able to manipulate the drama of woundedness to his or her own advantage. Although the body of the criminal might have been thoroughly stamped with the 'unrestrained presence of the sovereign,'[8] as Foucault, Elaine Scarry and others have argued, a counter-reaction by the transgressor could thus emerge as well – and one that was often just as powerful, with the antagonisms playing themselves out in displays of gashes, slashes, severed limbs, and other forms of bodily demolition.

Most historians have focused on the scaffold as a stable site of drama, but it should be pointed out that penal displays could also extend themselves into the streets and the flurry of the crowd.[9] In executions, for example, the event began with a relatively lengthy procession, as the offender (often dressed in his or her finest) interacted with balladeers, cherry sellers, and pickpockets along the way, perhaps stopping in a tavern in order to reach an appropriate level of intoxication for his pending departure from the world.[10] No less important were the more participatory, improvisational, or street-theatre aspects conveyed through the whipping post, stocks, ducking stool, and pillory that belonged to the realm of petty punishment; indeed, such traditions as carting, in which the culprit proceeded through the streets on a cart, usually for some sexual offence or another, could be perceived as a kind of mobile travelling stage show, alternatively pathetic and comic – the early modern equivalent, perhaps, of vaudeville.

As Martin Ingram and Paul Griffiths have pointed out, smaller penal punishments were intended to reach as wide an audience as possible, utilizing shame as a deterrent and a form of retributive justice (though whether or not that audience was always receptive to the state's message again remains unclear).[11] To heighten the spectacle, symbols were employed in the form of costumes and accessories, such as the striped hoods worn by prostitutes, the wands wielded by penitents in church, the strips of bacon worn by cheating butchers, or the yarn worn around the heads of pillory-fixed wool thieves. Musical accompaniment would also be supplied by minstrels or crowds that banged on pots and pans, to the point where the infliction of pain, even in whippings which became dominant among the lesser penalties,[12] was secondary to the sheer charivari-like presentation itself.

Despite the varying degrees of penal-theatrical formality, authorities were preoccupied if not obsessed with constructing precise rules of stage direction according to which an individual was to be punished or put to death. Important to the process was the role of the larger culture, which could play a significant part in the decisions and rituals undertaken in what may seem to us an otherwise arbitrary chop shop of abusive display. Particularly if the law, to quote Clifford Geertz, was a 'distinctive manner of imagining the real,'[13] then it is not surprising that the scaffold or whipping post was constituted by a range of other cultural representations, including past theatrical traditions. In the depiction of bodily tortures as both brutally base and salvific,[14] as well as its theological narrative of suffering and atonement,[15] the late medieval morality play, for example, might have influenced the actual proceedings that took place on the scaffold;[16] later, dramas of revenge (though the proper legal word was retribution)[17] were intertwined with the judicial process of punishment, as Elizabethan and Jacobean playwrights gave themselves over to a general preoccupation with public spectacles of the law that manifested itself in gruesome death.[18] Marlowe was particularly eloquent on the subject of the corporeal judgment, even if he ultimately exposed the essential hollowness behind such 'legal' violence; contemporaneously, Thomas Kyd's *Spanish Tragedy* presented a gore fest that was unrivalled in its depiction of innovatively rendered wounds and deaths, and that prefigured the more overt and promiscuous displays of stabbings, poisonings, and sundry other mutilations (particularly of women) in the Jacobean plays of Webster or Middleton.[19]

From the Middle Ages on, English authorities had also sought to infuse penal performance, and the performance of treason executions above all, with overt symbolic meanings that coexisted with the physical enactment of the law. Ceremony and ritual created and reinforced these symbolic and social projections of power, but it was during Henry VIII's reign that an act was passed rendering penal punishments even more formal and ritualized, and overseen by a number of titled, if bizarre, officials.[20] Though the penal stage would soon become less populated with the sovereign's titled agents – the executioner, his assistant, and crowd-controlling sheriffs and bailiffs would be sufficient – the elaborate nature of Henry's various judicial measures is significant, for it reveals the extent to which greater legalism, characteristic of the Tudors, was accompanied by an increasingly heightened ceremony and stage direction, as well as a change in consciousness brought about in part by a new kind of language that permeated legal discourse.[21] Law thus became intimately connected with performance, with the latter not upholding the former, but rather serving as a vital and mutually supporting force alongside it.

Running throughout these performances of the flesh's punishment was what Desmond Manderson and others have described as the purely aesthetic (as well as, one might add, the non-textual) aspects of the law.[22] Law in fact could only become tangible and even legitimated in terms of performance and flesh, whether the drama concluded with an execution or with lesser, wound-inflicting punishments.[23] Though physical deportment and protocols of speech were important in such performances, it was in the moment when the knife or whip met the skin that the law most intimately made itself visible and became, quite literally, a wounding force. But the role of the body in a state of injury – its subjection or its triumph – also reveals the manner in which the law in early modern England resided on particularly tenuous ground, despite the fact that the theatre of punishment ostensibly served to legitimate violence (and the power that wielded it) through a quasi-legal prism.[24]

It was significant that such judicial dramas were enacted on the skin, which itself constituted a kind of blank slate ready for the scrawlings of an external (or internal and subjective) authorship. In the early modern period, one read the body as well as the soul and the mind on this text of the fleshly borders, which could implicate an individual in thoughts or crimes beyond his or her control. The idea that sin or criminality could be reflected in outward deformity – an idea that extended back to biblical treatments of leprosy, for example – was beginning to decline in the new scientific culture of the seventeenth century. But 'immoral' diseases such as syphilis, for example, had long been recognized through 'spotted' skin, just as the proto-neurologist Thomas Willis sought in the 1660s to understand the passions at least in part through blushes and other unintended epidermal displays. On a judicial level, while the trial by ordeal may have been obsolete by the seventeenth century, when officials no longer 'read' the blistered wounds of the skin after an arm or even an entire body had been exposed to boiling water or the hot iron, skin's revealing signs continued in the detection of witches, who were examined and exposed by their bluish, red, black, or sunken flesh – all indicators, presumably, of the devil's mark.[25]

Punishments also continued to be intimately connected to and symbolized through the body. In his influential law dictionary entitled *The Interpreter* (1607), John Cowell took care to reiterate the traditional bodily punishments for treason, which included being drawn through the streets and then hanged, after which 'thys living thou shalt be cut downe, thy bowels to be cut out and burnt before thy face, thy head cut off, and thy body to be divided in foure quarters, and disposed at the Kings Majesties pleasure,' and 'God have mercy upon thee.'[26] Edward Coke, for his part, was also a prosecutor, and in that capacity displayed no mercy to what he (and others) believed to be a crime not simply against laws and the reason they embodied, but against God and nature itself. Treason was imagined by Coke to reside metaphorically (if not actually) in the body; it therefore resulted in punishments that should precisely target those symbolic parts. The traitor's blood is 'stained and corrupted,'[27] Coke wrote, and added elsewhere that 'it is the physic of state and government to let out corrupt blood from the heart.'[28] As the heart was the originator and instigator of the traitorous deed and the corrupted blood ('Thou hast an English face but a Spanish heart,' Coke told Raleigh),[29] its removal was therefore not arbitrary, but an integral part of a larger symbolization at work.

Other woundable body parts were also charged with traitorous significance and therefore targeted in punishment, with Coke, echoing Cowell, advocating that the traitor's 'privy parts [be] cut off and burnt before his face as being unworthily begotten' – to further insure that no generation would follow him.[30] Likewise, the head 'that imagined the treason' would have to be severed.[31] The traitor's body was finally to be quartered and its parts spread far and wide, not simply to provide biblical feed for the fowl and to demonstrate the punishments that lay in wait for traitors, but to destroy the body (and soul) once and for all by denying it stability and integrity in death. In this, Coke was not only reflecting contemporary sentiments in his advocacy of such execution devices, but also recalling the rhetorical tradition of Romans such as Cicero, who similarly wrote of depriving the traitor's body of the integrity and stability of proper burial, since the goal was to 'cut the culprit off and shut him out of the entire sphere of nature.'[32]

Modes of punishment and the offender's physical comportment during his tortures were equally important to the authorities who presented for the public the sight of bodies in extremis. Hanging, for example, offered for full viewing a body whose flesh pulled ever downwards in resignation, dislodged from any fixed zone of being, belonging neither to earth nor to heaven, in a fate of suspension that was also greeted with particular horror in early modern Europe. Hanging had been the traditional punishment for enemies of the church, evoking as it did the death of Judas; even early Christian hagiographers were loath to associate such a fate with their heroic martyrs, with mutilating deaths privileged over all.[33] While the heavily Christian associations were perhaps lessened by the seventeenth century, the stigma remained; hanging was not a death that was desired, as testified by John Gerhard, who in 1654 successfully petitioned after his treason trial that he receive a beheading instead.[34]

Gerhard was aware that traitors of the upper ranks had long been accorded this more 'dignified' beheading; in this sense, class and gender also determined the punishment of the offender, as the stage carried '[an] implicit hierarchization of theatrical violence [that] correspond[ed] to the social codes that governed the distribution of judicial penalties.'[35] But punishment, and the law enacted in performance, could also intentionally diminish the class, and therefore the identity, of the victim. The execution for treason in 1650 of James Graham, the Marquis of Montrose, was a case in point. While many of his Scottish associates were simply hanged for treason by the Civil War covenanters – again, a highly dishonourable punishment – Montrose was dealt the classic treatment of being hanged and quartered; though he died upon hanging, his limbs were distributed among the towns, his trunk buried in the public gallows, and his head placed upon a spike.[36] Such dismemberment served to ostensibly deter the public from harbouring their own treasonous thoughts, but it also pointedly reduced the majesty of the person, effecting a transformation in which physical dismantlement reflected the diminishment of identity and, in a military sense, of honour. After the king's restoration, the 1661 state funeral granted to the remains of Montrose, the Scottish Hector, was in a sense an act of redemption not only for his unjust fate, but for the degraded manner in which he had died.

For lesser criminals, to be fixed unmovingly in place, as in the pillory – where one's ears were sometimes nailed to the boards, to prevent movement when the tomatoes, rocks, and dead cats came flying – was similarly terrifying. Nor were such criminals spared from also being dragged through the streets from the back of a horse – an act that was not simply wounding and mutilating in its effects but effacing as well, as the skin, the border of one's identity, was quite literally ripped away, to leave a battered, debased and meat-like carcass, in the manner of a modern-day painting by Francis Bacon. Branding an individual with a single letter was another particularly resonant means by which the law quite literally transcribed itself on the body of the offender;[37] such was the case with vagabonds, branded with a V on the forehead or arm, or the letters 'SS,' to signify the stirring up of sedition.[38] Such a practice was not new, of course; slaves and prisoners in the ancient world were inscribed with single marks (often the letter 'D,' meaning slave) that rendered them possessions of particular owners;[39] centuries later, the ninth-century saints Theodorus and Theophanes were punished for their worship of images by having poetic verses cut into their skin, resulting in a wounding that led them to be known as 'graptoi,' or 'written on.'[40] In both cases, branding, of all the punishments, represented permanent ownership by the state, with the law appearing to claim its transgressor as forever subject (and abject) to its power.

The most seminal bearer of a judicial signature and statement, of course, was Cain – something of a mutilator himself, in his execution of Abel[41] – who is said by some commentators to have borne on his forehead the Hebrew character 'ot,' meaning 'sign' or 'character,' thus creating a mark that referred back to itself as a mark while forever transforming the identity of the one who endured it.[42] The mark of sin and criminality borne by Cain also rendered him barren of land and property, an exile whose 'partnership with the world,' so God told him, was 'dissolved.'[43] Yet his mark, of course, also protected Cain from the harm of others, with alternative commentators arguing that the mark consisted of two Hebrew letters meaning 'you shall live'; in other interpretations, which also conveyed the variability of such a stigma's meaning, the mark was said to resemble a unicorn, the first animal thought to be sacrificed by God and therefore indicative of holiness and of Cain's new dedication to Him, while on a less elevated level, the sign was claimed to represent a pig, an animal that supposedly produced universal revulsion.[44] Cain's offences were also manifested on his skin in the form of a branding on the arm and the disease of leprosy that made his flesh glisten and turn spotted-white, and which indicated, as mentioned, the festering manifestation of transgression within.

To cut into the skin on a deeper level than branding – to penetrate further past the body's seal through cuts and slashes – was a particularly disturbing act; as the art historian Mitchell Merback has put it, the wound that resulted appeared 'as if a fault line [had] opened up across the body's topography, one that threaten[ed] to tear open ever wider expanses of the body's hidden interior.'[45] Fissured flesh represented depletion, of life and identity as well as blood, though not necessarily, as some writers have claimed, an effacement of memory of that individual. On the one hand, to carve into, scrape away, and dismantle a body, and to follow up that process by throwing the remaining pieces in a dunghill or placing the quartered parts on various posts, was a ritual of humiliation as well as eradication, as the case of Montrose attests. According to Desmond Manderson, the mutilated bodies of criminals as well as traitors such as Montrose 'were displayed as if they were statues or icons on which state power had been etched'; indeed, 'their wounds were symbols for which their bodies had become a canvas of dissemination.'[46] In many respects, the authorities thus sought not to annihilate so much as reconfigure memory, to bring the transgressor's death and life to accord with their own controlled narrative. As will be seen, however, the question of controlling the memory of the dead could be a contested one; and it was on and in the body that this contest most overtly played itself out.

In surveying the brutalizing treatments of offenders, from common criminals to high traitors, one may question whether such wounds held the same degree of revulsion for seventeenth-century audiences that were acclimated to violence woven into the fabric of everyday life. As

Richard Rambuss has pointed out elsewhere in this volume, bodily excesses did not provoke the same responses as the equivalent corporeal spectacles of modernity. Though authorities did not intend it to be the case, punishments and executions, which conveyed their own bloody overload, were entertainment, with blood and pain – as well as a larger narrative of redemption – serving to compel, not repulse. But the very fact that injury existed as central to the drama of execution still attests to that injury's powerful nature, however normative or quotidian such executions might have been; rather than produce a disgust that, in Julia Kristeva's words, '[shows] me what I permanently thrust aside in order to live,'[47] wounds on the scaffold or the pillory invited in the gaze, by making those contusions and gashes, in all their horror, maximally perceptible for all to see.

In the face of such power, and with the law so thick with historical meaning in its performance of mutilation and humiliation, one may well question whether resistance by the transgressor himself was possible. For Pieter Spierenberg, the scaffold was a ceremonial and ritualistic 'mode of repression' that successfully 'served to underline the power of the rulers' and therefore, in its unilateral force, precluded any true agency on the part of the criminal.[48] Raymond Williams, by contrast, argued that the law instead was, and is, a 'moving hegemony,' its 'cultural aspects 'alive with the push and pull of contestation,' negotiation, and the fluidity of meaning – a statement that perhaps holds more accuracy when it comes to early modern penal displays.[49] Indeed, the role of the body in a state of injurious death and dismemberment reveals the manner in which the law in early modern England could be so contested and even fictive at times, not only in the legal treatises of a Coke but on the level of the scaffold body itself.

On the one hand, wounds were representative of vulnerability and humility;[50] yet injuries were also, of course, born by Christ, even in heaven. They could therefore be infused with godly meaning, not only by more overtly religious figures but even by traitors themselves, who claimed those wounds as tokens of spiritual identity, revealing not bodily abjection but, on the contrary, emblems of a final, defiant stand against the world. As Montrose himself famously wrote, in a foreshadowing of his death:

> Let them bestow on ev'ry airt [direction] a limb;
> Open all my veins, that I may swim
> To Thee my Saviour, in that crimson lake;

Then place my pur-boiled head upon a stake;
Scatter my ashes, throw them in the air:
Lord, since Thou know'st where all these atoms are,
I'm hopeful, once Thou'lt recollect my dust,
And confident Thou'lt raise me with the just.[51]

Montrose thus utilized and even embraced his debasement to affirm not only his own salvation but the justness of God, who would raise him once more to full spiritual integrity. Earthly and sinful men may wound and separate him, literally, from himself, yet in a play on the famous Crusade maxim ('Kill them all; God will know his own'), Montrose would be recognized and even saved by his scattered body parts, since 'Thou know'st where all these atoms are.' Montrose, however, did not have to wait for divine intervention to restore him, or a semblance of him, that lived through his body or its parts; after his death, and in addition to his state burial, his heart was allegedly retrieved by supporters and placed in a gold casket – a relic for the ages.

Executions were thus pervaded with Christian symbolism that could easily turn martyrological. Last speeches were extremely important in this regard, for if the victim was given the opportunity to reinforce the state's justice, he could also exploit his last words as a moment of agency in which to frame the meaning of his death towards his own ends.[52] In his sermon before death, for example, Archbishop William Laud cited his 'predecessors' and therefore attempted to elevate himself to the martyred level of John the Baptist or Bishop Cyprian, who 'submitted his head to a persecuting sword'; moreover, 'my charge . . . lookes somewhat like that against Saint Paul [in Acts] . . . for he was accused for the Law and as well as the Temple that is the Law and Religion.'[53] From the opposite religious spectrum, the death in 1651 of Christopher Love, convicted for treason in allegedly planning to raise money for the restoration of the monarchy, was equally deploying of religious iconography. Love's last speech, however, differed from previous spiritual set pieces, such as those conveyed in Foxe's *Acts and Monuments*, in the level of its defiance and overt and proclamatory political nature. Appearing at the scaffold to 'pay the wages of Death,' he stated that 'I am not in the least sorry'; more typically, he insisted on his innocence against the charges that he had a correspondence with the 'King of Scots' – the future Charles II – even though he had desired 'nothing more then [Charles's] restoration to Honour and Freedom.' As for his pending death, 'formerly I have been in more terror and fear for the drawing of a Tooth, then I am at his present, being in a moment of time ready to have my head severed from my shoulders.' But, he added in a typical last-speech trope, 'I beseech God to forgive my enemies, as I freely do.' A prayer then followed, in which Love combined sacrificial language ('I am now ready to be offered, and the Vine of my departure is at hand') with Christian soldierliness ('I have fought a good fight, I have finished my course.') The scarf which he gave to the executioner to lay on the block was red, signifying martyrdom; as the sympathetic pamphleteer described it, 'he would not change his condition from the Block for any Emperors throne, if he might get ten thousand worlds by it.'[54]

Jesuits or Quakers especially welcomed death for the new life that beckoned beyond, but the immediate wounds that prefigured that death were also to be embraced, as physical evidence of grace and salvation. Stories, and not all of them apocryphal, abound, describing this embrace: the priest John Almond, executed in 1612, may have, according to his martyrologist, 'craved no favour to be shown in cutting him up alive,' though ' he wished [his executioners] if they pleased to begin with his fingers' ends and so go forwards.'[55] Aware, as his fellow Jesuits were, of the symbolic weight he was publicly assuming, Almond sought to connect himself to a holy pantheon of martyred predecessors, stating further on in his mortal soliloquy that he wished 'to have there St Laurence in his gridiron to be broiled on, St Peter's cross to be hanged on, St Stephen's stones to be stoned with, to be ript, ript, ript, and ript again, to have a thousand lives to suffer so many deaths for Jesus Christ His sake.'[56]

Responses may have varied, but Catholic priests, trained on the Continent to die if need be in their missionizing task, knew the traditions of martyrdom that had preceded them. If they appeared to feel no pain before the executioner's knife, then they were joining the superhuman and impervious – and thus victorious – examples of the early Christian martyrs – and using their wounds to do so; for those who, on the other hand, did express visible anguish, such tortures were also welcomed as a form of salvific flesh mortification and a manifestation of what Esther Cohen has termed a philopassionism, or surrender to physical pain, which was most evident in the later Middle Ages, but which continued in the work of Ignatius of Loyola and his *Spiritual Exercises.*[57] At once highly personal and abstract, since priests were also taking on the burden of all mankind in the sacrificial manner of Christ, torment as enacted on the stage was thus both a display and a denial of self, as the individual priest emerged into the larger and more typological (yet in his pain highly subjective) figure of the saint. Mutilation for such Catholics could even be perceived as representing a quasi-sacramental ceremony, with its preparations of the knives, ropes, planks, fires, and cauldrons, and its high point – the equivalent of the cup elevation – of the cutting moment itself, a moment that raised the body to its most vulnerable and 'bodily,' yet also reverent, condition.

Almond, whose heart was said to have 'leapt' into the hands of a Jesuit spectator after his slaughter,[58] was utilizing his central presence on the stage to offer up a counter-performance, using the attendant props of his wounds and the language of his pain to forge a heroic identity. Catholics were not alone in this strategy, however; Protestants who had been martyred by Mary I in the previous century were highly attuned to the performances they were giving at the stake, particularly in their capacity to gain converts and strengthen an already existing community of faith; in the seventeenth century, such patterns continued, in the manner by which Nathaniel Butler, for example, announced his conversion and redemption at the gallows in 1657, in a script that was carefully written by Puritans, or even by Naylor, whose bloody procession through the streets was transformed by him and his followers into a kind of English *Via Dolorosa*.

Women's resistance to judicial torments also took on particular significance in their own right. Hanging was the most frequent method of execution, and female common criminals, as well as witches who merited such a fate, were more often represented in visual, pamphlet, and ballad material that in turn reflected the huge interest and audience for such female-centred spectacles. While spared the fate of being drawn and quartered, which would have required a degree of immodest flesh exposure, women were subject to other equally severe punishments as men, particularly in being whipped or pilloried: punishments that frequently led to death in any case.[59] In the courts of law, the crimes of drunkenness and sexual laxity were, on the surface, gender-neutral in that they made little distinction between men and women, who both received the punishment of a whipping; yet profound differences also remained, as women were more frequently targeted with sexual crimes, including the bearing of illegitimate children.

Stripped to the waist, emanating copious blood, women certainly presented a more charged and eroticized spectacle of pain. Broken flesh in particular was a stark reminder of the continuing connection between women and their frail flesh, now exposed to the world in uncontained and wilfully violated spectacle. Contradiction, however, pervaded such a presentation: on the one hand, it remained incumbent for women to protect the seal of their body's boundaries, with sin and crime representing women's forsaking of such an imperative;[60] yet it was the Virgin Mary, with her extended palms and upturned arms, who represented an iconographic model of openness, just as mystics such as Julian of Norwich had once sought out or embraced physical disintegration in order to cross boundaries and approximate in themselves the suffering of Christ. Women were also expected to manifest the ideal of their sex on the scaffold in the form of meek acceptance of their fate and a last dying speech that would convey these noble qualities. Yet as Frances Dolan has pointed out, women, like men, could also use the opportunity of the scaffold to take a stand against authority and unjust punishment, as when the alleged adulteress Elizabeth Caldwell proclaimed that she 'could teach as the Preachers . . . [since] she was able to speake from a feeling hart,' and proceeded to lead the audience in the singing of a psalm.[61] The theatre of punishment could thus serve as a forum in which to exploit these contradictions, with women utilizing their electrifying wounds or the moment of imminent death to express a distinct and superior spiritual experience.[62]

Men and women, criminals and martyrs, were thus aware that their capacity to feel pain and to die – and to live on in parts after death – would determine their ability to rewrite the script according to their own controlled narratives. Of course, not all were resigned to meeting their ends in peace or eliciting the sympathy of the crowd. The last moments of the priest John Shert, for example, were marked by a hand-wagging admonition to his spectators that 'whosoever dieth out of the catholique Church he dieth in the state of damnation.'[63] In addition, one must take care to mention that Jesuits died differently than Quakers (or at least they beckoned to a different god), and religious individuals in general were perceived as standing apart from thieves or counterfeiters, even if they were often executed together. Nevertheless, the mechanisms of punishment, and the very theatre itself, often did call forth similar responses from a repeating cast of actors. In anthropological terms, the performance of punishment, in its tension and its manipulations of pain, wounds, and identity, was a display of liminality, as the offender undertook a rite of passage into a new state of being, utilizing all the ambiguities and possibilities embedded within such a state.[64]

The judicial drama of the flesh did not end in death, however, for the body after it had been mortally wounded or dismembered could then live on in miraculously revived and theatricalized form, undermining the authority – and above all the law – that had sought to disgrace and kill it.[65] Spectators who had witnessed Charles's death, for example, not only groaned but famously dipped their hands in his blood, which was thought to carry life in its healing properties. This was not, needless to say, as the authorities wished, even if they sought to manipulate corporeal remains toward their own ends. The posting of a severed head on London Bridge, or the public display of a corpse's fragmented parts over the course of weeks, for example, presented – or so it was hoped – an exhibit commemorating the theatre of justice and an advertisement for the law's majesty, designed to dominate the ideological struggle that could sometimes ensue.[66] But posthumous, wounded body parts could, again, subvert the intentions of authorities, particularly when a continued life-like power seemed for many to emanate from those parts, which necessitated their quick removal to prevent their collection and transformation as artefacts of positive memory.

Early modern sensibilities were particularly subject to a fear of posthumous reanimation, and the sight of severed heads apparently continuing to breathe and to even speak on the scaffold did not alleviate the dread, even if at other times severed heads were used for sport before they were thrown into the kettle for parboiling or hideously disfigured in a kind of posthumous iconoclasm that nevertheless testified to their continued power.[67] Such revivifications, as well as the general power of the eloquent if severed head, had been a long-held theatrical trope,[68] but popular belief, pamphlets, and broadsides also continued to utilize the image, perhaps borrowing from a dramatic tradition. In the pamphlet entitled *Canterburies Amazement*, written in 1641, for example, the head of the youth Thomas Bensted, executed for conspiring against Archbishop Laud, engages in a surprisingly ecumenical discourse with the head of a Jesuit: 'who art thou, that dares come up without my consent, and stand[s] thus cheek to cheek with me?' asks Bensted's head, posted on London Bridge; both heads proceed to speak of their respective crimes, though Bensted insists that his crime was only against the archbishop of Canterbury, whereas the Jesuit acted against the entire kingdom (eventually the Jesuit retires from his defence, claiming to have a headache).[69]

The miracle of a body fragment or a severed head that had remained preserved and uncorrupted (and talking) long after its disattachment from the corpse also attested to secular authority being overridden by the God in whose name the government had claimed to act. For Catholics, it was the relic, of course, that comprised the most visible manifestation of the memorialization process;[70] thus would women supporters such as Luisa de Carvajel visit the remains of the theatre of death long after the crowd had passed on, searching for bodily remains that could be shipped on to protective repositories such as the English seminary of Douai. According to one account, followers of the executed priest Robert Sutton, for example, managed to recover a shoulder and an arm, though 'all the flesh was consumed, torn, and eaten by the birds'; nevertheless, a thumb and forefinger were salvaged as well, consecrated with holy oil, and placed 'in contact with the most holy Body of Christ, a special honor above all the other fingers [of the world].'[71] Even nonbelievers could be persuaded by the evidence presented by a limb or hand; thus would a Protestant retrieve a leg from the quartered priest Mark Barkworth and, noticing that the knee had been calloused from so much prayerful kneeling, declare to his fellows, 'Which of you Gospellers can show such a knee?'[72]

Montrose's heart, as mentioned, was also carefully preserved in an urn, and therefore redeemed, not only carrying with it the symbol of the man but of his inward self and thoughts, now purified in their golden containment. By contrast, Oliver Cromwell's body was exhumed, hanged, and disfigured in 1661, along with other regicides – an act that accorded with the intentions of authorities, even if it still attested to unease over the power of the corpse, particularly as it could autonomously control and direct memory.[73] What authorities feared that these seventeenth-century body parts and wounds could memorialize was not the particular sin or deed of the criminal or traitor, but rather the performance of pain and joy, victory and disability, repression and defiance, and the injustice of the law itself. As the bearer of treason, the offender had wounded the realm and born that offence in a body, or in body parts, that could live on after death; just as treason had to be utterly extirpated for the purification of the law, so did the body that carried the treasonous taint have to die.

If the organs, limbs, entrails, and other corporeal parts constituted, as Pascal once put it, 'a body full of thinking members,' each containing its own metaphorical significance and experience, then it is not surprising that what Donne called the 'scatter'd body,' as well as its wounds, would therefore assume a heightened somatic significance,[74] especially on the platform of a judicial stage. Over the course of the eighteenth and nineteenth centuries, however, a more vocal repugnance to such judicial displays, at least on the part of the elite and evangelical philanthropists,[75] began to signal the end of this mode of theatrical punishment, even if the performative and ritual aspects of executions would continue to live on. Paradoxically, coterminous with the rising abhorrence to such 'medieval' forms of death was the increasing number of crimes that merited capital punishment, from fifty in 1688 to over two hundred in the early nineteenth century.[76] As J.A. Sharpe has pointed out, however, the actual number of executions, despite the statutory increase, began to undergo a distinct decline,[77] particularly with the rise of the prison system, penal colonies, and other methods of punishment. While individuals would continue to be branded, whipped, and even quartered, on stage or off, for the next two centuries – with the eighteenth century constituting a particularly lively age in the theatre of death and punishment – the reasons for this ultimate decline or increasing abhorrence are open to interpretation. For Foucault, the goal (and achievement) of authorities was 'not to punish people less, but to punish them better.'[78] The decline of such overtly and publicly wounding judicial spectacles – and the emergence of new and modern forms of punishment, primarily in the form of prison containment – might also attest to the tenuousness and ultimate ineffectuality that such spectacles carried in the first place, particularly in the subversive potential contained within them.

On another level, and as far as wounds themselves were concerned, Mikhail Bakhtin's related notions of the grotesque body, boundless and open to the world through orifices that leaked, defecated, stained, and exposed the body's interior contents, might also be applicable. Wounds, after all, were orifices themselves, akin in their own way to mouths, noses, and other apertures;[79] in the age of the modern classical body, Bakhtin wrote, all that which 'protrudes, bulges, sprouts, or branches off . . . is eliminated, hidden or moderated,' as 'all orifices of the body are closed' with an 'impenetrable façade.'[80] Technologies of execution that involved extended and graphically open displays of injuries, such as quartering, thus became less palatable to modern sensibilities, leading to 'quicker' (if not necessarily more humane) methods of killing, or to the increasingly covert sequestration of holdovers such as hanging.[81] In this sense, changes in practices of punishment and execution accorded with an increasing closure of the body and its extremities, at least in terms of public display, with the mechanical regularity of the guillotine or the medicalized, quasi- (or pseudo-)scientific lethal injection of today overtaking the more overtly 'lurid' and symbolized – and messier and subversive – practices of a previous age.

Despite the intensity by which certain offenders embraced their pain in public, the symbolic and metaphorical meanings that attached themselves to such judicial injuries were also beginning to decline from their peak in the late Middle Ages, even if the ritual around those meanings continued to linger amid the intellectual and contradictory cacophony of the age. On the one hand, while William Harvey's revolutionizing understanding of circulation, for example, resulted in a kind of desacralization of blood, crowds nevertheless continued to surge forward to dip their handkerchiefs in or taste the sacred blood of a criminal;[82] nor did Richard Wiseman's more empirical and non-Galenic medicine prevent him from embracing, as a good royalist would, the doctrine of the king's sacred touch (and blood).

On the other hand, while physical pain continued to be seen by many as the price paid for sin,[83] which had been essential in making sense of traditional judicial punishment, new mechanical understandings of the body, at least among the elite, began to undermine traditional and moral notions of physical torment. Descartes, for example, not only conceptualized pain in the modern sense, as a sign of physical pathology, but he also refuted the notion that pain was the connective strand that united the soul and the body (in Descartes's dualistic scheme, pain was a perception not of the body, which was an automaton, but of the soul aware of itself in pain). Even those English Cartesians who refuted Descartes's notion of pain, such as Kenelm Digby, advanced their own distinctly corpuscular theories that served to dislodge pain from its previously moral-centred perch, and to influence an emerging notion of the automaton-body that had to be disciplined and punished absent the kind of symbolic ideas that had persisted in the past, and which no longer worked in accordance with changing social, philosophical, and religious realities.

Despite these transformations, and though the seventeenth century witnessed the decline of a penal philosophy that had lasted for centuries, the symbolisms of judgment, punishment, and the law – and wounds – would not, of course, end. In Kafka's exceedingly disturbing story entitled 'In the Penal Colony,' an unnamed officer in an unnamed land sings the praises of what he calls a 'harrow' machine, an execution contraption that utilizes a series of jabbing and moving needles to literally inscribe judgment onto the body of the condemned over the course of twelve excruciating hours – long enough for the victim to comprehend his judgment in the very marrow of his being. For Kafka, called the 'great twentieth-century fabulist of judicial stigmatization,' the law is both absurd and utterly serious,[84] with the torture machine representing, perhaps, a kind of 'mechanical' jurisprudence[85] that ultimately goes horribly awry, as it proceeds at the end of the story to stab the officer, now prostrate upon it, indiscriminately across the body and finish him off with a single spike through the forehead. It could be said that the officer shares his fate with the fate of the machine, and by extension with 'justice' itself, and is ultimately destroyed by it. But while Kafka's justice is a profoundly twentieth-century conception, one could also argue that many who were punished or went to their deaths in seventeenth-century England were also, like the officer, implicated in (if not quite responsible for) the mechanics of their own suffering and judgment, particularly when they sought to exploit their punishments and transform their identity on stage toward a larger abstract and no less ideological goal.

What these seventeenth-century body parts and wounds finally came to memorialize was not the particular sin or deed of the criminal or traitor, but rather the performance of pain and joy, victory and disability, repression and defiance; and the performance did not end there, either. The dying Quaker became a martyr; the bodily fragment of a Jesuit became an object of veneration; and if the offender continued to live, then a reminder in the form of a scar, a glistening brand or an amputated stump would survive on as a ghostly echo, or a kind of mechanical reproduction, of the long-ago performance. As the gallows was littered with blood and dismembered parts after the drama had ended, even those appendages took on an animated and performative spirit of their own, with one pamphlet describing algae growing on a severed hand, abandoned forlornly beneath the scaffold: evidence perhaps that life, and resurrection, were contingent, in the end, upon death.

NOTES

1 *A True Narrative of the Ecamination, Tryall, and Sufferings of James Naylor in the Cities of London and Westminster* . . . (London, 1657) [Anon.]

2 See, for example, J.A. Sharpe, *Judicial Punishment in England* (London: Faber and Faber, 1990); Richard J. Evans, *Rituals of Retribution: Capital Punishment in Germany, 1600–1987* (Oxford: Oxford University Press, 1996); V.A.C. Gatrell, *The Hanging Tree: Execution and the English People* (Oxford: Oxford University Press, 1994); Thomas Laqueur, 'Crowds, Carnivals and the State in English Executions, 1604–1868,' in A.L. Beier, et al, eds., *The First Modern Society* (Cambridge: Cambridge University Press, 1989), 305–55; Peter Lake and Michael Questier, 'Agency, Appropriation and Rhetoric under the Gallows: Puritans, Romanists and the State in Early Modern England,' *Past and Present* 153 (1996): 64–107.

3 Molly Smith, 'The Theater and the Scaffold: Death as Spectacle in *The Spanish Tragedy*,' *Studies in English Literature* 32 (1992): 218.

4 Michel Foucault, *Discipline and Punish: The Birth of the Prison*, trans. Alan Sheridan (New York: Pantheon, 1976), chap. 1.

5 *A True Narrative*; see also Leo Damrosch, *The Sorrows of the Quaker Jesus* (Cambridge, MA: Harvard University Press, 1996), 222–9.

6 See Erving Goffman, *Stigma: Notes on the Management of Spoiled Identity* (New York: Simon and Schuster, 1963).

7 J.M. Beattie, *Policing and Punishment in London, 1660–1750* (Oxford: Oxford University Press, 2001), 307.

8 Foucault, *Discipline and Punish*, 49.

9 Pieter Spierenburg, *The Spectacle of Suffering: Executions and the Evolution of Repression* (Cambridge: Cambridge University Press, 1984), 45.

10 For processions of punishment on the continent, see Lionello Puppi, *Torment in Art: Pain, Violence and Martyrdom* (New York: Rizzoli, 1991), 20.

11 Martin Ingram, 'Shame and Pain: Themes and Variations in Tudor Punishments,' in *Penal Practice and Culture, 1500–1900: Punishing the English*, ed. Simon Devereaux and Paul Griffiths (New York: Palgrave Macmillan, 2004), 48–9.

12 Ibid., 57–8.

13 Clifford Geertz, *Local Knowledge: Further Essays in Interpretative Anthropology* (New York: Basic Books), 173.

14 See John Spalding Gatton, "There must be blood': Mutilation and Martyrdom on the Medieval Stage,' in *Violence in Drama*, ed. James Redmond (Cambridge: Cambridge University Press, 1991); Claire Sponsler, 'Drama and Resistance: Bodies, Goods, and Theatricality in Late Medieval England' and 'Violated Bodies: The Spectacle of Suffering in Corpus Christi Pageants,' in her *Drama and Resistance: Bodies, Goods, and Theatricality in Late Medieval England* (Minneapolis: University of Minnesota Press, 1997), 136–60.

15 Randall McGowen, 'The Body and Punishment in Eighteenth-Century England,' *Journal of Modern History* 59 (1986): 654–6.

16 See Margaret E. Owens, *Stages of Dismemberment: The Fragmented Body in Late Medieval and Early Modern Drama* (Newark: University of Delaware Press, 2005).

17 Mitchell Merback, *The Thief, the Cross and the Wheel: Pain and the Spectacle of Punishment in Medieval and Renaissance Europe* (Chicago: University of Chicago Press, 1999), 134.

18 See Stephen Greenblatt, *Shakespearean Negotiations: The Circulation of Social Energy in Renaissance England* (Berkeley: University of California Press, 1988), 15; see also Molly Easo Smith, 'Spectacles of Torment in *Titus Andronicus*,' *Studies in English Literature* 36 (1996): 315–31.

19 See Leonard Tennenhouse, *Power on Display: The Politics of Shakespeare's Genres* (New York: Methuen, 1986), chap. 3, esp. 115–22; Owens, *Stages of Dismemberment,* chap. 8.

20 Cf. Charles Wriothesley, *A Chronicle of England during the Reigns of the Tudors* . . . (London, 1875), vol. 1. For executions in general see, for example, G.R. Elton, *Policy and Police: The Enforcement of the Reformation in the Age of Thomas Cromwell* (Cambridge: Cambridge University Press, 1972), 386, 392–4.

21 Desmond Manderson, *Songs without Music* (Berkeley: University of California Press, 2000), 76–81.

22 Ibid.

23 John Briggs, Christopher Harrison, et al., *Crime and Punishment in England* (New York: St Martin's Press, 1996), 73.

24 Susan Dwyer Amussen, 'Punishment, Discipline, and Power: The Social Meanings of Violence in Early Modern England,' *Journal of British Studies* 34 (1995): 2–6.

25 Richard Bernard, *A Guide to Grand-Jury Men* (London, 1627).

26 John Cowell, *The Interpreter: or Booke Containing the Signification of Words* . . . (Cambridge, 1607), Vvv2.

27 Edward Coke, *The First Part of the Institutes of the Laws of England* (London, 1794), 2: 746.

28 J. Bund, *A Selection of Cases from the State Trials: Trials for Treason (1327–1660)* (Cambridge, 1879), 1: 396.

29 Ibid., 351.

30 *Trial of Guy Fawkes and Others,* ed. Donald Carswell (1934), 89–90.

31 *State Trials,* 396.

32 Quoted from Allen D. Boyer, 'Sir Edward Coke, Ciceronianus: Classical Rhetoric and the Common Law,' *International Journal for the Semiotics of Law / Revue Internationale de Sémiotique Juridique* 10 (1997): 9.

33 Samuel Y. Edgerton, *Pictures and Punishment: Art and Criminal Prosecution during the Florentine Renaissance* (Ithaca, NY: Cornell University Press), 1985).

34 Thomas Bayly Howell and William Cobbett, eds., *A Complete Collection of State Trials and Proceedings for High Treason* (London, 1816), 531–7.

35 Owens, *Stages of Dismemberment,* 145.

36 See for example Mark Napier, *Montrose and Covenanters* (London, 1838), 559ff.

37 Branding, however, could also take on positive memorializing connotations; Luther, for example, spoke of the necessity for children to have faith 'branded' forever into their hearts. See Mitchell Merback, 'Torture

and Teaching: The Reception of Lucas Cranach the Elder's Martyrdom of the Twelve Apostles in the Protestant Era,' in *Art Journal* 57 (1998): 14–23.

38 Alan Brooke and David Brandon, *Tyburn: London's Fatal Tree* (London: Sutton, 2004), 65. See also the case of Sarah Swanton, who in 1616 was branded with the letters FA – false accuser.

39 See in general Israel Drapkin, *Crime and Punishment in the Ancient World* (Lexington, MA: Lexington Books, 1989), chap. 8.

40 Steven Connor, *The Book of Skin* (Ithaca, NY: Cornell University Press, 2003), 79.

41 David Max Eichhorn, *Cain: Son of the Serpent* (Chappaqua, NY: Rossel Books, 1985), 67–8; see also Ricardo J. Quionones, *The Changes of Cain: Violence and the Lost Brother in Cain and Abel Literature* (Princeton: Princeton University Press, 1991), chap. 3; and see Ruth Melinkoff, *The Mark of Cain* (Berkeley: University of Cailfornia Press, 1981).

42 Connor, 76.

43 Eichhorn, *Cain: Son of the Serpent*, 89.

44 Ibid., 98.

45 Merback, *The Thief*, 113.

46 Manderson, *Songs without Music*, 114.

47 Julia Kristeva, *Powers of Horror: An Essay on Abjection*, trans. L.S. Roudiez (New York: Columbia University Press, 1982), 3.

48 Pieter Spierenberg, *The Spectacle of Suffering: Executions and the Evolution of Repression from a Preindustrial Metropolis to the European Experience* (Cambridge: Cambridge University Press, 1984), 207.

49 Raymond Williams, *Marxism and Literature* (Oxford: Oxford University Press, 1977), 112.

50 Zvi Jagendorf, 'Coriolanus: Body Politic and Private Parts,' *Shakespeare Quarterly* 41 (1990): 466–7.

51 *The Memoirs of James, Marquis of Montrose, 1639–1650*, ed. George Wishart (London, 1893), 534.

52 See Lake and Questier, 'Agency, Appropriation and Rhetoric under the Gallows: Puritans, Romanists and the State in Early Modern England,' *Past and Present* 153 (1996), 64–107; see also J.A. Sharpe, 'Last Dying Speeches: Religion, Ideology and Public Execution in Seventeenth-Century England,' *Past and Present* 107 (1985), 144–67.

53 *Archbishop of Canterbury's Speech: or his Funerall Sermon preacht* . . . (London, 1644), 9.

54 *Mr Love His Funeral Sermon Preached by Himself on the Scaffold on Tower Hill* (London, 1651), 2–6.

55 *Acts of English Martyrs Hitherto Unpublished*, ed. John Hungerford Pollen (London: Burns and Oates, 1891), 193.
56 Ibid., 190.
57 Esther Cohen, 'Towards a History of European Physical Sensibility: Pain in the Later Middle Ages,' *Science in Context* 8 (1995): 54.
58 Pollen, ed., *Acts of English Martyrs*, 170–94.
59 E.J. Burford and Sandra Shulman, *Of Bridles and Burnings: The Punishment of Women* (New York: St Martin's Press, 1992), 63–72.
60 Karma Lochrie, *Margery Kempe and the Translations of the Flesh* (Philadelphia: University of Pennsylvania Press, 1994).
61 Gilbert Dugdale, *A True Discourse of the Practices of Elizabeth Caldwell* (London, 1604) sig. Dv. See also Dolan, '"Gentlemen, I have one more thing to say,"' *Modern Philology* 19 (1988): 170–1.
62 See also the case of Margret Clark in Dolan, 'Gentlemen,' 171–7.
63 Bede Camm, *Lives of the English Martyrs* (London, 1905), 2: 460.
64 See Victor Turner, *The Ritual Process* (Chicago: Aldine, 1969); Caroline W. Bynum, 'Women's Stories, Women's Symbols: A Critique of Victor Turner's Theory of Liminality,' in *Anthropology and the Study of Religion*, ed. Robert L. Moore and Frank E. Reynolds (Chicago: Center for the Study of Religion, 1984); Esther Cohen, *The Crossroads of Justice: Law and Culture in Late Medieval France* (Leiden: E.J. Brill, 1993), esp. 79–80.
65 According to William Allen, writing early in the previous century, 'euen [the Catholics'] bodies . . . though hanging on ports, pinnacles, poles & gibbets, though torne of beasts and birdes: yet rest in peace, and are more honorable, sacreed [*sic*], and soueraine then the embaumed bodies of what worldly state soeuer in their regal sepulchers . . . diuers deuoute people . . . come as it were on pilgramage to the places where their quarters or heades be set vp . . . to do their deuotion & praiers vnto them, whose liues they knew to be so innocent, and deaths so glorious befor God and the world.' William Allen, *A Briefe Historie of the Martyrdom of xii Priests* (London, 1582), cviir–cviiv.
66 Merback, *The Thief*, 139.
67 Christopher Hibbert, *The Roots of Evil: A Social History of Crime and Punishment* (Stroud: Sutton, 2003), 27. Lake and Questier, 'Agency, Appropriation and Rhetoric under the Gallows,' 102.
68 See for example Regina Janes, *Losing Our Heads: Beheadings in Literature and Culture* (New York: New York University Press, 2005); Patricia Palmer, '"An headlesse Ladie" and "a horses loade of heades": Writing the Beheading," *Renaissance Quarterly* 60 (2007): 25–57.

69 *Canterburies Amazement: or The Ghost of the yong fellow Thomas Bensted, who was Drawne, Hangd, and Quartered by the meanes of the Bishop of Canterburie; who appeared to him in the Tower, since the Iesuites Execution (With a Discourse between the two Heads on London Bridge, the one being Thomas Bensteds, the other the late Jesuites* (London [ck], 1641), 8v.

70 Lake and Questier, 'Agency, Appropriation and Rhetoric under the Gallows,' esp. 83–4.

71 *Acts of English Martyrs,* 325; Susanne Wofford, 'The Body Unseamed: Shakespeare's Late Tragedies,' in *Shakespeare's Late Tragedies: A Collection of Critical essays,* ed. Susanne L. Wofford (Upper Saddle River, NJ: Prentice Hall, 1996), 1–21.

72 Brooke and Brandon, *Tyburn,* 49.

73 Peter Gaunt, *Oliver Cromwell* (Oxford: Blackwell, 1996), 4.

74 See David Hillman and Carla Mazzio, 'Introduction,' in *The Body in Parts: Fantasies of Corporeality in Early Modern Europe* (New York: Routledge, 1997), xi–xxix.

75 Gatrell, *The Hanging Tree,* 266–72.

76 On the so-called 'Bloody Code,' see John Beattie, *Policing and Punishment in London, 1660–1750: Urban Crime and the Limits of Terror* (Oxford: Oxford University Press, 2001), esp. chaps. 7 and 9.

77 See J.A. Sharpe, *Crime in Seventeenth-Century England: A County Study* (Cambridge: Cambridge University Press, 1983), 144.

78 Evans, *Rituals of Retribution,* 10.

79 See Edgerton, *Pictures and Punishment.*

80 Mikhail Bakhtin, *Rabelais and His World* (Bloomington: Indiana University Press, 1984), 319.

81 Manderson, *Songs without Music,* 120–2.

82 On popular perceptions of blood, see Peter Linebaugh, 'The Tyburn Riots against the Surgeons,' in *Albion's Fatal Tree,* ed. Douglas Hay (New York: Penguin, 1988), 65–118.

83 Esther Cohen, 'Towards a History of European Physical Sensibility: Pain in the Later Middle Ages,' *Science in Context* 8 (1995): 48.

84 See Richard A. Posner, *Law and Literature: A Misunderstood Relation* (Cambridge, MA: Harvard University Press, 1988), 118.

85 Lida Kirchberger, *Franz Kafka's Use of Law in Fiction* (New York: New York University Press, 1986), chap. 2.

chapter eleven

Excursions to See 'Monsters': Odd Bodies and Itineraries of Knowledge in the Seventeenth Century

KATHRYN A. HOFFMANN

In 1649, the parents of conjoined twins made a dash to Paris to put their 'monsters' on display for profit.[1] They didn't make it in time, and the dead infants were dissected at the École de Médecine. In 1676 a pamphlet invited the public to see a horned woman at the Sign of the Swan in London.

As conjoined babies and a horned women found their places within the display spaces of the city, they reveal what McClary calls 'cultural stages' in the most literal sense of the term.[2] Cities, fairgrounds, inns, and medical amphitheatres were sites of display where entertainment, profit, and medical knowledge intersected. They offer perspectives not only on early modern urban pastimes such as city strolling and public displays, but on the ways in which disciplines, commercial practices, texts, and individuals consumed, collected, enjoyed, and constructed understanding of marvellous things.

Anomalous bodies circulated and performed within a variety of cultural sites. We find conjoined twins, hairy people, people with cutaneous horns, extra limbs, or missing limbs, the unusually short or tall in the royal courts, city inns, fairgrounds, coffee houses, marketplaces, and street corners. We can catch a hypertrichotic German woman performing on her harpsichord at a French fair in the company of a five-footed cow, a lioness, a dromedary, a dolphin, a man without hands, and a rope dancer.[3] An Italian man with a parasitic twin demonstrated his agility on a handball court. A little person served as a museum guide.[4] Dead bodies circulated whole and in parts, embalmed and in jars, sometimes fused to animal parts to make fairground monsters. Human specimens were displayed in the offices of anatomists and apothecaries, transported on carts by promoters, and incorporated into collections poised to become the great European museums.

The public for monstrous bodies travelled as well. The history of odd bodies on display is in part a history of the increased travels of physicians, philosophers, collectors, and brokers as they set out on the trail of marvels, to study them through the lenses of the new sciences, collect and trade specimens from them, write specialized treatises on them, or incorporate them into larger works on natural history, philosophy, anatomy, and marvel. The physicians Thomas Bartholin and Johann Caspar Bauhin, the collectors Elias Ashmole and Ole Worm, and leisured men like Elie Brackenhoffer, Hieronymus Welsch, and John Evelyn, all of whom spent years travelling for personal enrichment or professional development, left traces of their contacts with odd bodies.[5]

Marvels were an incitement not only to national or international excursions, but also to local trips. Physicians whose names might otherwise have been lost from history visited local marvels, publishing their experiences in small treatises. The general public visited monsters and marvels as well. Some encounters occurred by chance in the entertainment zones of the large fairs, among the food and drink stands, puppet shows, animal acts, musical and theatrical shows, and prostitutes. Other encounters took place in large city and town markets, inns, and coffee houses. Spectacles designed for the general public, with a range of entry fees, used techniques of advertising, from printed brochures and illustrated posters to promoters and servants banging on tambourines or blowing on trumpets to draw the public off the street or across town. Their very presence suggests that taking a walk was already a recognized social activity with commercial possibilities exploited by seventeenth-century merchants.

What Lorraine Daston calls the 'esoteric consumerism' of early modern intellectual culture was accompanied by the beginnings of an esoteric tourism that would involve intellectuals, merchants, and the general public as well.[6] Travel to see monsters was part of the developing modern world, particularly affecting urban spaces. It becomes possible to follow the tourism of anomaly in the seventeenth century because of the number of printed materials available, including posters, handbills, brochures, books, short treatises, letters, diaries, travelogues, historical memoirs, gazettes, and collection catalogues. To avoid losing my reader in the great expanses of the fairgrounds, the streets of dozens of European cities, the hundreds of miles of museum basements, and the

Figure 11.1 Mary Davis, from Joseph Mayer, 'On Shotwich Church and Its Saxon Foundation,' *Proceedings and Papers [of the] Historic Society of Lancashire and Cheshire*, Session VI, 1854 (Liverpool, 1854), unnumbered page preceding page 83. Accessed through Google Book Search.

astounding array of human anomalies that were put on display in the seventeenth century, I have limited discussion to several small incidents in the history of the tourism of anomalous bodies: a pamphlet advertising a horned woman, and a trio of small texts – a memoir, a doctor's treatise, and a letter written by a person who saw a monster next door – that told of exhibits of conjoined twins. There are other studies that more fully describe types of human anomalies, the history of some of the people discussed below, and the ways in which marvels were worked into developing theories on nature and curiosity, and into developing consumerism.[7] What I want to capture is an admittedly fragmentary assemblage of cultural spaces that help broaden the understanding of the ways in which spectacle, travel, and reveries on the body functioned in the seventeenth century. Nearly all of the bodies themselves, including most of the specimens that were put in museums, are gone today. What is left is a textual itinerary of lost bodies.

'Take but a Walk' to See a Woman with Horns

In 1676 a seven-page pamphlet circulated in London with the title: *A brief narrative of a strange and wonderful old woman, that hath a pair of horns growing upon her head, giving a true account of how they have several times after their being shed grown again. Declaring the place of her birth, her education, and conversation; with the first occasion of their growth, the time of their continuance; and where she is now to be seen, viz., at the sign of the Swan, near Charing Cross.*[8] The woman was Mary Davis of Cheshire. Among the pamphlet's declared narrative intentions – to describe Davis's physical anomaly, provide her personal history, and explain the origin of her anomaly – was an enticement to the visual. It directed visitors to the sign of the Swan in the Strand, near Charing Cross. I am unsure what exact business was conducted under the sign of the Swan. I have been unable to find a Swan inn, tavern, coffee shop, or small theatre on the Strand in that year; all were possibilities for this type of display. The Swan might have been the inn where Mary Davis was staying or perhaps a coffee house, as coffee houses served as sites of pseudo-medicine, where elixirs and potions were sold. Several coffee houses even became small popular cabinets of curiosities.[9] As there is no mention in the pamphlet of Davis doing anything in particular during her display, she likely simply sat at the Swan, awaiting visitors. She may have spoken about her horns. Since she was a poor woman from Cheshire, it may be that whoever promoted her and produced the pamphlet spoke for her. We may assume she submitted, willingly or not, to having her growth touched and pulled, as visitors attempted to ascertain for themselves whether she was real or a fake. Wherever Mary Davis was, it was probably a boisterous place filled with people who came and went, spent their money, heard a story, and likely argued over the merits of the story and the truth of the spectacle before them.

While Mary Davis was no hoax – her cutaneous growths were real – the pamphlet opened with an address to a London reader jaded by charlatanry, and wary of the seductions of the visual:

> Reader,
>
> It may be, upon the first view of the title of this short relation, thou wilst throw it down with all the carelessness imaginable, supposing it to be but an idle and impertinent fiction, such as some frontless persons have too frequently exposed to publick view, on purpose to impose upon the credulity of the gazing multitude, who are apt to gape at wonders, and to think all true as the gospel, they see in print. (3)

The pamphlet warned of the double visual traps of wonder display: the visual fictions that caused the 'gazing multitude' to gape in awe, and the printed word that passed for truth. The pamphlet and the display of Mary Davis would also employ the techniques of vision and text, but for a public whose acumen it flattered. The visitor who stepped into the Swan would, the pamphlet intimated, leave the realm of the multitude cheated by charlatans and duped by false texts, and enter the ranks of the initiates into the real.

The pamphlet was not devoid of exaggeration, but it is the familiar exaggeration of advertising. It claimed that Mary's horns were a 'wonder in nature, as hath neither been read or heard of (we may justly suppose) since the creation' (4–5). This was hardly the case. There had been several humans with cutaneous horns on display in Europe in the late sixteenth century, including the Welshwoman Margaret Gryffith and the Frenchman François Trouvillou. Closer in time to Mary were the Dutchwoman Margaretha Mainers and the Scotswoman Elizabeth Lowe. The same year that the pamphlet on Mary appeared, Georg Frank published his *Tractatus Philologico-Medicus de Cornutis* in Heidelberg.[10]

The pamphlet on Mary Davis suggested a scale by which the truth of a wonder show might be ascertained, based on the distance the gazer had to travel. It set faraway wonders as those most likely to be deceptive:

'That this may court thy more favorable thoughts, call to minde, that such as intend to deceive, tell of wonders that are remote, and too far distant from thee' (4). The horned woman, just a walk and a small expense away, was offered as a marvel easily seen in person and evaluated by the layperson:

> This gives thee an account of what thou mayest with little trouble, and as small expence, behold: Take but a walk to the Swan in the Strand, near Charing-Cross, and there thou mayest satisfie thy curiosity, and be able to tell the world whether this following narration be truth or invention. (4)

The public was offered a day excursion into marvel. The words 'take but a walk to the Strand' invited the public into a stroll for curiosity and towards marvellous truths gained from vision. Eschewing the hotly debated theories of anomaly of the day – including divine will, maternal imagination, whims of nature, excess of matter, and portents – the pamphlet offered the most mundane of explanations for Davis's horn: that perhaps it had been occasioned by her wearing a 'straight hat' that had been too tight and had rubbed. This was a distinct shift from sixteenth-century posters and pamphlets. For instance, a poster for François Trouvillou provided him with a back story involving his expulsion from his village on suspicion that bewitchment might have provoked his condition,[11] and the pamphlet for Gryffith was a tract on prodigies and God's work, and did not mention where in London Gryffith could be found.[12] The marvel of Mary's cutaneous growths was banalized and familiarized for a London public, likely set up to provoke consternation that imprudent headgear choices might result in the development of horns. It is a wonderful example of marketing anomaly for the general public.

Mary Davis may have travelled less than many other people with rare conditions, who sometimes spent most of their life shuttling about the European fairground and court routes. Still, Mary's departure from her village seems to have been an event, with neighbours and acquaintances who 'brought her many miles of her journey' (5), and her horns became itinerant objects on their own. According to the pamphlet, 'the two first, Mr. Hudson, minister of Shotwick (to whose wife this rarity was first discovered) obtained of the old woman, his parishioner.' With the third growth, Davis's horns entered the museum and cycles of noble exchange:

> one of them an English Lord obtained and presented to the French king; the other, which was the longest, was nine inches long and two inches

> broad. It is much valued for the novelty, a greater than any John Tradeskin can shew, or the greatest traveller can affirm to have seen. Sir Willoughby Aston hath also another horn dropped from this woman's head, and reserves it as a rarity. (6)

Mary Davis and other horned humans fell under the category I have called 'knickknack humans': humans who were in whole or in part, collected or put on display as rarities.[13] The actors in the processes of collection and display included the royalty, the nobility, natural philosophers, doctors, charlatans, mountebanks, fairground and coffee house owners, sellers specializing in marvels, and a myriad of purveyors of spectacles, who included spouse-touts. Mary Davis's horns became marvellous collectables that circulated among a range of collection sites, from a local minister to the English nobility and the royal court in France. The pamphlet, not devoid of nationalistic sentiment probably designed to appeal to the London public, notes that Louis XIV was not offered the longest one. After other trades, horns identified as belonging to Mary Davis ended up in the British Museum and the Tradescant.[14] There is no record of exactly how they were displayed. We do know that in Edinburgh, Elizabeth Lowe's horn, removed in 1671, was put into a glass jar. The horn dangled on a silver chain along with a silver plaque on which the history of its excision was elegantly inscribed.[15]

Stephen Asma has said of museum specimens: 'The odd thing about a specimen is that it's a kind of cipher when considered in isolation. Specimens are a lot like words: They don't mean anything unless they're in the context of a sentence or a system, and their meanings are extremely promiscuous.'[16] Elizabeth Lowe's horn suspended on its silver chain was an object of promiscuous meanings: simultaneously a medical specimen, a museum artefact bearing a number and a history, a rare curiosity with a tale that could be told on an oval plaque, and a precious *wunderkammer* object. Human horns made sense within histories of anatomy, popular shows for the general public, and the development of museum collections. To the modes of display which Robert Bogdan developed for nineteenth-century human displays – the exotic and the aggrandized modes, both applicable to earlier displays as well – we might add other categories for the early modern, such as the collectable.[17]

Mary Davis's horns, as collectable and displayable anatomy, became part of the history of the specimen and the development of early museums. We can follow the horns for some time: Robert Plot demonstrated one of Mary's horns for the Philosophical Society of London in 1685; the

German Zacharias Conrad von Uffenbach said he saw the Ashmolean horn in 1710; John Pointer said it was there in 1749; and Dr Erasmus Wilson said the horns were still in the museums in 1844.[18] Joseph Mayer, who included Davis in a paper prepared for the Historic Society of Lancashire and Cheshire in 1854, mentioned that the horns were on display, although there is the chance that Mayer might have simply repeated information from the original pamphlet.[19] All of Mary's horns have now disappeared. The reasons for that disappearance are as lost as the specimens themselves, but might have included the condition of the specimens, cataloguing or storage errors, decisions to privilege normalized anatomy, or more generalized efforts to purge museums of *wunderkammer* aspects and/or human specimens.

Stephen Greenblatt notes: 'The experience of wonder continually reminds us that our grasp of the world is incomplete.'[20] The history of Davis's horns reminds us as well that our grasp of the spaces in which we have organized wonder is incomplete; that museum spaces are deceptive, slippery spaces of moving objects, shifting with public or curatorial tastes, with early modern natural and anatomical material often poorly catalogued and maintained. It is difficult to study the realm of what might be termed 'curatorial ephemera' because it is difficult to catch the traces of things that have disappeared and the history of decisions or errors that led to their misplacement or loss. Human remains, including horns on silver chains or baby heads dressed in bonnets, once hoarded and displayed with a verve for the decorated human part, were discarded in times that did not share that verve. The horns of Mary Davis are part of the lost, discarded, hidden-in-the-basement knowledges of the early modern.[21] Yet those discarded knowledges help us reconstruct other histories, among them that of a society of collection that allowed for gifting and exchanges of objects, and that produced artefacts including images, letters, brochures, and treatises designed to circulate when the objects could not. A portrait of Mary Davis disappeared from the Ashmolean as well.

The public for whom the 1676 pamphlet was designed did not need to be a natural philosopher or a wealthy traveller; she or he could encounter a novelty 'greater than . . . the greatest traveller can affirm to have seen' simply by strolling to the Strand. The pamphlet marked the desirabilty of travel and offered a reduced and accessible outing for the masses. Von Uffenbach, who saw Davis's horn at the Ashmolean in 1710, complained about the public who 'imperiously handle everything in the usual English fashion and . . . even the women are allowed up here for sixpence; they run here and there, grabbing at everything and taking no rebuff from the *Sub-Custos*.'[22] Encouraged by pamphlets, annoying von Uffenbach, a public of city dwellers and country visitors on city trips can be glimpsed walking, running, grabbing, and eluding the control of museum staff in the spaces set up for them to experience marvel. Pamphlets, letters, and diaries reveal early practices of urban strolling tied to commerce, entertainment, and the pleasures of the gaze. Walter Benjamin constructed his immense reverie on nineteenth-century urban practices around Baudelarian *flânerie*, iron construction, the textile trade, and social power.[23] Foucault constructed his theories on the disciplinary will to control, partly on the basis of the immobilized city envisioned in plans to reduce the spread of urban plague.[24] Using examples of seventeenth-century urban and fairground shows, we find early incidents of the mobilized city, where urban strolling was incited by spectacle and anomaly, and urban popular movement was sought because it provided social advantages, including entertainment, education, and commerce. The disciplines of medicine and museums often invited the public to engage in pleasurable movement. Whether one chooses moments of extraordinary control or extraordinary pleasures through which to read centuries shapes our understanding of them in different ways.

Today, Mary Davis's horn remains an incitement to excursions. 'The Horn of Mary Davis of Saughall' is listed as one of the four 'exhibits from the permanent collections' at the Museum of Jurassic Technology, a modern-day *wunderkammer*/art exhibit in Culver City, California.[25] While others have seen some form of a horn at the museum and photographs are posted on the internet, all I encountered the day I took an excursion to Culver City was a wall of animal horns and antlers, and a label with a quote about Mary Davis's horn.[26] The vicissitudes of horns in museums inspire the ironic obverse of Jonah Siegel's reflection on museums:

> If the walls of the museums were to vanish, and with them their labels, what would happen to the works of art that the walls contain, the labels describe? Would those objects of aesthetic contemplation be liberated to a freedom they have lost, or would they become so much meaningless lumber?[27]

With no horn there to adorn them or be explained by them, are the walls of the Museum of Jurassic Technology and the descriptive label thus liberated to their own freedom from the collectable? Whether the Culver City museum is intentionally a cabinet with or without a faked curiosity, an artful reflection on lost objects, or just a bit of fun with horns probably doesn't matter much in a museum created by a man who prefaced a conversation about Mary Davis with 'confusion can be a very creative state of mind.' David Wilson's goal of 'helping people to achieve states of wonder' is fulfilled whether the wall is blank or carrying a horn.[28] Mary Davis's horn remains today an incitement to an outing from Los Angeles and an invitation to small expenditures: one can purchase a 'Horn of Mary Davis' candle and candle holder or a pair of Mary Davis horn earrings at the online gift shop.

Encounters with the Conjoined

Lazarus Colloredo was born in Genoa in 1617 with a partially formed twin (baptized as Joannes Baptista) joined to his belly. Colloredo was one of the most famed and well-travelled marvels of his day. He was shown in Rome the year he was born, and travelled as a child and as an adult throughout Europe, including France, the British Isles, Poland, Switzerland, Denmark, and perhaps Turkey. He was granted audiences with King Charles I and Queen Henrietta, and included in treatises by Fortunio Liceti and Thomas Bartholin, who saw him in person.[29] The texts on monstrosity, focused on Colloredo's anomaly, give few specifics about the ways in which he was displayed. A better sense is gained from John Spalding who described the 'Italian man monster' at an Aberdeen inn in 1642:

> About a day or tuo befoir Pashe, thair cam to Abirdene ane Italian Man Monster of about 24 yeires of aige, haveing from his birth growing fra the breist upward, face to face, as it war ane creature haveing heid and syd hair lyk the cullor of the man's hair; the heid still drouping bakuardis and dounward . . . When he cam to the toune he had tuo servandis auaiting upone him, who with him self were weill clad. He had his portraiture with the monster drawin, and hung out at his lodging, to the view of the people. The one servand had ane trumpettour who soundit at suche tyme as the people could cum and sie this monster, who flocked aboundantlie into his lodging. The uther servand receaved the moneyis fra ilk persone for his sight, sum less, sum mair. And efter there was so muche collectit as culd be gottin, he with his servandis schortlie left the toun and went southuard agane.[30]

Spalding's record is notable for the specifics of the display at the city inn: a portrait hanging outside an inn to draw a city public; a trumpeter announcing show times; and well-dressed servants determining and collecting fees from the public. All this suggests preparation and the targeting of publics of differing economic levels. We know from Henri Sauval that Lazarus also played handball in France: 'Il étoit si accoutumé à porter son frère, que ce fardeau ne l'empêchoit point de jouer à la paume' ['He was so used to carrying his brother, that the burden did not keep him from playing handball'].[31] With multiple display strategies for a range of exhibitionary spaces that included royal courts, handball courts, and public inns that could accommodate wider public crowds, Lazarus Colloredo seems to have made a good living by drawing tourists to see him.[32]

In 1650, a physician named Paul Dubé from Montargis in France published a work on a case of conjoining that he had apparently seen himself, entitled *Histoire de deux enfans monstrueux nées en la paroisse de Septfonds au duché de S. Fergeau, le 20 juillet 1649* [*History of two monstrous children born in the parish of Septfonds in the duchy of St Fergeau on July 20, 1649*].[33] Dubé showed his familiarity with other cases of conjoining shown in France, mentioning Colloredo and a man who had been displayed in 1530. The text is an interesting record of a local physician's trip to a display in his region, and he reports on his conversations with locals and the mother. According to Dubé, the townspeople were convinced that the conjoining was the product of maternal imagination provoked when the mother had seen a portrait of conjoined twins in a surgeon's boutique. The mother however, assured him that this had not been the case:

> On m'avoit asseuré dans le païs que cette femme voyât dans la boutique d'un Chirurgien un monstre en peinture qui avoit quelque rapport avec celluy-cy, ceste puissante imagination avoit laissé le mesme effet dans le fetus; ce que la mère n'avoüa point m'asseurant n'avoir point veu cet objet.[34]
>
> [People in the area assured me that this woman had seen a painted picture of a monster which resembled this one in the boutique of a surgeon, this powerful imagination had had the same effect on the fetus; all of which the mother absolutely would not admit, assuring me that she had never seen that thing.]

Dubé himself seemed open to interpretations beyond maternal impression, mentioning other possibilities such as a compressed uterus and the excess or absence of matter in the fetuses.

Dubé appears to have taken a trip to see the twins in Septfonds soon after their birth, and this lent his treatise an air of reportage and thus veracity. In a much-reprinted treatise on medical care for the poor, advising remedies that could be obtained locally and produced cheaply, Dubé gives the impression that he was a practical physician concerned for his patients, not a fame seeker inclined to fanciful monster-mongering.[35] What happened to the infants next was recorded by Dubé and repeated here by Henri Sauval: 'Le père et la mère accoururent à Paris pour les montrer, croyant s'enrichir; mais à peine y étoient-ils arrivés, que ces enfans moururent. Ils furent apportés au théâtre anatomique de l'Ecole de Médecine, pour être ouverts' ['The father and the mother ran to Paris to show them, thinking they would become rich; but they had barely arrived when the children died. They were taken to the anatomical theatre at the medical school to be opened'].[36] Live conjoined twins set a poor family on the run to the city. While the revenues of display might help such a family care for itself and its children, travel also put fragile infants at more risk. Still, dead infants with anomalies remained displayable. I wonder who took the parents, surely lost in the city of Paris, and their dead children to the anatomical theatre and if the École de Médecine paid the family for the bodies it dissected and likely used to attract its own audience. Wealth, knowledge, and display mingled in ways that can be guessed at from the texts.

An individual's encounter with conjoined twins can be found in a two-page printed letter from 1685 of a man named E.B., entitled 'Strange and Wonderful news of the birth of a monstrous child with two heads and three arms, which was lately born at Attenree, in the county of Meath, in Ireland.' The letter, written from Dublin on 31 January 1684, opened:

Sir,

> You may remember I made you a promise, that as soon as I had a sight of that monstrous birth mentioned in a former letter, I would send you a particular relation of it: and yesterday it being exposed next door to me, I accordingly took time to view every part of it, and make my particular observations on every point needful to be remembered.[37]

Here we catch a fortuitous encounter with bodies on display and the efforts of an unidentifiable E.B. to be a good ocular witness who 'took time to view every part of it':

> It hath two Heads upon two well-proportion'd necks: the heads of the bigness of any child of a quarter or half a year old; fair and large, well-

> proportion'd and comly faces, with hair upon each of the heads; not the least defect (as I could perceive) either in eyes, noses, ears, or mouths. The shoulders are as large as a child of two or three years of age, proportion'd to bear two heads. I had a long pipe that I was smoaking in, which I laid across between the shoulders, and found it to be seven inches by measure and better in breadth on the back, from one shoulder to the other. (1–2)

Among the curious, we see a visitor gazing carefully and with the tools available to him measuring the dead infants with his pipe. It is a tiny detail from a display that is telling of ways in which the general public attempted to observe, measure, and record events. E.B. said that 'It was born about ten days since at a place called Attenree, in the barony of Kelly, in the county of Meath; the parents but poor people' (2). As was the case with the infants seen by Dubé, one wonders how a poor ploughman – faced with a stillborn birth and a wife who barely survived – managed to get his infants to display in a large city. Perhaps they were embalmed and taken by the physician or surgeon, who dissected them and whose report on their two hearts was found in a printed 'relation' E.B. mentions at the show (2). Henri Sauval reported on another pair of twins shown first alive and later embalmed at a fair: 'Ceux qui ne les avoient point vû en vie, les purent voir mortes à la Foire Saint Germain, où on les montra' ['Those who had not seen them at all in life, could see them dead at the Saint Germain fair, where they were shown'].[38]

In the early modern world, 'seeing is believing' as Richard Leppert says in his chapter in this volume, but seeing is also what makes things, bodies, and knowledges pleasurable, commercial, displayable, and collectable. The complex histories of the pleasures and the force of seeing are still being unravelled.

Antoine Furetière said of travel in his *Dictionnaire universel*: 'One travels out of curiosity in order to see rare things . . . Nothing is more instructive than reading about travel.'[39] The texts and the museum collections that resulted from travel to see odd bodies in the seventeenth century help reveal strategies of social, philosophical, and professional exchange and practices of display that link anatomical shows, private cabinets, court, fairground, inn, and street-corner shows with the beginnings of the modern museum. As a man measures dead babies with a pipe or parents take their babies, intended for the fairground, to an anatomical theatre, we are clearly in spaces shaped by the gaze, knowledge, and power. They differ from the spaces dreamt by Bentham or Foucault. These are mobile spaces and disciplines, interwoven and slippery. E.B. devised his own measuring tools and informal reporting system from within an inn. The physician Dubé set off on a sort of medical tourism, drawn by famous twins. The anatomical theatre at the École de Médecine interrupted its routine one day to dissect the bodies of dead babies first intended to be displayed live for profit. The discipline of medicine was drawn by the fairground, and inns displayed bodies that would end up in museums, each realm repeating, with shifting emphasis, the scenarios offered by the others. If one leaves Foucault behind for a moment forging his imaginaries of power inside Bentham's panopticon, we can see the disciplines of medicine and museums caught in their own inquisitive turns towards anomaly and the fairground. Watching small events from the margins of history, we can begin to forge other theories in which the productive forces of pleasure, curiosity, and bodily movements make the disciplines turn their metaphorical heads and shift their focus. Bénigne de Bacilly's description of cadence or *mouvement* in music – 'it stirs up, I may say it excites, the listeners' attention' – could apply to other early modern movements as well.[40] In the travels of odd bodies and those who followed their paths, there are stories of vision caught in surprise, marvel, fear, fascination, and flimflam, in attempts to know, to be entertained, to sidle up to fame, to make fame, or to record the world by measuring dead babies with a pipe. There are functions of the gaze still waiting to be uncovered at the spaces where the fairground and medicine met, where people took trips to see monsters.

NOTES

1 The term 'monster' was routinely used in the seventeenth century for anyone with a corporeal anomaly and is used by a number of the authors of pamphlets and treatises discussed here.

2 See her introduction to this volume, as well as the essay by Sarah Covington.

3 On the display of the hypertrichotic Barbara Urslerin at a French fair, see Jan Bondeson, *The Two-Headed Boy and Other Medical Marvels* (Ithaca, NY: Cornell University Press, 2000), 1–6, and Kathryn A. Hoffmann, 'Of Hairy Girls and a Hog-Faced Gentlewoman: Marvel in Fairy Tales, Fairgrounds, and Cabinets of Curiosities,' *Marvels and Tales* 19, no. 1 (2005): 67–85.

4 Sebastiano Biavati was a guide, demonstrator, and human specimen in Ferdinando Cospi's museum in Bologna. See Zakiya Hanafi, *The Monster in the Machine: Magic, Medicine, and the Marvelous in the Time of the Scientific Revolution*

(Durham, NC: Duke University Press, 2000), 86. An engraving with Biavati demonstrating the museum served as the frontispiece in Lorenzo Legati's *Museo Cospiano* (Bologna, 1677).

5 For histories of several seventeenth-century travellers, see Zweder von Martels, ed., *Travel Fact and Travel Fiction: Studies on Fiction, Literary Tradition, Scholarly Discovery and Observation in Travel Writing* (Leiden: E.J. Brill, 1997).

6 Lorraine Daston, 'Curiosity in Early Modern Science,' *Word & Image* 2, no. 4 (1995): 391.

7 Lorraine Daston and Katharine Park, *Wonders and the Order of Nature 1150–1750* (New York: Zone Books, 1998); Bondeson, *The Two-Headed Boy*. On English popular shows, see Richard D. Altick, *The Shows of London* (Cambridge: Harvard University Press, 1978), and Paul Semonin, 'Monsters in the Marketplace: The Exhibition of Human Oddities in Early Modern England,' in *Freakery: Cultural Spectacles of the Extraordinary Body,* ed. Rosemarie Garland Thomson (New York: New York University Press, 1996), 69–81.

8 London: Printed by T.J., 1676. Page numbers will be given parenthetically.

9 On quacks in coffee houses, see Aytoun Ellis, *The Penny Universities: A History of the Coffee-Houses* (London: Secker and Warburg, 1956), 129–44, and 145–58 for the coffee-house museum. See also J. Pelzer and L. Pelzer, 'Coffee Houses of Augustan London,' *History Today* (October 1982): 40–7.

10 See Bondeson, *The Two-Headed Boy,* 120–40.

11 In the 1598 narrative that accompanied the poster, it was said that Trouvillou's village had expelled him under suspicion that his condition arose from sorcery. See Bondeson, *The Two-Headed Boy,* 124.

12 *A myraculous, and monstrous, but yet most true, and certayne discourse, of a woman (now to be seene in London) of the age of threescore yeares, or thereabouts, in the midst of whose fore-head (by the wonderful worke of God) there groweth out a crooked horne, of foure inches long.* By Thomas Orwin, and are to be sold by Edward White, dwelling at the little north dore of Paules Church, at the signe of the Gun (1588). *STC* 6910.7; microfilm *Early English Books,* reel 419. The pamphlet was summarized or paraphrased in a number of sources, including *Kirby's Wonderful and Eccentric Museum; or Magazine of Remarkable Characters,* (London: R.S. Kirby, 1820), vol. 6: 163–4.

13 K. Hoffmann, 'Of Hairy Girls and a Hog-Faced Gentlewoman,' 76–9.

14 *Book of the Dean of Christ Church* (compiled 1684–90), in Arthur MacGregor, et al., *Manuscript Catalogues of the Early Museum Collections 1683–1886, Part I* (Oxford: Ashmolean Museum, 2000), 48. See MacGregor, 'Mary Davis's Horn: A Vanished Curiosity,' *The Ashmolean* 3 (1983): 10–11.

15 A photo of the horn is reproduced in Bondeson, *The Two-Headed Boy,* 133. Today, the horn remains on display at the University of Edinburgh Anatomy Museum but is no longer in a jar.

16 Stephen T. Asma, *Stuffed Animals and Pickled Heads: The Culture and Evolution of Natural History Museums* (Oxford: Oxford University Press, 2001), xiii.

17 Robert Bogan, *Freak Show: Presenting Human Oddities for Amusement and Profit* (Chicago: University of Chicago Press, 1990), 94–116.

18 Bondeson, *Two-Headed* Boy, 130–1. The last Ashmolean catalogue to list the horns is the printed catalogue of 1836. See MacGregor, 'Mary Davis's Horn,' 10.

19 Joseph Mayer, 'On Shotwich Church and Its Saxon Foundation' *Proceedings and Papers [of the] Historic Society of Lancashire and Cheshire*, Session VI, 1854 (Liverpool, 1854), 77–83. Davis is discussed on 81–3.

20 Stephen Greenblatt, *Marvelous Possessions: The Wonder of the New World* (Chicago: University of Chicago Press, 1991), 24.

21 Among critical works that focus on early modern collections, see: Oliver Impey and A. MacGregor, eds., *The Origins of Museums: The Cabinet of Curiosities in Sixteenth- and Seventeenth-Century Europe* (Oxford: Clarendon Press, 1985); Krzystof Pomian, *Collectors and Curiosities: Paris and Venice, 1500–1800* (Cambridge: Polity Press, 1990); Antoine Schnapper, *Le Géant, la licorne et la tulipe: Collections et collectionneurs dans la France du XVIIe siècle*, vol. 1: *Histoire et histoire naturelle* (Paris: Flammarion, 1988); vol. 2: *Curieux du Grand siècle* (1994).

22 Martin Welch, 'The Ashmolean as Described by Its Earliest Visitors,' *Tradescant's Rarities: Essays on the Foundation of the Ashmolean Museum, 1683*, ed. Arthur MacGregor (Oxford: Clarendon Press, 1981), 62; cited in Amy Boesky, '"Outlandish-Fruits": Commissioning Nature for the Museum of Man,' *ELH* 58, no. 2 (Summer 1991): 305–30.

23 Walter Benjamin, *The Arcades Project*, translated by Howard Eiland and Kevin McLaughlin (Cambridge, MA, and London: The Belknap Press of Harvard University Press, 1999).

24 Foucault described the seventeenth-century city during attempts to control the plague: 'It is a segmented, immobile, frozen space. Each individual is fixed in his place. And, if he moves, he does so at the risk of his life, contagion or punishment.' *Discipline and Punish: The Birth of the Prison*, translated by Alan Sheridan (New York: Vintage Books, 1995), 195. Originally published as *Surveiller et punir: Naissance de la prison* (Paris: Gallimard, 1975).

25 http://www.mjt.org/exhibits/gallery1.html.

26 Several photographs of the horn are posted online, for example: http://www.metropolismag.com/story/20061229/how-does-a-museum-become-a-performance (accessed 2 October 2011).

27 Jonah Siegel, *Desire and Excess: The Nineteenth-Century Culture of Art* (Princeton, NJ: Princeton University Press, 2000), xv.

28 Lawrence Weschler, 'Museum of Jurassic Technology,' premiered 6 December 1996 on *All Things Considered* (Sound Portraits Productions, 1996), http://soundportraits.org/on-air/museum_of_jurassic_technology/ (accessed 2 October 2011). See also Weschler, *Mr. Wilson's Cabinet of Wonder* (New York: Vintage, 1995), 145.

29 See Bondeson, *The Two-Headed Boy*, vii–xix.

30 John Spalding, *The History of the Troubles and Memorable Transactions in Scotland and England from 1624 to 1645* (Edinburgh: Bannatyne Club, 1829; printed from the 4to. manuscript, apparently the original, of that work, preserved in the Skene Library, now, by inheritance, the property of the Earle of Fife), vol. 2: 30.

31 Henri Sauval, *Histoire et recherches des antiquités de la ville de Paris* (Paris: Charles Moette; Jacques Chardon, 1724), vol. 2: 564–5. The work was completed and published after Sauval's death in 1676. Unless otherwise noted, translations are mine.

32 Spalding noted he was well-dressed, and Sauval wrote: 'Il vit toutes les villes de France où il gagna bien de l'argent' ['He saw all the cities of France where he earned a good deal of money']. Sauval, *Histoire*, 565.

33 Dubé, *Histoire de deux enfans* (Paris: François Piot, 1650).

34 Ibid., 43.

35 *Le médecin des pauvres qui enseigne le moyen de guerir les maladies par des remèdes faciles à trouver dans le pays, et préparer à peu de frais par toutes sortes de personnes* (Paris: E. Couterot, 1669), saw at least fourteen editions from 1669 to 1700.

36 Sauval, *Histoire,* 565.

37 E.B., 'Strange and Wonderful' (London: John Smith, 1685), 1. Page numbers will be given parenthetically.

38 Sauval, *Histoire,* 566.

39 'On fait voyage par curiosité pour voir des choses rares . . . Rien n'est plus instructif que la lecture des voyages.' Antoine Furetière, *Dictionnaire universel,* 3 vols. (La Haye and Rotterdam, 1690; rpt. Paris: SNL–Le Robert, 1978), vol. 3: 'voyage' entry.

40 Quoted in McClary's essay in this volume.

PART V

TOWARD A HISTORY OF TIME AND SUBJECTIVITY

chapter twelve

Temporality and Ideology: Qualities of Motion in Seventeenth-Century French Music

SUSAN McCLARY

In a classic essay from 1973, art historian Michael Fried focused on a quality he had discerned in French eighteenth-century painting – a quality he called 'absorption.'[1]

The paintings he examines in the course of the article depict individuals so immersed in meditation that they seem withdrawn from the world. Those artists who excelled in this genre rarely chose heroic figures as their subjects; Jean-Baptiste Greuze, for instance, often preferred to present pretty children quietly pondering their dead canaries or gazing in distraction away from their school books. Today these paintings may strike viewers as precious and sentimental – certainly not the stuff to which one would turn in reconstructing socio-political history. Indeed, such paintings, much loved during their own moment, have long been dismissed by many critics as kitsch. Yet by interrogating this quality of absorption rather than the manifest content of the canvases, Fried identifies an elusive but persistent element for the period under consideration.

I first encountered Fried's article when I was seeking to understand a peculiar quality in French music of the ancien régime – a quality that seems designed to induce something like absorption in the listener, a quality of stillness in which consciousness hovers suspended outside linear time. As it turns out, Fried's absorption is but one of a very large cluster of privileged images and metaphors prevalent in France during the seventeenth and eighteenth centuries that converge around the ideal of timelessness: I would include here the Neoplatonic geometry that undergirds everything from landscape design to ballroom dance at Versailles, the obsession with Arcadian themes that pervades court life and its art, the warnings against thinking about the future in Jansenist theology, the quietist definition of ecstasy as a state of utter desirelessness.

To the consternation of historians who like to keep their categories separate, these images come from a wide variety of cultural domains, some of them (for instance, the absolutist court and the Jansenist philosophers of Port Royal) explicitly antagonistic. Moreover, they appear throughout the seventeenth and eighteenth centuries: a very long span of time during which many radical ideological and cultural changes occurred.[2] I will return later in this essay for a more detailed discussion of these problems. But first I wish to consider briefly the music that first motivated my own line of inquiry.

In my experience as a coach of early-music performance, the seventeenth-century French repertory presents more acute challenges to most present-day musicians than any other. Heinrich Schütz's complex modal allegories or Girolamo Frescobaldi's erratic toccatas may present them with temporary obstacles, but these gradually become accessible through the rhetorical sensibilities performers bring with them from later music. French music, however, stops them dead in their tracks; François Couperin taunts them from across the centuries when he boasts in *L'art de toucher le clavecin* (1716) that 'foreigners play our music less well than we do theirs.'[3] Yet most performers, before they will accept Couperin's chauvinistic diagnosis for their puzzlement, prefer to reverse the blame, to dismiss the music itself as incompetent.

Oddly enough, such dismissive assessments underlie a good many of our more prominent musicological accounts of this music. Several performing artists – foremost among them William Christie – have been producing exquisite recordings of the French seventeenth-century repertory for the last fifteen years, and they clearly have learned how to come to terms with the phenomena with which I am grappling. But of those who write on seventeenth-century French music, only David Fuller seems to me to have grappled sympathetically with how it produces its effects.[4] Most scholars – even those who create elaborate catalogues, exhaustive archival documentation, and detailed histories – go on to dismiss summarily the materials in question as unworthy of serious musical attention. In his introduction to a book devoted to Lully, for instance, Paul Henry Lang writes (with extravagantly feminized tropes):

> The music all these composers cultivated was in the sign of the dance, so congenial to the French, with its neat little forms, pregnant rhythms, great

> surface attraction, and in tone and structure so much in harmony with the spirit of the age. This music, though slight and short-breathed, was elegant and so different from any other that the whole of Europe became enamored of it.[5]

Similarly, James R. Anthony, in his *French Baroque Music* (long the definitive book on this repertory), damns with the faintest of praise one of its most characteristic genres:

> In summary, French lute music of the seventeenth century is mannered, precious, even decadent; its melodies are surcharged with ornaments, its rhythms fussy, its harmony often aimless, and its texture without unity. Yet at the same time, it is never pretentious, it never demands more from the instrument than the instrument can give. In its own fragile way, it is honest to itself.[6]

Recall, however, that the absolutist rulers who commissioned and listened to this music had access to the very best artistic talents money could buy. It is not likely that Louis XIV simply tolerated mediocrity in his compositional staff; indeed, we know that he intervened at every level of cultural production and even participated personally in auditions for new orchestral musicians. If this music now falls on figuratively deaf ears, it seems to have satisfied precisely what its highly discriminating makers and patrons required of it.

As the quotations above indicate, musicians encountering French seventeenth-century music today frequently experience it chiefly in terms of lack: they listen in vain for teleological tonal progressions ('its harmony often aimless'), patterns of motivic reiteration ('its texture without unity'), or imitative counterpoint – the very ingredients we have learned through our theoretical training to notice and value. Instead, this music arrests the attention with an ornament here, a sudden flurry and cessation of activity there, making it difficult or impossible to play the games of speculation and anticipation we usually bring to music of this and subsequent periods.

If we discern nothing in this music except manifestations of absence, we may indeed hear it as relatively arbitrary – as a series of events connected (if at all) only on a moment-to-moment basis. In phenomenological terms, it sounds static rather than dynamic. Yet most courtiers and artists during the ancien régime clearly preferred this music to its alternatives. Consequently, historians of seventeenth-century French culture face the difficult task of converting all those negatives into positive attributes. What kinds of rewards did this music offer to its devotees? What structures of feeling did it reinforce?

We might, of course, turn directly to the polemics of the time, in which Francophile connoisseurs sought to justify their predilections. In their attempts at pinpointing the essence of French music, they buttressed their documents with words such as *bon goût*, *plaisir*, and *raison* (good taste, pleasure, reason) – words obviously freighted with a great deal of cultural prestige. But those words speak meaningfully only to insiders who already count themselves aficionados; the rest of us must ask: *whose* taste? *which* pleasures? *what version* of reason?

I have selected as my example Jean Henry D'Anglebert's *Tombeau de Mr de Chambonnières*, from his print of 1689.[7] I acknowledge the danger of single examples: I too can produce lists of pieces that behave otherwise – most obviously, the unmeasured preludes that flourished during this period in the hands of Louis Couperin, Elisabeth-Claude Jacquet de la Guerre, and D'Anglebert himself, as well as the hybrids produced by composers such as Marc-Antoine Charpentier or François Couperin who self-consciously trafficked in Italianate styles. I know, moreover, that the genre of the tombeau virtually demands an elegiac, introspective quality. Yet D'Anglebert exemplifies in his tombeau (and in most of his pieces) so many of the points I wish to make, and he does so with what seems to me such beauty and skill, that I hope to avoid the charge that the music itself is inept, even if it works according to premises far removed from the ones within which we usually operate.

Let me begin with the usual series of negatives. First, D'Anglebert's tombeau displays no imitative counterpoint of the sort we like to celebrate in Bach. (Note, however, that if we were to turn the page in the print we would find a set of five quite extraordinary fugues on a single subject. D'Anglebert was, in other words, fully capable of contrapuntal complexity, even if he did not showcase it in most of his work.)

Second, this tombeau does not employ melodic motives to pull the various parts of the piece together; instead, the rhythmic groupings of the surface constantly shift. To be sure, as a gaillarde,[8] it offers the regularity of dance steps: the piece guarantees at least the rational structure of a slow triple metre with stresses on beats 3 and 1, and it thus choreographs the body in accordance with a Neoplatonic matrix. But the listener cannot predict when a metric unit will contain a surfeit of ornamental notes (e.g., the middle beat of m. 3) or when it will pause and hover with virtually no activity.

Example 12.1 Jean Henry D'Anglebert, 'Tombeau de Mr Chambonnières'

Finally, the piece never truly modulates. Binary dance forms tend to adhere closely to conservative harmonic conventions, but this example does not even establish its dominant as a secondary key at the end of the first half. Twice D'Anglebert implies the possibility of moving to the subdominant (both mm. 2–4 and 17–19 gesture toward G major), but neither passage concludes with a cadence. The key of A minor becomes a viable destination in mm. 14–15, but the would-be cadence on A never materializes. In the final analysis, the tombeau remains in D major from start to finish.

Yet this series of negatives seems to me an indictment less of D'Anglebert's skill as a composer than of our analytical habits, which were designed for illuminating particular repertories but then applied willy-nilly as universal standards to all music. I do find it noteworthy that D'Anglebert does not utilize imitative counterpoint, unifying motives, or a progressive modulatory schema in his tombeau. But his refusal of these devices – all of which he employs in other pieces – leads me to ask what these devices usually accomplish.

If we turn to the dance suites of Bach or the dance types (allemandes, gigues) in which the French also typically made use of imitative counterpoint, we find that this device produces relatively long rhythmic groupings, the reiterations of which invite listeners to project into the future.[9] As soon as a second voice enters to repeat what we have just heard in the first, we can leap forward in our imaginations to anticipate what will happen next. To be sure, the specific engagement between voices may offer us delight. Yet as soon as the imitation begins, we know from past experience with such techniques that we should jump ahead in time and start speculating. Something similar occurs with motivic play: when a composer indicates that a two-beat-long motive will saturate the texture of a piece, the listener quickly assumes a particular way of parsing out time.[10] Of course, motives produce a sense of identity, organic relatedness, and much else as well. But they also greatly influence our perception of temporality.

As does the rhetorical version of modulation that pervades contemporaneous Italian music, which works on the basis of instilled, heightened, and fulfilled desire. Developed as a means of expanding the simple linear formulas fundamental to modal practice, this set of procedures sustains each pillar of the background structure by deferring arrivals, barely granting each implied cadence before rushing off toward the next. Each moment serves principally to whet the appetite for its successor, maximizing the sense of a headlong race into the future – the immediate future of the next modulatory arrival, the final destination of the return to tonic.[11]

It is this element of multi-levelled goal orientation, I would argue, that people unaccustomed to French seventeenth-century music miss most: to the extent that propulsive tonality counts as 'the way music is supposed to work,' its absence spells pure and simple incompetence. Yet if we take seriously the choices made by D'Anglebert and his colleagues, we can glean insights into a society quite alien from the one that gave our own dominant tradition – not only its compositional techniques, but also its very sense of being. For D'Anglebert worked within a culture that for a wide variety of reasons wished to promote sensibilities of timelessness.

But how precisely does a composer go about producing such effects? Music by its very nature unfolds through time; of all media it would seem the most resistant to the project of simulating immobility.[12] Put briefly, D'Anglebert's task is to produce an experience of time in which the listener is absorbed by each present instant. He is obliged to satisfy the rules of orderly succession (the much vaunted *raison*) as he moves from moment to moment: the transgression of fundamental propriety would undermine the idyllic security of this prolonged stasis. He may even group together a couple of measures in a quasi-causal conspiracy, as in the case of the implied modulations, though none of these actually comes to fruition. Yet – and in contrast with superficially similar strategies in Italian music of the time – those missed cadences do not spark the rhetorical effects of disappointment or frustration; rather, the relatively low level of anticipation involved produces merely a bittersweet inconclusiveness. Gradually we learn from this music not to bother with future-oriented thought, but to embrace instead the serenity of each new configuration as it arises.

D'Anglebert thus needs to make every moment sufficiently full that we can desire nothing more, so that the attention moves on to the next instance of plenitude only with reluctance. And this he accomplishes in large part through his highly refined negotiations between two different conceptions of rhythmic activity: what the French referred to as *Mesure* and *Mouvement.* Couperin wrote that if '*Mesure* defines the number and equality of the beats,' '*Cadence* or *Mouvement* is properly the spirit and soul that it is necessary to add.' Bénigne de Bacilly further explains these important qualities thus:

> *Mouvement* is . . . a certain quality that gives soul to the song, and that it is called *Mouvement* because it stirs up, I may say it excites, the listeners' attention, in the same way as do those who are the most rebellious in harmony . . . it inspires in hearts such passion as the singer wishes to create, principally that of tenderness . . . I don't doubt at all that the variety of

> *Mesure*, whether quick or slow, contributes a great deal to the expression of the song. But there is certainly another quality, more refined and more spiritual, that always holds the listener attentive and ensures that the song is less tedious. It is the *Mouvement* that makes the most of a mediocre voice, making it better than a very beautiful voice without expression.[13]

Adopting these terms, we could say that listeners can follow quite easily the *raison* of the tombeau's *Mesure*, its metric structure, but might be hard pressed to anticipate the *bon goût* of its *Mouvement*, its particular way of inhabiting each successive beat. Couperin and Bacilly write primarily for performers, and they point to something beyond simple metrical accuracy for which keyboardists or singers must take responsibility. To the extent that a score such as D'Anglebert's represents a kind of recorded improvisation, we may discern at least some of the ways in which he composes in the effects so treasured by his contemporaries – the effects conducive to absorption.

One of D'Anglebert's principal strategies for playing *Mouvement* against *Mesure* is his lavish deployment of ever-changing ornaments. Unlike Italian ornaments, which typically lead forward impulsively to the next event, French *agréments* serve to ground any rhythmic excess that may have accumulated by securing the weight onto the strong beats, the markers of *Mesure*; the tension/release mechanisms that animate the music occur on the very local level of the half note. But even as the arrival on the beat reliably anchors the dance step, the *agréments* draw the ear down into the intricacies of those slight delays that flirt with the self-evident main pitch, thus sustaining a crucial quality of hovering and allowing for the constantly replenished novelty of *Mouvement*.

D'Anglebert also ensures that we will expect something beyond the luxury of the instant at hand through the judicious arrangement of harmonic dissonances, for he saturates the surface of his tombeau with lengthy suspensions and anticipations. These operate somewhat like a series of locks on a canal: they break down what otherwise might be an abrupt shift into tiny increments that release the pressure only gradually.

Thus the opening trajectory – a descent from tonic (D) down to the mediant (F#) in the bass – is both urged along by a tenor line that applies the pressure of 2–3 suspensions at irregular intervals and also delayed by the bass's seeming reluctance to part with each of its pitches (note, for instance, the *port de voix* that creates a pull on its move to C# in m. 1). No sooner is the basic trajectory of the progression clear to the ear (with the descent to C♮ in m. 1 and its refusal to move in keeping with the pitches added against it at the beginning of the next bar) than D'Anglebert begins playing with rates of motion: observe the way he sustains that dissonant C♮ for two full beats in m. 2 – enhancing the poignancy of the moment through the feathery mordent of the middle voice marking the second pulse. But as the bass descends to B (such a big deal for such an obvious move!), the tenor quickens its pace and coaxes the ear into the even richer sonority of m. 3 – suspended in turn with a wistful melisma in the soprano.

Note also that the chromatically inflected bass line alludes to the widespread seventeenth-century association of the descending tetrachord with laments. 'Tombeau,' of course, means 'tomb,' and the genre operates in a social and affective terrain similar to that of lamentation. The listener might well anticipate the progression in the bass to arrive on A and then return to D. But D'Anglebert thwarts this expectation by harmonizing the A of m. 3 in such a way as to tilt the line onward to G and thus away from the conventionalized lament. If we have been assuming that the bass would halt at A, then the entry of C♮ on the downbeat of m. 3 guides us gently away from the obsessive cycle of grief usually fundamental to laments and into a vista of sweet (if somewhat melancholy) continuation.

This is a moment of stoic self-restraint: a refusal of the histrionic display of sorrow that usually accompanies the tetrachord descent, a memorial at the tomb of D'Anglebert's mentor rather than an expression of raw anguish more suitable for the moment at which a tragic event is first announced.[14] The eventual arrival in the bass on F#, destined for the downbeat of m. 4, lingers so that the soprano reaches its melodic goal alone and in tension against the bass. Finally, the bass slips down to produce the desired pitch, though on the off-beat as a mere afterthought, and the right hand supplies its downward arpeggiation of the first-inversion tonic sonority – the affirmation of a quasi-caesura – over a rhythmic void in the bass.

I do not want to continue with an inchworm's-eye view of this piece. Yet D'Anglebert strives to focus our attention at precisely this level – on the fact of that exquisite mordent in m. 2, on the sudden awakening and repositioning that follows, on the swirl of circular activity in m. 3, on the C♮ that gently coaxes us out of conventional lament, on the nonsimultaneity of arrivals in m. 4. Consequently, one shouldn't even think about playing a piece like this unless one is willing to savour to the utmost every detail in turn. Harpsichordist Lisa Crawford used to smile with delight at her hands when they played these pieces, as though they were adorable pets who were frolicking of their own accord.

Compare the method behind my description of D'Anglebert's opening passage with Denis Diderot's celebrated review of Greuze's painting 'Young Girl Mourning her Dead Bird' (see fig. 12.1):

> The pretty elegy! The charming poem! . . . Delicious painting! . . . Oh, the pretty hand! The pretty hand! The beautiful arm! Notice the truthful details of these fingers; and these dimples, and this softness, and this blushing tint with which the pressure of the head has colored the tips of these delicate fingers, and the charm of all this . . . One would move closer to this hand in order to kiss it, if one didn't respect this child and her pain . . . This kerchief is thrown on the neck in such a fashion! So supple and light! When one sees this detail one says, *Delicious!* If one stops to look at it, or returns to it, one exclaims: *Delicious! delicious!*[15]

Or compare it with this eyewitness account of Chambonnières's performances of his own music: 'Every time he played a piece he incorporated new beauties with *ports-de-voix*, passages, and different *agréments*, with *doubles cadences*. In a word, he so varied them with all these different beauties that he continually revealed new charms.'[16] Or read Charles Rosen's exquisite analysis of how one of D'Anglebert's contemporaries – the poet and fabulist Jean de La Fontaine – manipulated minute shadings in French vowel sounds to produce his unparalleled effects of aural patterning.[17] None of these pays attention to the manifest content or the affective power of the work at hand. Instead, they home in on what may seem to be incidental details, much as Roland Barthes chose with apparent perversity to fixate in *Camera Lucida* on the Mary Jane shoes worn by a woman in a group photograph or in 'The Grain of the Voice' on the peculiar quality of Panzéra's basic sound rather than on his musical choices.[18]

To focus on – indeed, to *fetishize* – each moment of a piece goes quite contrary to our training as analysts and as musicians. Most of us descend philosophically from an anti-French tradition of German *Kultur* that insisted on the moral virtue of structural essence in express counterdistinction to the sensual surfaces of French *Civilisation*,[19] and we learn to brush away such details in order to get at a composition's formal and emotional truth. Accordingly, D'Anglebert's processes may well breed impatience to get on with things and not to dither about where exactly to locate the downward arpeggio demanded in the beat that serves as a pick-up to the

Figure 12.1 Jean-Baptiste Greuze, *Girl with Dead Bird.* Edinburgh, National Gallery of Scotland.

first full measure. We might be tempted to mutter in exasperation: 'It's a tonic triad – get over it!' But that beat (by far the most difficult to execute in the entire piece) sets the atmosphere for everything that follows: the appoggiatura (itself elaborately embellished) that delays the arrival on A before the arpeggio can commence already puts a nostalgic tug against the necessity of moving forward through time, and the eloquent repetition of A just before m. 1 produces a gesture of self-possessed resolve following the collapse performed by the arpeggio. *Delicious! delicious!*

A telling feature of this music, once it has seduced one into its phenomenological web, is that the performer actually *wants* to play the repeats – even the invitation at the end of each dance to recommence all over again from the very beginning. The longing to sustain this out-of-time state becomes almost a physical necessity, and one dives back in to revisit each exquisite moment as soon as one reaches the double-bar. After a summer of playing only this music and noticing in myself this odd compulsion to take repeats, I assumed I would bring this new-found reflex back with me when I played Bach. But no: even the most Francophilic of Bach's dances pushes inexorably forward through its series of destinations. Taking the repeats in Bach is, to be sure, always instructive and enjoyable, for we cannot truly grasp how he got from one place to another in a single hearing. Still, to go back and do it all over again feels a bit like turning back the clock, like a betrayal of the narrative impulse that propels Bach's music onward.[20]

When this Italianate impulse begins to infiltrate François Couperin's music, he often marks it programmatically as a special effect. See, for instance, the opening movement (an allemande) of his Second Order, titled '*La laborieuse*' (the laborious), in which a two-beat-long motive works hard to achieve every twist and turn along the course of the piece. Or, more famously, '*Les baricades mistérieuses*' (mysterious barricades, from the Sixth Order): a rondeau movement that enacts in its third couplet, however gently, the sense of striving to overcome invisible obstacles typical of the Italo-German version of tonality. It is as though the premises of such techniques – the very basis of what pass in Bach as 'purely musical' – demand some extramusical explanation within the French context. Interestingly, the one movement Couperin named after himself, '*La Couperin*' in the Twenty-first Order, identifies through its procedures with the Italian style.

The reader has no doubt noticed that I am once again committing the crime I think of as 'effing the ineffable': that is, translating into words the kinds of experiences that music can render so effortlessly and that speech does so clumsily and ineffectively. I have three reasons for doing so, however, two of which I have indicated throughout my discussion:

first, that performers often require extensive reorientation of this sort before they can make any sense of this music; second, that coming to terms with the French repertory can lead us to re-examine the cultural premises of the most basic units of the analytical methods taken for granted in North American musicology and to take seriously elements such as this elusive quality.

But I want to concentrate for the rest of my presentation on my third reason – namely, history. Historians such as Hayden White sometimes implore musicologists to give back to the discipline of history the kinds of information to which musicians have special access.[21] Too often, we restrict ourselves to the modes of evidence available to other historians while neglecting those issues to which they look to us, usually in vain; scholars who cannot read a note of music can produce inventories of archives, comparisons among verbal documents, or accounts of various moments of critical reception. Yet most of them cannot address how music itself participates as a cultural medium to articulate structures of feeling.

Let me begin with some of the common explanations for why much French seventeenth-century music works in the ways I have described. As mentioned earlier, some simply assume the mediocrity of the music, as the products of talentless composers. And many assign the blame for this abysmal absence of talent at the French court to Jean-Baptiste Lully, who exercised a ruthless monopoly over composition, driving would-be competitors to seek employment outside France and leaving behind only those who posed no challenges. Paul Henry Lang writes concerning Lully:

> In this ascent to a commanding position he deftly used everyone from the king down. The *lettres patentes* and the *privilèges* he secured from the king were so outrageous that they could not have stood the slightest legal scrutiny, but they could not be scrutinized because they came directly from the king. This adroit manipulator did succeed in becoming the virtual dictator of French musical life.[22]

But many political and cultural historians – among them Robert Isherwood, Norbert Elias, Michel Foucault, Kathryn Hoffmann, and Georgia Cowart – have pointed to the ideological centrality of Neoplatonic ideals for the perpetuation of the absolutist state.[23] Such critics understand seventeenth-century French cultural forms not as inept but as exceptionally powerful; they concentrate on how these media created the illusion of an eternal NOW so surfeited with pleasures and images of perfect order that thoughts of change never even had the chance to arise. In theory at least, Louis XIV arranged the daily lives of the nobility so as to distract them from fomenting rebellions such as the Fronde, to suspend them in an Arcadia of endless delights, in a condition of busy immobility. Hoffmann opens her book with the statement, 'The society of pleasures . . . was a reverie of power where the logic of pleasure always contained the trap of violent oppression, where desire and force, pleasure and knowledge, the caress and the chains of subservience always informed each other in strange couplings'; and Isherwood concludes his study with the sentence: 'Louis XIV made music the handmaiden of the politics of absolutism.'[24]

Thus we could explain the music as the pragmatic means to an autocratic end: the deliberate anaesthetizing of a potentially restless group of subjects. The geometrical gardens at Versailles, the carefully executed *divertissements,* the highly regulated dance manoeuvres, the complex etiquette of courtly manners, and many aspects of the music were deliberately designed to produce these political effects, to lull aristocrats into habits of activity-filled oblivion; in the words of a cynical contemporary critic: 'Let the people slumber away in their festivities, in their spectacles.'[25] I always marvel at accounts of French seventeenth-century music that somehow neglect to mention any of these issues. We should never minimize the efforts at social engineering that lent support to these cultural practices.

Yet I hate to fall back on a monolithic Adorno-esque explanation that appeals solely to false consciousness.[26] For if political establishments and their intentions must form part – even a large part – of the picture, they cannot account for the allure of the imagery, the material complexity of the practices, the ideals embodied and enacted through these processes. Moreover, a state, however powerful, cannot bring into being a viable structure of feeling purely by fiat.[27] At best it can privilege some qualities that seem consonant with its priorities and try to suppress others – which is, of course, precisely what happened under Louis XIV. But this mode of being has to have had broad-based support, had to have made sense, had to have genuinely counted as pleasurable for it to work, even at the political level.[28]

As it happens, this sense of timelessness was valued not only by the centres of power in France, but also by many of those disenfranchised by absolutism. In his classic study *The Hidden God,* Lucien Goldmann argues that the philosophers of Port Royal advocated withdrawal from the world in part as a way of coping with an eroded sense of political agency; he shows how they aspired to an ideal of attentive motionlessness while discouraging future-oriented thought and beliefs in progress.[29] Martin de Barcos (1600–78) wrote, for instance:

> Thoughts of the future are a dangerous and clever temptation of the Evil One, contrary to the spirit of the Gospel, and capable of ruining everything if not resisted; they must be rejected without even a first glance, since God's word tells us not only to take no thought for the morrow in things temporal but also in things spiritual, and it is these which hang much more on His will.[30]

Far from anticipating the advent of Enlightenment habits of thought, this philosophy recalls the sublime passivity advocated in the Parable of the Lilies in Matthew 6: 'Consider the lilies of the field, how they grow; they toil not, neither do they spin; And yet I say unto you, That even Solomon in all his glory was not arrayed like one of these.' Blaise Pascal, Barcos's more famous colleague, likewise wrestled with scepticism concerning agency in a world bounded by absolutist rule: 'We desire truth and find in ourselves nothing but uncertainty. We seek happiness and find only misery and death. We are incapable of not desiring truth and happiness and are incapable of either certainty or happiness. We have been left with this desire as much as a punishment as to make us feel from where we have fallen.'[31]

An entirely different religious domain, that of the quietist mystics, diverged in many important ways from the theology of Port Royal. Yet they too advocated withdrawal from time. St Francis de Sales (1567–1622), for instance, wrote concerning 'The Prayer of Quiet':

> The soul, then, being thus inwardly recollected in God or before God, now and then becomes so sweetly attentive to the goodness of her well-beloved, that her attention seems not to her to be attention, so purely and delicately is it exercised; as it happens to certain rivers, which glide so calmly and smoothly that beholders and such as float upon them, seem neither to see nor feel any motion, because the waters are not seen to ripple or flow at all.
>
> Now this repose sometimes goes so deep in its tranquility, that the whole soul and all its powers fall as it were asleep, and make no movement nor action whatever except the will alone, and even this does no more than

> receive the delight and satisfaction which the presence of the well-beloved affords . . . It is better to sleep upon this sacred breast than to watch elsewhere, wherever it be.[32]

Sales refers to the writings of St Teresa of Avila for corroboration of this experience of quiet, but it is very significant that Teresa regards quiet as the least ecstatic of the states she describes in her vivid prose. Her desire-driven descriptions of divine union, which inspired so much poetry, music, and visual art of the Counter-Reformation in Italy, found little resonance in her French counterparts;[33] the quietist mystic Mme Guyon, for instance, exalted most a condition in which the soul is 'without action, without desire, without inclination, without choice, without impatience, seeing things only as God sees them, and judging them only with God's judgment.'[34]

Note that although the absolutist court worked to suppress both Jansenism and quietism they all share similar phenomenological ideals. In other words, musical imagery need not correspond in a one-to-one relationship with the antagonisms or allegiances in the world of politics; the cultural meanings of music and the other arts are always much vaguer than we might wish. At the same time, music also offers experiential knowledge of a sort that makes far more palpable the qualities aspired to during former periods. Philosophers and theologians of the late seventeenth century could write all they wanted about qualities of being in time, but they could never attain the immediacy offered by immersion in, say, D'Anglebert's tombeau, in which we hover for the duration of about four minutes in an eternal present of *plaisir*, slightly tinged with a melancholy reminiscent of Watteau.[35]

Perhaps the most important cultural insight offered by this music, however, involves what polemicists referred to as *raison* – that sense of reason apparently guaranteed by French manners and found to be sorely lacking in the rambunctious music from Italy. We often conflate the *raison* of French style with the brand of reason elevated by the dawning Enlightenment. But they are not the same: indeed, they turn out to be diametrically opposed qualities.

As Norbert Elias has explained, the *raison* of court culture might better be translated 'regulation': it involves submission to the authority of tradition and etiquette.[36] Such acquiescence gained one entry into a Neoplatonic realm that embodied timeless truths; it allowed one to luxuriate in an idyllic cocoon, a paradise on earth. By contrast, the premises of contemporaneous Italian music enacted ideals of progressive thought:

the consistent sacrifice within the music of past and present for the sake of ongoing movement into the future. It is the Italian version of tonality that best approximates the habits of relentless questioning, discarding, and projecting forward on the quest toward distant goals we identify with Enlightenment reason.

To the extent that images of extroverted public rhetoric, progressive action, and investment in the future circulated within Italian repertories, that music needed to be quarantined: French authorities feared that a bite of the forbidden sonata would suffice to destroy the illusion of their carefully cultivated Eden, to bring about another fall from grace. We can still experience in the musical practices of this time the radical incompatibility of these two worlds. To those courtiers who had managed to live suspended in music such as D'Anglebert's, the head-on collision with the sweeping events of the later eighteenth century involved more than the loss of status and wealth; it brought with it the violent collapse of a way of being. The hermetically sealed jar broke open, and history rushed in.

This helps explain the vehemence with which so many in France denounced Italian music. In his account of the hysteria over music generated during the *Guerre des bouffons*, d'Alembert presented the following satirical version of the argument against foreign styles:

> All liberties are interrelated and are equally dangerous. Freedom in music entails freedom to feel, freedom to feel means freedom to act, and freedom to act means the ruin of states. So let us keep French opera as it is if we wish to preserve the kingdom and let us put a brake on singing if we do not want to have liberty in speaking to follow soon afterwards.[37]

Note d'Alembert's use of breathless phrasing and his deployment of a brand of logic that, once unleashed, runs rampant from music to insurrection. The irony is, of course, that if Italian music itself did not bring about the French Revolution, it did embody quite palpably the qualities of motion and habits of thought that eventually overthrew the court tradition. In the words of José Maravall: 'Static guidance controlling by presence had to give way before a dynamic guidance controlling by activity.'[38] And given French ideals such as Neoplatonic order, spiritual quiet, absolutist authority, and Arcadian timelessness, the awakening could not have been more rude.[39]

Of course, seventeenth-century France also produced Descartes, who advocated the individual subject's questioning and rejection of traditional authority in his famous slogan 'Cogito, ergo sum' (I think, therefore I am).[40] But Louis XIV effectively appropriated the terms of Descartes's egocentricity with his 'L'état, c'est moi!' (I am the State), according to which he became the supreme and only subject. As Hoffmann puts it, the French nobility 'were invited to desire their infinite subservience to the Other. It was a perfect dream of power . . . where the disciple is always desiring the body of the master and is turned to stare, in the posture of admiration, at the place where the renunciation of his own will is performed. Reverie of another's *cogito*.'[41]

I have no intention of trying to lure anyone back to take up permanent habitation in the always-vulnerable, spellbound utopia of seventeenth-century France. But historians of music need to be able to understand the *goût*, the *plaisir*, the *raison* that sustained this repertory: not only for the sake of performers, who must learn how to suspend their expectation of future-oriented procedures if they are to make sense of this music, but also for the sake of historians of culture, to whom we can offer invaluable pieces of a larger puzzle. Versailles has long since become a theme park safe for bourgeois tourists. Perhaps we can afford the occasional surrender to absorption in D'Anglebert without losing our investment in upward mobility.

NOTES

1 Michael Fried, 'Absorption: A Master Theme in Eighteenth Century French Painting and Criticism,' *Eighteenth Century Studies* 9, no. 2 (Winter 1975–6): 139–77. See also his *Absorption and Theatricality: Painting and Beholder in the Age of Diderot* (Berkeley and Los Angeles: University of California Press, 1980). Fried observes that 'there *had been* a tradition of absorptive painting, one whose almost universal efflorescence in the seventeenth century was everywhere followed by its relative decline' (*Absorption and Theatricality*, 43; emphasis in the original).

2 Gordon Pocock justifies a similar account of the *longue durée* in his book *Boileau and the Nature of Neo-Classicism* (Cambridge: Cambridge University Press, 1980), 14: '[neoclassicism is] a doctrine which flourished in such different social and intellectual contexts, beginning in France in the years when Richelieu was coming to power, consolidating itself in the 1630s, and enduring through the Frondes, the absolutism of Louis XIV, into the Regency, and well into the second half of the eighteenth century. These are years of profound social and intellectual change: of civil wars; of the establishment and partial

failure of absolutism; of recession followed by eighteenth-century prosperity; of the Counter-Reformation and Enlightenment. It surely requires some explanation that the same critical themes and doctrines should occupy such diverse minds as Chapelain, Boileau and Voltaire.'

3 François Couperin, *L'art de toucher le clavecin* (1716), from the paragraph just before the heading 'Examinons donc d'où vient cette contrarieté!'

4 See, for instance, David Fuller, entry on Chambonnières, *New Grove Dictionary of Music and Musicians*, ed. Stanley Sadie (London: Macmillan, 1980); 'French Harpsichord Playing in the 17th Century – *after Le Gallois*,' *Early Music* 4 (1976): 22–6; and '"Sous les doits de Chambonniere,"' *Early Music* (May 1993): 191–202. I wish to thank Professor Fuller for sharing with me some of his unpublished materials on this repertory.

5 Paul Henry Lang, introduction to *Jean-Baptiste Lully and the Music of the French Baroque: Essays in Honor of James R. Anthony*, ed. John Hajdu Heyer (Cambridge: Cambridge University Press, 1989), 1.

6 James R. Anthony, *French Baroque Music from Beaujoyeulx to Rameau* (New York: W.W. Norton, 1978), 243.

7 Jean Henry D'Anglebert, *Pièces de clavecin* (Paris, 1689; facsimile edition, New York: Broude Brothers, 1965), 109–10.

8 Two compositions specifically labelled 'gaillarde' appear in D'Anglebert's print, one virtually a transposition of the *Tombeau de Mr de Chambonnières* into the minor mode (see 81–2; the other gaillarde is on p. 50). It is not the same dance as the more familiar galliarde, a lively dance usually paired with a pavane. Jacques Champion de Chambonnières also includes one gaillarde in his collection, composed much earlier but printed in 1670 (facsimile edition New York: Broude Brothers, 1967), book II, 7–8.

9 See, for instance, my discussion of the Courante from Bach's Partita in D Major in *Conventional Wisdom: The Content of Musical Form* (Berkeley and Los Angeles: University of California Press, 2000), chapter 3.

10 For more on the very sophisticated ways listeners orient themselves with respect to music, see Lawrence M. Zbikowski, *Conceptualizing Music: Cognitive Structure, Theory, and Analysis* (New York and Oxford: Oxford University Press, 2002).

11 See the discussions of early Italian tonality in my *Conventional Wisdom*, chapters 1 and 3.

12 See Richard Leppert's essay in this volume, 'Temporal Interventions: Music, Modernity and the Presentation of the Self,' for an extended consideration of the contradictions between visual and aural media in the constructions of subjectivities.

13 The translations of both Couperin and Bacilly quotations appear in Beverly Scheibert, *D'Anglebert and the 17th-Century Clavecin School* (Bloomington: Indiana University Press, 1986), 40–1.

14 Famous tetrachord-based laments include Monteverdi's *Lamento della Ninfa*, Dido's 'When I am laid in earth' from Purcell's *Dido and Aeneas*, and the Crucifixus from Bach's B Minor Mass. French composers sometimes adopt this Italianate convention though they frequently bend it to accommodate the great premium put on self-control by the French court: see, for instance, Marin Marais's 'Tombeau pour Mr de Ste-Colombe,' played so memorably by Jordi Savall in the soundtrack to *Tous les matins du monde.*

15 Denis Diderot, 'Salon de 1765,' in *Oeuvres esthétiques*, ed. Paul Vernière (Paris: Garnier, 1959), 533. As quoted in Peter Brooks, *Body Work: Objects of Desire in Modern Narrative* (Cambridge, MA: Harvard University Press, 1993), 35–7. Diderot writes, of course, at a very different moment in French history. Yet Michael Fried argues persuasively throughout *Absorption and Theatricality* that Diderot attempts in his art criticism to teach viewers how to interact appropriately to paintings that play not to the taste for theatricality prevalent at his time, but rather to the contemplative states of mind associated with absorption – a value far more frequently appealed to art of the seventeenth century.

16 Jean Le Gallois, *Lettre de Mr Le Gallois à Mademoiselle Regnault de Solier touchant la musique* (Paris: Michallet, 1680), 68–86, quoted in Fuller, '"Sous les doits de Chambonniere,"' 196.

17 Charles Rosen, 'The Fabulous La Fontaine,' *New York Review of Books*, 18 December 1997, 38–46.

18 Roland Barthes, *Camera Lucida: Reflections on Photography*, trans. Richard Howard (New York: Hill and Wang, 1981), 43–4; 'The Grain of the Voice,' *Image – Music – Text*, trans. Stephen Heath (New York: Hill and Wang, 1977), 179–89. On p. 185 of 'The Grain,' Barthes celebrates this determined inattention to intended content as the escape from 'the tyranny of meaning.'

19 See the theoretical and historical discussion of *Kultur* versus *Civilisation* in Norbert Elias, *The History of Manners: The Civilizing Process*, trans. Edmund Jephcott (New York: Pantheon, 1978), vol. 1, chapter 1. See also my 'Unruly Passions and Courtly Dances: Technologies of the Body in Baroque Music,' in *From the Royal to the Republican Body: Incorporating the Political in Seventeenth and Eighteenth Century France*, ed. Sara Melzer and Kate Norberg (Berkeley and Los Angeles: University of California Press, 1998), 85–112.

20 See again my discussion in *Conventional Wisdom*, chapter 3. As the title of his recent book suggests, Karol Berger understands Bach's temporality in

a very different way. See *Bach's Cycle, Mozart's Arrow: An Essay on the Origins of Musical Modernity* (Berkeley and Los Angeles: University of California Press, 2007). I understand linear temporalities – arrows, in other words – to emerge very prominently in the early seventeenth century. We now call those arrows 'tonality,' and most of Bach's music is profoundly teleological. For a study of seventeenth-century musical grammars and temporalities, see my *Desire and Pleasure in Seventeenth-Century Music* (Berkeley and Los Angeles: University of California Press, forthcoming).

21 See Hayden White, 'Form, Reference, and Ideology in Musical Discourse,' in *Music and Text: Critical Inquiries*, ed. Steven Paul Scher (Cambridge: Cambridge University Press, 1992).

22 Lang, Introduction, Heyer, ed., *Jean-Baptiste Lully*, 2. See also Rosen, 'The Fabulous La Fontaine' for a discussion of how talented artists fled France during this period because of Louis's ruthless favouritism.

23 Robert Isherwood, *Music in the Service of the King* (Ithaca, NY: Cornell University Press, 1973); Norbert Elias, *The Court Society*, trans. Edmund Jephcott (New York: Pantheon, 1983); Michel Foucault, *Discipline and Punish: The Birth of the Prison*, trans. Alan Sheridan (New York: Vintage Books, 1979); Kathryn Hoffmann, *Society of Pleasures: Interdisciplinary Readings in Pleasure and Power during the Reign of Louis XIV* (New York: St Martin's Press, 1997); Georgia J. Cowart, *The Triumph of Pleasure: Louis XIV and the Politics of Spectacle* (Chicago: University of Chicago Press, 2008).

24 Hoffmann, *Society of Pleasures*, 1; Isherwood, *Music in the Service of the King*, 352.

25 'Laisser le peuple s'endormir dans les fêtes, dans les spectacles.' J. La Bruyère, *Les caractères* (1688), quoted in Peter Burke, *The Fabrication of Louis XIV* (New Haven, CT: Yale University Press, 1992), 6. In *Society of Pleasures*, Hoffmann traces in texts of this time the many recurrent images associated with slumber: dreams, reverie, trance, somnambulism, and so on. Hoffmann has moved to other areas of research, as is evident in her essay for this volume, 'Excursions to See "Monsters": Odd Bodies and Itineraries of Knowledge in the Seventeenth Century.' But her work always invites the reader to enter into a realm of perception very different from those characteristic of the early twenty-first century.

26 I pursued this line of argumentation to some extent in my 'Unruly Passions and Courtly Dances.' This essay is my penance.

27 For critiques of the explanation of this culture as simply imposed from above, see again Hoffmann and also Jonathan Dewald, *Aristocratic Experience and the Origins of Modern Culture: France, 1570–1715* (Berkeley and Los Angeles: University of California Press, 1993).

28 Cowart, *The Triumph of Pleasure.*

29 Lucien Goldmann, *The Hidden God: A Study of Tragic Vision in the* Pensées *of Pascal and the Tragedies of Racine,* trans. Philip Thody (London: Routledge and Kegan Paul, 1964; repr. 1977). For a more recent political interrogation of Racine and his relation to power, see Hoffmann, *Society of Pleasures,* chapter 2.

30 Quoted in Goldmann, *The Hidden God,* 34.

31 As quoted in Sara Melzer, *Discourses of the Fall: A Study of Pascal's* Pensées (Berkeley and Los Angeles: University of California Press, 1986), 86. ['Nous souhaitons la vérité et ne trouvons en nous qu'incertitude. Nous recherchons le bonheur et ne trouvons que misère et mort. Nous sommes incapables de ne pas souhaiter la vérité et le bonheur et sommes incapable ni de certitude ni de bonheur. Ce désir nous est laissé pour nous punir que pour nous faire sentir d'où nous sommes tombés.'] Blaise Pascal, *Pensées,* ed. Philippe Sellier (Paris: Mercure de France, 1976), fragment 20. Similar mixtures of philosophy and theology are also discussed in Daniel Garber's essay on Spinoza, 'Disciplining Feeling: The Seventeenth-Century Idea of a Mathematical Theory of the Emotions,' and Thomas Christensen's 'The Sound World of Father Mersenne,' both in this volume.

32 St Francis de Sales, as quoted in Paul de Jaegher, *An Anthology of Christian Mysticism* (Springfield, IL: Templegate Publishers, 1977), 124–7.

33 See, for instance, the discussion by Richard Rambuss of Richard Crashaw's verse elsewhere in this volume. See also my discussions of Italian representations of Divine Union in *Desire and Pleasure in Seventeenth-Century Music.*

34 Mme de Guyon, *Torrens spirituels,* part II, chap. 4, par. 12, as quoted in Ted Campbell, *The Religion of the Heart* (Columbia: University of South Carolina Press, 1991), 34. Campbell's book is a comparative study of subjective religious movements of the seventeenth century.

35 For detailed readings of Watteau stressing the qualities contributing to reverie, see Norman Bryson, *Word and Image: French Painting of the Ancien Régime* (Cambridge: Cambridge University Press, 1981), chapter 3. See also Georgia Cowart, 'Watteau's *Pilgrimage to Cythera* and the Subversive Utopia of the Opera-Ballet,' *Art Bulletin* 83 (September 2001): 460–78. Professor Cowart has mounted a major exhibition on Watteau and music at the Metropolitan Museum in New York, and she is completing a book titled *Watteau, Music and the Musical Theater.*

36 Elias, *The Court Society,* especially the section on court rationality, 110–16. See also Pocock, *Boileau and the Nature of Neo-Classicism,* 12–13.

37 J. le Rond d'Alembert, *La liberté de la musique* (1759), in *Oeuvres de d'Alembert* (Geneva: Slatkine Reprints, 1967), 1: 520; my translation.

38 José Antonio Maravall, *Culture of the Baroque: Analysis of a Historical Structure*, trans. Terry Cochran (Minneapolis: University of Minnesota Press, 1986), 68.

39 Of course, this is not the only moment in history to have experienced such a collision. Americanists such as David Noble have identified a similar confrontation at the turn of the last century between quietist isolationism (which many wanted to protect from the onslaught of modern urbanization) and the progressive political movements that eventually won the day. See his *The End of American History: Democracy, Capitalism, and the Metaphor of Two Worlds in Anglo-American Historical Writing, 1880–1980* (Minneapolis: University of Minnesota Press, 1985).

40 See the essays by Daniel Garber and Thomas Christensen in this volume on the ways Cartesian thought developed in the hands, respectively, of Spinoza and Mersenne. Spinoza attempts, for instance, to account mathematically for the unruly qualities of affect.

41 Hoffmann, *Society of Pleasures*, 34.

chapter thirteen

Temporal Interventions: Music, Modernity, and the Presentation of the Self

RICHARD LEPPERT

Music has long played an important role in myriad practices associated with cultural and ethical assessments of time and its use or abuse. Experienced *in* time and, in essence, *of* time, music invites a heightened experience and engagement with temporality. Adorno once put this nicely: 'The self-evident, that music is a temporal art, that it unfolds in time, means, in the dual sense, that time is not self-evident for [music], that [music] has time as its problem. It must create temporal relationships among its constituent parts, justify their temporal relationship, synthesize them through time. Conversely, it itself must act upon time, not lose itself to it; must stem itself against the empty flood.'[1]

My remarks in what follows will centre on the human senses of sight and hearing in the Low Countries in the early modernity of the seventeenth century, in conjunction with the conflicted relation governing time consciousness and the dialectics of pleasure, on the one hand, and the role played by music in organizing subjectivity, on the other. I will address both the acoustic phenomenon of music and also some typical visual tropes representing acoustic culture.

In the early seventeenth century, at a defining moment of early modernity, there developed an intense humanistic and scientific interest in the human senses, with principal interest centred on sight and hearing. The visual arts, literature, and philosophy, as well as the new sciences of anatomy, biology, and medicine delved into the subject. Humanistic and philosophical inquiry in particular addressed the senses as keys to human identity, principally as vehicles of our embodied apparatus for knowing. In northern painting, the theme of the Five Senses received particularly dramatic treatment.

The subject first established its pedigree as a mirror reflecting, hence putatively reinforcing, long-established religious belief: the old world theory of knowledge according to which the here and now makes ultimate sense only in terms of the hereafter. The way to knowledge was described as a series of pathways marked by the senses – but the senses' role, as it were, was to confirm principles of religious orthodoxy.[2]

> An alphabet of images related to the Scriptures was established: Sight, symbolized by the eagle, was linked with the theme of the healing of the blind man by Jesus; the mirror, with the theme of the expulsion of Adam and Eve from Paradise; Hearing with the preaching of John the Baptist; Taste with the miracle of the bread for the five thousand; Smell with Mary Magdalen's anointing of Christ's feet, and Touch with the miracle of Christ walking on the waters.[3]

Yet among the most striking of all the Five Senses paintings, those produced by the Fleming Jan Brueghel the Elder and, later, those by his son Jan the Younger (see figure 13.1), something else comes to the fore. With the Brueghels, the radical abstraction of the senses as theological metaphors is abandoned. What 'their' senses sense is this-worldly, made strikingly concrete, and super-charged with a visually gorgeous materialism. Accordingly, the senses' more traditional role as pathways to theological knowing is shifted toward the secular. Indeed, these paintings effectively argue for the earthly pleasures available to be consumed by the sensing body, at the same time that they provide a direct opportunity to experience the potentiality of the sensual. The Brueghel's Five Senses paintings, in other words, hail the *body* in the act of aestheticizing and valorizing sensibility and sensuality.

As viewers, Brueghel's *Hearing* calls us to our bodies by providing us a level of pleasure that vastly exceeds mere knowing. Brueghel gets us to look by giving us so much to look at. That we want to look in the first place is partly the result of the cultural value fixed on worldly goods, products of human manufacture that in virtually every instance are luxury items, and none a basic life necessity. To take in the myriad material contents of the painting we must look wholeheartedly. The act of visual consumption becomes a feast not a snack; it requires time and even focused attention simply to make basic identifications – that is, to name the objects.

Not the least pleasure we are invited to experience is derived from the naked muse, presumably Euterpe. Her bare flesh attracts our eyes

Figure 13.1 Jan Brueghel the Younger (1601–78) and Jan van Kessel the Elder (attr.) (1626–79), *Hearing*. Whereabouts unknown. Photo: IRPA-KIK-Brussels, B154569.

partly by its whiteness in contrast to the richly coloured materials surrounding her, including the drapery that frames her body, thereby setting it off as a kind of special sight. The fact that she is naked of course changes everything, for it marks the pleasure to be had as specifically erotic, that is, sensual (of the senses) – and also at odds with lived experience. Her body is made available as a sight in ways that profoundly exceed what is available for us to see in ordinary daily life. The painting's visual pleasures, in other words, are extra-ordinary, hence supplying all the more reason for us to look. Brueghel's painting illustrates a human sense (Hearing and, since it is a painting, Seeing as well). It also activates our own sensing bodies to the extent that it makes us *want* to look. In a culture where, already in Brueghel's own lifetime, seeing is believing, paintings of the human senses – no matter which sense is represented – mark the hold that looking as such enjoys in modernity. Brueghel's *Hearing*, accordingly, is Hearing for the eyes to the extent that the eyes can confirm hearing's function, even when there is literally nothing to hear. The painting also confirms the agency – the social power – of looking, for what is made available for seeing in this image are the accoutrements of extreme privilege and power. What is here for the visual taking is one among the infinite variety of over-determinations for modernity's claim that Man, in the Foucauldian sense of the modern We, is defined by what we have, or by what we are taught to desire: worldly goods. Brueghel's painting evokes extreme consumption as determinant of human worth. He also genders this worthiness as male, by granting access to the stark nudity of the woman who organizes the entire composition.

Since paintings are silent, what matters in this representation is not aural phenomena as such, but the social importance and function of certain kinds of sound and audition. Brueghel's painting illustrates not simply things that make sounds,[4] but things that make socially prestigious, and principally *private*, sounds. That is, the musical instruments illustrated are solely those of high-caste music; the hunting devices scattered on the floor at the left recall an activity restricted to the nobility; the timepieces placed here and there throughout the image were expensive collector's items at the time. All in all, human hearing is represented less as a natural phenomenon than as one of high social position. Hearing, in short, is politicized, and its politics are made to appear beautiful.

The pleasures immanent to Brueghel's picture are to no small extent produced by the degree to which the accumulated objects make no functional sense, except as a kind of archive of related objects. As an inventory, Brueghel's sound-making collections please by their function-*less* excess. Their visual logic, so to speak, lies in their apparent lack of logic, the degree to which the inventory seems impossible, a mere fantasy, except for the fact that nearly all the objects in the room not only are painted with notable precision but also are objects of contemporaneous use. They occupy, in effect, a space out of time, at the same time they themselves are, as it were, at once time-bound and entirely timely. The fantasy, in other words, has its feet planted in a recognizable reality. The view through the open archway looks onto a fanciful Italianate landscape apparently hosting a concert of muses (a popular northern trope at the time). But through the doorway at the left is something rather more mundane in the form of a carillon player, who, judging from his costume, is a quite ordinary mortal busy earning his keep at his keyboard. Thus pre-history and present history cohabit. And the same can be said of space, broadly conceived, to the extent that the fauna in the foreground constitute both the utterly ordinary and the notably exotic – the local and the foreign. In other words, time and space are radically concentrated. (The small stag functions, obviously enough, as a kind of internal label that identifies the painting's organizational principle to be that of Hearing.)

Norbert Schneider points out that Five Senses paintings of this sort work not so much to satisfy cravings as to produce them. In this regard, the seventeenth century marked the emergence of new wealth, and the accompanying demand for things to buy. The great port at Antwerp, Brueghel's hometown, later in the seventeenth century could accommodate two thousand ships at one time, bringing trade goods to northern Europe from the far corners of the already-fast-shrinking globe. 'The stimuli provided by the new range of luxury goods triggered off a compulsive urge in the viewer to enhance his own sensual pleasure and to keep increasing his long-term needs.'[5] More to the point of my concerns, these desires are both classified and structured in paintings like Brueghel's; that is, our consuming pleasures are organized for us, and their import is pedagogical.

Brueghel's Five Senses paintings isolate each sense, hence parallel the practices of contemporaneous anatomy lessons that examine one discrete body part after another. This parallel is neither accidental nor trivial. At the same historical moment that Brueghel's paintings both visualize and valorize sense-derived physical pleasure, the viewer's own sensing body itself is in effect objectified, taken apart, and appealed to in a kind of aestheticized science of pleasure. This science is structured as an inventory of the objects that reference and stimulate each sense in turn – wonderful sounds to 'hear,' exotic flowers to 'smell,' bountiful feasts to 'taste,' and so forth. Science meets and allies with consumption and the desires that drive consumption.[6]

Thus the same epistemology underwrites these pictures and contemporaneous scientific classificatory schemes generally. The images are doubly modern, despite the fact that their organizing principle is allegorical. They mark the pleasure of excess consumption, linking it directly to power, and they situate physical; embodied pleasure in a quasi-medical discourse about the *mechanics* of pleasure. Pleasure becomes something not simply to be enjoyed but to be isolated into its component parts, and then appealed to. More, these representations evoke modernity's troubling conflation of work and play (or perhaps the erasure of play).[7] That is, the pleasure of the seeing comes from the considerable effort expended to make sense of the classification schemes organizing the painting's material contents.

Five Senses paintings, unified by a philosophy of the hoard, are nonetheless underwritten by an anxiety about loss, in part driven by the fact that 'having' in the two dimensions of a painting is not analogous to having, in three dimensions, the actual objects represented. Imagery stimulates desire precisely by frustrating it, except for those individuals who have both the paintings *and* what the paintings represent. But for other viewers, those who have only the sight of what is represented, such paintings mark the enormous gap separating the realm of 'having' from the realm of 'having (merely) a look.'

By freezing time, paintings suspend action and reaction, and in the process the viewer is both permitted and encouraged to imagine a permanence that does not exist. The objects Brueghel represents are 'there' only for the eye, as a stimulation passing through the retina, and nothing more – apart from the literal value of the picture itself, no small matter to be sure. As such, what is seen in an image makes a promise it cannot fulfil. The 'seeing' in painting frustratingly leads no further – we cannot pick up one of the musical instruments and make it sound; we cannot smell a single bloom. We can only *imagine*. What seems in representation so concrete, so available, so 'real,' pulls back from us, always out of reach, as it were, to the very senses appealed to. When we move too close to a painting, what made perfect 'sense' from a short distance suddenly blurs into the coloured fog of the image's own material surface – just so much paint on wood or canvas. Thus the eye that establishes what a painting 'is' likewise confirms that it is not what it claims to be.

Brueghel's painting invokes the pleasures of hearing, so far as music is concerned, principally by its absence, a lack made the more pertinent given the extraordinary possibilities for musical (and other) sonority visually evident. The little background ensemble at the extreme right drives home the point. The pleasure of music resides in its possibility rather than actuality. Paintings are perforce silent, but their silence itself becomes a trope when so much potential music remains unrealized, with reference to the many instruments scattered carelessly in the foreground. So far as the musical performances are concerned, were we to be within earshot, it is hard to imagine that we would much want to listen. Two background ensembles perform, as does a bell ringer, the muse-organist, a child piper, and the shawm-blowing primate. And this says nothing about the possible acoustic contributions of clocks chiming, a dog barking, and exotic birds screeching. In brief, the painting invokes the possibilities accorded to hearing organized around the most privileged of sounds – accordingly, there is not a single instrument associated with the peasantry – but ones whose literal result, if we could somehow hear what is going on, would be cacophony. In other words, the beauty of the *visual* music exists in extreme tension with what is actually represented, namely, musical simultaneities that together produce noise: the price paid for too much of everything. But of course what matters most here is not reality, but the invocation to a fantasy of accumulated pleasure the foundation of which is structured from an immense degree of social power and accumulated wealth.

It is no accident that Dutch art of this early modern period represented musical subjects to a degree never previously equalled, and probably never since surpassed. The cultural reasons for employing music as a visual trope in the new age of the visual episteme is explained best, I think, by music's evocation of, and dependency upon, the aestheticization of time, at precisely the moment when modern time consciousness becomes obsessive – and obsessively linear: the moment when time truly becomes money, and the moment when human subjects stage their lives and experiences in increasingly self-reflexive relation to time, the pilgrim's progress to the secular heaven of worth as that form of self-worth that can be taken to the bank.

Modern time consciousness helps account for the inclusion of timepieces in the painting. Clocks, as Norbert Elias, reminds us, are 'nothing other than human-made physical continua of change which, in certain societies, are standardized as a framework of reference and a measure for other social and physical continua of changes.'[8] 'Whatever else they may be,' he noted, 'timing devices are always transmitters of messages to people.'[9] George Kubler complements Elias's insight, suggesting that 'Time, like mind, is not knowable as such. We know time only indirectly by what happens in it: by observing change and permanence; by marking the succession of events among stable settings; and by noting the contrast of varying rates of change.'[10]

What Elias says about clocks holds good for music, likewise a 'timing device.' Music is a form of time that draws attention to itself, either in time or in opposition to time. Music is time; time is life. But the life of music in modernity must be experienced in specific relation to the hegemonic and distinctly non-aesthetic dynamics of time that now organize life generally. Looking ahead, beyond the seventeenth century, within a quarter-century or so following the death of Mozart, is born the age of industry ('Be on time'), when time itself is internationally first regulated: Greenwich Mean Time; this is also the age of music regulated by the metronome ('Keep in time'). Time as we now know it, as though our time were somehow 'natural,' was defined in the early decades of the nineteenth century on account of money. Our 'time' was invented for the railroad schedule – so that raw materials could be gotten to the factories and keep them running, ostinato-fashion, ever same, and to get factories' production to the towns, cities, and ports for sale and consumption.[11] But what was fully realized only in the nineteenth century was predicated on the articulation of time consciousness that began shaping itself two centuries earlier. Elias marks modern time as 'the symbol of an inescapable and all-embracing compulsion.'[12] Time in modernity has a life of its own. It reaches beyond our capacity to control it. Thus pleasure and power are enjoyed in time; the difficulty is that the social, political, and economic base for pleasure and power, however apparently secure, is always challenged by the clock. Like music, it fades quickly when the efforts to produce it cease.

Music, in relation to time's hold on life, must either get in step, or refuse to march. And it is precisely that choice that the auditor is given to hear when listening. Sensitivity to the issue of choice, regarding music's articulation of time, is not least what makes music dangerous, read either as a waste of time or as an experience of difference distinctive from time-bound 'normality.' The functionlessness of art in an age of function can quite easily play the role of opponent to the here and now, a fact perfectly evident from the degree of effort expended to control both the training for, and the making of, music throughout history.

Brueghel's painting fetishizes time as a dimension of power and control. In this sense, time consciousness formulates the ultimate mark of prestige in a society so generally unaware, except for a relative few, that modern time operates not in circular fashion, in sync with the agricultural seasons, but in a straight line, and that within that time frame the world may be explained by its sounds, all of which are to be increasingly subject to external control. This adds up to a simple reality: the moderns have figured out that time is worth listening *to*.

Time, as a parameter of power, did not exist to be wasted. Subjecthood (identity marked by subjectivity), as a component of power, to be realized and thereafter preserved and manifested, likewise required time's wise use. Music, requiring time, realized through time, played a critical but contradictory role in modernity as regards the modern subject. And as is very well known, the story is different depending on who is making the music – whether amateur or professional, whether man or woman, whether high-class status or low – and depending as well on the kind of music made, though I am not going to address that question further here.

The *Bird Concert* (see figure 13.2), a quasi-popular trope in the Low Countries, provided painters with the opportunity to display their talents at rendering fauna of the most spectacular and distinctly colourful variety by means of a startling visual conceit that directly engages the dialectics of temporality. As with Brueghel's *Hearing*, the painting's visual appeal is obvious, likely in part because of the surreal suspension of reality demanded by the composition, which gathers together birds (as well as a bat) from the near and – mostly – from afar. The absurdity is plainly visible; indeed, it is made a point. This image is about ownership, built on a foundation of worldly dominion. Its apparent subject is birds; its real subject is people. The landscape is northern European, staffed by a peasant worker of sorts who gazes at the same sight that we gaze upon from outside the image. He looks; we look. And, no accident, the birds look. To be precise, and as the saying goes, they face the music: 'ours,' not theirs. They focus their eyes on a small book on which a few notes are scribbled; they are all following the same script in order to produce (an impossible) heteronomy, that point made emphatic by the contorted necks of some of the birds, as if straining to follow the acoustic-temporal

Figure 13.2 Flemish (17th century). *Bird Concert.* Whereabouts unknown. Photo: IRPA-KIK-Brussels, B115729.

orders. Here is the point: the birds have been put into time; they have been made historical. Culture trumps nature, and puts nature in its service. So busy are the birds doing our bidding that they suspend their natural instincts to hunt one another or even to defend territory, territory which in any event is no longer theirs.

The swan was considered the noblest of birds at the time in northern Europe, so much so that the legal right to hunt it was extremely restricted. Here this elegant bird has left its pond to perch impossibly in a tree, in order to do as it has been told. It is as though the new 'worth' of the swan and the other birds in the scene is determined not by what they are in nature but what we determine them to be, a worth measured against the degree to which they do our bidding. Man's rule over nature, long sanctioned, has here reached into new territory to the extent that the violent relation of man to nature has been radically aestheticized. The worth of these animals is determined by the success each manifests in singing our tune, and by modelling themselves as eye candy besides.

The little music book, inconsequential in size, nonetheless possesses more than sufficient cultural authority to determine the entire composition. Around the two tiny sheets touched by flecks of black notation there swirls a phenomenal array of colour – literally spectacular – like matter being pulled into a black hole, in this instance, the black hole of modernity. The image puts nature into time; nature marches in step, in a pretty rhythm. It does so for the pleasures of those, both inside and external to the painting, who look, and who expect to see what they are seeing, and also what they are invited to sense: the triumph of organizing the world around the human pleasures of sensing and, through the particularities of the appeals to sensing, the construction of modern subjectivity and selfhood. Aesthetics is never passive, and music is never drained of meaning. In aesthetics and music alike purposelessness is only a mask or a sweetener for something deemed more important, namely, the shape of society and the human subjects within it. Pleasure is never without consequences: it is a component of history and comes with a price to be paid.

Time, Elias reminds us, is 'a social institution.'[13] Regarding time in music, it is appropriate to raise a question similar to one Elias posed of clocks: 'What do clocks really show when we say that they show the time?'[14] Any answer demands more than I can give it, but at least this for starters. Like clocks, time in music provides a means by which human subjects 'orient ... themselves within the succession of social, biological and physical processes in which they find themselves placed.' Like clocks, music also serves people 'as a way of regulating their behaviour in relation to each other and themselves.'[15] In music, time demands attention, yet not necessarily or even specifically attention to clock time, though always in relation to it. That is, time *in* music and the time *of* music either play in time to clock time (rarely so, I would judge) or in distinction from clock time, and often in experiential opposition to it. Musical time commonly provides momentary distraction, if hardly escape, from time's general instrumentalization, at the same time that musical time, even while providing aesthetic cover for dystopian reality, seems to insist on an alternative. Musical time, in other words, can play both sides of the sociocultural street.

Early modernity confronts time as a moral issue, to the extent that earthly time, whether wasted or fetishized, runs the risk of earning one the eternal time of damnation. The tension between now-time and the non-time of eternity produced cultural ambivalence and moral contradiction, a dialectics that gave rise to a prominent genre of painting, the vanitas still life, which fed off the book of Ecclesiastes 1:2 ('Vanity of vanities, saith the Preacher, vanity of vanities; all is vanity'). Vanitas paintings transformed a rich array of textual allusions into emblems and attributes, based in particular on work by Calvinist scholars from the University of Leyden. Music featured prominently.

The still-life objects represented were intended to encourage the observer to contemplate the frailty and brevity of life: human skulls, instruments for measuring time (clocks, watches, hourglass), candles burning or extinguished but still smoking, soap bubbles that exist only for an instant, flowers at their height of bloom hence about to fade, ripe fruit hence about to rot. Luxury goods such as rare shells, jewellery, silver plate, gold coins, purses, deeds, and so on alluded to the vanity of earthly treasures. Musical instruments and music books fell among a related group of attributes referencing life's tastes and pleasures, the so-called *vita voluptuaria*, intended to be read as activities that waste precious time better spent saving one's soul.[16] Similarly, books and scientific instruments alluded to the *vita contemplativa*; and the inclusion of weapons and insignias of command to the *vita pratica*. Finally, as a putative antidote to the condemnation of things transitory, vanitas pictures often incorporated signs of the soul's eternal existence, such as a sprig of ripe wheat or ears of corn, which contain seeds of new life that will sprout after planting/burial. (Few individual vanitas paintings reference all of these categories.) The most severe examples of the genre, leaving nothing to doubt, incorporated mottoes as internal labels: 'Vanitas,' 'Vanitas, vanitatis,' 'Vanitas vanitatis et omnia vanitas,' 'Homo bulla' (man is but a bubble), 'mors omnia vincit' (death triumphs over everything), 'memento mori,' and the like.

In the vanitas still life all *movement* ceases in favour of a concentrated sorting of data. In this process, the end falls victim to the means, and data as such quickly become the imagery's real subject. In short, vanitas still-life paintings privilege *information*. To be sure, each object represented 'officially' meant something beyond its literal self, having 'attached' an elaborate set of textual conceits, each properly didactic. But all that textuality was nonetheless external to the image, hence literally invisible. The challenge set before the viewer was to 'see behind' or to 'see through' what was visible to the eye – gorgeous material goods, commonly luxurious – to the elaborate moral critique charted by Calvinist intellectuals. To achieve this didactic goal was no small feat; unquestionably, the moral challenge was commonly not met.[17]

To illustrate the problem, I would like to consider two quite different vanitas paintings. The first (figure 13.3), by the Fleming Jan van Oost the Elder, is something of a hybrid to the extent that it includes a human figure. The setting is a scholar's study furnished with a table on which rest numerous symbolic objects: a sword (*vita pratica*); violin, wine pitcher, glass, and dice (*vita voluptuaria*); and books and manuscripts (*vita contemplativa*). On the parchment is written: '*finis coronat opus*' (death crowns work). In the background is a zodiacal sphere that is stopped at the point where the Lion replaces Cancer, thus marking year's end. On the chair in the left foreground is an apple, fatal fruit of man's fall, thus referencing the introduction of sin and death into the world, although next to it is a piece of bread, one of the signs of the Eucharist, hence the promise of life after death. A small manuscript enumerates the letters of the alphabet from A to Z, apparently an allusion to the Alpha and Omega, Christ as the beginning and end of all things.[18] An old man, Faust-like, sits contemplating a skull.

The viewer is drawn to the sympathetically painted man, arranged so that we focus on his ancient face, downcast eyes, and wrinkled hands. Yet as affecting as his image may be, we are pulled away to the left, attracted by the clutter of objects on the table, so arranged that our eyes can find no repose among them. The composition is brilliantly conceived. Despite the individual detail each object offers, we are distracted by what lies in its proximity. Our eyes dart restlessly from one 'trinket' to another. The only space where visual repose is offered is that occupied by the old

Figure 13.3 Jan van Oost the Elder (1601–71), *Meditating Philosopher* [with Vanitas Still Life] (1647), Bruges, Comissies van Openbare Onderstand Museum, Burgelijke Godshuizen. Photo: IRPA-KIK-Brussels, B112471.

man's face. Yet in looking at him, we cannot avoid the temptation to look once again at the goods opposite. The painting's tension, the means by which it acts upon the viewer, thus transliterates a moral choice into a physical one: we can *feel* it. What our eyes can see, they can also sense in the urge to shift their glance.

Van Oost's painting references music with only a partial view of a violin. Something entirely different is evident in a still life by Joh. Fr. Grueber (figure 13.4), in which musical instruments are abundantly represented; they include a large viol (especially prominent), as well as a cittern, lute, rebec, violin, bagpipe, trumpet, two recorders (a soprano and perhaps a tenor), what is likely a mandora (partly visible), probably a shawm, as well as an open partbook, and two sheets of music (the artist has signed his name on the one at the left). Besides the musical instruments, there is a jumble of expensive plate, and an abundance of ripe fruit, alongside

Figure 13.4 Johann Friedrich Grueber [formerly attributed to Cornelis de Heem (1631–95)], *Still Life* [Vanitas] (1662–81). Amsterdam, Rijksmuseum, SK-A-2564. Photo: Rijksmuseum.

a box filled with gold coins and, apparently, jewellery – and so on. There is much to eat, but taken together it does not add up to a meal; the culinary logic fails. And obviously this is no set table: objects tilt precariously, leaning against each other, in momentary gravitational suspension. A peeled lemon is at the centre right, in the characteristic mode whereby it apparently exists in order to exhibit its spiral form, and nothing more. Magic is not in its astringent taste but in the look of contrasting colour and texture of the peel from outside to inside. Again, each of the individual objects represented is anchored to a moral text. But it is all too easy to lose track of the import of the moral imperative here.

Still life is the genre through which art and aesthetics most boldly encounter their entwined relation to privilege precisely because the still life's typical object-centredness seldom allows anyone to forget its relation to buying and having, and this is notably the case in the early history of still life. Not for nothing did the genre re-emerge in the early modernity of proto-capitalism in the Dutch seventeenth century. Roland Barthes aptly described these paintings' contents as an 'empire of merchandise'; speaking about Dutch paintings in general and their focus on the object world, he noted that they require the viewer to 'audit the painting like an accountant.'[19]

Still life is commonly about power, but of a raw and blunt kind, without the trapping and gilding of mythology's heroes, history's grand narratives, Scripture's saints, or portraiture's men of noble stature. Still life is about what power gets you. It is the one genre that blatantly tells the unwitting story underwriting money: you are what you have, all the more visually inescapable given the 'almost obsessive precision'[20] with which still life's objects were commonly painted. Still life ordinarily excludes persons (or at least de-emphasizes them), but still life is always ultimately about persons and not (or not merely) about the objects actually represented. In other words, still life is about the relation of the object world to the human subject who is unseen but imagined.

Perhaps more than any other sort of painting, still life reminds us of our own embodiment, to the extent that it so specifically connects us, as physical and sensory beings, to the material world. There's money, and what money will buy: abundant, gloriously perfect food and drink (the wine cooler on the floor), and acoustic richness provided by the full range of musics available in the region, from what we would understand as art music to the music of popular life. The music invokes the pleasures of leisure as well as those of taste and refinement; it likewise invokes the more sensual pleasures of the flesh, especially with the inclusion of the rebec and the bagpipe. The connection of music to sensual pleasures is designated by a small pocket fiddle and its bow, an instrument then exclusively associated with dancing, a practice condemned by Calvinist preachers as an occasion for sensual improprieties. There is also a bagpipe, another dance instrument, especially popular among the lower social orders, and the subject of a contemporary proverb: '*Met een goed gevulde buik wil het zingen beter lukken*' ('one sings better with a well-filled belly'; the instrument 'sings' best only when its sack is well filled), an earthy metaphor for male sexual performance, developing from the fact that the bagpipe's chanter pipe and wind sack together visually correspond to the male genitalia. Both the rebec and the bagpipe were peasant instruments, which is to suggest that the particular excesses to which they allude are more or less class-specific in their condemnation of sensuality.

The picture provides pleasure – altogether too much pleasure – less in contemplating than in looking – via the myriad beautiful material objects, each of which not coincidentally references specifically sensual-corporeal activities.[21] In this picture, the things of this world are rendered less with suspicion than with an admiration akin to fetish; each is afforded a nearly obsessive degree of the painter's attention. There is one thing more: vanitas paintings could themselves be very expensive; indeed, as with other paintings, they were in part bought for financial security and investment in *this* world. In other words, the very purchase of such pictures contradicts what their subject and supposed function otherwise claimed. Read against this grain, the vanitas issues a moral challenge by literally enacting a vanity.[22] In the end we're left to admit that the vanitas depends for its rhetorical impact on an irresolvable tension: the vanitas both represents and itself is what it condemns.

The visual referents to music, apart from those alluding to erotic pleasures, are those principally associated with official civic life and authority (shawms, as part of the typical Low Countries' town bands, and the trumpet) or with privatized art music. Two points emerge here with respect to time. Time privatized and acoustically aestheticized has gained a great deal of status, particularly to the extent that the music made is not hired but self-realized. Refined music, in other words, is a sign of self-reflexive and elevated selfhood. To acquire this goal takes time, to be sure (and here the ambivalence towards music was, and would remain, considerable, especially with regard to music's potential negative impact on the individual's larger responsibilities). But the performance of music, which functioned as a sign of an excess of time, hence power, also distinctly aestheticized the authority, wealth, and power available to control time – parenthetically, it is this that makes sensible the otherwise apparent incongruousness of choosing to decorate the case of a double-manual harpsichord with battle scenes (figures 13.5 and 13.6).[23]

I would like to conclude by looking at two images that represent house concerts involving amateur musicians. The first, attributed to Gonzales Coques (figure 13.7),[24] is, at least in subject, typical of large numbers of Dutch and Flemish paintings produced during the course of the seventeenth century representing private music making. Indeed, one of the more notable facts about this genre is how suddenly it appeared and how

Figure 13.5 *Double-manual Harpsichord* (1612, Antwerp; rebuilt 1774), case paintings by Adam Frans van der Meulen (1632–90). Brussels, Conservatoire Royal de Musique. Photo: IRPA-KIK-Brussels, B182534.

strikingly popular it became. That said, this particular painting is unusual in several ways, on account of which it is easier to make points concerning the cultural significance of what is 'happening' in the scene and in many other – if compositionally tamer – versions of the same subject.

The painting is oddly shaped (and there is nothing to suggest that it has been cut down): it is strikingly longitudinal compared to conventional picture sizing at the time. Its 'action' stretches out so as to break into three discrete events. At the extreme left, three musicians perform (a singer holding a sheet of music and marking time with his hand, a woman at the virginals, and a man playing a violino piccolo, with its characteristic scalloped outline). In the centre a wholly separate ensemble of five musicians sing and play from part books (three singers, one of whom marks time with his hand, a woman playing theorbo-lute, and a man playing a viol). Finally at the extreme right, a boy peeks in from the outside, as though an intruder, thereby acknowledging the restricted,

Figure 13.6 *Double-manual Harpsichord* (1612, Antwerp; rebuilt 1774), case paintings by Adam Frans van der Meulen (1632–90). Detail: Landscape with Louis XIV and Mounted Entourage; Siege of a Town. Brussels, Conservatoire Royal de Musique. Photo: IRPA-KIK-Brussels, B182535.

Figure 13.7 Gonzales Coques (1618–84, attr.), *House Concert.* Whereabouts unknown. Photo: IRPA-KIK-Brussels, C1716.

quasi-private nature of the event and also the fact that an external world lies beyond this special enclosure. His dress is not local. Instead, it is Italianate and distinctly flashy, the sort painted by northern Caravaggists. In Caravaggist-style paintings of the period where music was featured, it was commonly as an accompaniment to sexual excess, and even debauchery. Little wonder the degree of amazement evident on the boy's face; what he sees is not excess, but an extraordinary degree of *mesure*. The over-determined role played by music in the scene anchors associations of virtue and virtuous behaviour, visually obvious to be sure, but also textually sanctioned in period emblem books.[25] In other words, the role music played in vanitas paintings, namely, as a reference to time wasted, has here been entirely abandoned. Instead, music is honoured, and music in turn honours the musicians. The two ensembles separately order themselves so as to produce a musical harmony that mirrors social harmony (it is no accident that in both instances it is a man who beats time, reflecting standardized gender roles).

The Latin motto on the virginals reads '*Musica laetitae comes medicina dolorum*' (Music is the companion of joy, the healer of sadness). Music in short is about feelings, and feelings, or sensibility, in this instance constitute a valorized articulation of the self. Music is about me. Music made by me puts my 'me-ness' into acoustic reality. Music in short is my 'me' aestheticized. Is it any wonder that the joy promised by the virginals' motto is so little evident in the faces of the performers? Self-expression, to oneself and to others, after all, is serious business. Making one's selfhood evident to oneself and to others takes concentration. Selfhood is a performance – it is theatre – and these performers, as it were, are still learning their parts. It is also still necessary for there to be an outward, visible sign of *mesure*: not one man is sufficient to mark time; two are needed. The lessons of modern selfhood are by no means as yet culturally internalized as second-nature.

There is one performer, the theorbo-lutenist, who seems to have it down better than the others, and in this respect it is no accident that the painter has put her inside the elaborate frame of the fireplace behind her, thereby setting her off from the rest, visually featuring her, so to speak. Unlike all the other musicians, she is inspired, even self-decentred, yet appears to be in full command of her performance. Head thrust slightly back and to the side, and with eyes not on the printed music and certainly not focused on her fellow performers, she gazes towards the heavens, in essence towards nothing but herself, her sensibility, her acoustic signature, her inspiration. She becomes music, an embodied music, and in the process she becomes the more fully modern by becoming the more fully human. In effect, she defines the space that frames her; she gives purpose to what the other musicians work hard to accompany and themselves accomplish. She is in time and out of time simultaneously; her self-articulated selfhood acts out what music always is: in time and of time, an ordering of time and a commanding of space; via her musicianship she defines herself, just as she serves as the measure of the *mesure* towards which the other musicians strive. Arguably music articulates space to the extent that it gives sonic life to space. In this instance, two separate ensembles are called upon to make the point. Musically articulated space in turn enlivens and indeed decorates time. The fact that the music is of a particular sort, increasingly a music describing feelings and intimacies not public and official but private and personal, only increases the stakes of the degree to which modernity's structures of feeling are acoustically rich.

I will conclude by means of a leap forward in space and time to England perhaps one hundred and fifty years later, in order to look at one more image, a tiny pen and ink drawing (roughly 5 × 8 inches), by Nathaniel Dance-Holland (figure 13.8), very quickly executed, a kind of doodle – in the end, just a sketch, but a telling one, and not least on account of the spontaneity with which it is executed.

Figure 13.8 Sir Nathaniel Dance-Holland (1735–1811), *Musical Party*. Whereabouts unknown.

First off, Dance-Holland gives us a real performance, one he has witnessed, and not a tableau that he has staged, and upon which he will ultimately base an oil portrait. The arrangements of the subjects in the image are invariably 'wrong' for a portrait. What we have instead is something like 'real life,' despite the fact that the representation is so obviously unfinished, nothing like the precise, sometimes almost photographic attention to detail evident in contemporaneous paintings.

Besides the fact that a man sits at the keyboard, one more general visual element is striking: the music acts as a gravitational pull on everyone present. The left side is heavy with dark, fast pen strokes delineating the musician(s) and immediate audience. The right side, distinctly lighter in tone and pen stroke, shows two women in very different stance. The one more towards the centre is set at greater depth from those at the left, but she seems drawn toward them and unquestionably gives the music her attention. The woman farthest to the right is slightly ghostly, and still further removed from her companions. But her profile confirms her attentiveness. Indeed, both women are visually pulled toward the music, their lightly sketched bodies overwhelmed by the concentration of much darker lines to the left. As viewers, our eyes complete the task they themselves cannot accomplish, frozen as they are in time: our eyes make the shift from them towards the source of sonority. Something is happening here compositionally that seldom occurs in paintings. The experiential power of music is visually activated; its action on the body is both acknowledged and celebrated.

The participants listen, intently so, yet without the patently obvious self-consciousness – what might be named 'political correctness' – of the somewhat stiff decorum events in the earlier Flemish paintings, nothing if not highly staged fictions designed to promote the sitters' status. What is evident in the drawing, by contrast, hints (if only barely) of a paradigm shift according to which the modern subject morphs into a listening subject and by means of listening – as it were acute listening – is the more self-aestheticized, hence self-realized. This epistemic change is clearly not yet culturally official. Nonetheless, it presages a key turning point in the history of culture and the history of music. It is the moment when hearing can be imagined less as a parameter of power, whether real or imagined, as in Brueghel, and more as a gesture driven by a potentially more utopian form of desire to hear, simply stated, what Foucault's Man might become. That is, in close conjunction with this form of hearing lies music's invitation to ways of listening, new forms of imagining, and new forms of living life.

NOTES

1 Theodor W. Adorno, 'On Some Relationships between Music and Painting,' trans. Susan Gillespie, *Musical Quarterly* 79, no. 1 (Spring 1995): 66.

2 Norbert Schneider, *The Art of the Still Life: Still Life Painting in the Early Modern Period,* trans. Hugh Beyer (Cologne: Benedikt Taschen Verlag, 1990), 65; see further to 75.

3 Pierre Skira, *Still Life: A History,* trans. Jean-Marie Clarke (New York: Skira/ Rizzoli, 1989), 100; see further his discussion of the sacred associations, 100–1.

4 Concerning Brueghel's Five Senses paintings, see Klaus Ertz, *Jan Brueghel der Ältere (1568–1625): Der Gemälde, mit kritischem Oeuvrekatalog* (Cologne: DuMont Buchverlag, 1979), 328–62; see 329, 350–2, with regard to the paintings on Hearing; Fritz Baumgart, *Blumen Brueghel (Jan Brueghel d. Ä.): Leben und Werk* (Cologne: DuMont Buchverlag, 1978), 121–31; and Hans Kauffmann, 'Die Fünfsinne in der niederländischen Malerei des 17. Jahrhunderts,' in *Kunstgeschichtliche Studien: Festschrift für Dagobert Frey,* ed. Hans Tintelnot (Breslau: Gauverlag, 1943), 133–57. On the general subject, see Chu-tsing Li, 'The Five Senses in Art: An Analysis of Its Development in Northern Europe' (PhD diss., State University of Iowa, 1955).

5 Schneider, *Art of the Still Life,* 65.

6 Roland Barthes, 'The Plates of the *Encyclopaedia,*' in *New Critical Essays,* trans. Richard Howard (New York: Hill and Wang, 1980), 27: 'Ownership depends on a certain dividing up of things: to appropriate is to fragment the world, to divide it into finite objects subject to man in proportion to their very discontinuity: for we cannot separate without finally naming and classifying, and at that moment, property is born.'

7 See Roland Barthes, 'Dare to Be Lazy,' in *The Grain of the Voice: Interviews, 1962–1980,* trans. Linda Coverdale (New York: Hill and Wang, 1985), 38–45.

8 Norbert Elias, *Time: An Essay,* trans. Edmund Jephcott (Oxford: Blackwell, 1992), 46.

9 Ibid., 14.

10 George Kubler, *The Shape of Time: Remarks on the History of Things* (New Haven, CT: Yale University Press, 1962), 13.

11 See Donald M. Lowe, *History of Bourgeois Perception* (Chicago: University of Chicago Press, 1982), 37–8.

12 Elias, *Time: An Essay,* 21.

13 Ibid., 13.

14 Ibid., 12.

15 Ibid.

16 For other relevant Scriptural sources, as well as relevant secular literature and emblems relative to the vanitas topos, see Ingvar Bergström, *Dutch Still-Life Painting in the Seventeenth Century*, trans. Christina Hedström and Gerald Taylor (London: Faber and Faber, 1956), 155–6. For a general introduction to the vanitas theme, see 154–90, whence much of my basic information. Bergström is the best source in English for traditional interpretations of this genre. For an important revisionist view, see Svetlana Alpers, *The Art of Describing: Dutch Art in the Seventeenth Century* (Chicago: University of Chicago Press, 1983), especially 90–1, 103–9, 114–15.

17 For an excellent account of the tension between the visible and the invisible, the image and the unseen text in vanitas painting, see Norman Bryson, 'In Medusa's Gaze,' in the exhibition catalogue by Bernard Barryte, *In Medusa's Gaze: Still Life Paintings from Upstate New York Museums* (Rochester: Memorial Art Gallery of the University of Rochester, 1991), 9–14.

18 Albert Pomme de Mirimonde, 'Les sujets de musique chez les Caravagistes Flamands,' *Jaarboek, Koninklijk Museum for Schone Kunsten* [Antwerp] (1965): 165–7.

19 Roland Barthes, 'The World as Object,' trans. Richard Howard, in *A Barthes Reader*, ed. Susan Sontag (New York: Hill and Wang, 1982), 65 and 67, respectively.

20 Schneider, *Art of the Still Life*, 16.

21 On the matter of making a moral choice as a function of these images, see Anne Walter Lowenthal, 'Response to Peter Hecht,' *Simiolus* 16 (1986): 188–90; and by the same author, *Joachim Wtewael and Dutch Mannerism* (Doornspijk: Davaco, 1986), 57–60; and Bryson, 'In Medusa's Gaze,' 10–12.

22 Bryson, 'In Medusa's Gaze,' 11.

23 See further, Richard Leppert, *The Sight of Sound: Music, Representation, and the History of the Body* (Berkeley and Los Angeles: University of California Press, 1993), 127–31.

24 I have discussed this painting previously, though the argument I am advancing here is somewhat different. See Richard Leppert, '*Concert in a House*: Musical Iconography and Musical Thought,' *Early Music* 7, no. 1 (January 1979): 3–17.

25 See P.J.J. van Thiel, 'Marriage Symbolism in a Musical Party by Jan Miense Molenar,' *Simolus* 2, no. 2 (1967–8): 90–9, figure 13.8.

Contributors

Olivia Bloechl is Associate Professor of Musicology at UCLA. She is author of *Native American Song at the Frontiers of Early Modern Music* and is now writing *Opera and Politics in Old Regime France.*

Thomas Christensen, Professor of Music at the University of Chicago, is a theorist and historian of music theory. He is author of *Rameau and Musical Thought in the Enlightenment* and editor of the *Cambridge History of Western Music Theory.*

Sarah Covington, Professor of History at Queens College, CUNY, is author of *The Trail of Martyrdom: Persecution and Resistance in Sixteenth-Century England*; and *Wounds, Flesh, and Metaphor in Seventeenth-Century England.*

Daniel Garber, Stuart Professor of Philosophy at Princeton, is author of *Descartes' Metaphysical Physics, Descartes Embodied,* and *Leibniz: Body, Substance, Monad,* and is co-editor of the *Cambridge History of Seventeenth-Century Philosophy.* He is currently working on a monograph on the seminal writings of Jacobus Fonialis, along with a new edition of his Latin works.

Penelope Gouk, Honorary Research Fellow at the University of Manchester, is author of *Music, Science and Natural Magic in Seventeenth-Century England* and editor of *Music, Musical Healing in Cultural Contexts*; and *Representing Emotions: New Connections in the Histories of Art, Music, and Medicine.*

Wendy Heller, Professor, Department of Music at Princeton University, is author of *Emblems of Eloquence: Opera and Women's Voices in Seventeenth-*

Century Venice, and is currently completing *Animating Ovid: Opera and the Metamorphosis of Antiquity in Early Modern Italy.*

Kathryn A. Hoffmann, Professor of French at the University of Hawaii, is author of *Society of Pleasures: Interdisciplinary Readings in Pleasure and Power during the Reign of Louis XIV.* She is now writing *Phantasms of the Feminine: Strange Bodies and Monstrous Narration in the West.*

Richard Leppert, Professor of Comparative Studies in Discourse and Society in the Department of Cultural Studies and Comparative Literature at the University of Minnesota, is author of *The Sight of Sound: Music, Representation and the History of the Body*; *Art and the Committed Eye: The Cultural Functions of Imagery*; and *The Nude: The Cultural Rhetoric of the Body in the Art of Western Modernity.*

Susan McClary is Professor of Music at Case Western Reserve University. A MacArthur Fellow, she is author of *Feminine Endings: Music, Gender, and Sexuality*; *Conventional Wisdom: The Content of Musical Form*; *Modal Subjectivities: Self-Fashioning in the Italian Madrigal*; and *Desire and Pleasure in Seventeenth-Century Music.*

Sara E. Melzer, Professor of French and Francophone Studies at UCLA, is author of *Colonizer or Colonized: The Hidden Stories of Early Modern France* and *Discourses of the Fall: A Study of Pascal's Pensées.*

Richard Rambuss, Professor of English, Brown University, is author of *Spenser's Secret Career* and *Closet Devotions.* He has just completed a new critical edition of Richard Crashaw's poetry.

Louise K. Stein, Professor of Music at the University of Michigan, is a leading authority on Spanish music. She is author of *Songs of Mortals, Dialogues of the Gods: Music and Theatre in Seventeenth-Century Spain*, which won several awards, and the performing edition of the first American opera, *La púrpura de la rosa.*

Gary Tomlinson is John Hay Whitney Professor of Music and Humanities at Yale University and the Director of the Whitney Humanities Center there. A MacArthur Fellow, he is author of *Monteverdi and the End of the Renaissance*; *Music in Renaissance Magic*; *Metaphysical Song: An Essay on Opera*; and *The Singing of the New World: Indigenous Voice in the Era of European Contact.*

Index